Is Prussia Returning to Europe Instead of Pacifist Germany?

Sara Moore

For Walter

© Sara Moore
Published in 2025 by The Bruges Group

ISBN: 978-1-917743-08-2

The Bruges Group Publications Office
246 Linen Hall, 162-168 Regent Street, London W1B 5TB
www.brugesgroup.com

Bruges Group publications are not intended to represent a corporate view of European and international developments. Contributions are chosen on the basis of their intellectual rigour, and their ability to open up new avenues for debate.

Scan me for Bruges Group

Twitter @brugesgroup, LinkedIn @brugesgroup
GETTR @brugesgroup, Telegram t.me/brugesgroup, Facebook @brugesgroup
Instagram @brugesgroup, YouTube @brugesgroup

Contents

Introduction	1
1 Bismarck: Unifier or Conqueror of Germany	3
2 The Coming War	26
3 Bismarck's Responsibility for the First World War	53
4 Was there a moment for victory?	78
5 Peace without victory?	117
6 Germany's Great Inflation	137
7 The Wall Street Crash	165
8 The Pan-Germans Hitler and War	181
9 Germany and America in the Second World War	209
10 Who won the Peace after the Second World War?	233
11 How Germany achieved Reunification	261
12 Germany and the Lehman Brothers Crash	279
13 War in Ukraine	297
14 Conclusions	320
Bibliography	338
Index	347
References	356
About the Author	386
About the Bruges Group	387

Introduction

In 1996, German historian, Volker R Berghahn wrote in his book *Quest for a European Empire*

'It has become increasingly clear that Germany, which twice in the first half of the twentieth century vainly attempted to establish by force a formal empire stretching from the Atlantic coast to the Ural Mountains and beyond, now at the end of the 20th century finds itself on the verge of acquiring a similar empire without a shot being fired.'

Berghahn's account of history differs sharply from the popularly accepted view in the 1950s that all the European nations 'slithered' into war in 1914 and that their iniquitous reparations led to Hitler and the Second World War.

The popular legend promoted valuable friendships when Stalin was threatening Europe and has led to rapprochement between France and Germany and the formation of the European Union. However, it does not stand up to modern scrutiny, deters friendship between Britain and America, and encourages Germany to take advantage of her neighbours without censure from the international community.

This book starts with Prussia's militarist philosophy and reveals how guile and deception were part of Germany's armoury long before she expressed her innocence of starting the First World War.

Bismarck managed to blame all his wars on his foes. The German Reich initially blamed Russia for the start of the First World War. However, by the end of the 1920s German schools and universities were being taught that Britain was to blame.

The neglected German historian, Fritz Fischer's great achievement is in chronicling his country's aims throughout the First World War, including in Russia, where the victorious eastern army forced the prostrate Russians to agree to new painful territorial concessions, and an indemnity of '6,000 million roubles, 'in fine gold, currency and kind' less than three months before the army's collapse on the western front.

In the popular legend the European Allies wilfully mistreated Germany in the interwar period by imposing huge and impossible to pay reparations on her but investigation reveals that interwar Germany was far more powerful than outsiders imagined.

Indeed, this book lays much of the blame for the Great Depression of the 1930s on Germany herself and asserts that she deliberately impoverished America after Hitler came to power to deter her from helping the Allies in the coming war.

The book discovers that Bismarck's adoption of gold as a currency was primarily responsible for the 1873 stock market crash, which he managed to blame on Austria. Subsequently it scrutinizes the 1929 stock market collapse and the Great Depression of the 1930s, when Germany secretly maintained her economic power by trading with Stalin. It also examines the banking crash after the adoption of the euro to look at parallels with the past.

Finally, it looks at reunited Germany, and her ambitions for the future. The question is whether, despite Germany's cloak of pacifism, the country still possesses a powerful military industrial junta, which sees its power slipping in the world, and has sought to use NATO's money and armaments to realise its ambitions in 'Europe's' name.

CHAPTER 1

Bismarck: Unifier or Conqueror of Germany

In the eighteenth century, when Europe bade farewell to the medieval world, embraced Enlightenment and a new world in which the Rights of Man were declared, and Newton discovered gravity, a state on the edge of Eastern Europe, called Prussia, was creating a modern Sparta, idolising the virtues of war.

The popular vision of Germany before the First World War was of a nation that had produced some of western culture's greatest music, literature and thinkers. It was seen as a nation whose only concern was in unity. Bismarck was the 'great unifier and social reformer' who tried to lay the foundations for the future peace of Europe – or so we are led to believe.

The emphasis of this chapter is to focus on Prussia. It will show how the militarist state of Prussia fought and dominated Germany fiscally and militarily under Bismarck, promoting the philosophy for future wars.

Historically, the Prussian nobility regarded themselves as the descendants of the Teutonic Knights, who conquered the land of the Pruzzis in the thirteenth century, in the name of Christianity. The Teutonic Knights built a great empire in what is now the territory of Poland. At the centre of the empire stood the castle of Marienburg, which the Poles now call Malbork.

At the height of its power, Marienburg Castle housed three thousand knights and is still the largest castle in the world by surface area. Later, the Prussians lost their influence in the region but in the eighteenth century the Hohenzollern kings built the state of Prussia into a soldier state, whose citizens, like the warrior knights of old, believed in 'blind obedience' to their King – and in their King's right to invade his neighbours.[1]

In the seventeenth century, the Great Elector, Frederick Wilhelm, built up a sizeable army and used it to enlarge Prussia. The Great Elector's grandson, King Frederick Wilhelm I, created a huge army in Prussia in the early eighteenth century, recruiting ten percent of the entire population.

Frederick Wilhelm's son, Frederick II, who became known as Frederick the Great, was the first to use guile to achieve his aims. He published a book called *Anti-Machiavel* on achieving power which was a eulogy of peace. Peace was described as a country's greatest blessing and war as the greatest crime. Naturally, it created a sensation around Europe. Yet no sooner had Frederic published it than he invaded Silesia, with its rich seams of coal, and advised his successors to accumulate a might war chest before invading their neighbours. 'Money is like a sorcerer's wand' he declared.[2]

Prussia's General Gebhard von Blücher brought two corps to join the Duke of Wellington at the battle of Waterloo, arriving at a crucial time in the late afternoon. His intervention led to a decisive victory against Napoleon. Blücher became the highest-decorated Prussian soldier in history and the Congress of Vienna (1814-15), rewarded Prussia by giving her not only large parts of Saxony and Westphalia, but also the Rhineland with its coal, which would help bring her immense wealth and power.

The modern consensus seems to be that the Congress of Vienna was a great settlement, which brought peace to Europe for one hundred years. However, after the Second World War German Chancellor, Konrad Adenauer, disagreed, declaring that the greatest mistake the British had made was 'at the Congress of Vienna, when you foolishly put Prussia on the Rhine as a safeguard against France and another Napoleon' and that 'Prussianism in its turn culminated in National Socialism.'

The Congress of Vienna decided that the new German Confederation, comprised of German-speaking kingdoms and principalities, large and small, should agree upon a collective policy for trade, transport, and customs duties. As Prussia was the largest state in the Confederation, it was agreed that the 'collective policy' should be under Prussian rather than Austrian control. By 1834 Prussia had managed to create a *Zollverein* free trade zone of the twenty-six states, a microcosm in a purely

Germanic way, of the European Economic Community over a hundred years later. Austria was not invited to become a member.

Otto von Bismarck was born in 1815, at the time of Napoleon's defeat. He was eleven years younger than Disraeli and six years younger than Gladstone. Although a younger son of a Prussian Junker aristocrat, he was still entitled to call himself 'von' in contrast to the system in England, where only the first-born has the privilege of a title. Many of the Junker aristocracy owned huge estates, but Bismarck's was relatively small. Even on smaller estates, however, fifty years after serfdom had been abolished, the Junkers were the lords and masters, and the workers knew their lowly place.

Bismarck was a clever but bellicose youth who fought twenty-five duels at university. Initially viewed with the greatest suspicion by the conservative Prussian hierarchy, his marriage to a woman called Johanna von Puttkamer, from a strictly religious Protestant circle, alleviated their suspicions.

Bismarck resisted going into the army and found the civil service constricting and the management of the family's farmland dull; but eventually discovered the sort of challenge he relished when he became a member of the first Prussian Parliament. Because of his bellicose temperament, King Frederick Wilhelm IV refused to employ him, declaring that 'Bismarck, (was) only to be used when the bayonet rules unrestrictedly.' However, Bismarck made many useful friends during the 1850s, including General Albrecht von Roon.

By the time, the King Wilhelm I acceded to the throne in 1861, Prussia, with its great seams of coal, was prospering, and so were the independent states of Saxony, Bavaria and Hanover. Otto von Bismarck, who the great historian and liberal politician Theodor Mommson, asserted 'enlarged Germany and reduced the Germans,' had yet to become Chancellor.

One of the first things Wilhelm I did on becoming King was to invite Bismarck's friend, General, von Roon, to prepare a report on the army. Von Roon proposed that the King should enforce conscription for three years and more than double the size of Prussia's Standing Army.

Frederick the Great had lauded the discipline of the Prussian army in his political testament, declaring, 'Military discipline ... makes blindly obedient, the soldier to his officer, the officer to his colonel, the colonel to his general, and the generals to the commander-in-chief.'[3] The backbone of the Prussian army had always been the Officers Corps, which was recruited from the sons of the Junker landowners.

In England, officers used to be recruited from the landed gentry, and it was regarded as noble to die for one's country. The Junkers performed the same function in Germany. However, whereas in England army officers were always servants of the government, in Prussia soldiers were responsible only to the King.[4]

According to the Prussian military code, for a civilian to insult an officer was an offence to his uniform, for which it was his duty, without a moment's hesitation, to draw his sword. If a member of the Prussian Officer Corps committed a serious crime like murder, he was not subject to civilian law but was tried by a military court, where he might be 'honourably acquitted,' whereas under English law he would have certainly been sentenced to death. In war opponents could expect no mercy. The Prussian military theorist, von Clauswitz, begged his pupils to avoid a 'benevolent spirit towards a stricken foe' and denounced 'moderation' as an 'absurdity.'

Indeed, the General Staff manual expressly warned the Officers Corps to be on its guard against 'humanitarian notions', and the NCOs were expected to use their fists to discipline the men under their charge. Prussian soldiers therefore were far more terrified of their own officers than they were of the enemy.[5] No soldier would have dared disobey the order of an officer to fire upon a crowd, even if the crowd protested peacefully. 'Blind obedience' was the order of the Prussian army.

King Wilhelm asked the governmental treasury called the Landtag for the money to implement von Roon's proposals to quadruple the army's size. The issue threatened to become a constitutional crisis because Prussia's civilians were adamantly opposed to the proposals. In the May 1862 elections, the King's Conservative supporters were all but wiped out while the Progressive Party received a huge increase in votes. However, the aging King remained obdurate. In the end he found the one man who was happy to ignore the wishes of the people, Otto von Bismarck.

Bismarck was tall and powerfully built, with thinning red-blond hair, and a red-blond moustache. He enjoyed dispensing malice towards his opponents, declaring; 'I am no democrat and cannot be one' and caused further dismay by declaring 'The great questions of the time will not be resolved by speeches and majority decisions – but by blood and iron.'[6] His victory over parliament was complete when the King offered him the opportunity to not only become Minister President but also to be in charge of foreign affairs.

Bismarck assured King Wilhelm that as the economy was in such an excellent shape, that with the aid of the armaments' maker, Alfred Krupp, he could implement von Roon's plans to modernize and expand the army, without having to ask parliament to raise taxes.

Alfred Krupp, aged only fourteen, had inherited a nearly bankrupt business and seven sullen workers. However, he was a workaholic and a salesman. By the age of eighteen he had succeeded in making weldable crucible steel. Soon he was turning out forks and spoons. At an exhibition in 1844 he exhibited two hollow-forged, cold-drawn musket barrels. The ultra-Conservative Officers Corps was hostile to new weapons, but Alfred was not to be deterred. Tsar Nicholas was a potential client. Then Alfred met 'a reactionary' but clever man called Wilhelm Friedrich Ludwig von Hohenzollern, later to become King Wilhelm I.

King Wilhelm 1 had had an impressive army record, winning an Iron Cross against the French at the age of eighteen. When he saw Krupp's Potsdam gun at an exhibition at the Stadtschloss marble hall he expressed an interest in meeting 'this Herr Krupp.' He would soon help him financially, see that his key patents were extended, and let it be known that the Krupp works were 'ein vaterländisches Institut' (a national institution).

Through Wilhelm's sponsorship Alfred was able to vastly expand his business.[7] In 1852 he discovered the process of making seamless centrifugally produced wheels for the fast-expanding railways, but his military business was also expanding. Eventually he would become known as the 'cannon king.'

In January 1863 a rising broke out in the Russian part of Poland and public opinion throughout Europe expressed sympathy for the heroic down-trodden Poles. However, Bismarck's famous predecessor, Frederick the Great, had advocated allying Prussia with Russia, stating 'thus we have our back free as long as the alliance lasts.'[8] Bismarck agreed. He felt that he needed Russia's tacit support for his future ambitions, so he decided to support Russia's oppression. For the following thirty years, the Russo-Prussian entente would become the backbone of Bismarck's eastern policy as Bismarck was eager to deal with foreign policy opportunities in the West. Firstly, there was Denmark.

When King Frederick VII of Denmark died in 1863, the Duchies of Schleswig and Holstein were claimed both by his Danish heir and by a German Duke. Bismarck alleged that they legally belonged to the Danes under the London Protocol signed a decade before, but that as Schleswig was mostly German speaking it should be returned to its former status. When Denmark refused this solution, Bismarck persuaded Austria to join Prussia in invading Denmark on 1st February 1864.[9] After a second war, Denmark ceded both Duchies, nominally under Prussian and Austrian control.

However, Prussia did not allow this situation to last. Although, under the Gastein Convention, Schleswig was given to Prussia and Holstein to Austria, Prussia was given the right to build military roads through Holstein and establish a naval base at Kiel.[10] As time went on Prussia encroached more and more on Holstein's sovereignty until Austria's hostility was aroused.

The dispute with Austria over Holstein continued to smoulder until it provided a pretext for war. A hundred years' earlier Frederick the Great had declared: 'If sovereigns wish to make war they are not constrained by the need for a public protestation. They determine the course upon which they wish to embark, make war and leave to some industrious jurist the trouble of justifying their actions.'

Bismarck admired Frederick the Great's logic. It matched his own sentiments exactly. Frederick also wrote, 'It is necessary to have in one's neighbour's states, and especially among one's enemies, agents who report everything they see and hear.' Again, Bismarck agreed. He decided to employ Wilhelm Stieber, who had recently lost his job as Chief of Police and Head of Security of the Berlin police headquarters.

An autobiography of Wilhelm Stieber, called *The Chancellor's Spy*, was published nearly a hundred years after his death. In an explosive article, the magazine, *Der Spiegel* immediately declared it to be 'rubbish.' However, despite the inaccuracies of the book, Stieber's brilliance as a spy has been recognized by historians such as Jeffry T Richelson in *A Century of Spies, Intelligence in the 20th Century*, (1997) Jackson and Scott *Understanding Intelligence in the Twentieth-First Century*, (2000) Terry Crowdy in *A History of Spies, Spymasters and Espionage* and also Stephen Wade in *Victoria's Spymasters: Empire and Espionage* (2011) who went as far as to call Wilhelm Stieber, one of the founding fathers of military intelligence.

I have therefore inserted a few lines into this book to show the way Stieber operated to help Bismarck ascertain his foes readiness for war and to use the knowledge to prosecute his wars successfully.

Stieber asserted that to assess Austria's readiness for war against Prussia he would need a multitude of spies and suggested that the best way for them to operate without attracting attention was to set up a Press Bureau, like Reuters. Most of the agents would merely seem to be out to find a story and would not even need to know each other. Stieber also solved the question of payment, declaring that some brilliant forgers had been detained in Prussian prisons and that he was sure they would be able to forge undetectable bank notes.[11]

Soon Stieber had some interesting information to divulge. Firstly, he revealed that the Austrians wished to satisfy the 'longing of all Germans for unity by means of a federation of states with Austria at their head', and that this union was particularly desired by the Catholic South German states such as Bavaria and Hesse. Secondly, he reported that the authorities in Vienna had no idea that a war was in the offing; indeed, the Austrian people were resolutely against the idea of war. Thirdly, he revealed that three-quarters of Austria's military manoeuvres were purely defensive, and fourthly, that it would take a good two weeks longer for Austria to mobilize her forces than Prussia. Finally, he announced that, unlike Prussia,

Austria did not have the latest Dreyse 'needle gun,' said to be the first reliable breech-loading gun[12] guaranteed to mow down the enemy.

Bismarck declared that although it was 'repugnant' to him to take advantage of members of the same race, the Austrian Emperor, Franz Joseph, was determined to reduce Prussia to a powerless, petty state and so co-existence was impossible. He urged Stieber to stir up animosity between Austria and its neighbours and to persuade the Austrians to become dissatisfied with their government.

Soon tales of corruption swept the Austrian newspapers, also alarming reports of incidents where the police had exceeded their authority. Stieber also used eight hundred 'generously paid agitators' to incite the Hungarians, Slavs and Czechs against Austrian rule. An even more provocative plan, instigated with the help of counterfeit money, was to establish a 'Hungarian Freedom Legion,' made up of deserters from the Austrian army. Finally, Stieber promoted a report that Italy was about to invade Austria.[13]

Bismarck had managed to secure a defensive and offensive alliance with Italy 'in pursuit of the necessary reform of the German Confederation.'[14] Under this treaty Italy pledged to declare war on Austria, if and only if, Prussia attacked Austria within three months. This did not leave Bismarck much time to incite Austria into declaring war.

Prussia was by far the largest state in the German Confederation. The smaller German states had disliked Bismarck's predatory plans for Schleswig-Holstein and sided with Austria over the issue. On 27th March 1866 Prussia partially mobilized her troops. Then Bismarck, who had proclaimed, 'I am not a democrat and can never be one,' stated that the Federal Diet, through which the states were governed, was not legitimate, and that a new National Assembly must be elected by universal suffrage.

On 9th May the Federal Diet voted to demand why Prussia had mobilized her troops, but Bismarck gave no explanation. One month later a huge total of 330,000 Prussian soldiers assembled on the border with Austria. But Bismarck still had no pretext for war.

The Austrians asked the Federal Diet to intervene in the Schleswig-Holstein dispute and to mobilize the non-

Prussian army corps. They also ordered the Governor General in Holstein to call the estates of the Duchy into session. Unfortunately, by this action, Austria 'revoked' the recently signed Gastein Convention, and according to Bismarck's press office, 'endangered the sovereign rights of the king of Prussia as co-regent of Schleswig-Holstein.' His press release concluded menacingly: 'Our government will respond to the treaty violation with its full energy in defence of our rights.' Bismarck had managed to engineer war against Austria while proclaiming to his king and the wider world that Austria was responsible for the conflict.

A total of 120,000 soldiers from Saxony, Hanover, Bavaria, Württemberg, the Electorate of Hesse, Nassau, Frankfurt, and several other German principalities fought on Austria's side against Prussia. The Hungarians also forgot their grievances and rallied to Austria's support. Yet Austria was faced with war on two fronts. Although the Austrian army defeated Italy at Custoza, it was no match for the Prussians' 'needle gun' which produced a steady stream of 'lightning-fast' bursts of bullets, routing the Austrian armies at Königgrätz.

In 1742, after Frederick the Great succeeded in seizing Silesia from Austria, he wrote to his Minister, Podewils, 'At the present moment our task consists in making the capitals of Europe accustomed to see Prussia occupy the great position which she had obtained by her war with Austria, and I believe that great moderation and a conciliatory attitude towards our neighbours will help us in this.'[15]

Bismarck sensibly took the same course at the Peace of Prague on 23rd August 1866. Although he demanded a hefty indemnity, he did not actually grab any of Austria's territory. However, he was not so conciliatory to the German states who had opposed him. He absorbed the Duchies of Schleswig and Holstein into the Kingdom of Prussia, along with Hanover, Nassau and the free city of Frankfurt, while Bavaria and the other southern states had to pay war-indemnities and agree that their armies would fight for the Prussian King, if, (and when), war came again.

As the citizens of the former 'free' city of Frankfurt were unhappy about having to pay indemnities, Bismarck decided to make an example of the city, which had been home to Germany's largest Jewish Community from the fifteenth till the nineteenth century. Frankfurt was initially fined six million thalers and then another twenty-five million. When there was opposition to this impost Bismarck threatened Frankfurt with an additional fine for every day it failed to pay, and if the money was still not forthcoming, he declared that he would bring all traffic, mail and business dealings to a halt. No wonder the mayor of Frankfurt hanged himself![16]

After uncovering a stash of guns in a Hanoverian castle cellar and finding and appropriating the famous 'Guelph' treasure from a Hanoverian bank, Bismarck's spy Wilhelm Stieber was dispatched to Paris to assess France's readiness for war, with Bismarck's words ringing in his ears: 'Despite all the sympathy I feel for the poor Emperor of France because of his dwindling prestige in his own country, I do not believe that we can avoid going to war with him for very, long But I want to use the respite to give our army a head's start ... by arming it with the most modern weapons in the world.'[17] That sounded like good news for Alfred Krupp and his bourgeoning armaments firm.

Bismarck's surreptitious use of the Guelph treasure meant that the costs of Stieber's undercover operations in Paris would not appear in the official Prussian Defence Budget and therefore the entire operation could remain secret. Stieber set up a huge network of spies across France to find Frenchmen who might betray their homeland with the right inducements.

Yet it was one of his own agents who discovered the most exciting news. While posing as an Alsatian housepainter looking for work, he found employment with the French War Ministry, painting a dilapidated wall. As soon as he was alone, the agent scouted the area, found the right door and there 'on an ebony table gleamed the parti-coloured map, covered by a glass lid, which showed the deployment of French troops.'[18]

The Austrians had suffered in their war against Prussia from their lack of the most modern weapon, the Dreyse needle gun. In 1870 the French were equipped with the breech-loading Chassepot rifle, said to be one of the most modern mass-produced firearms in the world, with a far longer range than Prussia's needle gun. However, Stieber examined the Chassepot rifle and declared that it worked on the same principle as Prussia's guns and did not

12

constitute such a leap in technology as the French claimed. He regarded France's much vaunted precursor to the machine gun, the *mitrailleuse*, in the same light, stating that it was prone to jamming and ineffective against moving targets. Meanwhile, Prussia had Krupp's famous 6-pounder (3kg) steel breech-loading cannons in its armoury, ready to pound the enemy.

Stieber asserted that France was ill-prepared for war as many French troops were in Rome protecting the Papal States and Emperor Napoleon III's many illnesses, which included kidney disease, bladder stones, chronic bladder and prostrate infections, were affecting his ability to run the country, yet alone wage a war.

Bismarck declared the situation in France to be an 'invitation to the German soldier's boot.'[19] He would also have liked to have used a 'soldier's boot' to bring some of the recalcitrant German states into line but decided that might be unproductive. A glorious war against the historic enemy, France, was what was needed to persuade them to accept Prussian control. If only he could persuade the French to declare war!

Napoleon was already upset with the German Chancellor. Bismarck had reneged on his promise to give France the Duchy of Luxembourg as a reward for not intervening in Bismarck's war against Austria. Relations between Prussia and France deteriorated until eventually the British found a compromise. The Prussian garrison was removed from Luxembourg, and the Duchy was declared an independent neutral state. Yet Napoleon had been made to look a fool, and it rankled.

In 1868 the Spaniards expelled their delinquent Queen, Isabella, and started the search for a new King. Bismarck sensed an opportunity. He gave his Emissary, Theo von Bernhardi, £50,000 from the booty he had secured from the kingdom of Hanover, to bribe officials who could help Wilhelm I's young Hohenzollern relative, Prince Leopold, in his application to become King of Spain.[20] The Spanish duly offered their crown to the Prussian prince. King Wilhelm I, however, had obviously not been a party to Bismarck's scurrilous plan and was not keen on the idea.

On 20th April King Wilhelm and Leopold's father, Prince Anton, wrote to Madrid to refuse the proposal. Bismarck was annoyed. Prussia had a great army, ready to go to war against France but King Wilhelm would not help him create the opportunity. However, Bismarck did not give up hope. He secretly sent a letter to Spain's General Prim, through another confidant, Theodore von Bucher, asking Prim to write to King Wilhelm again, while insisting that Bismarck has nothing to do with his offer.

On 28th May Bismarck told young Prince Leopold's father, Prince Anton, that the Spanish had finally managed to change King Wilhelm's mind. General Adjutant, Alfred Waldersee, who was at Bad Elms with the King, wrote in his diary:

'... the Spaniards ... knocked on the door again and now, all of a sudden, the father and son Hohenzollerns have become passionately in favour ... They have allowed themselves to be talked into it by Bismarck, and the Prince who doubted that he had the guts to be King of Spain, is suddenly filled with the idea that he has a mission to make Spain happy.'[21]

On 19th June 1870 Prince Leopold sent his letter of acceptance of the Spanish crown. On 2nd July, the provisional Spanish government welcomed its arrival. The French were horrified. They did not want France to be hemmed in by Prussian kings to the north and south. Their ambassador, Count Benedetti, protested that the Hohenzollern candidacy for the Spanish throne constituted a serious attempt to alter the balance of power in Europe.

Leopold's father was pressured to withdraw his son's candidacy and King Wilhelm of Prussia, who had never been keen on the idea in the first place, renounced it in the name of the House of Hohenzollern. On 12th July 1870 Prince Leopold's candidature was officially withdrawn.

Bismarck did not give up. He decided upon a diplomatic offensive against France's Ambassador, emphasizing the restraint and moderation shown by Wilhelm I and his Ministry in withdrawing Prince Leopold's candidature.[22] The French were incensed. Egged on by the press, and the Empress Eugenie, Napoleon instructed Count Benedetti to demand that King Wilhelm never change his mind again. King Wilhelm, who was taking the waters at Bad Ems, was by now annoyed by the whole affair. He described the French request as 'impertinent', and sent a private report about it to Bismarck as follows:

'13th June. 1870. Count Benedetti intercepted me while I was out walking, and in what became a very importunate manner, demanded that I authorize him to immediately telegraph the message that I promised never again, at any time in the future, to give my consent if the Hohenzollerns were to renew their candidacy. Finally, I refused his demand somewhat sternly for, on no account, can one enter into undertakings of this kind. Naturally I told him that I had not received any information, and that, since he had been informed sooner than I about what was going on in Paris and Madrid, he could easily understand that my government had nothing to do with the matter.'[23]

Most of the King's government 'had nothing to do with the matter' but Bismarck had cooked the whole idea up in the first place and he was not going to let the opportunity slip. He quickly altered the dispatch which King Wilhelm had sent him so that it read:

'Ems, 13 June 1870. Today, France's Ambassador, Benedetti, intercepted the King of Prussia when he was out for a walk and importunately demanded that he promise to forbid the Hohenzollerns to assume the throne of Spain at any time in the future. In view of this unreasonable demand, the King of Prussia refused to reply to the French Ambassador and sent an adjutant on duty to inform him that he had nothing further to say to him.'[24]

The very next day Bismarck published his version of the Ems Dispatch in all the German newspapers and informed all the foreign courts that Benedetti had 'addressed the old and sickly King of Prussia, against his will and in a provocative manner.' The following day, the French voted for war.

The Prussians were ready to respond. Prussia's Chief of Staff, Helmuth von Moltke, had been devising a war plan since 1857, and had an intimate knowledge of the railway timetables so that he could send his troops to the front at lightning speed. Within a period of only fourteen days the Prussian army of 400,000 men was mobilized and ready to attack.

Frederick the Great used to lead his men in battle. This was impossible for Bismarck as he has never been in the army, but he admired the Prussian military tradition. Throughout the campaign he wore the silver helmet and yellow coat of a cavalry division, decorated either with the sparkling Order of the Eagle, or a gleaming white service cap.

Victories at Weissenburg and Wörth on the 4th and 6th August 1870 shook the morale of the French army. Von Moltke was a brilliant tactician, and he was helped by Krupp's new breech-loaded cast-steel cannons, which were far speedier and more accurate than the muzzle-loaded bronze cannons of France. Napoleon III surrendered, and the Germans marched on to Paris. After four months besieging Paris, Bismarck ordered 250 of Krupp's cannons to bombard the city. They silenced the defences and destroyed the tunnels bringing food to the starving population.

Wilhelm Stieber had been at Bismarck's right hand during the military campaign against France, so Bismarck ordered him to prepare well-guarded lodgings for the 'Revolutionary Minister,' Jules Favre. Jules Favre was the Vice-President and Secretary of State for Foreign Affairs in the new Republican government, and he had come with his stepson, Martinez del Roi, to negotiate peace terms.

There could not have been a more striking contrast between well-fed Bismarck, 'beaming' with health, and the two half-starved Frenchmen, who arrived to negotiate peace. Their ravenous appearance gave Stieber an idea. He decided that he would play the part of a valet to gain some inside information. He hurried back to where the secret police had their headquarters, made all his officers put on civilian clothes, and laid on a sumptuous meal. After dinner he gave Favre his feather 'coverlet' and led him to a bedroom he had prepared for him, where he had drilled a spy hole. Meanwhile Bismarck left for a Council of War with the Kaiser and army leaders.

Favre did not snuggle down under the coverlet in his bedroom but spent the whole night nervously pacing up and down, debating the peace options with his stepson. These were carefully listened to by Stieber's assistants before being passed on to Bismarck.

Favre was deceived by the solicitude of his valet, Stieber, and thanked Bismarck for providing him with such a good attendant. In return, Bismarck refused Favre's request for a month's truce and thirty-six thousand cattle for Paris's starving population, telling Stieber: 'We will keep them on scanty rations unless they agree to the peace terms we choose to set.' [25] Meanwhile Stieber oversaw the surveillance of the city using his secret police to make brutal arrests.

Eventually, Paris surrendered after 1323 days under siege. On 28th January 1871 Count Bismarck and Jules Favre signed a cease-fire agreement, and the city turned over all its arms. Stieber took hostages, who were forced to walk ahead of the soldiers until Bismarck made sure that the fortresses were not mined.

The Prussian army won the battle at the cost of over 138,000 French dead against 44,700 Prussian soldiers. It was a huge victory for Prussia. William I was proclaimed 'German Emperor' in the Gallery of the Hall of Mirrors at Versailles. Yet neither he nor his new Kaiser were happy. Bismarck was in a rage about the defects of the ceremony while William objected to being called 'German Emperor' instead of 'Emperor of Germany.'

It was still, however, a momentous occasion. The Holy Roman Empire was called the First (German) Reich. Bismarck and his Kaiser would name their new Empire the Second Reich, even though Wilhelm Stieber's spies related that the kings and princes and governmental leaders in the states of Hanover, Bavaria, Württemberg and Saxony would still far prefer Austria to regain her ascendancy in Germany and were all opposed to the idea of having a 'German Empire' under a Prussian king.[26]

Under the Peace Treaty of Frankfurt, France agreed to cede the French provinces of Alsace, (except the town of Belfort), and northeast Lorraine, and to pay a massive reparations bill. Then the Kaiser and his Chancellor returned to administer their discontented Reich.

Unsurprisingly, the new Reichstag was little more than a popular façade to hide the new Empire's autocratic structure. Although elected by universal franchise, its power was confined to making suggestions, which the government could refuse, to checking the income and expenditure of the budget and to passing bills which did not affect the emperor's right to appoint and control the military, and to appoint the Chancellor and deal with foreign affairs.

Yet, although more autocratic, Bismarck's new German Reich shared some remarkable similarities with the European Union.

It was comprised of twenty-six states, as opposed to the twenty-eight states in the European Union, and, as in the European Union, the states were of wildly differing sizes. There were four kingdoms, six grand duchies, five duchies, seven principalities and three republics, but each had its own constitution, representative system and divergent economy.[27] They retained practically the whole of their internal administration, but Prussia was the dominant state, just as Germany would become the dominant state in the European Union.

There was another similarity; both Bismarck's Reich, and the European Union, decided to adopt a new currency. On 1st January 1999, the European Union adopted the euro, instead of the mark, the franc, and other venerable European currencies. In 1871 Bismarck decided to adopt the gold mark instead of the less valuable silver vereinsthaler and other currencies prevailing in the different states of his new Reich.

Traditionally Prussia and many northern German states had the silver vereinsthaler for their currency. The Austro-Hungarian Empire also used silver for its currency although its coin was called the gulden and had a slightly lower silver content than Prussia's. Many of the southern states in Bismarck's new Reich had traditionally used the gulden too, although their gulden was slightly less valuable than Austria's.[28]

As with the arrival of the Euro, the gold mark initially created no problems. The French were forced to pay the stupendous sum of five billion gold marks in reparations after the Franco-Prussian war. ('If the sum is converted using RPI, it amounts to 342 billion today!'[29]) More than half of the money was earmarked to be spent on improving the German armies and modernizing the fortifications.[30] Yet there still seemed to be plenty of cash around. A bubble of money was created, and speculation ensued, just as happened after the arrival of the Euro. Even Austria joined in the fun.

After its defeat by Prussia, the Austrian Empire had devolved into the Austro-Hungarian Empire. To encourage confidence in the new regime Austria and Hungary sponsored building works. Some of the most beautiful buildings in their capital cities were built at this time. Mortgages were easy to come by, and a construction boom took off, not only in Vienna but also in Berlin and southern Germany. As land values soared, borrowers took added risks, using unbuilt or half-built houses as collateral for loans, just as would happen between 2001 and 2008.[31]

The party spread to America where Europeans and Americans speculated on American railroad shares. Ominously it was also announced that silver would no longer be used as currency in the German Reich from July 1873. 'The deflation of silver-backed currencies cascaded throughout the world'[32] as Bismarck's adoption of the gold mark, created a glut of silver on world markets. This hit the young burgeoning American economy hard as much of the silver used in European coins was mined in the US. The value of the silver Austrian gulden also plummeted. Then interest rates increased and increased again[33] and cash became scarce everywhere. On 9th May the Vienna Stock Exchange suffered a devastating crash, followed by a crash on Wall Street, and eventually in Berlin.

The stock market crash came at a handy time for Bismarck. One hundred and fifty years later, on 23 March 2006, the newspaper *Der Spiegel* would declare that the real divide in Germany was not between the former East Germans and those in the West, but between the Protestant North and the Catholic South. Bismarck was no longer indulging in military warfare but in political warfare against the Catholic Church, whose adherents in southern Germany yearned for ties with Catholic Austria, rather than with the autocratic Prussians. In 1871, he initiated his so-called *Kulturkampf* and abolished the Catholic Department of the Prussian Kultus-Ministerium.[34] Then, in May 1873, just as the stock market was crashing, he instituted his infamous May Laws,[35] which would eventually lead to hundreds of Catholics, and scores of priests and bishops, either being imprisoned or in exile.

Bismarck's experts argued that the Austrians were to blame for the stock market catastrophe in Vienna because of their irresponsible lending. Yet basically Bismarck had been responsible both for the easy money after 1870 and for its disappearance in 1873. Huge care should be taken in introducing a large new currency. Whether by accident or design, Bismarck's over hasty decision to abandon silver and to tighten the purse strings seemed to be the primary cause of the crash, both in Vienna and in New York because of collapse in the value of their currencies.

Nonetheless, Bismarck immediately accused the Austrian Emperor of allowing the Austrian State Bank to issue a larger volume of bank notes than had previously been authorized. Bismarck's experts argued that 'the

Vienna Stock Exchange had been the arena in which speculation had called forth a lot of companies ... for which the existing capital proved insufficient.' [36] The Austrian Emperor's brother, Archduke Ludwig Viktor, was alleged to have indulged in unwise speculation. Stephen Kelevich, a relative of Hungary's Royal Treasurer, was also declared bankrupt.

The Austro-Hungarian Empire received a grievous reverse. Thousands of Austrian public figures were ruined. They had hoped to recover their self-esteem after the joy of Bismarck's victory against France. Instead, they received a shattering blow. Naturally, they did not dare answer back. Indeed, they diverted all their anger against the Jews' 'unwise expansion, insolvency and dishonest manipulation' of the Vienna Stock Exchange. Their enmity against the Jews would extend beyond the First World War. Meanwhile, banks in Munich, Stuttgart, and Frankfurt which had links to Vienna, also suffered.

The Catholic southern states were horrified by the imprisonment of their bishops. However, there was little material that they could do about it. In future they would have to go cap-in-hand to Berlin rather than Vienna if they wanted money. After the Austrian stock market collapsed, the crash extended to New York and Berlin.

Then Bismarck's Reich adopted a policy of 'austerity', producing a lengthy economic depression in his new Reich. This caused an alarming increase in anti-Semitism which Bismarck was prepared to countenance in aid of his policy of 'negative integration.'

The official state historian, Heinrich von Treitschke, gave the movement respectability with his article, *Our Prospects* and *A Word about our Jews*. Soon anti-Semitic organizations like the Anti-Semitic People's Party, the Pan-German League and the German Reform Party would spring up. Von Treitschke gave them a scapegoat for all their misfortunes. He declared, 'From the inexhaustible womb of Poland von came an annual swarm of Jews ready to pollute the country,'[37] heightening the antagonism of the Junkers against them.

After Bismarck's victorious wars against France and Austria, the Reichstag had allowed the Prussian standing army to remain at the formidable figure of 400,000 men till 1874. The Reichstag then had the right to vote on reducing its size, but Bismarck and the generals were determined to keep the figure permanently at 400,000.[38] A confrontation with the Reichstag loomed while Bismarck searched for an excuse to maintain the army at its present level without creating a constitutional crisis.

France had paid her enormous reparations bill with astonishing haste to rid the country of the German occupying force. Yet this did not mean that the French were rich. Far from it. The French population would hardly increase in size over the next forty years because the country felt so poor. The sandy colonial empire that France acquired in North Africa was little compensation for the loss of mineral-rich Lorraine and the fertile land of Alsace. The German standing army of 400,000 battle-ready troops was threatening. In 1875 France decided to increase the number of her cavalry battalions from three to four.

Immediately, Bismarck seized on the news of France's cavalry increases with an article in the *Berlin Post* called 'Is war in sight?' He told every capital in Europe that France was bent on revenge. Russia's Ambassador in London, Count Peter Shuvalov commented cynically to British Foreign Secretary, Lord Derby, that it was the state of Bismarck's nerves that was a danger to Europe! The order for a German 'preventative war' was averted by British and Russian intervention[39] and Bismarck secured what he had been aiming for all along, the agreement of the Reichstag that the size of the German standing army could be fixed at 400,000 men for another seven years.

Meanwhile the German philosopher, Constantin Frantz, mourned for the German Confederation of States, which Bismarck had destroyed in 1866; 'It was of paramount importance for the whole European system... Its dissolution ... made the whole European system lose its former stability so that from that moment onward the relations of all European states became based on bayonets, and the whole continent groans under the burden of militarism.'[40]

The German people suffered from the Long Depression, instigated by Bismarck's austerity programme. However, the iron and steel barons prospered, owing to the rich coal seams of the Ruhr, the huge indemnity from France, a competitive exchange rate and indirect subsidies from the state. Nevertheless, the armament company A G Krupp had become over-extended after the war and was threatened with bankruptcy. The Emperor and his Chancellor said a public 'Nein' to coming to the aid of Europe's largest company. However, they were not going to let it go bankrupt. Before long, the company was prospering again. In 1878 and 1879 Alfred Krupp held cannon competitions for international buyers at his proving ground at Meppen, the largest in the world. Forty-six nations eventually signed up as customers.

After the railways spread to the corn-belt in America, America flooded the European market with cheap wheat. Under pressure from the Prussian Junkers, Bismarck introduced protectionist tariffs. Eventually this gave Germany a competitive advantage over Great Britain as many countries who wanted industrial goods had nothing to sell but agricultural produce. However, the workers in the great factories were incensed about the higher prices because so much of their income was spent on food. Anti-Semitism increased.

Ultimately, anti-Semitism would form a unifying force in Bismarck's Reich, especially after the arrival of his tariff. It would also become an increasingly violent expression for all those who feared the social and economic changes that were bound to result from the rapid pace of Germany's industrialization. In 1899 the programme of the United Anti-Semitic Parties called for the solution of the 'world problem' of the Jews by having them all rounded up and destroyed in what they called their *endlösing*.[41]

In answer to socialists' opposition to his expensive food policy, Bismarck adopted an aggressive policy. He exiled leading activists and adopted the 'Law concerning the Combating of the Criminal Aims of Social Democracy' which treated them like enemies of the state. He dissolved over 600 newspapers and prompted mass emigration to America; but later he tried to come to terms with the socialists by initiating innovative social legislation.

This legislation was probably inspired by the measures adopted by the armaments firm of Krupp. Alfred Krupp had started on the shop floor. He therefore had an intimate knowledge of the harsh conditions which shopfloor labourers had to endure. By 1900 he had over 45000 workers in his employment.

After his railway and armaments businesses racked up profits, he started building houses for his foremen. By

1905, 400 houses had been built, many being given rent-free to the widows of former employees. A boarding house was also built for single men, bath houses were provided, and employees received free medical treatment. Accident life and sickness insurance societies were in force, the firm contributing to their support. So, Bismarck decided to introduce progressive compulsory insurance schemes for the whole nation against sickness in 1883, against accidents in 1884 and for old age in 1889.

The national health insurance scheme was inspired by the cooperative model in the coal mining industry, which already offered cover for employees for accidents, with medical support, health payments and even pensions for invalids. Nevertheless, the employers pressed for a national scheme, with the workers paying two-thirds of the contributions.

The accident insurance Law of 1884 would make employers pay two thirds of the workers' wages after the 14th week provided that the worker was fully disabled. Lifetime pensions and widow's benefits were also provided by the scheme. Finally, the Old Age Pensions Scheme offered pensions to employees at 71 after 24 years of payment, equally financed by employers and workers.

British workers earned 'substantially more at engineering, coalmining, cotton-spinning and cotton-weaving than their German counterparts.' British unemployment was also half that of Germany.[42] However, the British workers were envious of the benefits that their German counterparts were going to receive. The German social security scheme was superior to anything that British or French workers had in their countries. Nevertheless, the scheme was widely resented in Germany. The employers regarded it as an intolerable burden at a time of public hardship, and their underpaid employees found the premiums expensive and the benefits inadequate.[43]

By 1900 the state was financed in large part by the high price of food, almost half the income of the Reich, coming from the agricultural tariffs.[44] This profited the Junkers with their great estates, but at a very, high social cost. It was the great industries of the Ruhr and other industrial centres which would create the German economic miracle but the cost to the German steel worker was hard. He would be paying contributions towards his pension with little chance of living to the age when it was due because of the expensive and poor quality of his food and the acrid polluted environment in which he lived and worked. Coal fires, 'used for heating, hot water and cooking' were lit every day an hour before the start of the morning shift, coals burnt in grates 'that had smouldered overnight, sending up plumes of smoke' from thousands of chimneys, fouling the atmosphere. [45]

German coal miners worked 51.5 hours a week in 1895, employees in the chemical industry worked 60 hours a week and steel workers 63 hours a week[46] while only in the 20th Century was legislation introduced against the exploitation of child labour.

Alfred Krupp was very reactionary. He disliked socialists, liberals, and Jews. In return for the social benefits that his employees gained, he demanded a loyalty oath, long working hours, strictly limited use of the toilet and an undertaking that his employees would not concern themselves with politics. In 1902 R S Baker in his book *Seen in Germany* declared: 'It is probable that no civilized workman in the world would change places with the German. Few indeed work longer hours for smaller pay, eat coarser and cheaper food, (and) live in more crowded homes.'[47]

Bismarck never returned to military warfare after 1870, but he did not appear peaceful! His large empire and huge standing army gave him political clout. He built up a complicated system of alliances in the early 1880s, which resulted in Germany being the dominant power in a weighty Central European bloc, containing Austria, Russia, Italy, Serbia, and Rumania.

Soon, however, relationships with Russia worsened. Germany's ever-heightening agricultural tariffs were seen in Russia as deliberately unfriendly.[48] Previously over thirty per cent of Russia's agricultural exports had gone to Germany to enable her to buy Germany's industrial goods, but Bismarck lost interest in trading with her.

Russia resigned from the Triple Alliance over a crisis in Bulgaria. Bismarck then concluded a Reinsurance Treaty with Russia but as the Russians refused to remain neutral in the event of a German war against France, he became deliberately unfriendly.

Bismarck's expulsion of over 30,000 Poles and Jews from German occupied Poland prompted the Czar to issue an edict prohibiting the tenure of land in Russia by any foreigners, most of whom seemed to be German. Then, the German press, with Bismarck's blessing, attacked the value of Russian State bonds. In November 1887, the Prussian State Bank stated officially that it would not offer any loans against the Russian State bonds. As Russia's shaky economy could not exist without foreign loans it had to turn to France.[49]

Bismarck was determined to secure a new seven-year mandate for the expansion of the army before ninety-year-old Emperor, Wilhelm I, died. So, even though he received a report from the German Ambassador in Paris, Georg Herbert zu Münster, saying that there was absolutely no sign of France preparing for war, he won a huge electoral victory in December 1887 by frightening the German electorate into believing that France was about to invade, with scary newspaper headlines like 'On the Razor's edge.'

Then he asked the newly elected members of the Reichstag to vote on the armaments bill proclaiming, 'Since 1870 there has been danger of war every year' but 'even if Germany were at war with France, a Russian war would not necessarily follow.' 'There is no need to fear the hatred of Russia'[50] he declared, further alarming the Reichstag, and winning its backing for increasing the German army to 491,000 men.[51]

Bismarck then triumphantly published the text of a new Austro-German Treaty, declaring: 'We no longer sue for love either in France or in Russia.' Soon afterwards, Wilhelm I died and Bismarck, aged 75, was sacked by the new young Kaiser, Wilhelm II. He left a powerful country in a 'chronic crisis of overproduction' looking for ways out of the depression[52] and he had some advice for the new Kaiser: 'The German Empire is just jogging along. You try and make Prussia strong!'[53]

CHAPTER TWO

The Coming War

On 15th June 1888 Queen Victoria's eldest grandson, Wilhelm II, became Emperor of Germany. 'Kaiser Bill', as he was popularly known in England, had a difficult birth at the hands of an English doctor and grew up with one arm paralysed and six inches shorter than the other. He blamed the British for his deformity, resented his mother's attempts to bring him up with British attitudes towards democracy, and regarded himself as a Prussian, with a great military destiny.

After he came to the throne he was seldom out of uniform. Bismarck had bequeathed him a powerful industrial base and a huge army. Wildly jealous of the British, Wilhelm decided that the path to glory was to build a great navy and to secure a colonial empire.

Bismarck had not professed much interest in colonies until the year 1884. Then he astonished the world by asking his Imperial Consul-General, Gustav Nachtigal, to take possession of Cameroon in the name of the German emperor. Up till that time, Bismarck had believed that the land that he had acquired in Europe to be of infinitely more value. However, later he divulged that he planned to grab a slice of the African cake on the cheap by playing off France against Britain.[54]

By 1889 Germany had four colonies but Bismarck had a new objective. He intended to use Germany's colonies as pawns to secure an 'appetizing plum in Europe.' On 11th January 1889, he offered British Prime Minister, Lord Salisbury, a defensive alliance against France. He asserted that British friendship was worth the whole of East Africa and asked Britain to swap Heligoland for Germany's African possessions, claiming that if French warships seized Heligoland during a Franco-Prussian war, it would create a threatening situation for his Reich.

The British were sympathetic. France had been their historic enemy and their friendship towards Germany was strong. The island of Heligoland was a few square miles of 'naked red sandstone' exposed to the wind and waves of the North Sea, forty miles west of the German town of Cuxhaven, at the mouth of the river Elbe.

Lord Salisbury was told that if France used Heligoland as a coaling station, she could seal off the Elbe River and block the new Kiel Canal, threatening the very existence of the German nation. Yet, despite this assertion, Bismarck and his new Kaiser felt less endangered by France than they made out. Their real purpose in acquiring Heligoland was because they felt that it could be developed into a major naval base, comparable to Britain's bases on the islands of Malta and Gibraltar.

Lord Salisbury did not immediately take the bait. However, eventually he listed four 'giant' demands in return for the barren island of Heligoland. They were, a British protectorate over Zanzibar, cession of the German protectorate of Witu and all territory north of the Tana; also access from Uganda to Lake Tanganyika, and the lion's share of the land west of Lake Nyasa.

The Kaiser accepted the swap without a murmur. One would have thought that Bismarck would also have been delighted. However, he was too clever for that. In 1890 his many followers - popularly called the 'Fronde'- were consumed with anger after Bismarck protested that Germany had been cheated in the deal.[55] As a result, powerful civil servant Dr. Alfred Hugenberg, later to become Chairman of Krupps armaments company, founded a new pressure group called the Pan-German League, with avid colonialist Carl Peters, to fight for Germany's interests at home and abroad.

Alfred Krupp had developed his armaments firm from practically nothing, into an industrial powerhouse, but he lacked the smooth edge which comes from being brought up among the rich and famous. His son, Fritz, was fat and myopic and suffered from asthma but had been raised amongst Europe's elite. A skilled negotiator, he moved seamlessly among the rulers of Europe, gaining military orders. He was also a firm supporter of the Pan-German League and Wilhelm dismissed General Julius von Verdy du Vernois, in 1890, and his successor Major General, Hans von Kaltenborn-Stachau, in 1893, for rejecting Fritz's design for the C-96 field gun, quipping 'I've canned three

War Ministers because of Krupp, and they still don't catch on.'56

In 1896 Wilhelm elevated a man with steely ambition and a magnificent two-pronged beard, called Alfred Tirpitz, to become State Secretary of the Imperial Navy Office while Fritz bought a shipping company called Germaniawerft.

Fritz lost no time in ensuring his new company's success. In 1898 he helped contribute to the foundation of a new promotional organization called the Navy League; then he and the Pan-German League poured money into promoting it.57 The Navy League soon became a wild success.

The Reichstag tried to resist Tirpitz's plans for making Germany 'the strongest naval power in the world' but the Navy League managed to create an uproar over Britain's seizure of the German merchant ship *Bundesrath*, which was on its way to South Africa loaded with help for the Boers. The Reichstag's objections to enlarging the navy were swept aside and thirty-eight battleships were authorized to be built, regardless of cost to be able to meet the British home fleet on equal terms.58

Fritz would die (some say that he committed suicide) after a scandal involving young boys. However, his company Friedrich Krupp Germaniawerft made a fortune from building dreadnoughts and submarines, managing to complete the building of the prestigious battleship *Kronprinz Wilhelm* by 1914.

Nevertheless, Wilhelm II's immediate aspirations were with territories of the 'dying' colonial powers, specifically Spain, Portugal, Denmark, and the Netherlands. It has recently been discovered that he also devised plans between 1897 and 1903 for invading the East Coast of America. The great general, von Schlieffen, poured cold water on the Kaiser's plans.59 However, America was without a large navy and Wilhelm sensed an opportunity.

Approximately 27% of Americans had at least one parent born in Germany in 1900.60 Wilhelm's plan was not to conquer the US physically. Instead, Wilhelm planned to launch an armada to attack the international systems of trade credit and insurance with the goal of bringing capitalist America to its knees.

Tirpitz toured America on his way back from the Far East. He reported that the country was filled with societies of German origin and organizers of pro-German sentiment. By early 1898 Naval Lieutenant (and later General) Eberhard von Mantey had drawn up his first plan. It called for a great German fleet to cross the Atlantic and destroy the Norfolk Naval Shipyard and the Newport News Shipbuilding centre, with another attack aimed at the 'the most sensitive point' of American defences, Portsmouth Naval Shipyard at the junction of Maine and New Hampshire.[61] But the Kaiser found the funding for the project difficult, and the Spanish-American War broke out in 1898.

Then the Kaiser had the idea of tempting Britain into forming a naval coalition with Germany and France against America during the Spanish War, but Arthur James Balfour, who commanded the world's most powerful navy, defended America, saying,

'No: if the British fleet takes any part in this war, it will be to put itself between the American fleet and those of your coalition.'[62]

So, the Kaiser reverted to his previous schemes against America. In 1899 he changed his plan to a two-pronged attack on America's Eastern Seaboard by sixty warships, with 100,000 soldiers and a large artillery force, but the designer of the famous Schlieffen Plan, General von Schlieffen, poured cold water on this and all his other American projects.[63]

Von Tirpitz and his Kaiser were frustrated but another opportunity presented itself in the New World. The Venezuelans had refused to pay their debts, so Wilhelm persuaded England and Italy to join him in blockading the Venezuelan coast until they were paid. After a while he threatened to bombard Venezuela's coastal towns too with a view to occupying them if he did not get satisfaction.

Ebullient extravert, Theodore Roosevelt, became US President in 1901. He had no illusions about what the Kaiser's threat to occupy the Venezuelan coastal towns would mean. If a German regiment managed to obtain a base within striking distance of the projected Panama Canal, Venezuela would be powerless to drive it out. So, he decided to kill the Kaiser's initiative. Having sounded out Italy and England, he warned the German Ambassador, Theodor von Holleben, that unless the Kaiser accepted arbitration over the debts within a strict timetable the

American fleet under Admiral Dewey would appear off the Venezuelan coast and defend it from German attack.

Holleben was aghast. 'Blind obedience' was not only expected of soldiers serving in the German Officers Corps but also of civil servants serving their imperial master. Holleben declared that when the Kaiser refused to accept arbitration that was the end of the matter. He asked Roosevelt if he realized what his words meant. President Roosevelt declared that it meant war.

A week went by without any communication from Berlin. Then Holleben called at the White House again. The President asked him if he had heard anything from Berlin. [64] 'No,' said von Holleben. 'Of course, His Majesty cannot arbitrate.'

'Very well' replied President Roosevelt. 'You may think it worthwhile to cable to Berlin that I have changed my mind. I am sending instructions to Admiral Dewey to take our fleet to Venezuela next Monday instead of Tuesday.'

Holleben shot out of the door and returned less than thirty-six hours later with the news: 'His Imperial Majesty consents to arbitrate.' The ambassador had consulted the German Consul-General in New York, who assured him that Roosevelt was not bluffing, and that Admiral Dewey could blow up all the German Navy in half an hour.

After this episode, the Kaiser turned his attention to Turkey and Africa. Hopefully, the Europeans would be easier to intimidate!

German heavy industry was interested in Turkey. The Kaiser had already visited Palestine and Syria in 1898 and declared himself the protector of all the Muslims. This found favour with Abdul Hamid II of Turkey, who alarmed the British by granting Germany a concession to build a railway from Constantinople to Baghdad. German heavy industrial leaders were excited by its possibilities. The projected route would eventually run close to the British oilfields of Persia (Iran). And beyond that lay India.

The railway concession was followed by military agreements. Most of the leaders of the Young Turks Revolt of 1908 would receive their military training from the German Reich. By December 1913, the Turkish army would be virtually under the control of the German general, Liman von Sanders, in a very strategic position.

Meanwhile relationships with Britain worsened. R J Unstead, in his *A Century of Change* (1963) declared: 'The German Emperor, who had neither brains nor manners, seemed to go out of his way to give and take offence. He wrote rudely to his grandmother, (Queen Victoria), openly sided with the Boers, and told Britain to mind her own business in Egypt.'

After France had lost valuable territory in the Franco-Prussian war, she had acquired an empire in North Africa. Much of it consisted of desert sand but Morocco contained valuable iron ore deposits. France's ally, Russia, had suffered from revolution after a disastrous war with Japan, and France herself was identified as vulnerable by the pugnacious German military establishment.

General von Schlieffen prepared a plan to invade France through Belgium. The Kaiser then spilled the beans and angered Belgium's King Leopold by saying that Leopold would have to guarantee the German Reich 'the use of Belgian railways and fortified places'[65] during the conflict, and informed Queen Wilhelmina of the Netherlands that Germany would need to occupy the entire Dutch coast to prevent the British from landing there.[66]

That might have been a more propitious moment for Germany to invade France, while Russia was still recovering from revolution, but the Kaiser's bellicose statements horrified Belgium and Holland, and France managed to sign an Entente Cordiale with Britain. So, Wilhelm I turned his attention to North Africa.

The first Moroccan crisis could be seen, as a German attempt to test the strength of France's Entente with Britain. The French 'with blissful disregard for international agreements had set about turning Morocco into a protectorate over which they would have a trade monopoly.[67] The British were torn because they believed in free trade. The Kaiser made a state visit and declared his support for a sovereign and independent Morocco, suggesting a conference to decide the matter.

After French Foreign Minister, Théophile Delcassé, opposed the idea of Moroccan independence, German Chancellor, Bernhard von Bülow, threatened war and Delcassé was forced to resign. The delighted Kaiser elevated von Bülow to the rank of Prince. Yet the 1906 conference at Algeciras was not a success for the German Reich. Indeed, it could have been called a crushing diplomatic defeat.

Just as Roosevelt had been alarmed by the threat to the Panama Canal if a German garrison was stationed in neighbouring Venezuela, so the British were aghast at the threat to the Strait of Gibraltar if German troops became entrenched in Tangier. Indeed, the Kaiser's sudden arrival in Tangier, and his procession through the city on horseback, was treated with the greatest suspicion by the whole of Europe. [68] Only Austria remained in his support.

The head of the giant armaments company, Fritz Krupp had supported the aggressive expansionist Pan-German League. After Fritz's suicide, the emperor, who was also a supporter. reputedly personally selected Gustav von Bohlen und Halbach to marry his daughter, Bertha Krupp, allowing Gustav to add the name Krupp to his surname.[69]

Bertha Krupp's mother, Martha had already chosen the Pan-German League founder, Alfred Hugenberg - who was regarded as a man 'of really superior intelligence' - to manage the family's armaments company.[70] Hugenberg would soon assume a leading role in the Central Association of German Industrialists and Gustav Krupp became a secret member of the Pan German League.

Alfred Hugenberg had been born in 1865, the same year as future General Erich Ludendorff, and was recruited for his first job in the Prussian province of Posen (now called Poznań in Poland), where Ludendorff was born and raised. Both Hugenberg and Ludendorff would come to hold similarly aggressive outlooks.

Hugenberg had been involved in the Prussian Settlement Commission to buy up land for German farmers from the Poles. He considered that a class of successful German farmers and small businessmen would stop the drift to the towns and act as a bulwark against Marxism. Evidently the Poles must have thwarted some of his plans to buy up their land for German farmers because in 1899 he frustratedly called for the 'annihilation of the Polish population.'[71] He also upset some of the vast Junker landowners in the East by wanting to break up their estates. So, he left the civil service and accepted a position on the board of the directors of the *Berg and Metallbank*, which eventually led to his exalted position at Krupps.

Hugenberg was described as 'not a man, but a wall'[72] because of his ability to destroy his opponents' arguments and refusal to alter his own. He liked to work behind the scenes and to keep out of the public eye. Nevertheless, under his administration the firm of Krupp adopted a ruthless attitude to business. When threatened with losing a contract in Brazil because of France's superior, French 75 weapon, the heavily guarded warehouse in which the French 75 was being kept, mysteriously burnt down in the night, and Krupp got the contract.

The trial of the company for industrial espionage in 1912 would be a rare moment when Hugenberg's name hit the limelight when he brushed aside irrefutable evidence of espionage with the argument that an attack against the firm of Krupp by international pacifists and socialists constituted an attack Germany's military preparedness.[73]

Certain members of Krupps were found guilty, but the emperor leapt to Gustav's defence by awarding him the Order of the Red Eagle, so Gustav Krupp and his company's supremo Alfred Hugenberg escaped scot-free.[74]

Afterwards, Hugenberg reverted to his low profile, using money from Krupps and the coal magnate (and future supporter of Hitler) Emil Kirdorf, to help pay for the Pan-German League.[75] He would effectively run Krupps vast manufacturing concern till 1918, and became a personal friend of Gustav Krupp, who nevertheless told Hugenberg that his membership of the Pan-German League must always remain a secret, which must never be divulged.

Morocco became the scene of another dispute between France and Germany in 2011. The growth of German steel production had been spectacular, rising from 0.9 million tons in 1886 to 13.6 million tons by 1912.[76] The income of the Ruhr's great iron and steel tycoons, like Hugo Stinnes, August Thyssen and Gustav Krupp surged between 1895 and 1907.[77] They forged their vast empires on a 'vertical plan' which meant that they owned or controlled the iron ore fields, the ships which brought the ore back home, the coal fields that provided the power to smelt the ore and the steel factories that produced the finished products.

Morocco contained iron ore and other valuable minerals, which were of acute interest to heavy industry. France's pre-eminence in Morocco had been upheld by the 2006 Algeciras Conference, but the Pan-German League began to champion the claims of the German Mannesmann brothers to the mineral rights in the southern and western regions of the country. German Foreign Secretary, Alfred von Kiderlen-Wächter, wanted to use the issue to help the government in the upcoming elections and in July 1911, the gunboat, the *Panther*, was sent to Agadir 'for the protection of German interests.'

The Pan-German League seems to have hi-jacked the negotiations as the Conservative journal, *Grenzboten*, asserted that Kiderlen had told the secretary of the Pan-German League on 19th April: 'I support the policy of the partition of Morocco. The Pan-German demand is thoroughly justified. We will see it out in Morocco. I am as Pan-German as you are.'

Under Secretary for Foreign Affairs Arthur Zimmerman seemed to have had even greater ambitions as he is reported to have said on the day of the arrival of the Panther at Agadir: 'We shall stick to Agadir, and we intend to stretch out our land over the whole district and to give up nothing ... We don't want compensation, we want Morocco.'[78]

This brought France and Germany to the brink of war. A tactful but firm speech by British Chancellor of the Exchequer, Lloyd George saved the situation. His hint that Britain would stand by France in her hour of need made Germany recoil. Germany had hoped at least to receive French Congo as the cornerstone of a great continuous German African Empire from her intervention but was merely given what she considered to be two 'meagre' strips of French territory on the Congo and Ubangi.

Pan-German publicist, Heinrich Claß quickly published a pamphlet on the Moroccan crisis which sold more than 50,000 copies. The Foreign Office managed to persuade Claß to withdraw the more extravagant excerpts, including the one in which he called for Germany to annexe most of eastern France 'in the event of war.'[79] However, the remainder of the pamphlet was still couched in such strong language that it alarmed the rest of Europe.[80]

A crucial factor in the German decision to retreat in Morocco was the lack of support from Austria. Austro-Hungarian Foreign Minister, Graf von Aehrenthal, vowed his perfect loyalty to the Triple Alliance but pointed out that Germany could count on Austria's support only when 'questions of European importance are at stake.'[81]

This virtually ensured that there would be no more colonial wars to achieve the Reich's coveted 'place in the sun.' Claß called the episode 'a shameful debasement of the international political prestige of the German Empire.' The Kaiser was blamed for Germany's colonial setbacks. In the eyes of the Pan-Germans and industrialists alike the episode was regarded as a national humiliation.[82]

So, the Pan-German League turned its attention to Europe. After Bismarck had defeated in battle his neighbours, Denmark Austria, and France in the nineteenth century. he had escaped international censure because his successful wars had been labelled by what could be called 'appeasing foreigners' as 'unification.' The Pan-German League wanted to bully more of Germany's neighbours into joining the Reich in the same fashion in the twentieth century. The enlarged European empire which they envisaged, they had already labelled *Mitteleuropa*.

The concept of a peaceful *Mitteleuropa* was attractive to many in industry. The economist, Julius Wolf had founded the *Mitteleuropäische Wirtschaftstag* (Middle European Economic Diet) in 1904, as an association of individuals and interest groups wedded to the idea of an informal Central European sphere. He had complained that Germany's main problem was that her trading area was too confined compared to other powers like America. What was needed was the creation of a *Großraum* stretching from the English Channel to the Balkans.[83]

The Pan-German League's concept of *Mitteleuropa* was more structured and potentially more bullying. Its publicist, Heinrich Claß, declared that 'Germany was incomplete because Bismarck failed to include all the people of German ethnicity.' Claß asserted that the borders of Bismarck's Reich were only temporary. Soon the moment would come for the national 'redemption' of all those unsuspecting mortals who the Pan-German League considered of German blood in the Hapsburg lands of the Austrian Empire, also in Switzerland, Holland, Luxemburg, Belgium, and Romania, (because of its strategic position at the mouth of the Danube). The Pan-Germans' plan was to attract these nations into their lair by means of a customs union like the Zollverein, which would prepare the way for community-wide legal and political institutions. Finally, if necessary, force might have had to be used to complete the unification process.[84] It seems that after the country's humiliation in Morocco the idea of 'force' to secure a

European Empire became more prominent in Pan-Germans' minds.

The pacifist Social Democratic Party's huge win in the national elections on 12th January 1912 elections had been a setback to the Pan-Germans' hopes for a colonial empire and even a threat to their very existence. To counter democracy, and to achieve Hugenberg's aim of securing more land for the increasing German population, Pan-German President, and virulent anti-Semite Heinrich Claß advocated increasing the German Empire in the traditional Prussian manner of invading her neighbours.

He also disliked the 'enemies within' writing in his book, *If I were the Kaiser*, (1912): 'all who stand in the service of socialist propaganda – should be expelled from the German Empire.'

Claß did realize that in a modern world the voice of the people could not be completely ignored but was determined to take up the 'struggle for the soul of the people.' He advocated holidays to celebrate the Fatherland and proposed that the army gave lectures drawn from German – or rather Prussian – history to entertain the masses. But the carrot was to be accompanied by the stick. Socialist strikers must be shown a firm hand. Claß was no fan of the Jewish community either.

In *If I were the Kaiser*, Claß, who would eventually become a member of Hitler's Nazi Party between 1933 and 1939, wrote: *Today the borders must be totally barred to any further Jewish immigration. ... foreign Jews who have not yet acquired citizenship rights must be speedily and unconditionally expelled, to the last man. And resident Jews be placed under an Aliens Law.*

Claß defined the Jews as anyone who belonged to a Jewish religious corporation as of 18th January 1871, as well as the descendants of such persons who were Jews at that date, even when only one parent was a Jew by that definition. Claß declared that the Kaiser should announce that all public offices remain closed to Jews ... and ... they would not be allowed to serve in the army or navy.

Claß also made clear that the Germans were a superior race, and that anyone who could claim German blood in Southern Russia, Galicia, Russian Poland, and North America should be welcomed home. Other nationals, however, were not welcomed in the lands his Volk had appropriated. Claß declared that Germany should pursue a resolutely militant policy against the Poles through the application of expropriation and the introduction of a prohibition against the parcelization of land.

In this respect Claß was copying Bismarck. Bismarck's 'expulsion law' of 1886, forced many Poles to leave their land, even though they were living on former Polish territory that had been annexed by Prussia. About 32,000 Poles had been evicted in a campaign which combined anti-Slav with anti-Semitic hatreds.

Claß was no kinder to the people of Alsace-Lorraine and Denmark, whose lands Bismarck had appropriated in his wars. He declared 'When we consider that in Alsace-Lorraine the number of French speakers has grown constantly since 1871, we need to speak out in cold blood. We didn't take the Reichsland for the sake of your beautiful eyes. We took it out of military necessity. The inhabitants are an extra. Every adult must declare publicly and without reservation ... that the French language will be used neither in the home nor outside it and that no newspapers, periodicals, or books will be brought in from France. The constitution will be abolished. The territory will be placed under a minister for Alsace-Lorraine ... and ruled dictatorially ... We must also consider the Danes and also place before them a new deciding choice. Whoever fails to declare himself unconditionally for the Prussian state must cross the border to Denmark.'

Claß felt that his initial idea, to create a larger Germany – or *Mitteleuropa* – gradually, initially by means of a customs union, had largely been overtaken by events. His answer to the German Reich's setback in Morocco was for it to grab European territory in the traditional Prussian manner.

He declared: 'We must pursue an active foreign policy – in a word, an aggressive one. ... Obviously, any expansion in Europe is to be brought about only through victorious wars ... If we have been victorious and force cessions of territory, we will thereby get regions inhabited by Frenchmen or Russians, people who are hostile toward us. We then have to ask whether such an increase in territory improves our situation ... Since we have broached the question of evacuation, (of native populations), in passing, so to speak, it is perhaps not out of order to speak of it publicly on occasion. By so doing, our enemies will recognize that such desperate measures already have their advocates in Germany ... In other words, we ought not to think of an aggressive war to take foreign territory for purposes of evacuating (inhabitants). But we ought to accustom ourselves to thinking of such a measure as an allowable response to foreign attack. A predatory war contradicts our principles. But a punishment for a ruthless attack justifies us, even to this severest measure, for there is such a thing as 'iron necessity.' A defensive war in this sense may legitimately be conducted in an aggressive way on the German side, for we must undertake to pre-empt the enemy.'[85]

Claß was making horrific remarks, but he had the support of Emil Kirdorf, the founder of the German Coal Syndicate, and of the broad-shouldered, pebble-spectacled lawyer, Alfred Hugenberg, who managed the Krupp armaments concern. French Ambassador François-Poncet would later observe that Hugenberg's 'round-gold-spectacles, his potbelly, his bristly white moustache, lend him the reassuring aspect of a worthy country doctor' but in reality, he is ... one of Germany's evil spirits.'[86]

The German Reich's population had multiplied since 1870. Afred Hugenberg had always felt towns to be the hotbeds of socialism and Marxism. He idealised the farming community and felt that it needed 'lebensraum' (more living space) outside the country's present borders to allow it to flourish. Hugenberg's aim was for the German Reich to expand, and he had the secret support of Gustav Krupp von Bohlen und Halbach, the firm's titular head, who was alleged to have closer ties with the German government than any other comparable firm in the world. [87]

Hugenberg revealed that his and Krupp's mission was 'to do practical work, and surreptitiously lay cuckoos' eggs all over the place – without insisting on taking credit for it.' The Pan-German League was suddenly awash with cash, and it supported books advocating enlarging the already huge German army.

In his book *Germany and the Next War* General Bernhardi revealed the anger that the German military-industrial cabal felt at its 'humiliation' in Morocco, declaring in his Preface: 'All the patriotic sections of the German people were greatly excited during the summer and autumn of 1911. The conviction lay heavy on all hearts that in the settlement of the Morocco dispute no mere commercial or colonial question of minor importance was being discussed, but that the honour and future of the German nation were at stake.'[88]

Bernhardi asserted in his introduction 'The Germans were formerly the best fighting men and the most warlike nation of Europe. ... In striking contrast to this ... they have to-day become an almost too peace-loving nation.' In the chapter headed 'The Right to make War' he wrote 'War ... will be regarded as a moral necessity, if it is waged to protect the highest and most valuable interests of a nation' while in the 'The Duty to make War' he asserted: 'The lessons of history thus confirm the view that wars which have been deliberately provoked by far seeing statesmen have had the happiest results.'[89]

Other scribes wrote in the same vein. Hans Delbrück, who succeeded the ardently nationalistic anti-Semite von Treischke as editor of the *Preussiche Jahrbücher*, was praised by the Pan-Germans as being almost one of them,[90] although he would voice his alarm at the growth of their power by December 1913.[91]

The Pan-German League also felt that the country should have a larger army and be prepared psychologically for war. So, it founded the promotional organization called the Army League and chose Major General August Keim, who had already successfully agitated for the Navy League, to head it. By the autumn of 1912, the Army League had secured 40,000 individual and 100,000 corporate members.[92]

The Kaiser had appointed former Prussian Minister for the Interior, Theobald von Bethmann-Hollweg, as Chancellor in 1909. Tall, elegant Bethmann-Hollweg, on whose soothing words the British would fatally come to rely, had a Swiss mother and eminent and cultured ancestors on his father's side.

Bethmann-Hollweg was a Prussian, but he was also a consummate politician. He told the Reichstag the army had to be increased because 'Nobody could do away with the chance of war. ... If there was a war it would become a world war, and we would have to fight on two fronts.' However, he asserted that Germany was rearming merely because she needed to negotiate from a position of strength and he asked his ambassador to London, Prince Lichnowsky, to stress that Germany and Britain had close links, and shared interests.[93]

The first army bill in 1912 raised the numbers of the already large standing army from 595,000 to 622,000 men. The second army bill in 1913 increased the German standing army to 694,000 with another 72,000 in the navy.[94] The Navy League had also been busy canvassing for funds for further expansion. It planned to construct another battleship, another large cruiser, two small cruisers, a flotilla of torpedo-boats and a quantity of submarines. Ten airships and fifty aeroplanes were also to be built.

One would have thought that the Social Democrats would have fought against the armaments bills as they had just won a huge electoral victory in the Reichstag, with both the conservative and Pan-German parties losing ground. Yet Bismarck had merely side-lined parliament when it opposed his armaments bill in the 1860s and his bitter campaign against the socialists in the 1870s and 1880s, exiling their spokesmen and banning their magazines, had made them wary of taking on the establishment again. Although as a pressure group they had been instrumental in prodding Bismarck to introduce progressive social legislation, they were subject to repeated threats of attack. So, after a half-hearted attempt at criticism, they accepted the army's new increases, their one consolation being that the increases would be paid by direct taxation instead of the usual indirect taxation, which hit the poor men's pockets.[95]

Britain was more anxious about Germany's construction of 'dreadnoughts' for the German navy. In February 1912 Viscount Haldane was sent to Germany to come to an agreement on halting the warship-building programme.

Haldane was born in Edinburgh and had the distinction of speaking fluent German. In December 1905 he had been appointed Secretary of State for War. Despite working on a very restricted budget, he had been very, effective. He had set up the British Expeditionary Force, 'the best trained, best organised and best equipped British Army ever to leave these shores.'[96] He had also inaugurated the Imperial General Staff, created the Territorial Force and had even met Wilhelm II so seemed an excellent choice for the current negotiations.

Yet Haldane had a very, different outlook from that of the aggressive Emperor and his Grand Admiral, Tirpitz. A supporter of women's suffrage, he had helped Sidney Webb in 1895 found the London School of Economics, whose aims was to 'teach political economy on more modern and more socialist lines.' He believed in peace and was not even of a military build. Indeed, Beatrice Webb felt that his 'bulky awkward form and pompous ways, his absolute lack of masculine vices and manly tastes ... would have made him an unattractive figure if it were not for the beaming kindness of his nature.'

Unfortunately, there was no meeting of minds between Haldane and the autocratic Emperor and his bellicose Admiral. Wilhelm II would not have noticed the 'beaming kindness,' of Haldane's nature and would have viewed his support for women's suffrage with the greatest suspicion. Germany offered Britain 'a naval holiday' if Britain promised that she would stay neutral in any future war that Germany was engaged in if Germany appeared as the defender. The offer seemed generous, but Britain was aware that Bismarck had asserted that Prussia/Germany was the defender in all the three wars that he had initiated. So, the talks failed.

The tactless Kaiser was warned against inflaming the British. Meanwhile, the more emollient Chancellor, Bethmann-Hollweg, attempted to portray his country's friendship with Britain like a business deal.[97] He felt that he made real progress in gaining Britain's friendship and must have been pleased that Britain was not increasing the size of her army in response to the German army's expansion.

Prussians liked to think of the coming war as a final settlement of accounts between the Germans or 'Teutons' and the Slavs because the Social Democrats had criticized Russia as a despotic regime. Yet the Austrians were not so keen on this portrayal, as about a third of their subjects could be called Slavs. The pretext for war would therefore have to constitute an affront to the Germanic race. The Balkan wars, of 1912 and 1913 did not fit into this category.

In the first Balkan War, which lasted from October 1912 to May 1913, Serbia, Greece, Montenegro, and Bulgaria fought the Ottoman Empire and captured nearly all its remaining European territories. When Austria-Hungary mobilized in the winter of 1912-13 to prevent Serbia from extending her frontier to the Adriatic, Chief of the German General Staff, Helmuth von Moltke, warned the Austrians that Germany could not be expected to excite her people over a border dispute.

Austria was filled with alarm at the thought of her empire disintegrating like Turkey's. She believed that Russia's ally and fellow Slav nation, Serbia's ambition was to gather all the South Slavs into an empire under her control. Archduke Franz Ferdinand, who later met with such an untimely end, had been against military adventures.[98] However, in the autumn of 1912, despite Austria's Foreign Minister, Count Berchtold advising caution, Franz Ferdinand urged that the Balkan 'Slavs' should not be allowed to advance further and be prevented by force from reaching the Adriatic and gaining a foothold there.[99]

On 21st November 1912 Franz Ferdinand's good friend, the Kaiser, promised that Germany would support Austria in a fight over the Balkans[100] but a newspaper article in the influential *Norddeutsche Allgemeine Zeitung* advised against military action. Austria was irate, yet as she was Germany's key ally Foreign Minister Gottlieb von Jagow eventually declared: 'If Austria is forced, *for whatever reason,* to fight for its position as a Great Power, then we must stand by her side.'

Unfortunately, these words sounded to Britain's Foreign Minister, Sir Edward Grey, too much like 'a blank cheque.' He made it known through Germanophile, Lord Haldane, that 'If Germany would not let Austria disappear as a great power, neither would England let France disappear.'[101]

On 3rd December 1912 the German Emperor vented his anger at Sir Edward Grey declaring: 'Because Britain is too cowardly openly to leave France and Russia in the lurch on this occasion and because it envies and hates us, other powers are not to be allowed to defend their interests with the sword.' He then called his army and navy chiefs to a conference on 8th December 1912. Chancellor Bethmann-Hollweg was not invited.

General von Wenninger, Bavaria's military plenipotentiary at the Military Supreme Command headquarters in Berlin, who would be decorated for his outstanding leadership in 1917, was in the vicinity but not actually present at Wilhelm's meeting. He summed it up as follows:

'A week ago, His Majesty summoned Moltke, Tirpitz and Müller (Bethmann, Heeringen and Kiderlen were not invited!) and informed them in a state of great excitement that he had heard from (his Ambassador) Lichnowsky that Haldane had come to tell him, probably on (Sir Edward) Grey's orders, that ... Britain could not look on while France was defeated, and a Power developed on the Continent which possessed absolute hegemony in Europe.'

(In the face of this affront to Prussian military ambitions, Chief of the Prussian General Staff) 'Moltke wanted to launch an immediate attack; there had not been a more favourable opportunity since the formation of the Triple Alliance. ... (however) Tirpitz demanded a postponement ... until the completion of the (Kiel) Canal and the U-boat harbour at Heligoland.

'The emperor was reluctant to agree to a postponement. The only thing which he told the Minister of War the following day was that he should prepare a new large army immediately. Tirpitz received the same order for the fleet. The Minister of War likewise demanded that the Army bill should be delayed because the entire structure of the army, instructors, barracks etc., could not digest more big increases; all drill grounds were crowded, the armaments industry could not keep pace ...

'The emperor ordered the General Staff and the Admiralty to prepare an invasion of England on a grand scale. ... Meanwhile his diplomats are to seek allies everywhere, Rumania (already partly secured), Bulgaria, Turkey etc.'[102]

Admiral George von Müller, Chief of the German Naval Cabinet, who was at the meeting, is said by Professor Röhl to have written that Tirpitz had pressed for 'a postponement of the great fight for one and a half years.' Röhl's conclusion was that the First World War broke out 'not by accident over a Balkan imbroglio but intentionally, as a result of a deliberate, (though disastrous) long-term policy.'

Some historians say that Röhl cannot draw the conclusion that the First World War was planned at this meeting in December 1912 as Admiral Müller's stated after the meeting with Wilhelm II: 'There were almost no results.'

However, Professor Röhl scrutinised the microfilm and discovered that Müller's remark merely emanated from his frustration that Germany had backed away from going to war immediately. Müller finished his diary entry with the words: 'I wrote to the chancellor about influencing the

Press.' The German army and navy commanders were not ready for war, but they were ready to contemplate it.

On three occasions, in 1912-1913, when Austria was on the brink of military intervention in the Balkans [103] Germany refused her support. German Foreign Secretary, Gottlieb von Jagow warned Austria-Hungary that before she went to war there must be an 'obviously hostile act by Serbia' and emphasized, 'It is very, important that we should appear to have been provoked because I believe that then - probably only then – Britain can remain neutral.'[104]

Meanwhile, Chancellor Bethmann-Hollweg agreed with Admiral Müller about influencing the Press. The task was to condition the peaceful German people to accept the prospect of war.

In December 1912 the Conservative East Prussian newspaper *Ostpreussische Zeitung* expressed itself in favour of a 'brisk, merry (fröhlich) war,'[105] while Gustav Krupp's newspaper, *Berliner Nuerste Nachtrichten* echoed Pan German President Heinrich Claß's demands for 'territorial expansion' and talked of 'the war that was needed to secure Germany's status as a world power,' and the *Post* largely financed by Hugenberg, announced at New Year in 1913, 'If, as a hundred years ago, a war is required, if the year of fire and flood was really to be followed by a year of blood – then the German people will demonstrate that today, as in the past, it can defy a world of enemies.' In the interim, over the border in France, France had elected a new Prime Minister and Minister for Foreign Affairs, called Raymond Poincaré.

Poincaré was small, neat, and punctilious. He loved literature and poetry but had a strong will, a formidable intellect, and a prodigious capacity for work. Before entering parliament, he had been a lawyer to the French iron ore magnates of Longwy and Briey in Lorraine, so he was acutely aware of how much the German the iron and steel bosses coveted France's iron.[106] He was convinced that France should present a strong negotiating front against German attempts at aggression, defending his attitude by declaring,

'I have studied all the documents relating to the Morocco affair. There results from this study a conviction: it is that each time that we have desired to be conciliatory towards Germany she has abused our overtures. Each time, on the other hand, that we have shown ourselves firm, she has retreated. Germany does not understand the language of right; she understands only the use of force.'

France would provide money for Russia to improve her ramshackle army, which had been defeated by the Japanese in 1905, and they both decided to espouse the doctrine of 'firmness' 'to safeguard the peace by the demonstration of force.'[107]

The Moroccan Agadir incident had been a shock to France. The Pan-Germans aggressive language over the incident had even been recorded in the British *Times*. Then the French had been faced with huge increases in the German army.

In the face of the German army's impending growth and the knowledge that must have percolated through to French intelligence of Pan-Germans wish to grab a portion of Eastern France,[108] Poincaré introduced a 'Three Year Law' in the summer of 1913 to equalise the number of soldiers on both sides of the border.

Putting the same number of soldiers as Germany into battle was a tall order for France as her population was only some forty million compared to Germany's sixty million. Although the smaller French field guns were superior in quality to their German counterparts, Gustav's Krupp's spies would have known that France's artillery was quantitively inferior, especially in heavy guns. Her fortresses guns were short of ammunition, and she lacked the heavy artillery and mortars,[109] so important in modern warfare. Yet Poincaré received mass support for three-year conscription. Only the radical socialists, led by former Prime Minister, Joseph Caillaux, opposed his bill.

In 1913 an astonishing incident occurred in the part of Alsace that Bismarck had grabbed in the Franco-Prussian war. A young Lieutenant named Forstner was reported to have stated to his recruits in Zaberne, (Saverne), that they would each be given a present of ten marks if they stab a Wackes, (a local expression for a native of Alsace), if the 'Wackes' insulted them. This caused outrage in the area.

That same evening some pupils from the secondary school were said to have made offensive remarks to the German officers returning from fencing school, whereupon Lieutenant von Forstner ordered his regiment to load their rifles and arrest all the civilians who were out of doors.

Forstner's regiment zealously carried out his orders and arrested twenty- seven people, including the Judge and Council of the Civil Court, who were leaving for home after a long day. A further aggravation was caused by Lieutenant Forstner's wounding of a lame cobbler, who he alleged insulted him 'by contemptuous cries.' The affair caused an explosion of indignation among the many peace-loving German civilians who disagreed with his excessive high-handedness. Bethmann-Hollweg tried to play down the incident by declaring that the authorities 'can make no progress in Alsace-Lorraine unless they abandon the fruitless attempt to turn the South Germans of the Reichsland into North German Prussians.' [110]2

Yet Bethmann-Hollweg's words were not enough to pacify the members of the Reichstag. A motion was proposed under the new rules of procedure, stating that the Reichstag disapproved of Bethmann-Hollweg's treatment of Forstner's conduct. It was adopted by the huge majority of 293 votes against 54. Forstner was sentenced by court-martial to forty-three-days detention for 'assault and wounding and the unlawful employment of weapons' in striking the lame cobbler with his sword.

However, the Officers' Corps fought back. It had always been the army's creed that 'the soldier, whether ... an officer, a N.C.O. or a private, (is) never subject, even in peacetime, so long as he (is) serving with the colours, to the civil courts, no matter what offence he might commit.'[111] On 5th January 1914 the military court of appeal reversed von Forstner's sentence, accepting his plea that the sword was only an ordinary military sword and had not been specially ground for the occasion and moreover that he was a Prussian officer and executed the orders of his King.'[112]

The battle lines were emerging between the Reichstag and the Emperor. Many in the military believed that the only way to retain their power and prestige was to wage a successful war. The Officers' Corps and the soldiers under their command did not believe that they would 'die as cattle' because of the greed of the industrialists, who paid their wages and coveted France's iron ore. Their fight was for their place in society, above the civilian herd, with their great estates subsidised and their rights secure from civilian courts. Members of the civil service owed their employment to the Kaiser too. The lower ranks of the civil service, (except for purely clerical and technical posts), were staffed exclusively by ex-servicemen 'hammered by years of discipline into the Prussian pattern.'

The postman who delivered the Officer's letters, the inspector who clipped the Officer's railway ticket, and the customs officer who examined the Officer's railway ticket, would all come smartly to attention whenever they met an Officer.[113] They were horrified at the modern concepts of liberty and equality emanating from revolutionary France and were prepared to die in an external war to preserve the status quo at home. In 1893 General von Haeseler, who commanded the German troops in Lorraine, declared: 'Our civilization must build its temple on mountains of corpses, an ocean of tears and the groans of innumerable dying men. It cannot be otherwise.' Most soldiers would not have used that language but essentially, they agreed.

Kaiser Bill and his military chiefs had created an immense army but had no war to use it in. Meanwhile increasing the size of the armed forces was so expensive that the country was running out of cash. By the autumn of 1913, the country's capital coverage had become extremely thin, and it was increasingly worried lest the Austria-Hungarian Empire slipped over to the Entente camp. By December 1913 both Turkey and Austria-Hungary began looking at enlisting Entente capital to help their projects. In May 1914, Chairman of the Deutsche Bank, Karl Helfferich, expressed his frustration.

'Not one man on our board can take the responsibility of going one step further with the advances for the construction of the Baghdad Railway without certain prospect that a Baghdad loan will come in the very, near future. If the market is upset for us by Bulgarian or Turkish armaments loans, we shall have to shut up shop.'[114]

However, help was at hand. A large Prussian loan had been launched on the international market in February 1914 and a second one immediately afterwards. They were oversubscribed. Yet the money did not go far enough. Deutsche Bank complained that it still had to make 'big uncovered, advances' for the construction of the Bagdad railway. However, Krupp's armaments company received a hefty slice of the money and Germany was able to offer Bulgaria a large loan, which ensured her friendly neutrality before the start of the war.[115]

In 1870 Bismarck had failed to invade enough of France to secure her iron ore deposits. France's iron ore was now desperately needed by the iron and steel and armaments magnates of the Ruhr.

German prospectors had been active in Asia, Australia, and Africa to fund their insatiable appetite for iron, but the French deposits in Lorraine, in the Briey basin were so much nearer and more convenient. August Thyssen was the first to buy an i62on ore concession in France. By 1913 seventeen concessions were partly or completely owned by German companies. Finally, in December 1913, alarmed by Germany's penetration 'pacifique,' the French halted the granting of new iron ore concessions to Germany. When it became apparent that there was no hope of continuing the peaceful penetration of France, a deputation of German industrialists spoke openly to the former Italian Minister of Commerce, Nitti, of their need to lay their hands on the iron ore basin of French Lorraine.[116] Indeed in 1917 Albert Vögler, future director of vast conglomerate, United Steel, would declare 'To obtain Briey we would fight for a further ten years.' [117]

The French had been frightened of another invasion since 1870. Sooner or later, they believed the 'Prussians' would invade again. The great iron and steel factories had initially expanded in Germany rather than France because of the simple fact that it was cheaper to move iron to coal rather than coal to iron. With the threat of war, France had expanded her iron production too, but it was far smaller and less profitable than Germany's.

Poincaré had offered to lend Russia money to modernize her armed forces so that the two countries could present a united front against German aggression. The Russian army was 300,000 larger than that of the German and Austrian armies combined but had suffered a humiliating defeat at the hands of the Japanese in 1905 and was short of artillery, shells, railway connections, motorised transport and even boots. Some money had already been received and the new treaty with France had been signed in December 1913, but it did not become law until June 1914.[118]

In the 1920s Poincaré would be accused of having been implacably opposed to a peaceful existence with Germany before the First World War because he was eager to help Russia modernise her armaments. However, it appears that he thought of re-arming Russia more as a protection against German aggression than as a step towards war. Indeed, he seems to have been ready and willing to appease his powerful northern neighbour in the early months of 1914 and dined at the German embassy in Paris on 15th January 1914 at a time when Bethmann-Hollweg already felt under pressure from the Pan-Germans 'naïve belief in force.'

During a discussion of the two countries' spheres of interest in Asia Minor and Syria, Bethmann-Hollweg declared that the government of 'monarchical and constitutional' Germany was guided by public opinion in general and was influenced by interested groups in particular. He declared that he was anxious to stand above group interests, but he was exposed to considerable pressure and his position was threatened. He complained:

'Je suis attaque et critqué de tous les côtés et il est possible que je ne reste pas longtemps à la tête des affaires ....' ('I am attacked and criticised from all sides, and it is possible that I will not remain long at the head of government)[119]

On 15th February, a Franco-German agreement was signed on the (French) financing of the Bagdad railway and on spheres of influence in Asiatic Turkey. It was followed by further talks between the two countries over spheres of interest in Central Africa[120] but the murder of the Archduke Ferdinand occurred before they reached fruition.

The German army had wanted the war to start before France's new help for Russia's inadequate railways and army produced results. On 1st June 1914 von Moltke declared: 'the sooner it comes, the better for us' asking Foreign Minister Jagow to precipitate a preventative war as soon as possible.[121] He seemed confident that even the Austrian army could hold the Russian army unaided for a period of time, telling Austrian General Conrad von Hötzendorf on 12th May 1914: 'We hope to be finished with France in six weeks after the commencement of operations, or at least have got so far that we can transfer our main forces to the east.'[122]

The Turkish Empire's collapse had not only affected Austrian Empire but also the creaky Russian Empire, which professed to be champion of the Slavs, but which had suffered from revolution in 1905 and was hit by huge strikes in July 1914. Russia was worried about the construction of the Baghdad railway. By December 1913, the Turkish army would be virtually placed under the control of the German general, Liman von Sanders. When the railway was complete Germany would be able to speed troops and guns to the area, impeding the Russian navy's access to the Mediterranean.

The Russians aimed to use the new French money to modernize their railways and to increase the army's peacetime strength by 480,000 by 1917 but they did not vote to approve the programme until June 1914, too late for the start of the First World War.[123]

Only the British were not preparing to arm. Although British Foreign Minister Sir Edward Grey had expressly told Haldane, in 1912, to emphasize that Britain 'could under no circumstances tolerate France being crushed' there was no doubt that France's historic enemies, the British, had enjoyed their friendship with Germany in the years before the war, and decided to believe in the German leadership's genuine love of peace.

In contrast to the rest of Europe, the British added no soldiers to their army between 1912 and 1914. The Liberal government had been excited by the German Social Democrats' great gains in the 1912 elections and believed that Germany was becoming truly democratic. Those on the Left in the Liberal Party sympathised with the ideas of the Fabian Society which looked forward to an evolutionary socialist society in Britain and felt that Germany was the model to follow. The founders of the London School of Economics Sidney and Beatrice Webb, had even been planning a six-months tour of Germany to study 'developments in state action and in German cooperation, trade unionism and professional organization' when war broke out in August 1914.[124]

Meanwhile, the Liberal party itself had been fatally weakened as it was dependent on the support of the Irish nationalists. Irish nationalist leader, John Redmond, had wanted Home Rule in return for his support for Prime Minister Herbert Henry Asquith's new administration. So, in April 1912, the Liberal government had introduced a bill, which declared that an Irish Parliament could deal with purely Irish questions, while Westminster dealt with Foreign Affairs and security. Protestants in the rich booming Belfast ship-building area were unhappy, and they prepared to fight, fearing that a Catholic administration in the poor rural South would discriminate against them.

This was exactly the sort of situation which Bismarck's spy, Wilhelm Stieber, would have enjoyed. He had been innovative in stoking up divisions between Austria and Hungary before Bismarck's invasion of Austria in 1866. And he taught his successors well. Germany offered tons of ammunition to the competing parties. Ulsterman Fred Crawford smuggled 25,000 rifles and three million rounds of ammunition from Hamburg in April 1914, while the Catholic Irish volunteers were caught landing a thousand rifles in broad daylight in July.

Meanwhile, in Germany, the *Post* had published a leading article, on 24th February, declaring that the prospects for a victorious preventative war were propitious. 'France is not yet ready to fight; England is involved in domestic and colonial difficulties. Russia shuns war because it is afraid of revolution at home. Are we to wait until our opponents are ready or shall we seize a propitious moment to bring about a decision?'[125]

On 12th May General von Moltke told his Austrian counterpart, Conrad von Hötozendorf, 'To wait any longer means a diminishing of our chances as far as manpower is concerned.'[126] He gave the same message to German Foreign Minister Gottlieb von Jagow a few days later as they drove from Potsdam to Berlin, warning that Russia would have completed her armaments modernisation in two or three years.

In June Emperor Wilhelm II also voiced his anxieties about Russia's armaments modernisation programme to the banker Max Warburg. He complained about the inadequacy of the rail links ... to the Western Front against France; and hinted ... (at) whether it would not be better to strike now, rather than to wait.'[127]

The conservative press had no doubts. It advocated 'a brisk and merry war' to quell the power of the workers, while the employers' federation spokesman, Walter Lambach, called for a war to achieve an 'economic unit stretching from the North Sea to the frontiers of Egypt.'[128] As usual the Pan-German League had the final say by quoting from Bismarck,

'It is very, useful to follow the example of Frederick the Great before the Seven Years War, who instead of waiting for the net in which he was to be caught to envelop him, tore it with a quick thrust ... In such situations it is the duty of the government, and the nation has the right to demand from the government, that if war is really impossible to avoid, the government shall choose to fight it at a time when it can be fought with the least sacrifice and the least danger to the nation.'[129]

CHAPTER THREE

Bismarck's Responsibility for the First World War

In 1961, after Lloyd George's belief that we all 'slithered' into war in 1914 was accepted throughout the Western world, the celebrated German historian Fritz Fischer published his book, *Griff nach der Weltmacht,*(*Grasp at World Power*, later published in England under the less explosive title of *Germany's aims in the First World War.*) That book and his later *War of Illusions* make a convincing case that the Prussians and in particular the Pan-Germans were responsible for starting the conflict.

    This book returns to Fischer's thesis about how the war began, with many supporting quotes from other modern eminent historians. Finally, it reveals the American journalist, Raymond Gram Swing's interesting meeting with Chancellor Bethmann-Hollweg and Sir Edward Grey just before the conflict took place.

The opportunity for Chancellor Bethmann-Hollweg and the German military to provoke a major European war came at a most convenient moment on 28th June 1914. On that fateful day, a Serb extremist committed a crime which could be presented as a crime against the whole Germanic race. He assassinated the heir presumptive to the Austro-Hungarian throne, Archduke Franz Ferdinand, in the city of Sarajevo.

    Franz Ferdinand's murder did not cause quite the amount of weeping and gnashing of teeth that might have been expected in Austrian court circles. Indeed, bellicose Chief of the Austro-Hungarian General Staff, Baron Conrad von Hötzendorf, and his military friends welcomed the news because it presented them with the opportunity of securing Germany's help in crushing Serbia and her territorial ambitions.

The Austrian army had wanted to crush the Serbians for a long time, but it had been difficult to persuade Germany to help. Many Germans had a low view of the Austro-Hungarian Empire. Indeed, balding, long-serving Ambassador to Vienna, Heinrich von Tschirschky, asked wearily on 22nd May 1914 'whether it is really still worth our while to tie ourselves so closely to this decrepit construct of states and to continue the irksome task of dragging it along.'[130] Yet the hierarchy needed the Austrians for their 'brisk and merry war' against France. The murder of the Archduke, with his Teutonic blood, could stir the sympathy of the German people, and provide the pretext for the conflict. Indeed, the timing of the Archduke's murder was so propitious that conspiracy theorists could even believe that a German spy like Bismarck's Wilhelm Stieber might be behind it.

Der Post spoke the truth in February when it declared that Britain and France were 'in disarray.' William Stieber himself could not have done a better job of stirring up turmoil in France and Britain at this critical time.

Britain was facing near civil war in Ireland, and the French were also totally pre-occupied at home after Henriette Caillaux, the former mistress and now wife of leading left-winger and former Prime Minister, Joseph Caillaux, murdered France's most powerful journalist, Gaston Calmette.[131]

Joseph Caillaux had been accused of having German sympathies. He was the most prominent opponent of the Three-Year Conscription Law which France had adopted in response to the large increases in Germany's army.

The iron ore magnates of Lorraine had a very, strong influence in French government circles, just like Krupp and the iron and steel magnates in Germany. The President of the French iron and steel association, the Comité des Forges, had been criticized by Joseph Caillaux as an undeserving plutocrat. Yet the French iron magnates knew far better than Caillaux that the Germans coveted their iron ore fields, lying as they did so temptingly close to the French border, and it was precisely to avoid them marching into their country and grabbing them that they had supported their citizens enduring three-years of conscription.

The conservative press was determined to discredit Caillaux for trying to undermine the three-year law. So, the journalist Gaston Calmette resorted to an underhand trick in publishing a letter in *Le Figaro* revealing that Caillaux had written love letters to his new wife, Henriette, whilst he was still married to her predecessor. An enraged Henriette then followed Calmette to his office. 'Do you know why I have come?' Henriette asked.

'Not at all, Madame' Calmette replied. But he soon found out. Henriette Caillaux took out a revolver and shot Calmette six times. Hours later, he died of his wounds.

The French public were convulsed by Calmette's murder and forgot about the assassination of the Arch-Duke Franz Ferdinand. Henriette Caillaux's trial would start on 20th July three days before Austria-Hungary's ultimatum to Serbia.

Emperor, Kaiser Bill had a close relationship with Franz Ferdinand and was stunned by his death. His vision of the two Emperors ruling the Continent of Europe together, after the death of Austria's present emperor Franz Joseph, was shattered by the Arch-Duke's murder. The Austrian Ambassador to Berlin was summoned forthwith to send a message to Vienna that the Kaiser 'would regret it if we let this present chance ... (to go to war) go by without utilising it.'[132]

The Kaiser was very, close to the Krupp family. He had been accused by the Pan-Germans of being weak during the Morocco crises but now he promised Gustav Krupp, that he would declare war at once if Russia mobilized, assuring him that this time he was not 'falling out.'

Gustav Krupp von Bohlen und Halbach was a head shorter and sixteen years older than his wife, Bertha. Portrayed as a man with a fanatical love of order, he forbade all talk of politics, never lost his temper, and rarely displayed emotion of any sort. One biographer even declared of him: 'It is ... doubtful that he entertained a single original thought in his entire life.'[133]

Yet that portrayal is grossly to underestimate Gustav's ability, ambition, and the threat he posed to peace in Europe before the First World War. His father-in-law, Fritz Krupp, had been the first of the family to bankroll the Pan-German League. His firm had developed the 420 mm Big Bertha howitzer, capable of breaking down any foreign defences, and his secret finance for the Pan-German League had borne fruit, with vast increases in the size of the German army agreed by the Reichstag in 1912 and 1913.

Indeed, Wilhelm II was so nervous of Gustav Krupp in 1914 that his 'repeated protestations' that no one would be able to reproach him, ever again, for his failure to declare war at the appropriate moment, were to the Kaiser's confidant, 'almost comical to hear.'[134]

At the time of Franz Ferdinand's death, Austrian Emperor, Franz Joseph had been on the throne for over sixty years. He had become nervous and brittle with age. Following his defeat by Bismarck, he had been forced to share his empire with the Hungarians. Each day he rose at 5.0 am and worked long lonely hours at his Dispatch boxes. Now he wrote a letter in his own quivering hand appealing for Germany's help to 'eliminate Serbia' and prevent his empire from being swallowed up in the 'Pan Slav flood.'

In the 1970s another German historian, Fritz Fellner, discovered that not all Austrians were as bellicose in 1914 as their aged Emperor. Chef de Cabinet, Count Hoyos later claimed that Foreign Minister, Count Berchtold told Hoyos that although Austria-Hungary considered a military clash with Serbia to be unavoidable sooner or later, she was prepared at present to content herself with closer ties to Bulgaria – 'in case Germany believed that a later moment would be more favourable from a European point of view.'

However, German Chancellor, Bethmann-Hollweg, who has received an enviable reputation in Britain as a responsible statesman, immediately promised Germany's 'entire might' if Austria-Hungary deemed it necessary to proceed against Serbia,[135] 'twice' urging 'immediate action,' as the international situation was 'entirely in our favour.'[136]

After initial hesitation, Wilhelm declared that Austria-Hungary could 'count on Germany's full support' even in the case of 'grave European complications', consoling himself that 'Russia is not at all ready for war and would certainly think long before appealing to arms.'[137]

Austria's partners, the Hungarians, also had to give their consent to reprisals being taken against Serbia. Hungarian Prime Minister, Count Stephen Tisza, was alarmed that an Austrian attack on Serbia might lead to 'intervention by Russia and consequently to world war.' However, Germany's 'unconditional attitude' that 'the Monarchy had to reach an energetic conclusion' persuaded him to change his mind.[138]

Germany had already been told of the contents of the Ultimatum to Serbia but both countries decided that it should be delivered only after French President Raymond Poincaré had finished his trip to St Petersburg, and was on the sea journey home, cut off from communications.[139]

'What a pity!' about the lateness of the date, declared the Kaiser, who had already set off on a cruise and was trying to keep abreast of developments by telegram. German Ambassador to Britain, small, thin aristocratic Prince Karl von Lichnowsky, had languished on his estates in Silesia for thirteen years before the Kaiser chose him to become British Ambassador. He was instructed to mobilize the British press against Serbia whilst being careful not to give the impression that Germany is 'egging Austria on to war.'[140]

In Vienna, German Ambassador, von Tschirschky, was confident that Britain 'will not at this juncture intervene in a war which breaks out over a Balkan state, even if this should lead to a conflict with Russia, possibly also France.

He declared. 'Not only have Anglo-German relations so improved that Germany feels that she need no longer fear a directly hostile attitude by Britain, but above all Britain at this moment is anything but anxious for war and has no wish whatever to pull the chestnuts out of the fire for Serbia, or in the last instance, for Russia.'[141]

Gustav Krupp had industrial spies everywhere. His agents had stolen over a thousand documents from the German War Office files in 1912. Moreover, his firm had fomented anti-German attacks in the French press to rattle the German government into giving him more orders.[142] When he declared in 1914 that the Russian artillery was 'far from being either good or complete, while Germany's has never been better' people believed him.[143] Foreign Secretary, Gottlieb von Jagow, said happily: 'if the conflict cannot be localised, and Russia attacks Austria, this gives the *casus foederis*.'[144]

Jagow was a close friend of Gustav Krupp.[145] On the 18th if July he suggested to Wilhelm II that 'His Majesty might spend the last days of his cruise closer to home in the Baltic' ... 'in case unpredictable developments should force us to take important decisions, such as (the army's) mobilization.'[146]

On 19th July, the text of the Austrian ultimatum to Serbia was finalised by Germany and Austria-Hungary.

Jagow promised that Germany would stand behind Austria 'unreservedly and with all her power.'[147]

On 20th July, while the French were still mesmerized by the wife of the former Prime Minister, Joseph Caillaux's actual appearance in court on a charge of murder, the Directors of the Hapag and Norddeutscher Lloyd were given warning of the Austrian Emperor's impending Ultimatum, so that they could take measures for the protection of their ships in foreign waters. The Kaiser also ordered the concentration of the fleet.[148]

Meanwhile Britain's attention was still diverted by the dispute over Irish Home Rule. The Protestant Unionists in the north-east of Ireland, and the Catholic majority in the south, both illegally armed by German armaments manufacturers, 'were still squaring up for a civil war.' In a leading article, on 22nd July, *The Times* issued an alarm to the British governing classes to forget Ireland for the moment ... and to examine 'a situation in European politics too serious to be ignored.'[149]

The 23rd of July was decided as the day for the ultimatum's delivery, and the time of the delivery was put back an hour to make quite sure that President Poincaré and his Prime Minister Viviani had left St Petersburg and were on the high seas when it arrived.[150]

At 6 pm on 23rd July, the ultimatum was presented. Besides the trial of those involved in the Archduke's assassination, the ultimatum demanded that the Serbian state formally and publicly condemned its 'dangerous propaganda' against Austria-Hungary, whose ultimate aim it alleged, was to 'detach from the Monarchy territories that belonged to it.' The ultimatum also demanded that the Serbs 'suppress by every means this criminal and terrorist propaganda' which it alleged was propagated in subversive magazines and in 'schoolbooks.'

In addition, it demanded that Serbia remove all the people from public office that Austria-Hungary disliked and accepted in their stead Austro-Hungarian government officials who could seek out and suppress all the elements in Serbia they consider insurrectionary. Finally, the ultimatum demanded a response in only two days-time, at 5 pm on Saturday evening, 25th July.

The wording of the ultimatum caused consternation in European capitals. Britain had been completely unaware of the impending conflict on her doorstep. First Lord of the Admiralty, Winston Churchill, wrote: 'Europe is trembling on the verge of a general war, the Austrian Ultimatum being the most insolent document of its kind ever devised.'

The collapse of the Turkish Empire had destabilized the Balkans. The Austrian Empire was affected by it, but so was the creaky Russian Empire, which professed to be the champion of the Slavs, but which had suffered from revolution in 1905 and was hit by strikes in July 1914.[151] The Russian leadership wanted to avoid war but feared that failure to support Serbia would lead to a loss of their credibility.

Long-serving British Foreign Minister, Sir Edward Grey, was held in high esteem in Europe.[152] Although rooted in love of the countryside, and with a passion for fishing in his spare time, he had been sorting out international problems for years. In 1913, he had persuaded the Germans to curb Austrian ambitions in return for Britain preaching moderation in St Petersburg [153] and he was confident that he and his German 'friends' could sort out the present situation. He told Ambassador Lichnowsky, that Germany should impress upon Austria-Hungary the need to retract some of its 'impossible demands' while Britain worked on Russia to influence Serbia.

This did not produce positive results. Ambassador, Prince Lichnowsky, was told to tell the British, 'We did not know what Austria was going to demand but regarded the question as an internal affair of Austria-Hungary, in which we had no standing to intervene.'

This did not satisfy Sir Edward Grey. On 24th July, he suggested mediation over the ultimatum by the four powers not directly affected – Britain, France, Germany and Italy – in the event of 'dangerous tension between Russia and Austria' but the suggestion was not sent on until after the time limit given in the ultimatum. [154]

Meanwhile the Austrians' resolve seemed to waver. Serbian Crown Prince Alexander had already visited the Russian Legation in Belgrade on the night of 23rd/24th to express his despair over the Austrian Ultimatum.[155] Subsequently the Austrians received the Russian chargé d'affaires to discuss the situation.

Russia was naturally alarmed at the thought of the obliteration of her fellow Slav and Eastern Orthodox, friend,

Serbia. The maintenance of the balance of power in the Balkans was vital to Russia. The Berlin-Baghdad railway, on which so many German ambitions were pinned, was alleged by alarmists to threaten Russia's very existence because Russia's only access from the Black Sea to the Mediterranean was through the narrow channel of the Bosphorus, the so-called boundary between Europe and Asia. When the Bosphorus Straits were briefly closed in 1911-12 'the economy of southern Russia nearly shut down as well.'[156]

In 1913 a German general, Liman von Sanders, had been appointed to command an Ottoman army corps at Constantinople. This caused uproar in the Russian press. Although Sanders was eventually appointed to the less provocative role of Inspector-General of the Turkish army, Russian anxieties remained. Yet Russia had only received the first 665-million-franc tranche of a large French loan to improve her strategic railways and enlarge the army on 9th February 1914.[157] So she confined herself to declaring in an official communiqué that it could not remain 'uninterested' if Austria annexed Serbian territory.[158]

On 25th July Serbia's answer the ultimatum was received. Serbia accepted all the onerous terms of Austria's ultimatum except for the demand that Austro-Hungarian police should be allowed a free hand in Serbia.

Grey said that Berlin should intervene in Vienna to say that it found Serbia's answer satisfactory. He differentiated sharply between the Austria-Serbia dispute and an Austria-Russian conflict. Lichnowsky sent three increasingly urgent messages asking Germany to give Austria 'the hint,' and in 1915, he would express his frustration at Bethmann-Hollweg's slow and inadequate replies to Sir Edward Grey's peace initiatives in 1914:

'On our side nothing, absolutely nothing was done to preserve peace, and when we at last decided to do what I had advocated from the first, it was too late. By then Russia, as a result of our harsh attitude, and that of Count Berchtold, (the Austrian Prime Minister) had lost all confidence and mobilized. The (Russian) war party gained the upper hand. ... Such a policy is comprehensible only if war was our aim, not otherwise.'[159]

On 25th July Austrian Emperor, Franz Joseph, decided that Serbia's response to the ultimatum had been inadequate. He signed the order mobilizing eight army corps. Hungarian Prime Minister, Tisza, revealed that Germany had influenced Franz Joseph's decision by declaring that hesitation would 'greatly impair belief in the Monarchy's energy and capacity for action, in the eyes of both friend and foe.'[160]

Late in the evening of 25th July, Jagow agreed to Grey's proposal to 'localise' the conflict, but Chancellor Bethmann-Hollweg destroyed his happy moment by threatening that Germany would mobilize if reports of an alleged call-up of Russian reservists were confirmed.[161]

Sunday 26th July came and went. President Poincaré and French Prime Minister Viviani were on the high seas at this crucial time. Poincaré would later write: 'In our floating home there reached us only the deadened echoes of the outside world. We received nothing precise, either from St. Petersburg or from Paris. We were more and more anxious in our solitude and in our remoteness and Sunday passed away without bringing us, lost between the sky and the waves, positive news from land.'[162]

That same Sunday, 26th July, while Poincaré was stuck on the sea, Chief of the German General Staff, General von Moltke, was plotting his French invasion, busily drafting a demand to Belgium to allow the passage of German troops in the event of 'the imminent war against France and Russia.'[163]

Moltke had little respect for the French armed forces. When asked how long the Austro-Hungarian armies would have to hold out against the Russian armies unaided, he confidently declared, 'We hope to be finished with France in six weeks after the commencement of operations, or at least to have got so far that we can transfer our main forces to the East.'[164]

At last, late in the evening on 26th July, the Kaiser arrived back from his cruise at Potsdam station.[165] He was met by Bethmann-Hollweg, whose apprehension stemmed 'not from the dangers of the looming war, but rather from his fear of the Kaiser's wrath when the extent of his deceptions are revealed.'

'How did it all happen?' asked the Kaiser brusquely. Bethmann-Hollweg quickly offered his resignation. Unfortunately, the Kaiser refused to accept it. So Bethmann-Hollweg continued to deceive his Kaiser, but he realized that he must act quickly to induce Russia to mobilize because the Kaiser would almost certainly try and quell the coming storm when he actually saw Serbia's answer to the Austrian ultimatum.

Emperor Franz Joseph had already mobilized eight army corps. On 27th July, Grey's trusted aide in the Foreign Office, Sir Eyre Crowe, warned that Austria's mobilization could have serious consequences.

'I am afraid that the real difficulty to be overcome will be found in the question of mobilization. Austria is already mobilizing. This, if the war does come, is a serious menace to Russia, who cannot be expected to delay her own mobilization which, as it is, can only become effective in something like double the time required by Austria and Germany. If Russia mobilizes, we have been warned that Germany will do the same, and as German mobilization is directed almost entirely against France, the latter cannot possibly delay her own mobilization for the fraction of a day. This however means that within twenty-four hours His Majesty's Government will be faced with the question whether ... Great Britain will stand idly by or take sides.'[166]

Sir Eyre Crowe had a German mother and a German wife. He spoke German as his first language and knew 'the Prussians' well. He warned Sir Edward Grey that Britain had been too soft in her approach to his mother country. The German newspapers were, to use Crowe's phrase, 'egging on Austria-Hungary.'[167]

Grey was growing frustrated. He asserted that if Germany really wanted peace, she could prevent Austria from pursuing a 'foolhardy policy.'[168]

But the 'Prussians' had other ideas, and they were in a hurry. On the 27th, Austria's actual 'declaration of war' was laid before the old Emperor for his signature. German Ambassador to Austria, Tschirschky, promised Berlin that it would go off on the 28th or 29th at latest 'in order to eliminate any possibility of intervention.'[169] Meanwhile, Germany's Ambassador in Britain, Lichnowsky, warned Bethmann- Hollweg: 'If we rejected every attempt at mediation the whole world would hold us responsible for the conflagration and represent us as the real warmongers. *That would also make our position impossible here in Germany where we have got to appear as though the war had been forced upon us.* Our position is the more difficult because Serbia seems to have given way extensively. We cannot therefore reject the role of mediator; we have to pass on the British proposal to Vienna for consideration, especially since London and Paris are continuously using their influence on Petersburg.'[170]

Bethmann-Hollweg and Foreign Minister Jagow did belatedly pass on Grey's latest peace initiative to Austria, but left out the all-important last line of the latest British telegram, which read: 'Also, the whole world here is convinced ... that the key to the situaton lies in Berlin, and that if Berlin seriously wants peace, it will prevent Vienna from following a foolhardy path.'[171]

Meanwhile Grey was sent a soothing message which read: 'We have immediately initiated mediation in Vienna in the sense desired by Sir Edward Grey.'[172]

The Kaiser had arrived back from his cruise. Yet it was only on the morning of 28th July, a full day after Serbia's reply to the ultimatum arrived, that he, in fact, had sight of it. [173]

Wilhelm II had been full of spite against the Serbs. Even just before he landed at Kiel, he had declared: 'These fellows (the Serbs) have been intriguing and murdering, and they must be taken down a peg.'[174] Yet when at last he saw Serbia's response to the ultimatum he immediately declared that it represented Serb 'capitulation of the most humiliating kind' and asserted 'because of it there no longer exists any reason for war.'

However, because it would mean that the Austro-Hungarian army had been mobilized three times in vain against Serbia, Wilhelm suggested, on the lines of Sir Edward Grey's proposal (which had been altered and sent on late by Bethmann-Hollweg) that as a *satisfaction d'honneur* Austria should occupy various areas of Serbia as a pledge until definite assurances had been received that she would behave herself in the future.[175]

This was the moment that the military, the armaments manufacturers and their Pan-German friends in government had been dreading, the moment that their Emperor's nerve would give way before the certainty of war, like it allegedly had in 1905 and 1911. But the Chancellor had a solution, and it had, to him, the merit of historical precedent.

In 1870 Bismarck decided to change the Kaiser William I's Ems telegram to goad France into war. In 1914 Bethmann-Hollweg decided to change the text of Kaiser

William II's so-called 'Halt in Belgrade' to ensure that war came in 1914.

The only condition that the Kaiser insisted upon in his 'Halt in Belgrade' was that Austria had 'to have a guarantee that the promises are carried out by a 'temporary' occupation of parts of Serbia'.

Bethmann-Hollweg changed the wording to stress that the Austrian Hungarian occupation must be the means of compelling 'complete fulfilment by the Serbian government of the Austrian demands,' emphasising to his Ambassador in Vienna, Heinrich von Tschirschky,(telegram no. 174), 'You must most carefully avoid giving any impression that we want *to hold Austria back. We are concerned only to find a modus to enable the realization of Austria-Hungary's aim without at the same time unleashing a world war, and should this after all prove unavoidable, to improve as far as possible the conditions under which it is to be waged.*'[176]

At 11 am on 28th July 1914, Austria presented her declaration of war on Serbia. Tschirschky did not even bother to show Bethmann-Hollweg's amended version of the Kaiser's 'Halt in Belgrade' to the Austrians until the afternoon.

The same day Bethmann-Hollweg offered Turkey an alliance guaranteeing Turkey's territorial integrity in relation to Russia if Turkey would bind herself to Germany and place her army under German control during the war. Negotiations also began with the aim of making Turkey the centre of revolution against Britain. [177]

Russia became alarmed by events in the Balkans. She had already stated that she could not remain 'uninterested' if Austria annexed Serbia. She ordered a partial mobilization of her troops as a warning.

Bethmann was pleased. He declared: 'Meanwhile should, contrary to our hopes, an intervention by Russia spread the conflagration. Then we should be bound under our alliance to support our neighbour with the whole might of the Reich. ... Russia alone must bear the responsibility if a European war breaks out.'[178]

Nevertheless, after Austria-Hungary presented her declaration of war against Serbia, Bethmann suddenly realized with horror that Austria was physically unable to begin hostilities until 12th August. He complained: 'The

Imperial government is thus put into the extraordinarily difficult position of being exposed during the intervening period to the other Powers' proposals for mediation and conferences ... It is imperative that the responsibility for any extension of the conflict to Powers not directly concerned should under all circumstances fall on Russia alone.'[179]

Under the Schlieffen Plan Germany's plan to invade France through Belgium would be triggered not when countries formally declared war but simply when they ordered mobilization.[180] Bethmann believed that he could count on the pacifist Social Democrats' support and on Britain's neutrality in the coming war, provided the detested Russian Tsar appeared to be the warmonger. So, he refused Generals von Moltke and von Falkenhayn permission to go to war after Russia's partial mobilization, and redoubled his efforts to secure Russia's general mobilization, to provide the pretext for war, which his country could unite upon.

Meanwhile, he continued to emphasize Germany's wish for peace to British Ambassador Sir William Goschen. However, the army's pressure was mounting. In two interviews with Generals, Falkenhayn and Moltke, in the morning and evening of the 29th, each time before meeting the British Ambassador, Bethmann had argued that Germany must wait until Russia had begun general mobilization; for unless the blame for 'the whole shemozzle' could be pushed on to Russia, it was vain to hope for Britain's neutrality. Nevertheless, the generals' troops were ready; they wanted to go to war and had, that day, sent a demand to the German Minister in Brussels to allow the passage of the German armies through Belgium.[181]

Once again Bethmann told them that Russia's partial mobilization did not create a *casus foederis* for them to go to war against France; they must wait till Russia's general mobilization to ensure German Social Democrat support and British neutrality.[182] But he couldn't put the army off for ever. Under Bismarck's Prussian structure for the German Reich, the leaders of the armed forces carried more weight with the emperor than the Chancellor.

Austria had already declared war on Serbia on 28th July. On 29th Austria bombed Belgrade. Even the German hierarchy agreed that Russia's partial mobilization had been undertaken in a weak and muddled fashion. Philipp Oscar von Chelius, German military plenipotentiary in St. Petersburg, wrote: 'I have the impression that they have mobilised because without having aggressive intentions, they are afraid of what will happen and that they are now frightened of what they have done.[183]

Yet the Tsar of Russia and his advisors were still racked with anxiety that if Russia mobilized partially and there was a war with Austria-Hungary, Russia would be completely unprepared for a war against Germany. At last, on the 29th of July, the boat bringing French President Poincaréand Prime Minister Viviani from Russia, arrived at Dunkirk. The two men took the train to Paris. All the members of the government were waiting for them at the Gare du Nord and people crammed the windows and pavements to see their four-wheeled carriage as it passed. Their attention had abruptly shifted from the murder trial of Madame Caillaux, whose husband did not see the point of France adopting three-year conscription, to the horror of an imminent war. The three-year conscription had been adopted to deter the Germans from marching into France, but it had not worked! [184]

At 11.05 at night on 29th Bethmann-Hollweg summoned Russia in almost ultimatum terms, not to provoke any warlike conflict with Austria. An hour and a half later, he informed Vienna of Russia's partial mobilization and added,

To avert a general catastrophe, or in any case to put Russia in the wrong, we must urgently wish to begin and to continue conversations with Austria in accordance with telegram 174.'[185] Telegram 174 was the one where Bethmann-Hollweg had written: 'You must most carefully avoid giving any impression that we want to hold Austria back. We are concerned only to find a modus to enable the realization of Austria-Hungary's aim without at the same time unleashing a world war, and should this after all prove unavoidable, to improve as far as possible the conditions under which it is to be waged.'

Then late in the night of 29th and into the early hours of 30th, encouraged by hearing that Georgy (George V) wanted Britain to remain neutral, Bethmann-Hollweg met the British Ambassador Sir Edward Goschen to explain to him the naked truth of the matter. Previously Bethmann-Hollweg had dissuaded the British from joining the arms race by stressing his country's peaceful intent and encouraging Britain to join Germany in solving the Balkan disputes. Now that Germany had the ascendancy, with an immense army about to fall upon her neighbours, he decided that the time had come to show his hand, to ensure deluded Britain's neutrality in the coming war.

Bethmann-Hollweg spilled the beans to Goschen - who was of German descent, and therefore hopefully would understand the German Empire's needs – to tell Sir Edward Grey that Germany would soon be going to war against France. He affirmed that the French colonies, which Germany had so long coveted, would be forfeited but promised that Germany would not grab any French territory unless Britain entered the war, in which case Germany would claim a free hand. He also spoke of Belgium, saying that Belgium's 'integrity' should not be impaired by the war 'provided Belgium does not take sides against us' but did not mention Belgium's sovereignty.[186]

Tall, slim Sir Edward Grey came from a long line of liberal politicians. He had been Foreign Minister since 1905 and carried immense prestige in England. In October 1908, the Kaiser had caused disquiet in Britain when he published an article in the *Daily Telegraph*, in which he declared:

'Germany is a young and growing empire. She has a world-wide commerce which is rapidly expanding and to which the legitimate ambition of patriotic Germans refuses to assign any bounds. Germany must have a powerful fleet to protect that commerce and her manifold interests in even the most distant seas.'

Grey had realized that the Kaiser was reflecting a view shared by a wide section of the Prussian establishment at the time, so he stated in his response in 2008:

'He (the Kaiser) has the strongest army in the world and the Germans ... are looking for somebody on whom to vent their anger and use their strength. ... It is thirty-eight years since Germany had her last war, and she is very strong and very restless ... I don't think there will be war at present, but it will be difficult to keep the peace of Europe for another five years.'[187]

Grey's assessment of the situation in 1908 was correct. Six years later the 'Prussians' were looking to upset the peace of Europe. They understood only too well that it was England's backing for France which had thwarted their colonial ambitions in 1911. So, they had concentrated their efforts on lulling Grey and his country into a false sense of security and friendship in 1913.

The British had responded enthusiastically. Their artistic and cultural links with Germany went back a long way. It was the French, after all, who had been Britain's historic enemies not the Germans; yet the British government had not realized that the country which had been chatting them up in 1912 and 1913 was not Germany but the Prussian Empire writ large. The Social Democrats, who had won such a large victory in the Reichstag in 1912 had little real power. In 1912 between 75% and 85% of the whole net revenue of the German Empire had been spent on the army, skewing its economy, unless justified in war.[188] In 1913 Germany voted for further army increases, leaving it critically short of funds.[189]

Unfortunately, Britain had a great navy but if she wanted to keep the peace in Europe, she needed a land force. Although the British Expeditionary Force was 'the best trained, best organized and best equipped British army ever, its size was insufficient to command German respect, while her projected armaments expenditure in 1914 was less in real terms than in it had been in the year 1907-8.

Grey realized that he had been fooled when he turned a blind eye to Germany's armaments drive in 1913. He did not believe that warfare was the way to conduct negotiations in the twentieth century, but he understood that Prussia/Germany took a different view. However, even with the knowledge of Bismarck's wars against France and Austria, a man as intelligent and civilized as Grey would have found it difficult to accept that Germany was prepared to go to war against both Russia and France. Finally, on the night of 29/30th, he did.

So, he sent a telegram to the German Ambassador to Vienna, Tschirschky, via Ambassador Lichnowsky, stating that Britain as a neutral power was prepared, with German help, to mediate between Austria-Hungary on the one side and Serbia and Russia on the other, but that the moment that France was drawn into the war, Britain would not be able to stand aside.[190]

Bethmann was momentarily shattered by Grey's telegram. At 3 am on the 30th he sent his Ambassador Tschirschky, a message, telling him that circumstances had changed and that he no longer supported Austria's fight against Serbia:

'If therefore, Austria should reject all mediation, we are faced with a conflagration in which Britain would be against us, Italy and Romania in all probability not with us. We should be two Great Powers against four. With Britain an enemy, the weight of the operations would fall on Germany ... Under these circumstances we must urgently and emphatically suggest to the Vienna cabinet acceptance of mediation under the present honourable conditions. The responsibility falling on us and Austria for the consequences, which would ensue in case of refusal, would be uncommonly heavy.'

And at 3.05 am Bethmann sent another telegram ordering Austria-Hungary to stop 'refusing any exchange of views with Russia.' He declared to the no doubt astonished Austrians, 'We are prepared to fulfil our duty as allies but must refuse to allow Vienna to draw us into a world conflagration frivolously and without regard to our advice.'[191]

Had he continued in this vein, a European war might have been averted but the powerful generals were already clamouring for a declaration of war and in this situation, they were more powerful. Wilhelm II had nominally the greatest power in the land, but he had already been side-lined. Now he was fooled again. When he was shown the news that Russia had partially mobilized, at 7 am on the 30th (two days after it had happened),[192] he commented in his marginal notes on the information 'Then I must mobilize too. ... He (Tsar Nicholas II) is taking on himself the guilt. ... I regard my attempted mediation as having failed.'[193]

The Foreign Ministry quickly passed the Kaiser's marginal notes on the necessity for Germany's mobilization onto the army's General Staff. As it was Wilhelm who was in titular charge of the country, not Bethmann-Hollwag, when General von Moltke saw that the Kaiser had said, 'Then I must mobilize 'he felt justified in pressing Austria-Hungary to adopt general mobilization, (without actually declaring war on Russia), and also to mobilize against Russia rather than Serbia.[194]

The Kaiser was a loud-mouthed fool, but it was not his fault that his 'Halt in Belgrade' had failed to stop the war. He had been deceived big time. Neither Austria-Hungary nor Serbia, let alone Russia, had seen the Kaiser's 'Halt in Belgrade' before Bethmann doctored it. He was distraught at the thought of war and at midday on 30th July he received more unsubstantiated news from his naval attaché in

London, to the effect that the 'British fleet would launch an instant and immediate attack on us at sea if it comes to war between Britain and France.' This statement drove the Kaiser crazy. After venting his anger against 'that filthy cur, Grey' he declared that 'England alone is responsible for the war, not we, anymore!'[195]

Although Bethmann-Hollweg was still reluctant to proclaim an 'imminent threat of war' General Moltke took independent action. He sent an urgent warning to the Chief of the Austro-Hungarian General Staff, Conrad, to mobilize immediately against Russia (letting the dispositions against Serbia take second place) and to announce as his reason the Russian proclamation of partial mobilization (so as to make Russia appear the aggressor).[196]

Meanwhile Sir Eyre Crowe and the permanent under-secretary at the Foreign Office, Sir Arthur Nicolson, discovered that forts were being manned and submarine defences installed all along Germany's North Sea coast, a sign which they interpreted as an expectation that Germany expected to fight Britain. Crowe declared that Germany 'is throwing dust in our eyes for the purpose of delaying if not hindering ... British preparations.'[197]

The French were acutely aware of the threat to their nation. The covering troops of the German army were already massed all along the frontier between Luxemburg and Alsace.[198] They had adopted three-year conscription to deter them from attacking France. As this had proved ineffectual, they felt that their only hope was to withdraw France's troops well behind her frontier to avoid giving the Germans the slightest pretext to invade. In an unprecedented move, Prime Minister René Viviani, (who had only been appointed by Poincaré a couple of weeks earlier), ordered the French troops to leave a zone of ten kilometres, (six miles), between the French army outposts and the border.[199]

This did not worry the 'Prussian' leadership but before attacking France, it thought it absolutely, essential to identify Russia as the aggressor to secure the support of the peace-loving German people. At last reports came in that Russia was mobilizing all her forces. At 9 pm on the 30th Bethmann-Hollweg and Foreign Minister Jagow yielded to generals Moltke and Falkenhayn's insistence that the 'state of imminent war' had to be proclaimed the next day.[200]

At midnight, only three hours after the evening meeting, Moltke had his adjutant, Hans von Haeften, draft the Kaiser's proclamation to his people, his army, and his navy. The report of Russia's general mobilization was confirmed at noon on 31st July.[201] To make certain of German and British socialist-backing, Bethmann-Hollweg postponed the date for Germany's general mobilization to 1st August.[202]

Threatened with war against Austria-Hungary (and Germany) the Russian Tsar had ordered the 'general mobilization' of his albeit woefully ill-equipped, but enormous number of troops from the depths of his huge country. However, Nicholas II promised Wilhelm: 'As long as the negotiations with Austria on Serbia's account are taking place, my troops will not take any *Provocative* action. I give you my word on this.'

And when he heard of Germany's mobilization on 1st August, he wrote to Wilhelm saying, 'I should like to have the same guarantee from you that I gave you myself – that these measures do not mean war.'[203]

Many historians have since agreed that unloved Russia's general mobilization did not amount to a declaration of war.[204] Yet Russia's refusal to demobilize within the ultimatum of twelve hours was accepted in Germany as exactly that. In Prussian military circles it was greeted with a huge sigh of relief. There would be no more trouble from the pacifist German people, who had voted en-masse for peace and prosperity only two years earlier. On 31st July Bavarian Minister at Berlin, Count Lerchenfeld, reported that the Social Democrats had 'in duty bound, demonstrated in favour of peace' but were now 'keeping quite quiet.'[205]

Persuading the German Social Democrats that Russia was the aggressor had been of fundamental importance because of their hatred of the Tsar's repressive regime and their traditional fear of the Slavs. On 1st August, the Press Office of the German Foreign Ministry declared: 'Russia alone forces a war on Europe which nobody has wanted except Russia; the full force of responsibility falls on Russia alone.'[206]

It was a brilliant move by Bethmann-Hollweg. Bethmann's assertion that Russia was the culprit had resonance in America as well as with the Left in Allied countries.

Although Colonel House would later assert that Germany had gone to war partly so that the 'group of militarists and financiers' who governed her could 'conserve their selfish interests," he had told his impressionable President, Woodrow Wilson on 29th May: 'The situation is extraordinary. It is jingoism run stark mad. Unless someone acting for you can bring about a different understanding, there is some day to be an awful cataclysm. ... Whenever England consents, France and Russia will close in on Germany and Austria.'[207]

Britain's socialists shared their German and American counterparts' fear and dislike of Russia. They admired German states like Saxony, which had been in the forefront of introducing garden cities and clearing slums and promoting elementary and adult education. In Würtemberg and Baden art, theatre, music and literature were generously supported.[208] A large portrait of the Kaiser hung in the Oxford Examination Schools and a host of distinguished German figures such as the ambassador, Prince Lichnowsky, and the composer Richard Strauss had just received honorary degrees.[209] On 1st August when a number of British academics realized that Britain was on the brink of war against the country that they so admired, they expressed their opposition in a letter to the Times:

'We regard Germany as a nation leading the way in the Arts and Sciences and have all learnt and are learning from German scholars. War upon her in the interest of Serbia and Russia will be a sin against civilization.'

Influential journalist, Norman Angell wrote in the same vein, declaring: 'The object and effect of our entering this war would be to ensure the victory of Russia and her Slavonic allies. Will a dominant Slavonic federation of say 200,000,000 autocratically governed people with very rudimentary civilization but heavily equipped for military aggression, be a less dangerous factor in Europe than a dominant Germany of 65,000,000 highly civilized people, mainly given to the arts of trade and commerce?'[210]

Norman Angell had already published a manifesto with half a million copies circulated, contending that for Britain to support Russia, would lead to Russia dominating Europe to the detriment of Germany, a nation 'racially allied to ourselves and with moral ideals largely resembling our own.'[211] His words had influence. British Prime Minister, Henry Asquith was concerned that although the powerful Unionist Party had affirmed its support for the war,[212] three-quarters of Liberal MPs remained to be convinced or were outright pacifists.[213]

On 1st August, after the German order for mobilization had been signed, the British King, George V, sent a direct personal telegram to the Tsar.[214] An offer also arrived in Germany to guarantee France's neutrality. The Kaiser accepted the offer and ordered Moltke 'to hold up the advance westward.'[215] However, Moltke protested that he could not; the patrols had already penetrated Luxembourg. When the Emperor persisted with his demand Moltke remarked bitterly, 'Now it only remains for Russia to back out too.' After sharp arguments, Bethmann-Hollweg and Moltke agreed that the military advance would have to go on 'for technical reasons.' George V's offer had come too late.

An American journalist named Raymond Gram Swing, who worked for the *Chicago Daily News*, has given an interesting insight into Bethmann-Hollweg and Sir Edward Grey at this time. He had met Bethmann through the offices of Baroness von Schroeder, the Canadian wife of a 'Junker nobleman of wealth and station.'

Swing later wrote about the Baroness's intervention. 'She was a socialite supporting moderate Bethmann-Hollweg against army extremists. She gave dinners to which the Chancellor and his friends were pleased to come. She repeatedly told me that Bethmann-Hollweg was a moderate, opposed to any annexations after the war. I said that if that were true, he should tell me and let me repeat it to Sir Edward Grey for the British certainly had a different view of him. And that was precisely what she brought to pass.

'I was received by the Chancellor in the sombre palace where his office was situated. I was invited to sit in the ample chair at the side of his huge desk, and there I was told, without any preliminary conversation, just what I was to repeat to Sir Edward Grey. Germany would not annex any Belgian territory after the war and would guarantee Belgium's independence. But he added a fateful phrase. I was also to tell Sir Edward that Germany would want an indemnity for having been forced into the war.'

'Herr von Bethmann-Hollweg may have noted my disappointment at hearing this. 'Can I trust you? He asked. 'Not a word of this must be published in the newspapers.

You understand that?' 'Of course,' I said. 'And you are able to deliver the message to Sir Edward Grey in person? I said that I was confident the London office of my newspaper could assure this. 'Then come back and tell me what he says. The Chancellor, a tall figure of a man, with gaunt cheeks above his short beard, rose from his desk. 'I must caution you again,' he said, 'not a word in the newspapers. If it is published, I shall have to say I never said it.' I repeated that I understood, and he held out his hand gravely.'

Raymond Swing was disconcerted by the sentence about an indemnity. He knew it would make the mission to Sir Edward Grey futile. He shared his fears with Baroness von Schroeder.

'Don't be so stupid,' she replied. 'The Chancellor was simply protecting himself. He has to do that. If the army hears that he has been talking peace with Sir Edward Grey, he can point to the demand for an indemnity. After all, he has to take precautions. This is a risky step for him. Sir Edward need only say that an indemnity is out of the question, but that he is interested in the proposal about Belgium. He will be smart enough to see why the indemnity has to be mentioned.'

So, Raymond Swing travelled to England, and it was arranged that he should meet Sir Edward Grey the next day.

Swing had little first-hand knowledge of the British. He wrote: 'I knew how the Germans regarded them Sir Edward in particular. He was the arch-conspirator, the passionless builder of Germany's ring of enemies, and especially dangerous because of his ability to speak hypocritically about moral virtues. ... The Sir Edward I met was a revelation. He had the personal appearance of a shaggy ascetic. He was tall, erect, slender with thin, and untidy hair. His clothes were not well pressed. At the time, I knew nothing about Sir Edward, the naturalist, of the breed of Englishmen he represented - sensitive, shy, and complex - or that he was one of the best educated men in the world.

'I delivered my message from Herr von Bethmann-Hollweg and ended with the instructions I had received to return to him and repeat what Sir Edward had to say in reply. Sir Edward's face turned crimson when I spoke the word 'Indemnity.' I thought of Baroness von Schroeders' explanation of it and almost blurted it out. But Sir Edward gave me no time to blurt out anything. He ignored what I said about no annexations in Belgium and Belgian independence. He struck at the word 'indemnity' with a kind of high moral fury and launched into one of the finest speeches I had heard. Did not Herr von Bethmann-Hollweg know what must come from the war? It must be a world of international law where treaties were observed, where men welcomed conferences and did not scheme for war. I was to tell Herr von Bethmann-Hollweg that his suggestion of an indemnity was an insult, and that Great Britain was fighting for a new basis of foreign relations, a new international morality.'

Grey had been horrified by Bethmann-Hollweg's talk of disrespecting Belgium's neutrality. He was also aghast at the idea of the German fleet steaming down the Channel, bombarding France within sight of the British coast. On 2nd August he told the French ambassador, Paul Cambon: 'I am authorized to give an assurance that if the German fleet comes into the Channel or through the North Sea to undertake hostile operations against the French coasts or shipping the British fleet will give all the protection in its power.'[216]

The Conservative Party promised Grey its patriotic support. Its leader, Andrew Bonar Law, was sure that Grey and the government, had done everything possible to preserve peace. He offered the 'unhesitating support' of the Opposition in whatever the government did for the 'honour and security of the country.'[217]

France knew that Bismarck had managed to blame every country he invaded as the aggressor, so she had withdrawn her troops ten kilometres, (six miles), behind her frontier to avoid giving Germany the slightest excuse to invade. On 1st August, the French Minister of War ordered the High Command:

'No patrol, no reconnaissance, no post, no element whatsoever, must go east of the said line. Whoever crosses it will be liable to court martial and it is only in the event of a full-scale attack that it will be possible to transgress this order, which will be communicated to all the troops.'[218]

At 11.0 am on that day, the German Ambassador declared that even if France promised to remain neutral in the forthcoming conflict between Germany and Russia, she would still have to surrender her principal fortresses along her eastern frontier as a guarantee of her 'sincerity.'[219]

France replied that she would act according to her national interests and made a formal protest against German troop incursions across her eastern borders.

Germany then asserted that the French had violated her territory and that French aeroplanes had dropped bombs on the railway near Karlsruhe and Nuremberg.[220] At 6 pm on 3rd August, the German Ambassador in Paris was instructed to inform the French government that Germany considered that a state of war existed between the two countries.

On 4th August Germany invaded neutral Belgium. The neutrality of Belgium was guaranteed by international law – a treaty that all the European states, including Germany, had signed as long ago as 1839. Belgium's neutral status was an integral part of the web of agreements that had preserved the peace in Europe for years. Although the bankers were upset, and the army was unready it was a moral issue.[221] The British declared war.

Chancellor Bethmann-Hollweg was reputedly upset. He realized that he had failed in his task to keep Britain neutral. Some historians have asserted that he secretly sympathized with the Pan-Germans. Yet the evidence suggests that he disliked their 'arrogance.' Indeed, it is said that he came to fear them and early in 1914 had complained of the 'shameless, chronic persecution from all sides' which was ruining his nerves as the Pan-Germans came 'uncomfortably close' in their attempts to undermine his position with the emperor.[222]

Even though the army held an exalted position in 1914 in Prussianised Germany, the responsibility of secret Pan-German Gustav Krupp and the Chairman of his company Alfred Hugenberg for the First World War seems to have been discounted.

The armaments' makers sold weapons to all sides in the run-up to war in 1914. However, all the armaments makers except Krupp were public companies, which held shares in each other's concerns. Krupp was a private company which could spend its profits as it pleased. Its managing director Alfred Hugenberg had been one of the founders of the Pan-German League and Gustav himself had been one of its two principal funders,[223] enabling the firm of Krupp to use its money secure popular support for the massive expansion of the army in 1912 and 1913. It was a huge company, a state within a state, dedicatedly anti-socialist, determined to keep its exalted status at the emperor's right hand, and confident of Germany winning the war through her superior armaments.

Krupp's immense, new 'Big Bertha' howitzer was more powerful than any cannon in the world.[224] The Belgian city of Liège had soon capitulated before the oncoming German army but the thirty-mile circle of strongpoints held out, holding up the progress of two million men into France.[225] The Belgians had ordered new heavy artillery from Krupp the year before, but it had never arrived.[226] They still thought that their forts were impregnable, but Gustav Krupp knew better. Late in the afternoon of 12th August 1914, the first of Krupp's giant Big Bertha howitzers was hauled into position and started its bombardment. 'Hour after hour this nightmare went on until the maze of subterranean corridors linking the thirty miles of redoubts became choked with gas, fire and men ...' Slowly the Big Berthas achieved Krupp's aim of destroying all the Belgian defences, allowing the German army to stream into France.[227]

British journalist, Norman Angell, had stated that Germany would not make money from invading France. Yet the Pan-German League did not agree. Despite France's introduction of three-year conscription, it envisaged the German army fighting a lightning six-week military campaign to demolish the French army. And it would soon be publishing its war aims.

CHAPTER FOUR

Was there a moment for Victory?

Chancellor Bethmann-Hollweg of Germany and Sir Edward Grey of Britain seem to have represented two rival philosophies in August 1914. Prussia/Germany believed that 'might is right.' She deserved to be able to march into her neighbours and grab their coal, iron, and territory because she was a stronger more capable race and able to use her neighbours' land and raw materials more efficiently. She had always expanded by going to war. Even if there was a mountain of corpses in the short-term, the future was bright. A short, sharp war against France and Russia, like Bismarck had waged against Denmark the Austrian Empire and France, would achieve her objectives.

Grey on the other hand believed that in the modern, civilised world there should be an international law, so that one country would not march into its neighbour, grabbing their land and stealing their wealth. Britain might have had to use minimum force for the security of her empire but in cultured northern Europe she believed that war was totally inappropriate, and she had the support of her dominions in her wish for law and order.

The 'Prussians' felt very, confident. The Social Democrats had been told that their country was threatened by a ring of enemies. Yet Russia had been defeated in battle less than ten years earlier by Japan and was separated from Germany by hundreds of kilometres of inadequate roads and railways, while Britain was a maritime nation, which had largely depended on the navy for her expansion. In contrast, Germany's battle-ready army was positioned in the centre of Europe, facing France which had almost as many troops, but a third-less population.

In fact, Germany had already gone to war before she invaded Belgium. The military strategist von Clausewitz had expressly warned the army against 'kindness.' In Consequence, on 2nd August 1914, the city of Kalisz in the Russian part of Poland had been sacked and set on fire.

Prior to the war it had 65,000 inhabitants. By the end of August, it would be left with 5,000. The Prussian army then invaded Belgium, ravaging the city of Leuven, setting fire to the university library, murdering civilians, and expelling the population, before sweeping on towards Paris.

Yet all did not go quite to plan. General Gallieni, Paris's Military Governor, redeployed troops so that they could attack General von Kluck's First Army on its exposed flank, bringing in extra troops in a fleet of taxis to avert catastrophe. Paris was saved. The German army was repelled by six French Field armies and 70,000 British Expeditionary troops along the River Marne.

The first Battle of the Marne, from 6th to 12th September, was an immense strategic victory for the Allies, wrecking Germany's bid for a swift victory. The German army had to retreat 64 kilometres and dig trenches north of the River Aisne. Despite this setback German morale remained high. Generals Paul von Hindenburg and Erich Ludendorff had won a major victory against Russia at Tannenberg between 26th and 30th August and in France their army occupied the area that Krupp the Pan-Germans and German heavy industry had most coveted in France in the years before the war, the Longwy-Briey iron ore-field.

As many German businessmen and industrialists had disliked the Pan- German League before the war, Krupp's Chairman, Alfred Hugenberg, had distanced himself from the movement. Once the conflict started, however, he renewed his ties with Pan-German League's President, Heinrich Claß, [228] who now asserted its war aims.

'France must be crushed ...' and Russia 'be required to make territorial concessions which give us a better frontier at the same time as land for settlers.'

On 28th August 1914 he produced a full list of the Pan-Germans' war aims. France was to cede the area down to the Somme, with a high enough war indemnity charged, 'so ... as to prevent her becoming dangerous to Germany for many years.'

Claß also wanted Germany to permanently grab the Longwy-Briey iron ore field and the Channel coast facing Britain, while in the east he declared that 'Russia's face must be forcibly turned back ... and her frontiers must be reduced, approximately to those of Peter the Great.' Finally, and most importantly, he wanted to create *Mitteleuropa*, a huge economic and political conglomeration of states in central Europe under 'Prussian' control.[229]

Claß claimed: 'The Netherlands and Switzerland, the three Scandinavian states and Finland, Italy, Rumania and Bulgaria will attach themselves to this nucleus gradually and of compulsive necessity, without need to the least pressure from the nucleus-States. If one includes the dependencies and colonies of these States, the result will be a vast economic unit capable of asserting and maintaining its economic-political independence against any other in the world.'

Gustav Krupp distanced himself from his fellow Pan-Germans by producing his own set of war aims. He shared the Pan-Germans' ambition to secure *Mitteleuropa* and wanted France eliminated as a great power. However, he viewed Britain as the real enemy and as a result demanded military domination over Belgium and the north of France. He believed, like Tirpitz, that the establishment of German military power on the Channel coast would force Britain to come to the negotiating table.

The Pan-German League had been accused of putting intense pressure on Bethmann-Hollweg before the war. On 9th September, the Chancellor produced 'provisional notes,' which looked suspiciously similar, to those of the Pan-Germans.[230]

Bethmann-Hollweg wrote that as Germany was surrounded by enemies 'the general aim of the war' must be the 'security for the German Reich in west and east for all time.' 'We must create a *European economic association* through common customs treaties, to include, France, Belgium, Holland, Denmark, Austria-Hungary, Poland and perhaps Italy, Sweden and Norway. This association will not have any common constitutional authority, and all its members will be formally equal, but in practice will be under German leadership and must stabilize Germany's dominance over *Mitteleuropa*.'

As to the countries his country was in the process of defeating, he declared that 'Belgium, even if allowed to continue to exist as a state, must be reduced to a vassal state, must allow us to occupy any militarily important ports, and 'must be economically dependent on us,' and 'France must be so weakened that she never again recovers as a great power.'[231] France would also lose her colonies and a commercial treaty would make her economically dependent on Germany and exclude British commerce from the country.

'The military to decide whether we should demand cession of Belfort and the western slopes of the Vosges and the coast from Dunkirk to Boulogne... French Flanders, with Dunkirk, Calais and Boulogne, where most of the population is Flemish, can without danger be attached to Belgium.' That would be in compensation for the loss of Liége and Verviers, which Bethmann envisaged being attached to Prussia.

Little Belgium, the third most industrialized small state in the world, was a prize conquest. Industrial magnate, Hugo Stinnes, who would fight a venomous and ultimately successful campaign against the eight-hour day in German mines in 1923, would be called upon to organize Belgium's coal and industrial production for Germany's benefit. Meanwhile Bethmann-Hollweg rejoiced in the capture of Germany's primary physical objective in France, the Longwy-Briey iron ore field.

Other nations may have coveted owning France's Notre Dame and the Arc de Triomphe in Paris, but Prussia/Germany coveted France's 'iron.' The loss of Longwy-Briey's ore would ensure that France lost 80% of her blast furnaces and 85% of her iron ore production, 'destroying' her as an industrial power.[232]

Heavy industry lost no time in exploiting the mines. They were put under a special 'Imperial Protective Administration' before being placed directly under the Supreme Army Command. The total reserves were put at 2,775 million tons of ore. August Thyssen declared ecstatically:

'The incorporation of the Briey basin will make it only a question of a little time before Germany catches up with and passes America, which will ensure Germany's world domination on the iron market.'[233]

The acquisition of Longwy-Briey and Belgium's industrial riches so close to the Ruhr made it infinitely cheaper for Germany to wage the war, as Britain would become increasingly dependent on expensive imports, [234] perilously transported across the ocean. Naturally, Germany rejected American President Wilson's tentative peace initiative at this time. Prince Gottfried Hohenlohe, Austro-Hungarian Ambassador to Berlin, believed that

Germany was resolved 'to thrash France and England as soundly as possible', and 'Russia as soundly as the enemies in the west, or even more so.'[235]

It is easy to march into a country, less easy to hang onto it. German General Erich von Falkenhayn was determined to win on the Western Front where General von Moltke had failed. After the battle of the Marne, there was the so-called 'race to the sea.' The British wanted at all costs to protect the French Channel ports from falling into German hands. In the battles fought in Picardy Artois and Flanders, neither side could gain the military advantage while the Belgian army, later reinforced by the British Royal Naval Division, held out in Antwerp.

In October and November Falkenhayn tried a breakthrough at the strategic town of Ypres in western Belgium. Although the 150,000 British Expeditionary Force was almost wiped out by the end of the battle, the Allies temporarily won the fight. Meanwhile German public opinion spun round from blaming Russia for starting the war to blaming Britain.

Well-meaning British Labour Leader, Ramsay Macdonald, had foolishly accused Sir Edward Grey of being a warmonger. He could not have imagined the impact his accusation would have in censored Germany, where freedom of speech was far more circumscribed, even in peacetime. His words were seized upon by the German Press. On 2nd December 1914, Chancellor Bethmann-Hollweg dressed himself up in the grey service uniform of a German General and asserted: 'England and Russia have, before God and man, the responsibility for the catastrophe which has fallen on Europe. Belgian neutrality, which England pretended to defend, was nothing but a disguise.'[236]

Now that the war had begun Bethmann-Hollweg took a tougher stance with the German Social Democrats. He told Social Democrat Minister for the Interior, Clemens von Delbrück

'The Social Democrat leaders must realise that the German Reich, and in particular the Prussian State, can never allow any loosening of the firm ground on which they have grown up, the firm acceptance of the State and the system which Social Democracy has been accustomed to stigmatise as 'militarism.' [237]

Naturally, Bethmann-Hollweg forbade the Pan-Germans from publishing their expansionist war aims. They would have horrified American President Woodrow Wilson, the huge German Social Democrat party and the British Labour movement, as Germany had explicitly renounced the annexation of any territory belonging to another country and Wilson and the British pacifists fervently believed her claim. Nevertheless, Krupp's supremo, Alfred Hugenberg, was determined that Germany's war aims should be advertised to the troops to give them a goal to aim for, maintaining that after President Woodrow's recent peace initiative, only the intervention of the Kaiser and the military could prevent the German government from accepting a humiliating treaty, and the demise of the monarchy.

Hugenberg's strength lay in his powers of organization. On 7th November he approached the League of German Farmers, the Central Association of German Industrialists, and the Union of Industrialists for support.[238] Hugenberg claimed that the soldiers would fight more valiantly if they knew that they were fighting to gain the empire they deserved. His pressure group then hassled the Chancellor to publicly declare that Germany was fighting for extra territory to protect her encircled *Reich*.[239]

Meanwhile, General Falkenhayn fought a second battle for control [240]of Ypres using poison gas to be sure of victory. After the battle of Frezenberg between 8th and 13th May Sir John French declared 'The effect of the gas was so overwhelming that the whole of the positions occupied by the French divisions were rendered incapable of movement. ... Fumes and smoke were thrown into a stupor and after an hour the whole position had to be abandoned.'

The Allies now had no option but to use poison gas too, but they were in a poor position to fight as their shells were antiquated, and the Kaiser's magnificently equipped army already had the latest military equipment. Indeed, until the Allies produced tanks in 1916, the 'Prussian' army was the first to produce poison gas, flame-throwers, extra-heavyweight artillery, Zeppelins, effective submarines and machineguns which could fire through aircraft propellers to crush their opponents.

Although Bethmann-Hollweg had made notes of his aggressive war aims, he continued to ban all public discussion of them. The Pan-Germans were frustrated. They felt that for the war to succeed, both the army and the home front needed constant positive progress reports. This meant that they had to have more complete control the press and the message it put out. Former founder of the Pan-Germans, Alfred Hugenberg was the head of Krupp's armaments company. As it had excellent contacts with its suppliers, he was able to form trust funds into which the largest coal and steel companies could secretly funnel the necessary cash to buy a large newspaper company to promote the war.[241]

Pan-German President, Heinrich Claß, had already circulated two thousand copies of his war aims. He was taken to court for disobeying government instructions. So, the Pan-German League mobilized the Prussian House of Deputies, which immediately asked for the nation to be allowed to debate its war aims and let Claß out of prison.

Bethmann-Hollweg maintained that the one and only essential, at present, was to achieve victory on the Western Front. But this did not satisfy Hugenberg. He invited the leaders of the trade associations to a meeting in Berlin. the unanimous outcome of which[242] was for it to tell the government to exploit the favourable situation that the army found itself in the East after Hindenburg and Ludendorff's great military victories at Tannenberg and Masurian Lakes.

Through dazzlingly successful wars, Hindenburg and Ludendorff had managed to acquire an area almost the size of France in the East, comprising present day Lithuania, western Latvia, and north-eastern Poland. The Pan-Germans supported the aim of creating a Polish border strip, approximately the size of Belgium. It was envisaged that up to three million Poles and Jews would be evicted from their land to make way for German settlers.[243] Although, later, this aim would be rescinded and the Kingdom of Poland would be proclaimed in November 1916 so as to persuade the Polish soldiers to fight for the Central Powers, the future determination of Poland's frontiers with Russia and Prussia-Germany would be reserved,[244] and the idea of expelling the Poles and the Jews from a large area would be resurrected in 1918.[245]

But first the government had the home front to attend to. With deaths rising and food scarce, Hugenberg stressed that it was necessary to present the Social Democrats with a 'fait accompli' and to openly pitch the country's war aims high to preserve national morale. A memorandum representing all the country's major business interests therefore demanded a colonial empire sufficient for Germany's economic interests, 'security' in the fields of tariff and commercial policy, 'an adequately guaranteed war indemnity' and territorial acquisitions in the East and the West.

While the people suffered at home, the Pan-Germans war-aims seemed to rise rather than fall. They demanded the Belgian and French Channel coasts, the military and economic domination of Belgium, and the annexation of the ore-fields of Longwy-Briey and the coalfields of the department of the Nord and the Pas de Calais. [246] To help promote these ambitions Hugenberg managed to raise nearly twenty-nine million marks to purchase the major publishing company August Scherl G.m.b.H.

No doubt in making his purchase, Hugenberg was impressed by the influence that Britain's premier newspaper baron, Viscount Northcliffe, had been able to achieve through his newspapers. Northcliffe, like Hugenberg, was a self-made man. He had long had a fear and a hatred of 'Prussian militarism,' which he had managed to instil in the readers of his newspapers. By 1914 the *Daily Mail*, which he had started from scratch, had a million readers. Northcliffe also managed to triple the sales of *The Times* after its purchase because he slashed the price and employed an editor called Geoffrey Robinson (later surnamed Dawson) who was held in high esteem.

Unlike the Pan-Germans, Northcliffe had never expressed any desire for Britain to grab territory in Europe, merely called for his country to rearm and modernize her navy because of the danger that he perceived from the German Reich. When he visited Germany in 1909, he reported to H W Wilson on the *Daily Mail* staff that, 'every one of the new factory chimneys here is a gun pointed at England'.[247] Nevertheless, in the last two years before the war even his newspapers became more concerned with events in Ireland than with the threat of war in Europe. Once the battle began, however, Northcliffe was a tireless campaigner for conscription and for the British army to be equipped with adequate shells.

His newspapers attacked Secretary of State for War and former Field Marshall, Herbert Kitchener for sending the British soldiers to fight equipped with shrapnel shells, which were 'useless' in trench warfare and unable to destroy barbed wire.[248] 'The kind of shell required,' Northcliffe declared, 'was a violently explosive bomb which would dynamite its way through the German trenches and entanglements and enable our brave men to advance safely.' Although Northcliffe was initially condemned because he dared to criticize Britain's national hero, his advice was eventually adopted and before long he was described as the 'most powerful man in the country.'[249] Indeed, the Germans were so alarmed about his propaganda that a German warship was sent to shell his house in Broadstairs in their attempt to assassinate him.

German newspaper proprietor, August Scherl, was also a colourful character. He enjoyed the theatre and published two major daily papers, *Der Tag* aimed at intellectual circles, and the popular newspaper, *Berliner Lokal-Anzeiger*, with a circulation of almost 250,000. However, he was a less successful businessman than Northcliffe and had experienced financial difficulties at the start of the war.

Armaments Tsar, Alfred Hugenberg felt that it was essential to secure Scherl's company because the owners of the other two major publishing houses in Berlin were Jewish-owned and favoured democracy. Naturally Hugenberg himself kept out of the picture, but his envoys insisted that they would only take on Scherl's debts if the new company acquired complete editorial control. The negotiations were prolonged and tortuous. Meanwhile, despite the Pan-Germans aspirations, the war on the Western Front was grinding to a halt.

In early 1916 Falkenhayn had decided on a massive battle of attrition against the French at Verdun. Falkenhayn reasoned that if France, which had a third less inhabitants than Germany, bled to death, Britain would be left fighting alone on the Western Front and could be starved into submission by a submarine blockade. The battle of Verdun lasted from 21st February till 18th December 1916. The Russian general, Brusilov's brilliant offensive, in June, was designed to force Germany to halt its attack. A primary reason for the British starting the Battle of the Somme in July, when nearly 20,000 raw young soldiers were killed on the first day, was also to take the pressure off France. The bloodshed was horrific and the gains seemingly negligible.

The Battle of the Somme was a terrible blow to Britain. It also gave the German Reich a huge and unwelcome shock. Her citizens were sickened by the bloodshed. However, Krupp's supremo Hugenberg had managed to gain complete control of the Scherl newspaper concern by July and immediately changed its editorial policy. Scherl's newspapers urged the troops not to squander the huge victories the army had gained in the East by failing to hold fast in the mud and blood of the trenches on the Western Front. They also warned the Home Front to remain steadfast.

Already in May, Chancellor Bethmann-Hollweg had felt that the economic position of Germany was so serious and the longing of her people for peace so widespread, that she must 'grasp at every possibility of achieving peace.' Housewives were even scrambling and fighting over obtaining meat, the 1915 grain harvest had been consumed and even supplies of potatoes were running short.[250] Yet, Bethmann-Hollweg was faced with the military/industrial junta's implacable opposition to responding to any peace-feeler.

When President Wilson's aide, Colonel House arrived in Britain in February 1916, he was told that Britain's only peace conditions were the evacuation of Belgium and northern France and that she would ask for no war indemnity. Lloyd George assured Colonel House that all Germany's colonial possessions would be returned, and that she would be allowed a free hand allowed against Russia.[251]

Lloyd George's generous peace initiative was rejected. Nevertheless, on 27th May the German Ambassador to Washington, Heinrich von Bernstorff, reported to his superiors that Wilson still wanted to broker peace between the belligerents and that he had the support of the entire American people for his initiative.

German warmonger, State Secretary Gottlieb von Jagow did not fancy his country being condemned by America and neutral Holland for turning Wilson's peace proposal down so he instructed his Ambassador von

Bernstorff: 'As soon as Mr Wilson's intentions of mediation threatens to assume more concrete forms and Britain shows signs of readiness to accept them, it will be Your Excellency's task to prevent President Wilson from approaching us with a positive offer of mediation.'[252]

Jagow was confident of winning the war on the battlefield and wanted the British to be blamed for the failure of Wilson's peace initiative. He called Wilson 'naïve' and declared: We can only welcome it (the peace offer) if the refusal comes from England. For it is obvious that we must be sceptical about the mediation of a statesman ... so naïve as President Wilson, if only because the President would presumably attempt to bring about a peace essentially based on the *status quo ante*, in particular as regards Belgium. ...'[253]

German heavy industry whole-heartedly supported Jagow's refusal to consider relinquishing Belgium with its huge Cockerill steel factory and countless other valuable manufacturing plants. It was also not about to surrender the French iron ore field of Longwy-Briey. American journalist, Raymond Gram Swing went to Dusseldorf to make a study of German industrial production at this time. There he met a steel manufacturer, who graphically explained the situation to him.

Swing reported, 'What he wanted me to understand was that on one side of the frontier between Germany and France lay coal mines in the Ruhr Basin. These were in Germany. On the other side were the iron mines in the Briey Basin. These were in France. German industry in the Ruhr and the remainder of highly industrialized western Germany lived from both iron and coal, and to have them divided by national frontiers was an absurdity. It was this absurdity Germany was fighting the war to end. Germany had to have the iron along with the coal.'

Swing commented, 'He said this simply and with 2conviction. The catch I could see at once in his proposition was that it was completely contrary to the war aims Germany had proclaimed, which explicitly renounced the annexation of any territory belonging to another country. However, I did not say this to the German industrialist. The official war aims, I knew were propaganda. What the industrialist said was sincere.'[254]

German Ambassador, Heinrich von Bernstorff, told Jagow that if Wilson's mediation broke down and Germany resumed unrestricted submarine warfare, war with America was inevitable. Nevertheless, despite the continuing German death-toll on the Somme and the abject misery at home, Jagow's outlook was relentless.

Falkenhayn lost his job on the Western Front after his failures on the Somme, but from a German military viewpoint, his effort had not been fruitless. France's total casualties at the Somme and Verdun amounted to the sickening total of 579,798. The war costs for Britain and France also kept mounting and not only in horrific human terms. They were finding it more and more expensive to buy their raw materials from overseas. Meanwhile France's Pas de Calais was producing coal for Germany's furnaces, Longwy-Briey was producing iron to make Krupp's Big Bertha guns and Belgium's factories were turning French iron into German steel.

With the help of his industrial associates, Stinnes, Kirdorf and Beukenberg, Hugenberg established three hefty companies to help Germany exploit Belgium's resources.[255] Satisfactorily, also for Germany, whereas the Flemish and the Walloons in Belgium had been united against the German invasion, the German government's attempts to split the two different racial groups in the country, by offering concessions to the Flemish, began to show results. Krupps profits would double in 1916-1917.[256]

The total carnage on the Somme was horrific. While the Central Powers had suffered 465,181 casualties, Britain and her Commonwealth suffered 419,654.[257] Naturally this caused political repercussions in Britain as well as in Germany.

British Prime Minister Henry Asquith had felt that the generals should be left to run the war while he ran the country. However, after the Somme's sickening bloodshed, criticism of him mounted; on 13th August Churchill wrote to a colleague that he thought that Asquith would survive

'but his position is not at all good. The Tories outside the Gvt. despise him: the Irish have lost faith in him & many of the Liberals are estranged or sore. There are hostile forces at work in the Cabinet and at any time a collapse is possible.'[258]

The pressure against Asquith continued. On 4th December, an article written with what was said to be 'calculated offensiveness' by Geoffrey Robinson (later to become famous as Geoffrey Dawson in the 1930s) appeared in *The Times*.

Lord Northcliffe was presumed to have written the article, but Dawson would later claim that he had written it on his own initiative. It proved to be the final straw for Asquith.[259] He resigned. The new regime would be led by 'the man of the people' Lloyd George, who assumed greater powers.

The Battle of the Somme had political repercussions in Germany as well. After Falkenhayn left the Western Front, 70-year-old General Hindenburg, who had been raised to a peak of adulation after his victories at Tannenberg, took military control of Germany and the German army withdrew to the more easily defendable Hindenburg Line on the Western Front, adopting a scorched earth policy on its retreat. Meanwhile, the big economic associations felt that the most effective, and least costly means of bringing the war to a successful end, was to return to unrestricted submarine warfare to force Britain to her knees.

In America, the political landscape was also in the balance as an election was due on 7th November. German Ambassador, von Bernstorff, had done his best to influence the electors to vote for the incumbent President Woodrow Wilson.

The British were condemned by the New-Yorker Staats-Zeitung as 'murderers' after the Easter Rising failed in Ireland. Other pro-German publications like The Fatherland, The Vital Issue and The International, whose material supplied some 500-800 newspapers across the country, took the same line in calling on German-speaking America to support the Irish.

After the British executed the rebel leaders, the New-Yorker Staats-Zeitung declared on 25th May: 'One hardly needs to be reminded, that the Irish have always stood with the Germans shoulder to shoulder at all times and on all questions, which have become pressing as a consequence of the war.'[260]

Both the Republicans and the Democrats favoured neutrality at this time, but Bethmann-Hollweg hoped that Wilson would win the forthcoming elections.

It was a close call. However, after his narrow win, the former Professor of Jurisprudence, lost no time in declaring his outrage as what he saw as British malpractice in searching seizing and censoring American transatlantic mail and issuing a 'blacklist' of American firms suspected of trading with the central powers. Wilson also warned that the US would not tolerate the continuation of 'repeated violations of international law.'[261]

In this situation, tall, stooped, and by now silver haired Bethmann-Hollweg was given the task of reneging on his promise not to return to unrestricted submarine warfare, while keeping America and the neutral countries on side. Bethmann-Hollweg told Hindenburg and Ludendorff his plan:

'Count Bernstorff has been instructed on the personal orders of His Majesty to induce President Wilson to issue an appeal for peace. If Wilson can be got to do this, the probable rejection of the appeal by England and her Allies, while we accept it, would give us a moral justification in the eyes of the world, and in particular of the European neutrals, for withdrawing our promise to America.'[262]

On 16th November 1916 German Ambassador Count Bernstorff relayed the good news that Wilson would be receptive to a peace initiative from Germany, the most important proviso being that there should be as little talk as possible about it in Germany so that the Entente powers would believe that it originated in America.[263]

Wilson had, by now, decided that all the Europeans had been guilty of war lust in 1914. His aim was 'peace without victory.' He knew that Britain was becoming more and more dependent on America to finance the war. To make quite sure that Britain responded to the German peace offer, he put Britain under such financial pressure that her reserves were almost exhausted.[264] On 4th December von Bernstorff reported that everything was 'ready for a peace action in Washington' and on 12th December Bethmann-Hollweg submitted his offer. He was a model for all negotiators to copy. Knowing that America could not put the same financial pressure on Germany she had done on Britain, he behaved as though Germany was making a concession even thinking about peace. His proposal was characterized by its strong confidence in victory and its absence of any commitments. He merely declared that the Central Powers were ready to enter negotiations 'calculated to assure the existence, honour and freedom of their people.'

Wilson was disappointed. On 18th December 1916 he asked all the belligerents to make public the conditions on which they would make peace. After Germany refused this initiative, the Entente refused to comply too. Yet Wilson clung to his trust in Germany, prohibiting the export of arms and foodstuff to Britain while fruitlessly begging the German government to communicate its war aims to him in confidence.[265] Republican ex-President Theodore Roosevelt declared 'I don't believe that Wilson will go to war unless Germany literally kicks him into it.'[266]

The German hierarchy was certain that Wilson would eventually be pushed into declaring war by American public opinion. However, they were confident that their use of unrestricted submarine warfare would win the war before America intervened and believed that their 'peace offer' had secured a propaganda victory among the neutral nations.

Large, red-blond haired and red-blooded Arthur Zimmermann, who had recently replaced the 'rodent' Jagow, as Foreign Minister, believed that 'unconditional submarine warfare' would force the British nation to surrender, telling a Danish journalist bluntly: 'If only the United States will keep its hands off and leave us alone, two or three months will be enough.'[267] Yet to make sure that American troops lingered in the US, rather than pouring over to Europe immediately to help the Allies, he decided to persuade the Americans that Mexico was just about to invade America.

In 1916 the revolutionary General Pancho Villa had raided Columbus, New Mexico, killing twenty Americans. Twelve thousand troops were sent in vain to chase him while four-fifths of the regular army were tied up along the Mexican borders. So, in 1917 Zimmermann sent a coded telegram to Mexico by three different routes to make sure that it arrived. It said:

We intend to begin unrestricted submarine warfare on the first of February. We shall endeavour in spite of this to keep the United States neutral. In the event of this not succeeding, we make Mexico a proposal of alliance on the following basis; make war together, make peace together, generous financial support, and an understanding on our part that Mexico is to reconquer the lost territory in Texas, New Mexico, and Arizona. The settlement in detail is left to you.[268]

Zimmermann's telegram created a huge stir in America. However, the Mexicans denied ever having received it and the cream of intellectual society in New York declared it to be a forgery. At Zimmermann's press conference he was asked straight out to deny 'this story.' 'I cannot deny it,' Zimmermann replied. 'It is true.'[269]

Zimmermann dared to admit that he sent the telegram because he believed that American anxieties lest Mexico invade their southern states would delay their troops' arrival in Europe until Germany had won the war. The British exchequer was in a parlous state,[270] and the German naval staff promised that unrestricted submarine warfare would sink an average of 600,000 tons of enemy and neutral shipping monthly and force Britain to accept terms within five months.[271] France was also fragile. The French army had been battered by Falkenhayn's policy of attrition in 1916, and a major mutiny would occur after General Nivelle's failed offensive in April.

Yet all Americans, including German Americans, were horrified by Zimmermann's admission that Germany had been inciting Mexico to go to war against America. The *Omaha World Herald* declared, 'The issue shifts... from Germany against Great Britain to Germany against the United States.' Overnight the Midwest isolationist press changed tack.[272] American sentiment became pro-British and war fever set in. The US number one popular song 'I didn't raise my boy to be a soldier' was swiftly replaced with the jingoistic tune 'Over There.' Zimmerman's telegram helped to unite American opinion in favour of war.

Wilson declared war on Germany on 2nd April 1917 as an 'associate power'. Yet even though Wilson's fears about a military incursion from Mexico might have contributed to his caution in sending large numbers of G Is over to Europe in 1917, Zimmermann's calculations about unrestricted submarine warfare forcing Britain into submission would prove false.

German submarines achieved extraordinary initial successes up to May and June, but defensive weapons and the convoy system gradually stemmed British shipping losses. Wilson's declaration of war also gave a tremendous boost to Britain's morale and on 14th June Britain's General Plumer took the Messines Ridge just south-east of Ypres, which had been held by the German army since December 1914. Yet Britain was spending ever more of her national treasure to replace her navy and to finance Russia's crumbling war effort.

Meanwhile, Emperor Wilhelm II had come round to Bethmann-Hollweg's point of view that his country should concentrate on tackling 'Russia militarily, so as to push her out of the coalition, which would probably drag France after her, and we should get a free hand against England.'[273] However, Germany did not only use military force against Russia but also used subversion, which was meeting with success.

In 1915 the German Foreign Office had discovered a Russian revolutionary in Turkey called Alexander Helphand, (also called Parvis) who declared: 'Russian democracy can only achieve its goals through the complete destruction of Tsarism and the dismemberment of Russia into smaller states. Germany, for her part, will not achieve full success unless she succeeds in starting a major revolution in Russia.'

Helphand was brought to Germany and promised that thousands of émigrés would return to Russia to create mayhem, provided that the émigrés were given finance. The German government gave him two million marks. Helphand recommended a conference of all Russian socialists in Switzerland, including Lenin, the radical leader, who was residing there.

Few in Zurich public library had remarked on the bald little Russian with a red moustache and a neat short beard, who, unknown to them, worked from morning till night demonizing less, extreme revolutionaries. For Lenin, the war had only one purpose – the destruction of the capitalist system and the substitution of the 'dictatorship of the proletariat.' [274]

An Estonian called Keskūla assured the German Foreign Office that it could bank on Lenin to achieve its ambitions. In September 1915 Lenin stated his conditions, including Germany renouncing annexations and a war indemnity. The German negotiators were happy to say 'Yes' to anything; the serious negotiations could proceed once Lenin was in place. In the winter of 1915-16 Helphand was given another twenty million roubles to create revolution in Russia, but Helphland found the Mensheviks, like their Social Democrat counterparts in Germany, unwilling to renounce their government in the middle of a war.275

At last, in mid-March 1917, the German hierarchy heard that the Russian Tsar had been toppled. This gave rise to a major German conference on Germany's war aims in the East. The idea was considered of securing a second security belt, to protect the German Reich in addition to the Polish 'frontier strip.' It would be filled with re-patriated Russian Germans, and other German minorities from the non-German parts of the Austro-Hungarian Empire and was envisaged to run between a reduced Lithuania and a reduced Prussia to Brest-Litovsk, which would become 'a Prussian provincial town.'276

Unfortunately, the democrats in Russia did not realize the danger their country was in. They split into two factions, those who wanted to carry on the war and implement moderate reforms and those who were ready to conclude peace with Germany on the basis, of 'no big annexations' only 'frontier rectifications.' German Russian expert, Count Brockdorff-Rantzau, advised Berlin to 'create the greatest possible chaos in Russia' and on 31st March Lenin and fellow Bolsheviks received permission to travel home in a sealed train, accompanied by a larger group of pro Entente Mensheviks so that they were not compromised as German agents.277

After reaching Russia, Lenin at once pressed for peace with the Central Powers. Yet he took months to achieve power. He had to flee after his attempted Bolshevik coups failed in May and June 1917, but the German Foreign Office continued to help 'inflame the anti-English feeling of the masses' and to strengthen the Russians' longing for peace.278

Despite the Russian General Brusilov's final offensive in June there were increasing reports that Russia was in chaos. Both Ludendorff and Bethmann-Hollweg believed that 'time has become our latest ally'279 but on the Western Front the submarine war was failing to defeat Britain and Germany was facing another winter of war when the navy had been expecting victory by August.280

Public confidence in Germany was at an all-time low. In April 300,000 workers had joined a strike, sparked by a reduction in the bread ration. In Leipzig workers wanted not just more bread but also the introduction of equal and universal suffrage. They were pacified by an increase in wages and a reduction in their working hours.[281] However, the industrial unrest would continue. The Social Democrats leader, Friedrich Ebert, warned that the Reichstag must not underestimate America, as it had underestimated England, and called for the unequal voting franchise in Germany's largest state, Prussia, to be removed.[282]

On 6th July, former arch annexationist Matthias Erzberger called for the Reichstag to vote for a 'compromise' peace. Social Democrat, Philipp Scheidemann, went further and asked for a peace without annexations. This horrified the military, already envisaging grabbing great swathes of the Russian Empire if only the Western Front remained firm. Bethmann-Hollweg finessed the situation by declaring that Germany had always favoured a defensive standpoint but had to include 'safeguards for Germany's future.'[283] His stance was supported by the newspaper empire that Hugenberg was expanding with the acquisition of the *Deutscher Überseedienst G.m.b.H* and the *Telegraphen-Union*.[284]

However, the pressure on the government from the left was tangible. It was in these circumstances that Bethmann-Hollweg agreed to consider the idea of equal franchise for Prussian voters.[285]

Prussia was by far the largest state in Germany. It was governed by an oral three-class franchise method, under which the richest got the lion's share of the votes. The socialists had long wanted to change the system. It seemed at last that their wishes had been granted. The emperor supported the idea, but the very next day Chancellor Bethmann-Hollweg was overthrown by General Ludendorff.

New Chancellor, Michaelis, realized that he must give the socialists one concession, so allowed the Reichstag to vote on a so-called 'Peace of Understanding.' The Reichstag proclaimed, just as it had on 4th August 1914, that Germany was waging war solely to retain 'the integrity of its own territory.' It would never aim at any other end than a 'peace of understanding.' Nevertheless, the

Reichstag had never been in control of Germany and the new Chancellor confided to the Crown Prince 'I have deprived it (The Peace of Understanding) of its most dangerous features by my interpretation of it. One can make any peace one likes with this interpretation.'286

Pan-German publicist Heinrich Claß and former Navy Minister Tirpitz quickly formed a new political movement called The Fatherland Party to discredit the socialists and to campaign for red-blooded war aims. Alfred Hugenberg would become one of The Fatherland Party's most powerful if unobtrusive members, emphasising territorial expansion and anti-Semitism as his two main themes.287

It was a period of misery for both the Central powers and the Allies. In the spring French General Robert Nivelle's offensive had ended in failure and a mutiny that was hushed up by the Allies. Winston Churchill was credited with the being the first to mention it in his history book, *The World Crisis, Part I*, in 1927, writing: 'Want of confidence in their leaders, cruel losses and an active defeatist propaganda had produced an intense spasm throughout its (the French army's) ranks. Mutinies of a very, dangerous kind occurred in sixteen separate Army Corps. Some of the finest troops were involved. Divisions elected councils. Whole regiments set out for Paris to demand a peace by negotiation and more home leave.'288

Although General Haig had told Prime Minister, Lloyd George, about the French Army's loss of discipline before Nivelle's offensive,289 he may not have been aware of the full extent of its collapse after its failure. Nevertheless, he seems to have been aware of the German people's loss of morale. So, he decided that now was the time to start another major attack. 'The German was now on his last legs and there was only one sound plan to follow quickly 'viz: Send to France, every possible man, possible aeroplane, gun.'290

Had 'arrogant' 'blinkered' Haig been able to go into battle in the spring the history of the Battle of Passchendaele in 1917 might have been very different as the Passchendaele area was very dry in May, with scarcely a drop of rain.

Unfortunately, the offensive did not start till the very last day of July, and August 1917 turned out to be the wettest for decades. The heavens opened the day that the fight began, rain soaked the ground below, and the soldiers were soon floundering in the mud, waiting numbly in water-logged holes 'with the mud gusts tugging the wire, like the twitching agonies of men among its (barbed wire) brambles'[291]

Meanwhile the Prussians had strengthened their grip on the home front and the Pan-Germans newspapers kept spreading the word that victory on the Eastern Front was in sight.

The rain, the bloodshed, and the agony of the Allies on the Western Front continued but Germany's efforts to put Lenin in place were nearly complete. Tirpitz expressed his loathing for Britain and America and his confidence in the future: *'The question today is whether we can hold our own against Anglo-Americanism or whether we must sink down and become mere manure for others ... Germany is fighting for a great deal, and therefore I would cry out to every corner of our Fatherland: Germany awake! Thine hour of destiny has arrived.'*[292]

At last, on 7th November 1917, forces led by Lenin overthrew Alexander Kerensky's provisional government. Zimmermann's successor at the Foreign Office, Richard von Kühlmann, responded immediately to Lenin's call for peace because he was alarmed that the Bolshevik government would collapse. Meanwhile he patted his spy department on the back, declaring 'It was only the resources which the Bolsheviks received regularly from our side ... that enabled them to ... greatly to expand the originally narrow basis of their party.'

Then, to the world's astonishment Kühlmann agreed to negotiate with the Bolsheviks on the base of a peace without 'annexations or reparations.'

It seemed to idealistic President Wilson that Germany held the moral high ground. Germany had agreed to a peace without annexations or reparations, while Lenin's right-hand man, Leon Trotsky, had revealed some shady agreements that Britain and France had made with Russia and Italy. The publication of the Allies agreements to keep Russia and Italy's battered armies fighting on their side caused uproar in America. The Allies were castigated for their rapaciousness and Wilson felt that he had to come out with a statement of his altruistic war aims to compete with Germany's philanthropy in denying herself the spoils of war.293

On 8th January 1918, Wilson produced his later to become famous Fourteen Points for Peace:

(1) open covenants of peace, openly arrived at, (2) absolute freedom of navigation upon the seas, alike in peace and in war, (3) the removal, so far as possible, of all economic barriers, (4) national armaments to be reduced to the lowest level consistent with domestic safety, (5) a free, openminded and absolutely, impartial adjustment of all colonial claims, (6) the evacuation of all Russian territory, (7) Belgium to be evacuated and restored, (8) all French territory to be freed and the former portions taken by Bismarck to be restored, (9) the frontiers of Italy to be readjusted along clearly recognizable lines of nationality, (10) the nations of Austria-Hungary should be accorded the freest opportunity for autonomous development, (11) Rumania, and the Balkan provinces of Serbia and Montenegro should be evacuated, (12) the Turkish portion of the Ottoman Empire should be restored but the rest of the nationalities should be allowed an absolutely, unmolested opportunity of autonomous development, (13) an independent Polish state should be erected, with access to the sea, (14) a general association of nations must be formed (to police these many new territories).

Hundreds of thousands of copies of Wilson's speech were distributed in Russia but the Russians were in no position to take advantage of it and the German leadership completely ignored it.

Kühlmann had been happy to agree to Lenin's request for 'no annexations' and 'no indemnities' because he was a warrior and lies and deceit were part of his armoury. Many years later he described his approach to the negotiations:

'My plan was to entangle Trotsky in a purely academic discussion on the right of self-determination ... to get for ourselves ... whatever territorial concessions we absolutely needed.294

Soon Germany found that she 'absolutely needed' a lot of territory and the spoils of war too. The Treaty with the Ukraine was signed on 22nd January 1918. The advantage of making a separate treaty with Ukraine was that Ukraine's government had absolutely no authority. Its rule, according to Lenin's irate negotiator, Leon Trotsky, did not even extend beyond its own living rooms in Brest-Litovsk.295

Yet Ukraine was full of natural resources, waiting for plunder. Heavy industry coveted Ukrainian manganese and its high-grade iron ore. It also wanted the seventy per cent of Russia's coal and one third of Russia's agricultural production which currently came from Ukraine but would in future be travelling towards Germany.296

The negotiations dragged on. German industry wanted complete freedom to acquire and work the mines formerly owned by the Russian state. It also wanted Russia's rubber, cotton, asbestos, copper, nickel, and tin and insisted that Russia becomes a supplier of raw materials, dependent on Germany.297

On 9th February General Hoffman demanded both Russia's Black Sea and her Baltic coast. To avoid this diktat, Trotsky declared: 'No war, no peace!' Yet, this merely gave the German army the chance to use 'the soldier's boot' in the name of 'chasing out the bandits!'

The *Allgemeine Evangelische-Lutherische Kirchenzeitung* commented: 'Germany's armies pressed on, took city after city ... Russia, who wanted to give no indemnity, was forced at the last minute to yield up uncountable booty; 800 locomotives, 8,000 railway trucks with every kind of treasure and supply. God knew that we needed it. And we also needed guns and munitions for the last blow against the enemy in the west. God knew that too. So, he freely gave us, since God is rich, 2,600 guns, 5,000 machine guns, two million shells for the artillery rifles, aircraft, lorries, and innumerable other things.298

On 3rd March 1918 in the charred and blackened ruins of the town of Brest-Litovsk, Russia ceded Poland, Lithuania and Courland and consented to the separate peace with the Ukraine. Livonia and Estonia remained Russian but were to be occupied by German 'police forces.'299 The Treaty of Brest-Litovsk pleased the Pan-Germans. Alfred Hugenberg believed in *lebensraum* for the German population. He founded two large corporations with a total of 37 million marks to establish funds to make loans to the thousands of German farmers that he expected soon to be settled in Eastern Europe at the expense of the local inhabitants.300

The 'Prussian' army was now at the height of its power. Its final ambition was to win the war on the Western Front. 'Some' forty divisions were transferred from the Eastern Front to knock first Britain, and then France out of the war before the trickle of American troops became a flood.[301] However, neither Britain nor France was defeated, and the weary German army never reached Paris. In the middle of July, it suffered a reverse on the Western Front. Soon the Allies were pushing it back to its homeland, but the army in the East was still making great progress.

After Germany had concluded the rapacious Treaty of Brest-Litovsk, its triumphant army surrounded Ukraine's parliament on 28th April 1918 and asked the government to surrender. Two days later Germany took control of Ukraine and decided that heavy industry, under such famous names as Krupp, would organise Ukraine's coal, iron ore, manganese, electrical and chemical industries, with the agricultural sector restructured so that its precious Black Earth could produce food for the Reich.

The industrialists were so excited by Ukraine's treasures, their ambition was for Ukraine to be sealed off from what they termed 'Great Russia' and 'any third power,' (through altering its railway gauge?!) and for its economic system to be aligned to Germany's.'[302] Meanwhile General Ludendorff occupied Crimea and campaigned for it to be peopled with German colonists.

Under supplementary treaties Rumania became a satellite state in May,[303] agreeing to give up eighty per cent of its oil and all surplus food. Marching eastwards the German army then captured the strategic city of Rostov-on-Don,[304] cutting the main line of communication between Russia and the resource-rich Caucasus.

Subsequently, to persuade the German army to evacuate Rostov and cease its advance, the Bolsheviks agreed to painful new demands on 27th August; half of Russia's raw material production was to be delivered to Germany, a joint commission would decide what industrial goods would be sent in return. Russia also surrendered Estonia and Livonia and agreed to the independence of Georgia, and the payment of an indemnity of 6,000 million roubles, in fine gold, currency and kind, delivery to start straight away![305] Russia also promised to deliver one-third of the Baku oil in return for its surrender by the Turks.

The German leadership reflected: 'The Bolsheviks are very evil and antipathetic people ... (Nevertheless) Politics have always been utilitarian, and will be so for a long time to come ... What ... do we want in the East? The military paralysis of Russia. The Bolsheviks are producing this better and more thoroughly than any other Russian could do, without our giving a man or a mark for it.'

Yet the German/military industrialists' greed in the East meant that the Western Front was starved of troops. It has been estimated that Germany had three quarters of a million troops on the Eastern Front, when they were desperately needed in the West.[306] On the 8th of August the British army delivered a telling defeat on the German army on the Western Front. Ludendorff called it the 'black day.' The German soldiers began to surrender in large numbers.[307]

On 23rd and 26th August, influential heavy industrialist, Hugo Stinnes discussed the seriousness of the situation with shipping magnate, Albert Ballin. Stinnes was close to Gustav Krupp and suggested that Ballin ask Wilhelm II to conclude an early peace so that, even if the war was 'liquidated' in the West, at least Germany's eastern conquests could be saved.

Ballin found the emperor 'very badly misinformed.' He urged Wilhelm to put forward a peace feeler, which, he argued, should be sought not through Britain, but through the 'idealist' Wilson, who was not seeking any territorial advantages in Europe. Wilhelm agreed in principle but said that he thought that the peace initiative could wait for another ten days, until the retreat to the Hindenburg line had been completed.[308]

On 2nd September, the Allies recovered the important Drocourt Queant-Switch line. By 3rd September, the Minister of State was told, 'The reserves (of the Central Powers) are running out.'[309]

On 13th September, the *Daily Mirror* recorded von Payer, the German Vice-Chancellor's first peace initiative. He reserved the right for Germany to keep its eastern territorial acquisitions, especially Poland and Finland, stating bluntly, 'We can never permit anyone to meddle with us in this matter.' 'Just as little will we submit to the Entente for its gracious approval or alteration of our peace treaties with the Ukraine, Russia and Rumania.' But he said that Germany was prepared to withdraw from France and Belgium.' However, the war was proceeding fast. Soon Britain's General Haig secured his war cabinet's grudging permission to pierce the Hindenburg Line and capture the Passchendaele salient by making it clear to them

'The discipline of the German army, is quickly going, and the German officer is not what he was.'

On 28th September, 'in bog-like conditions' the Allies won a great victory over the crater-strewn ground at Passchendaele.

Unfortunately, with military victory seemingly 'in the bag,' President Wilson was no longer concerned about German militarism. His prejudice was against Britain and France.

He sent a coded note to his emissary, Colonel House, which said: 'My deliberate judgement is that our whole weight should be thrown for an armistice which .... which will be as moderate as possible ... because it is certain that too much success or security on the part of the Allies will make a genuine peace settlement exceedingly difficult if not impossible.'[310]

Many Europeans had been horrified by the endless bloodshed of the war. Wilson's ideals expressed in his 14 points seemed to promise a new world order where war would have no place. Writing in 1933 former British diplomat and Member of Parliament, Harold Nicolson, reflected people's belief in Wilson's altruism:

'I believed, with him, (Wilson) that the standard of political and international conduct should be as high, as sensitive, as the standard of personal conduct. ... I believed, and I still believe, that the only true patriotism is an active desire that one's tribe or country should, in every particular, minister to that ideal.'

Wilson had great principles, which inspired a war-weary world. However, he was also guilty of prejudice. He allowed his prejudice against the British and French, and his realization that he controlled their purse-strings at this critical time, to cloud his better judgement. On the very day that the Allies surmounted the Passchendaele salient, he offered Germany peace, on the base of the fourteen points that Germany had flatly rejected in January 1918, with an added sweetener to persuade her to come to the negotiating table, 'impartial justice' which he declared *'must involve no discrimination between those to whom we* wish to be just and those to whom we do not wish to be just.'[311]

By 1st October, the combined Allied and American armies were nearing the French and Belgian frontiers. In his diary Colonel von Thaer related what Ludendorff told them about the state of the German army. '... our military situation was terribly grave. Our Western Front might be breached any day ... There was no relying on the troops any longer. ... Thus, it was to be anticipated that in future with the help of the high battle morale of the Americans the enemy would gain a major victory and break through on a very, large scale; our army on the West would then get out of control and flood back across the Rhine in complete disorder, bringing revolution to Germany.' Panic-stricken Ludendorff then declared:

The army cannot wait forty-eight hours longer. ... Today the troops are holding their own; what may happen tomorrow cannot be foreseen ... I have ... begged H M now to draw into the government those circles whom we have chiefly to thank for being in this position. ... Let them conclude the peace that must now be concluded. Let them cope with the mess! It is their mess after all.

On 2nd October General Haig commented that the German army on his Front was 'completely breaking.' In haste, Prince Max, leader of the new 'democratic' government, which had hurriedly been installed, grasped at the life-line Wilson had offered.

On 5th October, the new German Chancellor told the Reichstag that he was going to respond favourably to Wilson's offer of an armistice, saying: 'I have taken this step not only for the salvation of Germany and its Allies, but of all humanity, which had been suffering for years through the war.' Wilson then offered the German government an armistice without consulting the Allies.

On 7th October, Republican contender and ex-President Theodore Roosevelt voiced the anxiety, which was increasingly shared by the American public: 'At this point, if we make an armistice, we have lost the war, and we shall leave Germany about where she started. I am sure that the American people want a complete victory and an unconditional surrender.' However, President Wilson continued talking to the German government without taking Roosevelt or the Republican opposition into his confidence.

On 8th October Colonel House recorded: 'I found the President's viewpoint had changed during the night ... He did not seem to realize before the nearly unanimous sentiment in this country against anything but unconditional surrender. He did not realize how war-mad our people have become. This had to be taken into consideration, but not, of course, to the extent of meeting it where it was wrong.'

Colonel House was correct in his belief that Americans desire for "unconditional surrender' was not completely unanimous. Some of the European minorities Wilson was proposing to give independence to, supported his initiative. Some Irish Americans supported Wilson's peace initiative because they hoped that his principle of 'self-determination' would bring them a united Ireland. And they were a powerful lobby. Their pressure to address 'the Irish question' would reach a head with a full-floor discussion in Congress in March 1919, 'which passed a resolution calling on the US delegation at the Paris peace conference to make Irish self-determination an urgent matter.'[312]

Many German Americans also wanted their former homeland given a compassionate peace. Out of 92 million Americans, 2.5 million had been born in Germany and at least 5.8 million had one German parent,[313] making them the largest ethnic group in America. However, a large number had come to the United States to escape from Prussian militarism and felt that 'unconditional surrender' was the only way to extinguish it.

On 9th October Cambrai was taken by the Allies. The German army was said to be 'hard in flight, blowing up bridges and burning villages.'[314]

Meanwhile the battle continued. On 10th October Haig declared: 'We have got the enemy down; in fact, he is a beaten army, and my plan is to go on hitting him as hard as we possibly can, till he begs for mercy.' However, President Wilson's peace initiative and the setbacks of the American army at Meuse-Argonne which started at the end of September, would soon raise the confidence of the German army's leadership.

The American army's morale had been very high when it first reached France. Until the end of May the American troops had not seen serious action. However, on 28th May, the 28th Regiment of the American army's First

Division, plus two companies of the 18th Infantry Regiment had attacked and held the ridge at the village of Cantigny against successive German counterattacks, even after the French withdrew their heavy artillery. It was a small-scale operation. Yet the American army's fighting spirit had not only made an impact with the French but also with the German High Command.

Ludendorff had hoped to defeat the Allies before the American forces could be fully operational. On 21st March he had launched Operation Michael against the British army, hoping to capture the Chanel ports and drive the British Army into the sea before he dealt with France. On 23rd March, Chairman of Krupps, Alfred Hugenberg had sent a telegram of congratulations to General Hindenburg which declared: 'The peace with Russia ... and the great victory of these days against the English ...are like two powerfully ringing hammer blows to all German hearts' [315] Yet despite dreadful casualties the German army did not reach the Chanel ports, and the smaller British army, despite 70,000 more casualties than during the fourteen weeks at Passchendaele the previous autumn,[316] remained unbroken.

In April Ludendorff launched a new offensive against one Portuguese and eight British divisions, which were standing between German lines and the strategically important railway junction of Hazebrouck, controlling the vital Allied supply lines. After initial success, it ground to a failure, partly due to the exhaustion of the German soldiers who had fought in Operation Michael.[317]

Undaunted, on 27th May Ludendorff launched the Aisne offensive with 2.5 million shells fired in four and a half hours, the largest barrage of the war. Soon his troops had reached the north bank of the Marne River at Château-Thierry, sixty miles from Paris. On 1st June Château-Thierry and Vaux fell, and the German troops moved into Belleau wood as part of a major offensive to cross the river. The battle of Belleau Wood raged between 1st and 26th June, but the Americans had arrived to help the French defeat the marauding 'Prussian' army.

During the battle of Belleau Wood, the American troops, including a brigade of Marines, behaved with the utmost bravery. Some were cut down by machine-gun fire, others drenched with mustard gas, and they also fought in hand-to hand combat. There were many casualties.

Nevertheless, by 28th June, the battle was won. Belleau Wood was renamed *Bois de la Brigade de Marine* in honour of the American Marine's' heroism.

In July, the Americans combined with the Allied forces to thwart Ludendorff's last offensive. The German army was forced to evacuate the Marne and relinquish all the gains it had previously made. On the 8th of August, the British army delivered a telling defeat to the German army. Now General Pershing was anxious to begin his first major offensive on his own, as he had been commanded to by his President, Woodrow Wilson.[318]

Saint-Mihiel, east of Verdun, formed a salient inside the French lines, blocking communications between Nancy and Verdun. By 12th September Pershing had assembled a force of 550,000 Americans and 110,000 French to attack the salient. The visibility was poor and many of the tanks got bogged down in the mud. Nevertheless, the German army had been informed of the attack and had already begun a step-by-step withdrawal. By the evening of the 13th, the American army had captured all its objectives at Saint Mihiel.

It may have been Pershing's comfortable victory at Saint Mihiel which encouraged him to believe reports that the fighting spirit of the German army was low and that his offensive at Meuse-Argonne, timed to kick off Allied supremo General Foch's autumn campaign, would be simple.

Foch wanted General Pershing to spearhead his giant Allied and American offensive. Pershing would launch his campaign at Meuse-Argonne on 26th September. Then General Haig's First and Third armies would commence their campaign at Passchendaele and Cambrai on the 27th. The next day the Flanders group of Armies under the control of the Belgian king would launch an attack between the sea and the Lys River. And finally, on the 29th, Haig's Fourth Army, supported by the French First army would attack the beleaguered German Army in the centre.

Pershing had a huge army of 1,200,000 troops and support personnel, and an overwhelming superiority in fighting strength of roughly eight to one for his battle at Meuse-Argonne.[319] At 5.30 am on 26th September, after three hours' intense bombardment by 2,700 guns, nine American divisions advanced to the assault along a twenty-mile front. However, the German army had adopted the method of elastic defence – with the real resistance being safely some miles in the rear. [320] It had held the Montfaucon (Falcon Mountain) for most of the war, with its commanding views of the surrounding area. Massive barbed-wire entanglements and defensive positions had been installed from which its machine-guns could mow down the enemy.

Lined against the German army at Meuse-Argonne were not hardened American soldiers, like the Marines who had helped defeat the German army at Belleau Wood, but raw young troops, who had had only a few months' training. The area was pocked with old trenches, and shell-craters three to four feet deep from the Verdun battles. After the huge initial artillery barrage, artillery cover was lacking, and communications extremely poor. The roads soon became clogged, and the troops even suffered from a lack of food. They also had had little training against gas warfare as their commanders had entered the war believing that gas warfare was barbaric, and not in keeping with the soldiers' code of honour.

Unfortunately, that did not stop the German army from using gas at Meuse-Argonne, causing horror and dread amongst the raw young troops.[321] Montfaucon was taken by the 27th of September, but the German High Command rushed in six extra battle-hardy divisions who fought for every yard of the rest of the area.

On 5th October, the German command threw troops into counterattacks all along the front. Proportionately, the American casualties of nearly 75,000 up to 6th October were nearly as great as those suffered by General Haig's army during a similar period on the Somme. However, the Americans were learning fast. They soon discovered not to pass a German machine gun post whose personnel appeared to be dead, but who opened-up on them as soon as they were passed. They also found that booby traps had been placed in houses and on dead bodies.

Many of the German machine gun emplacements forward of the main positions were manned by well-trained fatalistic veterans, some of the 'sacrifice' gunners being chained to their machine guns [322]Ludendorff was reinforcing the Meuse-Argonne, even at the expense of his defences in Flanders. He knew that the end was fast approaching with 300,000 American reinforcements arriving every month. An armistice on Woodrow Wilson's woolly terms would be favourable to Germany, who had lived off her neighbours' industries during the war and was resolved to destroy them on her retreat.

On 7th October Major General Liggett flung his troops in a westward drive across the Argonne Hills and cut off the forest. He rescued the heroic 'lost Battalion,' and cleared the way for the French Fourth Army to advance on the west of the Argonne. On 14th October, the Americans attacked the German Kriemhilde Stellung, and though at first repulsed, they captured the highest point of the ridge on the succeeding days, with only one last defensive line ahead, the Freya Stellung.[323] The Metz-Sedan-Mezières railway now lay within heavy artillery range. However, the attack had been costly, and the important railway was not shelled. Instead, Pershing was relieved of his post with a promotion and General Liggett was given charge of the American First Army.

Unfortunately, now Liggett 'showed a surprising firmness with his boss.' He was faced with a huge number of deserters, stragglers, shirkers and men who had lost contact with their units, whose numbers he estimated as high as 100,000. They had all started with such good morale but had become 'depressed and dead beat'[324] Although Pershing repeatedly urged Liggett to continue the offensive, he refused to attack again 'before the army was 'tightened up.'[325]

The casualties at the Battle of Meuse-Argonne were horrific. However, the pause in the American army's campaign in the last two weeks of October, was most unfortunate because it arrived at a critical moment during the armistice negotiations. Ludendorff had called for an armistice because he had not only been afraid of the arrival of the large number of American troops, but also because of their high morale. Yet over a million American troops and support staff had been fought to a stand-still by his few brave troops at Meuse-Argonne.

French Premier, Georges Clemenceau declared frustratedly: 'Nobody can maintain that these fine American troops are unusable. They are merely unused.'

Meanwhile the retreating German troops had started to implement the military/industrial cohort's plans to turn military defeat into economic victory.

In 1916 the German High Command had examined 4,000 industrial firms in occupied northern France, to see how Germany could benefit from destroying France's industry in the event of defeat. The research showed that the destruction would bring German industry benefits:

... *iron and smelting works, will not be able to resume work before one or two years ... as a result of this long interruption of activity, production, and therefore receipts will fall off heavily, and industries will be so prejudiced ... that it will be difficult for them to resume operation or to restore it to its former level.*

Textiles: the French textile industry will during the War have lost its markets. To reconquer them, and to derive some use of the terrible blow suffered by the textile industry in occupied regions, it is particularly important for Germany to start its intact industries working as quickly as possible after the War. Coal mines: the districts will be unproductive for years to come, owing to the removal of machinery and the flooding of shafts ... France will have to buy her machinery from Germany[326] ...'

The retreating German army did not only devastate the industrial production of North France; Belgian industry was also laid waste. A *New York Times* reporter revealed the Germany army's systematic of the ruin of Belgium's largest steel concern:

'This morning, I visited the great Cockerill plant at Seraing near Liège. It is the largest engineering concern in Belgium and was founded 100 years ago. In normal times it employs 10,000 hands. The area covered by the works is immense and the multitude of buildings present the appearance of a town ... Now not an ingot of steel can be made at Cockerill's for the Germans with devilish ingenuity have dismantled the essential machinery and either smashed it up or taken it off to Germany. ... A favourite method is to drop heavy weights on the machinery from a rolling crane. As one of the directors explained to me, the Germans deliberately aimed at crippling Belgian industry for several years so as to enable their own mills and factories to capture markets.'[327]

On 17th October Ludendorff told his Secretary of State that he felt that he could hold out (till the armistice?) if he received sufficient reinforcements. At the same time, the German newspapers published an official notification that the German armies had ceased all destruction 'unless absolutely forced to follow this course by the military situation for defensive reasons.' However, before this change of policy was adopted Cambrai, Laon, Lens, and other cities were looted and burned.328

Naturally, the armistice talks and the success of the German army's efforts at Meuse-Argonne gave the German troops on other sectors of the battlefront the belief that they would not suffer a humiliating defeat on the battlefield if they just held out till the armistice. On 19th October Haig observed that the enemy was not ready for 'unconditional surrender.'

On 24th October irate ex-President Theodore Roosevelt declared that he believed that it was unconstitutional for Wilson to give Germany an armistice and peace treaty without the support of the Senate, and he pleaded 'Let us dictate peace by the hammering of guns and not chat about peace to the accompaniment of the clicking of typewriters. ... Moreover, we should find out what the President means by continually referring to this country merely as an associate instead of the ally of the nations, with whose troops our own troops are actually brigaded in battle.'

Theodore Roosevelt had known of the Kaiser's audacious plan to invade the US in 1901. He had no doubt that Germany had been responsible for war in 1914. An isolated figure at one stage during the conflict, he now represented a large majority of public opinion. The mid-term elections were approaching in two weeks' time; he was alarmed that Wilson was not going to let Americans have a vote on the vital question of war and peace. A flood of American newspapers echoed his anxiety.

The *New York Times* commented bitterly: 'They (the Germans) have manoeuvred for an armistice which would save their precious Fatherland ... and omits to mention moral punishment or reparations.'

The *Boston Herald* declared: 'Unconditional surrender is not only the sole course for us, but it is the best for our enemies. ... The hour of reckoning has come, and the reckoning cannot be a matter of bargain and sale.'

The *Chicago Tribune* affirmed: 'There is but one mind in America on this war – that it shall go on to victory, to the utter destruction of Prussian militarism.'

President Wilson was acutely aware that the mid-term elections were looming. Threatened with a crushing defeat at the polls he made one final peace condition for granting Germany an armistice, the Kaiser must abdicate. He did not stipulate on how Wilhelm II's abdication was going to be achieved, but he was resolute that this must happen, presumably before the armistice was finally signed by the warring parties on 11th November. Then, happy in the belief that he had secured German democracy, he turned to the Allies to force them to accept his peace terms.

Wilson's emissary, soft-speaking, Colonel House reassured Wilson that he was confident of forcing the Allies to accept Wilson's ambitions for a peace settlement when he met them on 29th October, telling him confidentially:

'It is my intention to tell the Prime Ministers today that if their conditions of peace are essentially different from the points you have laid down ... that you will probably feel obliged to go before Congress and state the new conditions and ask their advice as to whether the United States shall continue to fight for the aims of Great Britain, France and Italy. [329]

'I told the British privately you anticipate that their policy would lead to the establishment of the greatest naval programme by the United States that the world had ever seen ... I would suggest that you quietly diminish the transport of troops giving as an excuse the prevalence of influenza or any other reason but the real one ...'

Colonel House's words must have had a huge impact on the Allied leadership because President Wilson had ultimate control of the American army and navy, and the American army had already stopped fighting.

Lloyd George had only just encouraged the British public to 'Hold fast!' declaring. The great militarist autocracy of Prussia will still endeavour by violence or guile to avoid defeat and so give militarism a new breath of life. Having set our hands to the task we must see it through till a just and lasting settlement is reached.'

However, many of the British people who did not know about 'Prussian militarism', would have viewed Wilson's ideas for peace as 'a just and lasting settlement,' So, having won the concession that 'freedom of the seas' would be removed from Wilson's demands so that Britain could at least legitimately protect the water off her shores, Lloyd George fatefully agreed to the armistice, little realising that the German hierarchy would wilfully misrepresent it and that the majority of Americans were against it, and would become opponents of the Allies in the postwar years.

Lloyd George did have support for his position. The British shop floor was delighted as it had been told that Wilson would listen to the pleas of the working man and introduce humane working conditions throughout the world.330 In addition, the financial position of the country was appalling. In 1916 Britain had practically run out of money after Wilson put a financial squeeze on the country to respond to Germany's spurious 'peace offer.' In 1918 she was even weaker as she had to supply eighty per cent of the aircraft and virtually all the tanks and artillery for the American army.331

Also, crucially, the Commander in Chief of the British armies, Douglas Haig had also advised accepting the armistice. Haig spoke for many British people when he declared:

'The British army has done much of the fighting latterly, and everyone wants to have done with the war, *provided* that we get what we want. I therefore advise that we only ask in the armistice for what we intend to hold and that we set our faces against the French entering Germany to pay off old scores.'332

Many people in Britain would have agreed with Haig. He had embarked on the Battle of the Somme in 1916, in part to relieve the French while they were embroiled in their battle at Verdun. He may have been unaware of the extent of the collapse in French army's morale after General Nivelle's reverse in 1917, but the carnage at Passchendaele had certainly helped take the pressure off France at a critical time. He had felt that he could win the war on the field of battle, but his expectations had been dented by Pershing's failure at Meuse-Argonne.

Haig was already upset with America's General Pershing. At the end of August 1918 Pershing had removed five American divisions (150,000 men), which Haig had trained to help him deal the decisive blow. By October 1918, the American Army was larger than Britain's, but its supply lines had broken down during Pershing's offensive on Meuse-Argonne and divisions had to be relieved, according to a frustrated Haig, because they were literally 'starving.'333

Haig had thought that the battle could be won but he had lost confidence in the Americans and felt that Britain would have to continue to shoulder the burden of the war in 1919, with an unsupportive home-front snapping at his heals.

Yet in October 1918, the rifle strength on the battlefield was 2:1 in favour of America and the Allies. As the most successful general in the field, Haig should have known that it was vital that he joined with French supremo, Marshall Foch, (who would later be bitterly criticized by the French for his decision to accept the armistice) and America's General Pershing in advising that 'Prussian militarism' must be destroyed on the battlefield.

General Pershing was the only American commander who opposed the armistice. He sent an urgent message to the Supreme War Council at Versailles, stating that the Allies were in a favourable position to secure an overwhelming victory over Germany. He believed that any cessation of hostilities short of capitulation would postpone or render impossible the imposition of satisfactory peace terms. In his view an armistice would also lead the Allies to believe that fighting was at an end. After that it would be difficult – if not impossible – to persuade them to fight again if Germany refused to accept the peace terms. Indeed, he maintained that by accepting a negotiated peace the Allies would jeopardize the moral high ground which they then held and possibly lost the chance to secure world peace on terms that would ensure its permanence.[334]

In democratic countries generals can only advise governments, not dictate policy. Nevertheless, Pershing was correct on every point he made. Yet he himself had contributed to the Allies acceptance of the armistice by insisting on having a separate army and then failing to achieve a knock-out victory at Meuse-Argonne.

Undoubtedly President Wilson's offer of an armistice had had an impact on the troops on the battlefield. Besides giving hope to the 'Prussians' that if their troops fought like tigers, they would gain more favourable terms, rumours of a forthcoming armistice would also have contributed to the American troops unwillingness to keep fighting and dying when the war would soon be over.

Only on 1st November, after the armistice terms had been agreed, did General Liggett take up arms again at

Meuse-Argonne. He was very, successful. By 4th November, the First army had advanced twenty kilometres and the German forces on the Western Front began a phased, general withdrawal. Yet Liggett's initiative had come too late. The terms of the armistice had already been accepted, and the Allies had agreed peace on President Woodrow Wilson's nebulous terms.

The American people had not had a chance to vote on whether their nation should give Germany an armistice or fight on for unconditional surrender. They had wanted their army to fight on for a clear-cut victory and would come to believe that the perfidious Allies had thwarted them from securing it.

Even though Wilson's final decision to force the abdication of the German Emperor as a condition for giving Germany an armistice had helped bolster his support with the electorate, especially when a revolution seemed to loom in Germany, the American people still voted against Wilson in the mid-term elections on 5th November. The President had been viewed as a democrat, but he had not respected democracy. The American people would turn against him in 1919 and against the Allies who had supported him.

Unfortunately, by the autumn of 1918 Britain already had a dwindling number of friends in the US. American sentiment had been neutral for much of the war. Ex-President and future Presidential contender, Theodore Roosevelt, had been a consistent supporter of the Allied cause. The Allies' acceptance of President Wilson's peace offer to Germany would be a mortal blow for Roosevelt, for the Allies and for the long-term peace of Europe.

At this point, former founder of the Pan German League, Alfred Hugenberg, decided to relinquish his exalted position at the armaments firm of Krupp. He knew that unless he acted fast, he and his friends would be blamed for the 1,773,700 German soldiers who had died in the war and the 2.7 million German soldiers who were permanently disabled by their war wounds.[335] So, he concentrated on expanding his press syndicate to persuade the war-wounded and their families to understand that the noble German army would have won the war if it had not been 'stabbed in the back by socialists and Jews.'

Hugenberg left the firm of Krupps and decided to become a politician, and to use his formidable organizational ability to develop a national opposition' to the Weimar republic.[336] The 'national opposition' would become increasingly powerful in the post-war years.

Although Woodrow Wilson lost the mid-term elections on 5th November, he maintained his faith in Germany and in December 1918 he gave a kick in the teeth to the impoverished Allies by declaring that he would be asking for 'no indemnities' from Germany and would soon be sending his troops home.

In January 1919 Theodore Roosevelt died. Unfortunately, the Republicans, bereft of their leader, and un-consulted about the terms of the Treaty of Versailles, would later refuse to ratify the Versailles Treaty, and turn their backs on Europe. In the 1920s they would also eventually become Germany's staunch supporters. Meanwhile the Allied governments' PR machines went into overdrive to celebrate the end of the war and justify the stunning loss of human life, however, the reality was that in an economic sense Germany was barely dented by the First World War while Britain was in a parlous state and had lost the friendship of America.

CHAPTER FIVE

Peace Without Victory?

In 1759, after the battle of Kunersdorf, Frederick the Great wrote: *Prussia would have been lost if her enemies, who knew how to defeat her, had known equally well how to take advantage of their victories.*337

Frederick the Great's words about Prussia in 1759 were equally applicable in 1918. America and the Allies were in sight of victory but had begun to show discord and had sued for an armistice. So, the German army on the Western Front smashed northern France and Belgium's mines and industry on its retreat, and the German troops from the Eastern Front hastened to do battle with the 'enemies within,' who had, so they were told, 'stabbed the ... army in the back' just as it was about to achieve victory in the West.

Germany's civilians were confused because their tightly censored press had also given them nothing but tales of victory. Suddenly their newly elected Chancellor, Prince Max of Baden, astonished them by telling them that the fledgling democratic government was responding to Wilson's offer of an armistice. The Berlin stock market collapsed. Former Pan-German League publicist, Heinrich Claß, who knew that the Pan-German League was in danger of being accused of being responsible for the deaths of millions of German citizens, immediately called for 'the resolute struggle of a spirited nationalist party against Jewry, against whom the legitimate anger of the people must be diverted,'338 while former Pan-German co-founder and ex-Chairman of Krupp's industrial empire, Alfred Hugenberg, called for a newspaper's war against President Wilson and the socialists.

The German shopfloor, the Hugenberg Press asserted, had undermined the army's morale just as it was about to win the war, by going on strike and telling their loved ones at the front of the undernourishment and starvation at home. Hugenberg's propaganda would eventually have an immense impact. Whereas the Social Democrats had held the moral high ground before the war, Hugenberg and his 'Nationalists' would ultimately be successful in their efforts to tarnish the Social Democrats' image afterwards, by repeating over, and over again, that Germany was guiltless of causing the bloodshed, and had been viciously 'stabbed in the back' when she was on the verge of victory.

Funds from Hugenberg's office also helped establish right-wing groups, such as Martin Spahn's political office, the National Club in Berlin, and Heinrich von Gleichen's June Club. They also provided subsidies for radical political groups like the Organization Escherich, in Bavaria, and the *Deutschvölkischer Schutz-und Trutzbund*. Heinrich Claß was also interested in promoting the anti-Semite, Adolf Hitler, as a popular orator.[339]

President Wilson knew nothing of the Prussian mentality and could not envisage, in his wildest dreams, the propaganda campaign which the Pan-Germans would wage against him. He had convinced himself that Germany had been no guiltier of war lust in 1914 than the Allies, telling Colonel House that 'freedom of the seas' should be included in the peace terms dictated to the Allies because of his pledge 'not only to do away with Prussian militarism but with militarism everywhere.'[340] His aim was to administer what he considered to be a fair peace to all, especially to defeated Germany. However, he was playing a foolish and dangerous game. Although he had the power to create his own foreign policy, any subsequent treaty would have to be ratified by the American Senate.

In October 1918, American pressure had mounted for Wilson to demand 'unconditional surrender.' Wilson's negotiations with the hastily assembled German government had caused great disquiet in America. *Everybody's Magazine* had even carried the uncannily predictive headline: THE GREAT WAR OF 1938: IF ONLY WE HAD SEEN IT THROUGH IN 1918 and many commentators shared *Everybody's Magazine*'s anxiety.

Wilson had realized that he must make one more gesture if he wanted to give Germany a benevolent peace and escape a crushing defeat in the mid-term elections. On 23rd October he told the new German government: 'If it (the government of the United States) must deal with the military masters and the monarchical autocrats of Germany ... it must demand not peace negotiations but surrender.'

The German military/industrial junta realized that it had to obey Wilson's order to get rid of the emperor fast to secure the armistice by the 11th of November. In the words of the historian Erich Eyck, 'Wilhelm was now little more than ballast that might well have to be tossed overboard in this time of distress.' But the question was. How?

It was the Admirals of the fleet who provided the solution. They decided to steam out and fight a decisive engagement with the British navy without any authorization from the German government. In 1917 discontent in the German fleet had been severely dealt with, but there had been no indication of trouble since. However, on 30th October 1918, the very day that Wilson's envoy, Colonel House, was dictating peace terms to the Allies, the German Naval High Command secretly ordered its sailors to put out to sea to confront the British.

The crews of several ships mutinied when they received the order. There were a few tense moments, during which the ships that had mutinied and those that had not, aimed their guns at each other at point blank range, but then the mutineers surrendered. One thousand men were flung into prison, where they faced court martial and the execution squad. Protest meetings were held, and the revolt spread. The way was open for Germany's excellent secret service to spread the virus of disorder, just as Wilhelm Stieber had taught them to do in Bismarck's day. Even the soldiers flung open their barracks. By 8th November, all major German cities seemed to be in the grip of revolution, but the Kaiser still refused to abdicate, declaring that he would place himself at the head of the Army immediately after the armistice was signed. At last, General Gröner told the Kaiser bluntly: 'The Army will march back to the homeland in closed ranks and good order under its leaders and commanding generals, but not under the leadership of Your Majesty.'[341]

Still the unhappy, the Kaiser hung on. Finally, caretaker President, Prince Max, lost his patience and a proclamation was read out: 'The Emperor and King has decided to renounce the throne.'[342]

Hugenberg's newspapers hastened to proclaim that Germany's Emperor and his noble army had been 'stabbed in the back' by socialists and Jews. The story would feed extreme-right wing opinion in the future and lead to Hitler's rise to power. However, the Emperor's abdication helped pacify democratic public opinion abroad and Americans began to worry about the spectre of Bolshevism sweeping across Germany. They still voted against Wilson's peace proposals in the mid-term American elections on 5th November, but not by the huge margin which Wilson was originally threatened with.

On 11th November 1918, after a long wait in the fog, the German Reichstag delegation was authorized to sign the armistice after General Foch accepted the Allies' first concession; the Allies allowed the German army to retain 5,000 of its 30,000 machine guns, as well as its small arms, so that they could preserve order in the face of the 'revolution' erupting in Germany.[343] This would prove to be a mistake.

Naturally, once the revolution was started, it was difficult to quell. New Chancellor, Friedrich Ebert, a small, unprepossessing but authoritative son of a tailor, was given the task of saving the country from anarchy. From his lonely desk in the Chancellor's Palace, he could hear the extreme left advancing from their stronghold in the Imperial Palace. To whom could he turn to prevent a Bolshevik revolution in Germany? It was General Gröner on the telephone: 'The High Command expects the Government to co-operate with the Officer Corps in the suppression of Bolshevism, and in the maintenance of discipline.'

Chancellor Ebert accepted Gröner's terms. So, on 11th December,1918, exactly one month after the armistice, the German legions marched up the Unter den Linden brandishing their weapons, while Ebert declared: 'I salute you, who return unvanquished from the field of battle.'[344] It was a huge propaganda coup. The Allies' foolishness, in allowing the German army to keep its small arms had become glaringly obvious.

The Pan-Germans may have felt that Germany could salvage victory over its enemies from defeat, but it was clear that President Woodrow Wilson had won a great victory over the Allies. After British Premier Lloyd George declared that he was going to ask for a huge indemnity from Germany, Woodrow Wilson caused consternation by declaring that he was going to ask for no indemnity at all.

Lloyd George was in a quandary and not only because of his grave shortage of money. Britain is an island, and crucially in December 1918, acutely short of ships. Britain urgently needed Germany's merchant fleet to bring her troops home after the war. However, France was in desperate straits too. All her coal mines had been destroyed and without the power that they produced she could not exist.

Brigadier-General Morgan recorded how French factories had been wrecked '... not by shell fire but by the sabotage of German sappers all along the line of the Meuse between Liège and Namur'[345] while Monsieur Gruener, the President of the Civil Engineers of France, declared that some 220 coal mines had been made unworkable for years.[346] Nearly two million hectares of agricultural land lay devasted. The German army had also destroyed 2,245 kilometres of railway lines, 1,160 bridges and 500,000 houses, and 460,000 tons of industrial materials had been being carted off to Germany.[347]

The German government professed itself quite unable to surrender the country's merchant fleet to Britain or to pay reparations to France. Nevertheless, she declared that she was willing to use some of the 2,550,240,000 gold marks which she had amassed in the Reichsbank during the war - representing twice the value of gold as the 1,253,199,000 in 1914,[348] - to buy food from America.

The Americans had been generously donating mammoth quantities of food to bankrupt Europe and their farmers urgently needed paying by one of the few countries able and willing to reimburse them for their largesse. But France and Belgium would not agree to the gold in the Reichsbank being used to feed the German people until the Treaty of Versailles was signed and sealed, with the German authorities giving a cast-iron undertaking to pay for the repair of their ravaged mines and cities.

The Pan Germans lost no time in using starvation as a propaganda weapon. The German granaries were thrown open after the war and six months' supplies were consumed in six weeks.[349] Then the government threw itself upon the mercy of the Americans.[350] It pleaded to be allowed to buy corn to feed its starving population - but the Allies refused.

The American agricultural community ached to sell corn to the one country in Europe able to pay for it - but France was adamant. The devastation of France's land was so horrific that the German delegation en-route to Paris could scarcely bear to look at it.[351] However, the German press continued to publish such harrowing tales of German misery and starvation that the British people were impressed. 'Bolshevism' was an ever-present fear after the First World War. The British people believed that revolution had forced the departure of the Kaiser and feared that their own country would be next. Lloyd George decided to side with the Americans over the food issue because Germany promised that she would surrender her merchant fleet if Britain agreed to the deal. But the French would not give way.

Finally, an absolutely, despairing Lloyd George, had an idea. He pulled out a telegram from Field Marshall Plumer, Commander in Chief of the British Army on the Rhine, which said that the 'mortality amongst (German) women, children and sick is most grave, and sickness due to hunger is spreading. The attitude of the population is becoming one of despair, and the people feel that an end by bullets is preferable to death by starvation ... I request therefore that a definite date be fixed for the arrival of first supplies.' The French weakened but still declared that Germany could pay for the food in any way she chose but not with the gold, which must stand as surety for France's reparations.

Eventually, Lloyd George brought the matter up at the conference table in Paris, lambasting French Finance Minister, Louis-Lucien Klotz. The story of the unfortunate saga was related by none other than John Maynard Keynes in 1945.

Keynes recorded how Lloyd George attacked the poor Jewish Finance Minister: 'Never have I seen the equal of the onslaught with which that poor man was overwhelmed. Do you know Klotz by sight? – a short, plump, heavy-moustached Jew, well-groomed, well-kept, but with an unsteady roving eye, and his shoulders a little bent in an instinctive depreciation. Lloyd George had always hated and despised him; and now saw in a twinkling that he could kill him. Women and children were starving, he cried, and here was M. Klotz prating and prating of his 'goold.' He leant forward and with a gesture of his hands indicated to everyone the image of a hideous Jew, clutching a money bag. His eyes flashed and the words came out with a contempt so violent that he seemed almost to be spitting at him. ...

Everyone looked at Klotz with a momentary contempt and hatred; the poor man was bent over his seat, visibly cowering. We hardly knew what Lloyd George was saying but the words 'goold' and Klotz were repeated, and each time with exaggerated contempt. Then turning, he called on Clemenceau to put a stop to these obtrusive tactics, otherwise, he cried, M. Klotz would rank with Lenin and Trotsky among those who had spread Bolshevism in Europe. ...[352]

Lloyd George's anti-Semitic phrases were relayed throughout the world by avid newspaper reporters and the French gave way. In a three-way deal, Britain received Germany's merchant ships, Germany received America's food and America received cash from Germany's gold reserves to pay for it.

It was only after the Second World War that Keynes would reveal that General Plumer's telegram about the German people's starvation was not due to the general's anxieties over the food situation in Germany but in reply to a request from Lloyd George.

All Europe was short of food in the war's aftermath but dark, handsome British occupation General, Harry Lewin maintained that while the Germans in his area were quite well fed 'the Belgians were yellow with hunger and as for the French ... the women were gaunt spectres and the children listless little skeletons with skins like parchment.'[353] Indeed, Keynes remarked in his comment on the subject: 'It was a curious feature of the negotiations of the next three months that British anxiety over the German food supplies was, so far as concerned its urgency in point of time, decidedly greater, to all appearance, than the anxiety of the Germans themselves.'[354]

Statistics supported General Lewin's observation[355] that the French people suffered worse than the Germans in 1919. However, the French did not tell the world of their people's hunger, and the Paris talks were full of pomp and ceremony, so the fair-minded British people did not realize that Lloyd George's tales of German 'starvation' had been a propaganda exercise. Pan German publicists relished the propaganda opportunity. 'Starvation' was an emotive issue. It would be used with devastating effect when the treaty was handed to the German delegates at Versailles.

American Republicans had campaigned for the German army's 'unconditional surrender' and then to allow some former independent regions of Bismarck's Empire, particularly Bavaria, to regain their independence. However, Wilson decided that 'self-determination' on the base of language, was how he would determine the future of Europe, which meant that, although Wilson was keen to reconstitute the nation of Poland, Bismarck's fifty-year old empire would be left intact, with the Bavarians chained to Prussia.

Indemnities were usually charged to a defeated foe to pay for all the damage they had caused and ensure that the offending country was too weak to rampage over its neighbours again. Germany had emerged unscathed from the First World War, while invading all her neighbours. Nevertheless, Wilson had declared on 12th December that he would be charging 'no' indemnities.

As Wilson had won the war and was the arbiter of the peace, this meant that indemnities could not be charged. However, the Allies had to be recompensed in some way for their sufferings, and so the term 'reparations' was coined, and the War Guilt Clause inserted into the Treaty of Versailles, because all the nations had to have a legal framework for making their demands.

Indeed, restitution also needed to be made because uninvaded Germany seemed to be ready to embark on a trade war. In contrast to 'victorious' France with her ruined countryside and her coal mines 'unproductive for years owing to the removal of machinery and the flooding of shafts' the ubiquitous reporter from the *New York Times* declared:

'It is true that in some respects Germany is ready for a trade war. They have undoubtedly a considerable stock of glassware, cutlery, electrical appliances, photographic materials and iron and steel goods, admirably equipped and using electric power throughout, whose manager said proudly that he had enough mine pumps built during the intervals of big gun orders, through which he admitted he had made enormous profits, to supply all the flooded mines of France and Belgium.[356]

Lloyd George had been elected on a promise to demand the fullest indemnities from Germany. British Lords Cunliffe and Sumner therefore called for a sum of £8 billion. John Foster Dulles countered that there had been a contract with Germany and that the Allies could ask for no more than £5 or £6 billion in total.[357] Finally, much maligned French Finance Minister, Louis-Lucien Klotz suggested that it would be better to leave the full amount to be decided until May 1921.

Germany, which was supposed to be more powerful than Britain before the First World War, and now had twice the gold reserves it had possessed in 1914, was ordered to pay 20 milliard marks (approx. £1,000,000,000) in the years up till 1921, the amount to 'be made in such instalments and in such a manner (whether in gold, commodities, ships or otherwise) as the Reparations Commission may fix.'[358] One might ask how Germany had managed to finish the war with twice as much gold as at the outset.

Partly this was due to the German government's 'relentless' wartime campaign to encourage its citizens to surrender their gold. The public were assured of the value of the new paper Reichsbank notes and were promised 'the extraction of a gigantic indemnity' after their enemies had been defeated.[359] So, they had surrendered all their gold. In addition, the countries Germany had invaded had to pay indemnities too. After Russia was defeated, she was asked to pay 6,000 million roubles in fine gold currency and kind. Other vanquished foes like Belgium had contributed lesser amounts. As a result, defeated Germany's exchequer was in excellent shape in 1919.

History books give a long list of the indignities that Germany was made to suffer under the terms of the Treaty of Versailles. If you take the view that Germany was no guiltier than Britain or France for causing the First World War, they sound severe. Germany lost her colonies. Tanganyika was to be administered by Britain and the Cameroons to France as 'mandates.' However, Wilson's idea of the mandates was not that Tanganyika, and the Cameroons should become colonies but that they should be under the eagle eye of the United Nations, as a precursor to them achieving self-government.

Alsace and Lorraine were returned to France. The Saar coal fields were to be ruled by the League for fifteen years, with France controlling the mines because her mines had been destroyed. The German port of Danzig, with 300,000 Germans, was to be ruled by the League as a 'Free City.' Memel, another German port with 141,000 German inhabitants, was 'seized' by the new state of Lithuania. Malmedy and Eupen went to Belgium and the Rhineland was to have an army of occupation for fifteen years before becoming a demilitarized zone.

In Eastern Europe, Germany had to recognize the independence of Czechoslovakia and to cede parts of the province of Upper Silesia. Poland was reconstituted as a state with access to the sea. An area of 51,800 square miles of land was given to Poland, a massive blow to Prussia, whose military leadership had spent so many wartime hours, planning to syphon off huge chunks of Polish territory and to people the area with German farmers.

France wanted Wilson to allow her frontier to be moved to the Rhine so that she could defend herself against the 'Prussian' hordes. However, despite 'being smitten with a temperature of 103, looking utterly beaten, worn out, his face haggard ... and the eye twitching painfully' Wilson was determined to defend Germany's interests. His biographer, Ray Stannard Baker takes up the story:

'I went to see President Wilson at 6.30 – the first time since he fell ill and had a long talk. I found him fully dressed, in his study, looking thin and pale. A slight hollowness around the eyes emphasised a characteristic I had often noted before – the size and luminosity of his eyes.

'Then Italy will not get Fiume?' I asked.

'Absolutely not – as long as I am here,' he said sharply.

'Nor France the Saar?'

'No.'

'The time has come to bring this thing to a head,' he said.

'We agreed among ourselves, and we agreed with Germany upon certain general principles. The whole course of the Conference has been made up of a series of attempts, especially by France, to break down this agreement, to get territory and to impose crushing indemnities.'

Wilson was a pacifist, who was sympathetic to Germany. Nevertheless, he would eventually become impressed with the desperation of the French delegation.

Meanwhile, the Allied armies had to contend with the aftermath of the war on the ground. The American army had been ordered to return to the US four months after the Peace Treaty was signed, and Britain's army was also due to disband, although Germany still had over 400,000 Reichswehr under arms, and gun factories pumping out weapons.

General Haig declared: 'If the existing orders are continued ... there will be no organised army of occupation left.' How then can our government hope to dictate peace terms to the enemy?' Therefore, the conference decided that the German army should be reduced to 100,000 men. However, it made no recommendations as to how the decision was to be enforced.

The Prussian Officer had always had a special place in Germany, regarding himself as being above the common herd. [360] In view of the 'revolution' accompanying the Kaiser's departure, the German government insisted that the Prussian officers belonging to Sicherheitspolizei, (security police), were not to be treated as part of the army and could be armed, not only with machine-guns and trench mortars, but also with field guns and planes. Controlling the Communist 'enemies within' Germany, therefore, should not have been as difficult as outsiders imagined. Indeed, at this point 7,000 munitions plants had their factories intact, and Krupp was still manufacturing weapons.[361]

Wilson's most treasured ambition was to create a League of Nations to keep the unruly European nations in order. Britain supported him. She was tired of trying to do it herself. Yet the Republicans were surly.

Lord Northcliffe had been warned by the *Times* correspondent in Washington, Authur Willert, of the generally sour feeling towards Britain in the US after the British had supported Wilson's armistice.[362] The Republicans did not know of their army's tribulations at Meuse-Argonne. They believed that America had sent its soldiers over to Europe to win the war, and Britain had connived with their unpopular President to prevent victory on the battlefield. After the war, Wilson had had few discussions with them, and they had little faith in the League of Nations being able to control a resurgent Germany.

Nevertheless, Wilson was happy with the peace he had negotiated until the day he met the German representative, Count Brockdorff-Rantzau, at Versailles. To begin with the haughty, monocled Count refused to have the courtesy to rise when he addressed the Chamber. Then, in a loud voice, heard all over the world, he declared:

'It is demanded from us that we shall confess ourselves to be the only ones guilty of the war. We are far from declining any responsibility for this great World War ... but we energetically deny that Germany and its people, who were convinced that they were waging a war of defence, were alone guilty.'

Brockdoff-Rantzau went on to declare that hundreds of thousands of innocent German people had died since the armistice because of the Allies blockade on food shipments ... They had been killed 'with cold deliberation, after our adversaries had conquered and victory had been assured to them.'

Lloyd George wanted to hit Count Brockdorff-Rantzau presumably for using the propaganda weapon he had handed to him over the 'starvation' issue so adroitly. President Wilson also knew that Brockdorff-Rantzau was telling a lie. It seems that President Wilson was rapidly changing his mind over the war guilt issue too. He originally had been prejudiced against the Allies, but the anguish of the French over the future protection of their country and his meeting with Brockdorff-Rantzau persuaded him that he had made a huge mistake.

Meanwhile the German press screamed defiance over signing the Treaty. When Lloyd George and future President Herbert Hoover met Wilson and suggested the Treaty of Versailles might be altered to persuade the German delegation to sign, President Wilson answered: '... don't you think that if we regard the treaty as just, the argument of expediency ought not to govern, because, after all we must not give up what we fought for? We might have to fight for it again.'

Woodrow Wilson had been prejudiced against the Allies, but he had principles too. After he finally met the German negotiators at Versailles, he was brave enough to admit that he had made a terrible mistake in giving Germany a compassionate peace, telling the American people in September 1919 at St. Louis, 'For nearly fifty years the French had expected a war. ... The terror had been there all the time, and the war was its flame and consummation.'

And a few days later at Minneapolis, 'the only people in Europe who instinctively realized what was going to happen and what did happen in 1914 was the French people.'[363]

Unfortunately, the American people had been on one abortive military trip to Europe to save France and did not want to contemplate another. The Republicans had wanted a very, different kind of peace to President Wilson's with some of the component parts of Bismarck's Reich, like Bavaria, becoming separate counties again, but their most powerful representatives had not even been allowed to participate in the Paris negotiations.

Republicans were also upset by Count Brockdorff-Rantzau's accusation that the Allies had wantonly 'starved' the German people. His words were deeply shocking to hard-pressed Americans farmers, so many of whom had parents and grandparents in Germany, who had food in abundance to send to Germany.

Then the former British conscientious objector and economist John Maynard Keynes wrote a riveting page-turning condemnation of the Treaty of Versailles called *The Economic Consequences of the Peace*, which stated that America's inept President had been taken for a ride by the Allies and that Treaty's 'dishonourable' reparations clauses would reduce Germany to hunger and famine.

Passages from the book like 'There can seldom have been a statesman of the first rank more incompetent than the President in the abilities of the Council Chamber' were even read in the American Senate. The Republicans refused to ratify the Versailles Treaty and ousted Wilson from office in the next Presidential election. Over time Keynes's view that the Treaty of Versailles was outrageous would become dogma in the United States.

The Economic Consequences of the Peace had an equally unfortunate impact in Germany. German Social

Democrat member, Erich Eyck, who later fled and came to London, declared in his book, *A History of the Weimar Republic, vol 1*, that Keynes *Economic Consequence of the Peace* '... served as a complete confirmation to all those had been shrieking about the 'shameful peace' and the 'Diktat of Versailles...

'No German with any serious hope of a political career dared even imply the thought that Germany was legally obligated to pay for even part of the damages she had inflicted on the neighbours she had attacked. And if the Germans finally went so far as to attribute all their economic ills not to having lost a war but simply to the reparations that they paid, Keynes cannot be relieved of his share of the blame.

In his recent book, *A Perfidious Distortion of History, The Versailles Peace Treaty and the success of the Nazis*, published in 2017, German-born Professor Jürgen Tampke stated that a relatively modest increase in taxation, coupled by a modest reduction in consumption, would have enabled the Weimar Republic to pay the reparations demanded by the Treaty.[364]

Unfortunately, Keynes's *The Economic Consequences of the Peace*, published in 1919, had a deeper impact. The German hierarchy had asked America for an armistice, not the Allies. Without America's ratification of the subsequent Treaty of Versailles, and America's troops on the grounds to enforce it, the former military/industrial cabal felt no compunction to adhere to its demands at all.

Small, brave French general, Ferdinand Foch, who had campaigned for the French border to be moved to the Rhine as the only way to prevent the Germans invading France again, declared prophetically 'This is not a peace. It is an armistice for twenty years.'

After the American troops soon went home, the Allies who had largely disbanded their armies, were on their own, confronted by Germany, revitalised by the return of her victorious troops from Russia. On 1st January 1920, *The Times* gave chilling evidence of its military strength; 400,000 Reichswehr, 150 Zeitfreiwillingen, (emergency volunteers), 40,000 to 50,000 Sicherheitspolizei and 300,000 Einwohnenwehren, (home defence), from which, later, tens of thousands of Hitler's storm troopers would emerge.

Faced with the unenviable task of enforcing the Treaty of Versailles without America, the Allies decided to abandon Article 227 of the Treaty of Versailles, which called for the trial of the Kaiser, after Holland, reaping rich rewards from the country's transfer of trade from Antwerp to Rotterdam, refused to hand him over for trial.

Holland hinted that if, and hopefully when, the Associate power (USA) eventually ratified the Treaty of Versailles and was willing to take a full part in the League of Nations, the situation might be different.[365]

The Allies also abandoned Article 228 of the Treaty, which authorized them to try Generals Ludendorff and Hindenburg, Chancellor Bethmann-Hollweg, Admiral Tirpitz and 890 other persons or groups.[366] They just did not feel strong enough to enforce the Treaty's terms and renegade elements of the military were about to try and jettison the Weimar Republic.

Indeed, as soon as America decided against ratifying the Treaty, ex-soldiers from the victorious Eastern Front, egged on by a Pan-German Wolfgang Kapp, tried to stage a military coup. Small, squat, Social Democrat, Friedrich Ebert, with his snub nose and shabby overcoat, was faced with another desperate situation, only this time it came from the Fascists rather than the Bolsheviks. 'Cease work,' he cried. 'Stifle the opportunity of this military dictatorship! Fight with all the means at your command to retain the Republic. Strike along the whole line.'[367]

The effect of his words was miraculous. The workers downed tools. There was a general strike and after five days stalemate, the renegade soldiers retreated, firing at onlookers as they went. This was a great victory for the ordinary working man. The Republic won this time. The army was reduced in size and illegal military organizations were ordered to disband. However, the Republic was already under attack and the great industrialists would soon have their revenge.

The Pan-Germans decided to change the name of their organization. Alfred Hugenberg and his friends decided to create a 'National Opposition' to the Weimar Republic.[368] Britain's Brigadier General Morgan soon found that 'official obstruction' and 'newspaper vituperation' against the Allied Military Control Commission went hand in hand. His depressing verdict was that while the Republicans were, 'in office in the Weimar Republic, the Nationalists (ie. the former Pan-Germans!) were in actual control!'[369]

The 'Nationalists' discovered Hitler and were impressed by his oratory. Ex-Pan-German publicist, Heinrich Claß, blamed the Jews for the loss of the war, saying 'Kill them, the world court is not asking for your reasons!'[370] Hitler was captivated by Claß's ideas and enlisted to become a 'drummer' for the Nationalist cause. Then the industrial magnates started to flex their muscles. Germany had been able to defy Articles 227 and 228 of the treaty, ordering them to surrender the major war offenders for trial, so the coal barons decided to defy the Allies' request for reparations too.

At the Versailles peace conference, Monsieur Gruener, President of the Civil Engineers of France, had described how the German army had ruined 220 French coal mines on its retreat in 1918. The country was therefore required to send coal in 'deliveries in kind' reparations to France - and to sell her the mine pumps to repair her coal mines too. But neither the coal pumps nor the reparations coal, seemed to be forthcoming. In 1920, while Berlin's lights blazed and Germany exported coal to Denmark, Holland and Switzerland, Paris lay in darkness.[371] Yet when unrepentant coal magnate, Hugo Stinnes, was asked to explain the difficulties which had held up the delivery of France's coal, he merely referred to the Allies as 'our insane conquerors.'[372]

Hugo Stinnes was an anti-social man with a huge homburg hat, a black Assyrian beard and ill-fitting clothes but he was reputed to own some 4,500 businesses abroad after the First World War, in Russia, Romania, Italy, Scandinavia, Spain, Luxembourg, France, Britain, Holland, Belgium, North America, China, Japan and elsewhere.[373] He and his friends had put millions abroad while encouraging the government to run down the value of the mark. Meanwhile Germany was murdering its neighbours' industries. While the Danes were being flooded with 'iron and steel goods' 'stored up for exportation at rock bottom prices,' Britain's vital coal, steel and shipbuilding industries were in a desperate state too.

Prime Minister, Lloyd George, declared darkly that 'there is undoubtedly in existence what is in effect a substantial bounty on export from certain countries whose exchanges are in a very abnormal states' and that 'the government will do everything in its power 'to shield essential industries for the defence of this country to ensure that 'the exchange situation in Europe may not be utilised as a means of destroying our industries.'[374] But the Treaty of Versailles had not given the British or French the power to enter Germany, stabilise her currency, and control her finances and without American support they hesitated to use force, although their industries were being crucified.[375]

Looking at the map of the world after the First World War it seemed that Britain had become the most powerful nation on earth, enlarged by the inclusion of the 'mandated' colonies from the former German and Ottoman Empires. Yet Bismarck had declared that colonies, for the most part, were a burden on the public purse. This appeared to be true for the British Empire in the 1920s too. Britain had been acutely impoverished by the war; her industry was being hit by German competition and the costs of administering her Empire kept mounting because President Wilson's heady doctrine of 'self-determination' had opened-up a hornets-nest of discontent.

America, herself, was not feeling rich anymore. She had made a fortune out of the war, but her farming industry was in trouble because it had overexpanded, and German industry was hurting her industrial base.[376] On 11th February 1921 America asked the Germans to furnish them with all the data on their production to see if they were indulging in unfair practices.

In 1922 new Republican President, Warren G Harding, slapped on the Ford McCumber tariff to protect American industry, but as he dared not tell his countrymen that defeated Germany was the culprit, Britain and France's exports would be discriminated against too.

The British people were alarmed and angry after the huge sacrifices of war. Many were beginning to ask why they fought at all. Britain had spent nearly all her national treasure on the conflict and, unknown to her citizens, Germany's coal and steel magnates were doing their best to ensure that her great industrial heart died too. By 1921 with the help of the printing press, the German debt burden (internal and external) was slightly less than the ratio of the total British internal and external national debt to gross national product in the same year.[377] But that did not mean that Germany was going to pay her reparations. She felt herself powerful enough to defy the Allies' demands.

France was also suffering. She had received no money to restore her shattered provinces. Even obtaining coal reparations from the Ruhr magnates was fruitless until the offer of a bribe from Lloyd George.[378] Lloyd George's appeasing gesture, for the present, facilitated German coal deliveries to France, but it would encourage the German coal owners to take greater liberties in the future to the detriment of the world economy.

Former Pan-German, Alfred Hugenberg, had left Krupp's armaments firm at the end of the war to concentrate on his newspaper empire. He had a field day with his campaign against the Versailles Treaty. As early as 5th April 1921, the French legation in Bavaria sent a dispatch to the Quai d'Orsay, protesting that 'a violent campaign using the press, posters and meetings is underway in Germany to undermine the legal basis of the Versailles treaty: Germany's guilt in the war.'[379] Subsequently forty volumes of carefully edited documents called *Die Grosse Politik* were published in record time to demonstrate that the war had merely started as a breakdown of international relations. Therefore, Germany should not be compelled to pay any reparations.

In his article, '*Clio Deceived, Patriotic Self-Censorship in Germany after the Great War*' (1996) Holger H Herwig was most censorious of *Die Grosse Politik*. He claimed that it omitted all material from the General Staff, the War Ministry, the Navy Ministry, and the bureau responsible for the economic preparations for the war. It had merely been assembled from Foreign Office records but even so failed to include a number of critical documents, including the discussions on July 5th and 6th, the detailed analysis of the Viennese ultimatum to Serbia, virtually any and all talks held by Chancellor Bethmann-Hollweg with representatives of foreign powers in July 1914; 'and finally 'any and all contacts between Willhelm II and his political as well as his military leaders after the monarch's return from his northern cruise on 27th July.'[380]

Nevertheless, the Foreign Ministry decided that *Die Grosse Politik* was the standard work of reference into the causes of the First World War. No further documents were to be made available. Once completed the Foreign Ministry was ready to go on the offensive about the war guilt issue. It had been told by the Hamburg banker, Max Warburg, that it could not possibly hope to obtain to obtain loans unless it could refute the Allies war-guilt accusations[381] but it had 'proved' itself capable of the task. Between 1921 and 1923 one million marks was given to the pseudo-historical think-tank, 'The Centre for the study of the Causes of the War,' for propaganda purposes. An additional 200,000 marks was released to support the efforts of diplomatic missions abroad to 'prove' to the public at large that Germany was no guiltier than other nations of starting the First World War.

Under the Treaty of Versailles agreement, Germany was obliged to pay £1,000 million in reparations in cash and kind by 1921. Rolling stock valued at 1,102.5 million (approx. £55 million) was surrendered, stolen livestock valued at 146.9 million gold marks returned (£7.5 million) and stolen agricultural machinery valued at 20.8 (£1 million).[382] Germany would also be credited £250 million for the buildings, that she had erected in the French areas swiped by Bismarck in 1870 and returned under the terms of the treaty. All in all, including the Saar, merchant ships, deliveries of coal and other items, the Reparations Commission valued the 'reparations in kind' received at £400 million.

However, cash was also due to be paid in reparations. Some of that gold sitting in the Reichsbank should have been used towards the £1,000,000,000 due by 1921. But no 'actual cash' had arrived. The only cash payments made to Reparations Commission prior to May 1921 amounted to some 84 million marks (£4.2 million) which came not from Germany, but from France and Denmark, as credits for the value of property ceded under the terms of the Treaty. [383]

Eventually the Allies decided that they had to be seen to be getting tough. Public opinion was irate. German industry was rampaging across their lands stealing their business and not a single war criminal had been tried. They occupied the German towns of Düsseldorf, Duisburg and Ruhroht and gave Germany seven days to fulfil her disarmament provisions, try some of her lesser war criminals like the 'brutal' camp guards, and to pay her war reparations. To reassure the public a high headline figure of £6.6 billion was set as the total reparations due, although the small print revealed that the Allies were only expecting to receive £2.5 billion.

In the event the first £50 million was only eventually paid with the help of short-term loans from abroad. After paying another £25 million Germany put in her first official request for a moratorium.[384] Extracting cash reparations from Germany was going to be like getting blood out of a stone.

CHAPTER SIX

Germany's Great Inflation

By the early 1920s Germany had already succeeded in defying the edicts of the Treaty of Versailles to bring the Kaiser, Chancellor Bethmann-Hollweg and General Hindenburg and Ludendorff to trial. She was also in an excellent position to compete in the post-war world. Having destroyed France and Belgium's mines and industry with her scorched earth policy on her retreat, she was now maiming British industry with the low value of the mark.

The popular picture of Germany in the early 1920s was of the country on the verge of revolution. It was nothing of the sort. Germany had been made to sign the Treaty of Versailles by the Western Allies, but her fledgling democracy was in for no easy ride. The left was easily quashed, and the industrialists were in a perfect position to reduce the workers' power before the currency was stabilized.

The advent of the Weimar Republic had been treated with enthusiasm in Germany when it was first introduced. Although it was to be a federal republic it aimed to cement Bismarck's Reich into one country. Individual states like Saxony and Bavaria, which had been independent before Bismarck became Chancellor, were to become 'lands' in the future and it was proposed that the new, centralised government could impose direct taxation on them as well as the indirect taxation, which was all that Bismarck had felt powerful enough to levy.

Parliament was to be modelled on the American example but with proportional representation and everyone over twenty was given the vote. Germany's first President, Friedrich Ebert, had impeccable democratic credentials, being the son of a tailor. Nevertheless, he had incurred the enduring enmity of many on the right by formulating the Reichstag's famous 'peace resolution' in July 1917 and leading a huge strike in the munitions industry in 1918. Before the war, Ebert's party, the Social Democrats or SPD, had been impotent but had public opinion on their side.

After the war, although they had at last been given the longed-for legislative power that they craved, they rapidly lost cross-party public support over the 'nationalists' increasingly shrill accusations that they had 'stabbed the nation in the back' by accepting President Wilson's armistice.

The Social Democrat's enemies, the German Nationalists or DNVP, who were determined to avoid any trace of blame for starting and losing the war, won only 42 out of 421 seats in the first elections after the war. Newspaper magnate and former Chairman of Krupp, Alfred Hugenberg decided to become a member.

Besides what would become the two main parties, there were the People's Party, or DVP, which was founded by powerful steel magnate Albert Vögler, and Gustav Stresemann, who had supported the extreme Right when a member of the Reichstag during the war. There was also the Democratic Party, the Communist Workers Party of Germany, the Independent Social Democratic Party, the Bavarian People's Party, and the well-supported Centre Party, which was identified with the Catholic Church.

The anti-Republican parties could count on the support of many of the newly returned soldiers from the East, who had won a huge victory in Russia, only to find that the Western Front had collapsed. The main villain to war veterans like them was President Wilson of America, who had denied Germany military victory. Instead, he had offered the German socialists 'intrinsic justice,' 'impartial adjustment of colonial claims,' 'open covenants of peace openly arrived at' and had reneged on his promises.

Amongst the 354 people who were murdered in Germany in the savage post-war period, were many prominent people who wanted to fulfil the edicts of the Treaty of Versailles. Amongst other notables, Deputy Chancellor and Finance Minister, Matthias Erzberger, who had proposed stabilizing the currency and paying reparations, was murdered in 1920, and Foreign Minister, Walter Rathenau, who was accused of the 'pulverization of our middle classes,' by adopting a 'fulfilment' policy over the reparations demands was assassinated in 1922.

The French had received no monetary reparations by 1921. Before Rathenau's murder, German heavy industry had turned down Rathenau's plan to pay France's reparations 'in kind' with deliveries of coal. It had also vetoed any increase in taxation on profits or a levy on private wealth.   In desperation Germany was offered a mortgage secured on the collective wealth of German business and landowners.   In return Hugo Stinnes, arguably the richest coal baron in Germany, demanded that the socialists repeal the eight-hour working day and privatise all the productive assets of the state. However, the socialists were determined to keep the eight-hour day, so the mark crashed in value from 99.1 marks to the dollar to 262.96.[385]

Meanwhile the French lost faith in their government. They had received no cash to repair their textile factories, whose machines had been sabotaged by the retreating German army. Their railway tracks had been torn up, and their coalmines flooded. Towns, villages, and farmsteads had been looted and razed mercilessly by order of the German High Command.[386] but they had received no recompense. They threw socialist Prime Minister, Aristide Briand, out of office, and replaced him with ex-President Raymond Poincaré, who was determined to make Germany pay for the destruction her army had caused.

There was no meeting of minds between Poincaré and Lloyd George. Poincaré believed that Lloyd George had forgotten 'the 438,000' Frenchmen 'martyred in German prisons' while Lloyd George, safely across the Channel, wanted bygones to be bygones and for Britain to renew her ties with Germany. Indeed, that had already happened. Over a hundred British companies had taken advantage of Germany's low exchange rate to set up operations in Cologne. The British and the Hanoverians had fought side by side with Frederick the Great in the eighteenth century and the British began to believe Germany's new claim that she was a bulwark against Bolshevism.

The Hugenberg Press seized this moment to accuse Poincaré of causing the war in 1914. It asserted that Poincaré had agreed plans with Emperor Nicholas II in 1912 to dismember Bismarck's empire. The French Communist newspaper *L'Humanité* ran a front-page story on the issue called *Poincaré-la-guerre* and the German Reichstag voted credits to propagandise its allegations world-wide.[387] Britain had started to empathise with Germany when she seemed overwhelmed by revolution and starvation after the war. In the *Economic Consequences of the Peace* a sympathetic Keynes had denounced French

Premier Clemenceau for trying to impose a Carthaginian Peace on 'prostrate' Germany. Now even parts of the French press were accusing France of being the warmonger in 1914. Slowly British antagonism grew towards her historic enemy, France. In 1921 Britain's *New Statesman*, even published an article asserting that France was more bellicose than Germany and that 'there was no conceivable reason ... why Germany should not possess as many aeroplanes as France.'[388] Those on the Left knew nothing of Germany's great victories in the East. They began to forget that Prussian militarism had ever existed and hoped that the First World War had been the war to end all wars.

Nevertheless, powerful 'Prussians' did still exist, including the owner of one of Europe's largest companies, Gustav Krupp. Although his company was reputedly in financial trouble after the war, Gustav managed to gain control of the Swedish steel company, Bofors, by 1921. He was not allowed to manufacture armaments in Germany. However, in Sweden Bofors would churn out 'the latest type of heavy guns, tanks armed with machine guns ... anti-aircraft guns, and gas bombs ...' for the next fourteen years.

In Holland, meanwhile, Krupp operated through a company called Siderius, which was the holding company for three Dutch shipyards. By 1922 two of Krupp's directors held all the shares. They moved to the Netherlands with forty German engineers 'the vanguard as it turned out of a much larger force.' Their object was to set up 'a German U-boat construction office' on Dutch territory in contravention of articles 168, 170, and 179 of the Treaty of Versailles.[389]

Lloyd George did not know of Gustav Krupp's nefarious machinations. In 1922, his ambition was to encourage Germany not to trade with the Bolsheviks until they had paid their war debts - but his plan misfired. Under the Treaty of Rapallo, Germany and the Soviet Union forged a new friendship, under which 'impoverished' Germany waived all governmental – and private - IOUs against the Bolsheviks, provided that the Russians treated other (Allied) claimants in the same fashion. Britain was left with a multitude of Russian IOUs from the First World War, which would never be repaid, while the German army was secretly permitted to establish officer training courses in Russia and given tracts of land for testing rockets and heavy artillery.[390]

Balding, bearded Bolshevik Vladimir Lenin had just had a bullet removed from his neck by a German surgeon. He desperately needed German help. The full horror of Russia's famine, which has been estimated to have killed five million people had leaked out to the wider world and American Journalist, Raymond Swing was sent by his newspaper to investigate.

Swing reported: 'We went to the Volga port of Samara by train, then overnight down the river on a filthy and vermin-infested boat. ... I have never seen a more harrowing sight than people starving to death ... Several hundred of them had come to the river from the interior in the hope of being taken away by the government to regions where they could find food and lodging. They had built shelters of leafless branches, but they had little to eat but grass.' ... '

This group of refugees had a leader, an old, gaunt, tall, and white-bearded figure. He took us to the adjoining field where the dead were buried, each tomb decently identified with some primitive wooden marker. ... The children were the most heart-rending with their pallid faces and swollen bellies. It needed no expert eye to know that they were doomed to die.'

'What made the plight of these people both tragic and – if I may use the word – beautiful was the fact in a field within plain view ... was a great mound of sacks filled with grain and guarded by a single soldier. ... I asked the patriarch why he and his hungry people did not overpower the soldier and bring their fast to an end. He replied: "That is seed grain. We do not steal from the future."'[391]

Yet eventually people became so desperate that cannibalism was recorded in Russia and America was finally allowed to provide food for millions of people. The causes of the famine were said to be numerous, with the civil war a contributing factor. However, it may be that the fight between the Bolsheviks and their kulak peasant farmers had already begun, with the kulaks refusing to be paid for their produce in worthless currency.

The North Caucasus was a traditional wheat growing area and Germany had been a good customer for wheat in the 19th century. So, in 1922, former Pan-German, Gustav Krupp took a lease on 50,000 hectares of land in the North Caucasus to produce wheat to help Lenin export wheat without having to rely on his recalcitrant farmers.[392] Krupp promised that at least 60 per cent of his concession would be producing wheat by 1928, while Lenin approved the allocation of 40 per cent of all his gold reserves for the import of, so it was rumoured, as many as 5,000 new trains and 100,000 wagons.[393]

Meanwhile, in Germany herself, although the German middle classes on fixed incomes were seeing their savings wiped out by their country's inflation, unemployment was low, and those in industry with land and property, and money abroad, were getting richer. On 12th July 1922, a special correspondent for the *New York Times* wrote an article in bold headlines PROSPERITY SEEN IN GERMAN JOURNEY in which he remarked on the abundance of 'pretty luxurious things, including watches and jewellery' in the shops, and the absence of 'maimed men' in the streets. Yet seemingly Germany had no money to pay reparations.

After Jewish Foreign Minister, Walter Rathenau, was murdered, the value of the mark collapsed and Germany asked the alarmed Allies for a moratorium on paying war reparations not only for 1922, but also for 1923 and 1924.

The strength or weakness of a currency is usually an indicator of the strength of a country's economy, but not in this case. Having managed to evade surrendering for trial, amongst others, Generals Falkenhayn, who tried to bleed the French 'white' at Verdun, and Ludendorff who would become the Godfather of Hitler's Nazi Party, the German leadership were never going to pay any monetary war reparations except under duress. However, they did not want to repay their debts to their own citizens either.

All through the war German citizens had been called upon to subscribe to war bonds. By the time that they were asked to donate to the seventh War Loan bond in the autumn of 1917 national morale was at an all-time low. However, the German people were told that if their country was defeated Britain would 'annihilate us so we never recover.' 'World history' they were warned had 'proven again and again that England takes everything from her vanquished and treats the poor, robbed people just as slaves.' So, the nation rallied to the cause. The campaign collected 5,530,285 signatures and 12,626 million marks which would never be repaid.[394]

After the war, the German people who had rallied so nobly to the cause, saw the value of their war bonds slowly being reduced to zero. The German leadership felt that to flourish and to conquer internal debt must be eliminated. So, they ruined the value of their citizens savings through inflation, blaming the rapacious Allies for the robbery. By 1922 the German national debt had been reduced to the same as it had been at the onset of war in 1914, compared to the huge national war debt which remained in Britain and America.[395]

This gave German industry a competitive advantage. However, her industrial leaders wanted to destroy socialism at home. Ruining the currency so that the workers were completely bankrupt was an attractive option. The eight-hour day was one of the workers' principal ambitions secured after the war. Trashing the value of the mark until it was completely worthless would bankrupt the shop floor and halt their defiance to their bosses.

It was easy to incite Poincaré into occupying the Ruhr, just cut off the coal supply! In January 1923 Poincaré embarked on a low-key intervention to collect coal and monetary reparations due to pay for the repair of his devastated provinces. The German coal syndicate, including Kirdorff, Krupp, Klöckner, Hugo Stinnes and Fritz Thyssen, decided to whip up public opinion against the French.[396] Dr Grimm, who appeared as attorney for the coal barons, and Fritz Thyssen... led the crowd in the singing of 'Deutschland über Alles.'[397]

The companies in the Ruhr decided on a policy of 'passive resistance,' and the workers were encouraged to go on a general strike to save their beloved country from invasion by the 'rapacious French.'

The Americans realized that their war loans were at risk and came hot-foot over to Europe to secure water-tight agreements. Poincaré declared doggedly that he could pay no war debts until he received reparations from Germany, maintaining stoutly that Germany's 'present state of ruin is not consequent upon the occupation of the Ruhr but is the work of Germany herself.'[398]

The Americans were not going to allow the British to shilly-shally about paying their war debts, however. American Democrats had become increasingly anti-British during the war and since 1918 the British had lost the respect of the Republicans too. It is not known whether America had ever repaid Britain for the tanks and ships and artillery that her troops used during the conflict. General Pershing himself admitted; 'We were literally beggars as to every important weapon, except the rifle.'[399] However, Britain's Chancellor of the Exchequer, Stanley Baldwin, did not want to lose the few American friends Britain had left, so he agreed to repay the £938 million that Britain owed in war debts without, as yet having received any 'actual cash' in reparations, except the £80 million extracted in tariffs.[400]

Wilson's advisor, Bernard Baruch, declared that Britain's sincere offer to pay her war debts to America at this time was made 'at a cost almost impossible for others to realize.' Britain's industries were being crucified by German competition. Even her foremost business ship production was almost being overtaken by Germany's.[401]

At first the British press showed great sympathy with France's efforts to secure reparations from Germany but soon there was an incident at Krupp's factory in Essen, which alarmed the British public. Six employees were killed and thirteen wounded in the fracas. France was criticized for the carnage, and for her decision to increase her troop numbers in Germany too. The British began to sympathize with Germany's struggle against what seemed like the high-handedness of Britain's historic enemy, France.

Interwar Germany was an amalgam of different states like Saxony, Bavaria and Hanover that had been 'united' by Bismarck and cemented through war. With the currency collapsing, Bismarck's Reich was now in danger of disintegrating. The Rhineland was getting restive, but it was the secessionist movement in Bavaria that gave the greatest concern to the 'National Opposition,' which had been developed and bankrolled by former Krupp's Chairman Alfred Hugenberg.[402]

Catholic Bavaria had an illustrious history before being sucked into Bismarck's empire. In 1923 it made careful plans to seek independence again. On 26th

September, the Bavarian government proclaimed a state of martial law and appointed Gustav von Kahr as head of state. Von Kahr declared that everything he did was for Bavaria's traditional monarch, Prince Utrecht, who would soon be in a position to take responsibility.

Yet the 'Nationalists' had already taken steps to counter this threat. On 2nd September Hitler was invited to make a rousing speech in front of 100,000 Nationalists at the anniversary of the French defeat at Sedan in 1870. On 25th September, the leaders of the newly formed Deutscher Kampfbund assembled in Munich and elected Hitler as their leader.

Hitler told the Bavarian leader, von Kahr, that he wanted to march on Berlin and overthrow the Weimar Republic. Von Kahr said that he would forbid any *coup d'etat* except the one he was making. Hitler and his accomplices then disturbed von Kahr while he was addressing a meeting in an Eastern suburb of Munich. They led von Kahr and his associates to an anteroom to meet a hastily summoned General Ludendorff. After a brief discussion, Ludendorff and von Kahr and his associates walked back into the hall, swore loyalty to Hitler and shook hands. But the next day von Kahr reneged on the deal, and when Hitler and Ludendorff marched through Munich with about two thousand men, they were met with police fire.

The Hugenberg press criticized Hitler, stating that his organization had been poor, and his undisciplined antics could have provoked anarchy, but the newspaper chain did not utterly condemn him. It judged that he was an 'exceptionally popular speaker' who had the ability to free 'innumerable workers from the bond of international socialism' and convert them to the nationalist cause.'[403]

Although Hitler's attempt to start an insurrection against the Weimar Republic failed, it killed Bavaria's effort to cede from Germany. Hitler was put in prison, but he was rewarded by being treated as an officer, and encouraged to write his memoirs, in which many of the Pan-Germans' themes would reappear, such as their anti-Semitism and their idea of Germany gaining Lebensraum in the East.[404] Hitler's book would be called *Mein Kampf*.

On 23rd September 1923, the German government declared that it had abandoned 'passive resistance' over the payment of the reparations but Hugo Stinnes and his friends in heavy industry refused to agree terms over renewing payments unless the government gave them compensation for all coal 'confiscated by the French during their occupation', and a free hand to lengthen the working day in the mines 'to eight and half hours underground and ten hours above ground.'[405]

Hugo Stinnes had stated, in 1921, that he wanted to get rid of the shop floor's eight-hour working day.[406] With the workers now destitute, he was in an excellent position to achieve his aim.

The French and Belgian engineers at the head of the Control Commission argued that the delivery price of coal in Düsseldorf was already so far below the delivery price of English coal that even after delivering twenty per cent of their output as reparations, the German mine owners could far undercut the British coal owners, without lengthening the miners' working hours. However, the spokesman for the German coal magnates, Hugo Stinnes, disagreed, declaring:

'I do not hesitate to say that I am convinced that the German people will have to work two extra hours per day for the next ten to fifteen years.' As the value of the German currency had reduced to wastepaper, he was in a strong position to persuade his workers to work for longer hours.

In the autumn, conditions grew desperate. On 2nd November, the *New York Times* reported on the food riots in Berlin and how, in their desperation, people had been turning against the Jews: 'Mass food riots and plunderings ... occurred today in Berlin and they continue tonight in all sections of the city. A mass mob attack on the Bourse was one feature of the outbreak, and for the first time a pogrom spirit manifested itself in brutal treatment of Jews and others who looked like Jews...'

On 8th November under the banner heading: RUHR WORK HANGS ON THE TEN-HOUR DAY, the *New York Times* described how the negotiations had proceeded: 'The German industrialists told their workforce that they could only afford to make reparations deliveries to the French and what they called 'the resumption of economic life' provided that the workforce worked a ten-hour day above ground and eight and a half below.'

It commented, 'Already grim starvation is staring several hundred thousand workmen in the face with the cold dark winter nights creeping in'... 'If all the industrial plants close as threatened the total unemployed will reach from 700,000 to 800,000.' [407]

Beaten, with the value of their wages reduced to waste paper, and their savings exhausted, the German workers finally agreed to work the longer hours for wages between 14% and 18% lower than they had been in 1913.[408] In return the employees gained an arbitration system for industrial disputes which seemed, on the face of it, to be highly advantageous to the shop floor.[409] However, as the German workers were by now all penniless, and destitute, it would be difficult for them to complain.

Hugo Stinnes and his friends in heavy industry had refused to agree terms over renewing reparations payments unless the government gave them compensation for all coal 'confiscated by the French during their occupation,' and a free hand to lengthen the working day in the mines 'to eight and half hours underground and ten hours above ground.'[410] By November 1923 Stinnes had managed to destroy the most precious socialist aim after the First World War, the eight-hour working day. In 1925, in accordance with Stinnes 1923 demands, the Ruhr industrialists would be paid 707 million gold Reichsmarks (roughly £35 million) in compensation for all the coal 'confiscated by the French during their occupation' while the Allies received a mere 65 million Reichsmarks (£3 million) in reparations.

The British socialists did not realize the terrible defeat that the Grman socialists had suffered in 1923. They were filled with horror at what they viewed as France's rapaciousness in invading Germany and reducing the German people to destitution.

Former British First World War pacifist Philip Snowden, who became Britain's Chancellor of the Exchequer in 1924, was one of many who drank in Germany's protestations of penury and became 'virulently anti-French.' The economist, John Maynard Keynes, who had predicted Germany's misery, had a wider audience. People remembered that Keynes had denounced the Treaty of Versailles reparations provisions as 'dishonourable', abhorrent and detestable.' 'Year by year' he had maintained in the *Economic Consequences of the Peace* 'Germany must be kept impoverished, and her children starved and crippled.' His prophecy seemed to be coming true. His words resonated not only in the Labour Party, but also in the wider British community, who had come to believe in the inhumanity of their politicians and returned to their traditional distrust of France.

Even contemporary historians, who had doubted that Germany was as poor as she made out, were impressed by the documentation emanating from Germany which purported to show that their country had been less guilty of war lust in 1914 than the Allies had asserted. British historian G P Gooch went as far as to claim that all the European countries shared guilt for the start of the First World War. Other historians soon followed. Some, like Raymond Beazley and William H Dawson even received financial support from the German War Guilt Section.

After Raymond Beazley had seen the 'evidence' produced by the War Guilt Section in *Die Grosse Politik* he declared decisively that Germany 'had not plotted the Great War, had not desired a war, and had made genuine, though belated and ill-organized efforts to avert it.'[411]

Nevertheless, ailing ex-President Woodrow Wilson, now not only believed in Germany's 'war guilt' but also in the necessity of charging her adequate war reparations. He asked his financial adviser, Bernard Baruch, to persuade the British Imperial Conference to ensure that Germany paid a meaningful amount, stating:

'There seems to be little realization in England and America of what it would mean to them if Germany should escape too lightly. In the United States of America, the increased borrowing of the Federal Government continues; industries and dues to the war have piled up and added tax burdens; our federal budget has risen from one billion to four billion dollars annually. While the amount of money that we have to raise in taxes because of these increased expenses and borrowings has risen so greatly, the taxes of the German government and the fixed charge on German industries have been practically wiped out owing to the use of the printing press. This means that there must be taken from the efforts of our people in taxes for the Federal Government four billion dollars a year and nothing from the Germans unless they are compelled to pay some fixed tax in the way of reparations. Unless this is done Germany will conquer the world industrially.'[412]

The *New York Times* agreed with Woodrow Wilson and Baruch's assessment. Its reporters were astonished that despite the German people's suffering, Germany was the best customer for America's valuable cotton crop in 1923, importing 'approximately double' the amount of cotton going to either France or England in the first eight months of the year. It also noted that Germany's copper imports were 'larger than those of any other country.'

It concluded: 'It may be true that today Germany is not able to pay appreciable sums on her reparations account, ... but what she may be able to pay in five or ten-years' time is significantly indicated by what she is doing now through putting her hand upon great supplies of the raw material of manufacture to make ready for an immense economic expansion in the future.'[413]

French Prime Minister Raymond Poincaré, whose cousin was a famous mathematician, was also sceptical of tales of Germany's destitution. He ordered a commission to locate and repatriate the German money, which the *New York Times* estimated at 2 billion dollars[414] but his initiative in occupying the Ruhr had merely subjected his country to odium, and he was ejected from his position as Prime Minister.

Unfortunately, whether one looks upon Germany's Great Inflation as an internal initiative to eliminate her internal debts and undo the power of the workers, or as a fight to gain the economic structure to defeat British industry after the stabilisation of the mark, or as most people believed, as a protest against paying the war reparations, the sufferings that the German people endured ensured a huge dent in their respect for democracy. On 23rd December 1923, the socialist President of the Republic, Friedrich Ebert, was deemed guilty of treason for taking part in the strike against the armaments' manufacturers in 1918.

During Ebert's trial a letter was read out that he had written to one of his two sons killed in action. It had been returned unopened because his son had died on the battlefield. In the letter Ebert had written: 'During the last few days some useless strikes have broken out ... Such fool's tricks do not serve the cause of peace but only strengthen the fighting spirit of the enemy.' But his words made no difference to the guilty verdict. He died two months later with his reputation in tatters.

In December 1924, the avowed enemy of the Republic, the DNVP (or German Nationalist party) which counted ex- supremo of Krupps, Alfred Hugenberg as a member, secured 103 seats in the Reichstag elections and the Nazis, 14. German citizens flocked in even greater numbers to give the Social Democrat Party 131 seats, but the socialists were on the defensive. The anti-Republican monarchist, General Paul von Hindenburg, became President of the Republic.

Hindenburg had been born and raised in the Prussian heartland about 100 kilometres south of Danzig. He had participated in the Franco-Prussian war of 1870/71 and had been present in the Hall of Mirrors when Wilhelm I was proclaimed German Emperor. He had become a hugely popular war hero, largely because of the efforts of his Chief of Staff, Erich Ludendorff at the battle of Tannenberg. Although Germany subsequently lost the war and Hindenburg should have been tried for treason, he retained his status and now achieved the highest position in the government with the words,

'Just as the first German President, as Protector of the Constitution, never concealed his origin from the ranks of labour, no one will be able to expect of me that I should surrender my political convictions.'

As the DNVP was stuffed with former Pan-Germans like Hugenberg, it could have formed a party with Hitler, the National Liberal Party and other minority groups but it declined to take office to avoid the stigma of agreeing to the new Dawes Plan reparations proposals, preferring to ensure the bill's success through the Reichstag[415] while instigating a virulent personal campaign against Foreign Minister Gustav Stresemann for agreeing to it.

The American negotiators were acutely anxious that Germany might debase her currency again so the country was given 'transfer protection' so that if it seemed to be heading for a depression, the payment of reparations could be suspended to ensure the currency's stability. Unfortunately, this would give Germany a strategic incentive to drive out reparations through foreign borrowing[416] and made it virtually certain that the next German bid for a downward revision would be successful.[417] As part of the agreement Germany also received the Dawes Loan to get the arrangement off to a good start.

But the Dawes Plan Loan was not enough. The DNVP wanted more. At last America agreed that if

Germany agreed to stabilize her currency on the bases of a 'gold-exchange in effect' the Fed (American Federal Reserve Bank) would consider as eligible for their open market purchases certain German dollar trade bills in the United States, if endorsed by the newly established German Gold Rediscount Bank, the so-called Schacht Bank.[418]

Many Americans had wanted to invest in the land of their forefathers now that the currency had been stabilised. The main drawback was the size of the reparations bill. The American government speedily sent a delegation over to Europe in 1924 to judge if Germany had been overcharged.

The German negotiators had a field day exaggerating the cost of the ships they had surrendered, the railway carriages and the value of the German factories and schools in the territories they had occupied before the war, in order to claim that most of the reparations bill had already been paid. They even tried to claim for the fleet that they scuppered at Scapa Flow!

Luckily, France's Raymond Poincaré looked at payments in a more grounded fashion. The Germans had only paid £80 million in cash since 1919[419] and that was with the help of the British tariff. Poincaré insisted that the new Dawes Plan must only look at Germany's present capacity to pay, not to fix the final amount. He also put French inspectors into the German treasury to ensure that France was not short-changed.

As the German negotiators declared that their country had no ready cash to pay the reparations because of their Great Inflation, Britain agreed to accept her reparations through the thirty per cent tariff on imports, which she had already levied in Germany's inflationary years[420] while the French had to accept an unsatisfactory system through which the Ruhr magnates delivered coal free to France in reparations and were then reimbursed by their government through a tax on the railways, sugar, etc.

Meanwhile neat new President of the Reichsbank, Hjalmar Schacht, with his high stiff collar and accountant's pince-nez, who had been acclaimed as an 'economic wizard' for ending Germany's Great Inflation, set about establishing the Gold Discount Bank. He contacted Britain's Governor of the Bank of England, Montagu Norman, and asked him if he could visit him in London. Wispy-bearded Norman, who had spent much time in the past in Dresden, was delighted. Yet when Schacht arrived on a foggy winter's day, he alarmed Norman with a tale of a group of Rhineland and French bankers intending to set up their own Central Bank in the Rhineland, with the blessing of the German government.

This was an unlikely story. The Right was on the ascendant in Germany. It would not countenance French banks controlling Germany's richest area. Yet Montagu Norman was perturbed by what he saw as a threat to the City of London and attracted by Schacht's idea of stabilizing the mark on gold.

Schacht promised Norman that if Norman lent him the money to start his new Gold Discount Bank; he would raise one hundred million gold marks in foreign currency in Germany and issue Germany's notes entirely in sterling.[421] This sounded like a wonderful opportunity to Norman - but there was a catch. Because of Britain's impotence, Britain had publicly accepted the lie that Germany herself was a weak country in 1923, as opposed to her impoverished citizens. If Montagu Norman agreed to back Schacht's new Gold Discount Bank, he would immediately be pressurized to return Britain to the Gold Standard at the same rate as Germany before the war. And that would crucify British industry.

Montagu Norman had been at the helm of the Bank of England since 1920. If the Bank of England's selection process for governor had been made on the ground of pedigree, he would have been an obvious choice because his grandfather on his mother's side had been Governor and his grandfather on his father's side, a director. Yet Norman had been a sickly, neurotic youth and viewed as a misfit during his years with the merchant bank, Brown Shipley. Nevertheless, he had many useful traits for a central banker; a formidable memory for places, names and facts, restless, abundant energy and, when he chose to use it, persuasive charm. So eventually he became the Bank of England's most famous and 'infamous' Governor.

It may be that Norman did not know that the German industrialists had slashed wages and re-introduced the ten-hour day to make German industry more competitive in those last dark days of autumn before Schacht contacted him. At any event Schacht left him spell-bound with talk of the Reichsbank's 'supreme power within the German Reich'. Norman trusted Schacht. He would soon become completely under the thumb of the brilliantly able and deceitful German financier, Hjalmar Schacht.

On 3rd February 1924 ex-President, Woodrow Wilson died. Republican Americans ruled the country. They regarded Germany as their friend. They were thrilled that Germany now believed in stable currencies and wanted to return to the Gold Standard.[422]

The Gold Standard was vital to America because the anti-Republican German Nationalists (or DNVP) Party, stuffed with members like the former Pan-German Alfred Hugenberg, had refused to sign the Dawes Plan agreement unless America accepted German loans, which they temptingly promised would be endorsed by Schacht's Gold Discount Bank.[423]

It was essential to America, therefore, that the British government would return to the Gold Standard to set a good example to Germany. To accomplish their aim the Americans were prepared to offer a bribe. They had agreed to give a large bribe to Germany to stabilise her economy in the shape of an offer of a multitude of loans. The bribe to Britain was smaller.

Governor of the Federal Reserve Bank of New York, Benjamin Strong, was a close friend of Montagu Norman's. He promised $200 million from the Fed for the British Exchequer and another $300 from J P Morgan if Britain returned to the Gold Standard and Norman remained in office.

Norman was overcome with gratitude for Benjamin Strong's vote of confidence in him. He fervently believed in the Gold Standard and viewed Strong's offer not as a bribe but as a vote of thanks from a friend who was coming to help the Allies persuade Germany to return to the international norms of economic behaviour. He wrote warmly to Strong:

'As you know, Ben, I am grateful for all your welcome and hospitality; and for all you do for me and are for me. God bless you.'[424]

Benjamin Strong Jr. came from a banking family with a strong Presbyterian social conscience. Tall, slim and 'good-looking but for a prematurely receding hairline and a large nose that spoke of ruthlessness' Benjamin Strong was always going to succeed in his chosen profession. His personal life was less happy, however. His first wife Margaret committed suicide after the birth of their fourth child and he developed TB in 1916, struggling with its effects for the rest of his life.

Strong had chosen to accept the immensely prestigious job of becoming Governor of the newly created Federal Reserve Bank but it only offered a salary, which was a fraction of what he would have received as President of a large New York bank. In 1920 he was divorced by his second wife, Katherine, whose father had always been against him taking the job. By the mid-1920s, he lived in a small two-bedroom apartment and was using morphine to control the pain of his TB. He was an ardent advocate of Britain returning to the Gold Standard, however. It was true that the Bank of England would have to raise interest rates if there was a run on its gold reserves[425] but Strong genuinely believed in the security of the Gold Standard to keep the world economy on track and looked upon himself as Norman's guardian angel until he died in 1928.

Norman did not understand that Germany had ruthlessly reorganised her finances and mechanised her industry before she returned to the Gold Standard in order to destroy British industrial competition. He was concerned about restoring peace and financial stability not only at home but also in Britain's great empire and the wider world.

Britain was not only the repository of Great Britain and her empire's savings; the US, Russia, Japan and Argentina also kept a portion of their cash reserves in London.[426] A measure of devaluation would have been prudent, but it could have caused an international upset. Norman had taken the precaution of retaining the 30 per cent tariff against German goods under the terms of the Dawes Plan before he advised the Chancellor of the Exchequer, Winston Churchill, to take Britain back on the Gold Standard at the same rate as Germany before the war. He felt that with the 30% tariff in place, he could secure the reparations and retain Britain's industrial base.

Winston Churchill was a flamboyant figure and a great administrator, but economics was not his forte. Former pacifist, John Maynard Keynes had been wrong about Germany's economic power at the end of the First World

War. It seems that he was finally beginning to realise her latent economic might. At any rate he fought against Britain's return to the Gold Standard at the pre-war rate, saying that it would condemn the British people to unemployment and political unrest, but the establishment did not trust him. Churchill reluctantly accepted Norman's advice and Norman promised him 'I will make you the golden Chancellor.'[427]

France's unloved French Bank Governor, Émile Moreau, described Norman at this time; 'He does not like the French. ... On the other hand, he seems to feel the deepest sympathy for the Germans. He is very, close to Dr. Schacht. They see each other often and hatch secret plans.'

As soon as the Great War was over France had embarked upon restoring her devastated provinces, but Germany had never paid any cash for their restoration. After Germany engineered her Great Inflation, the only way forward, France believed, was to embark on a great inflation of her own and use her own citizens' savings to pay for the war. France wanted to leave her savers with a modicum of money, however, so the franc was finally stabilized at twenty per cent of its former value. Unfortunately, the French middle classes were irate at the loss of their savings and became very anti-Semitic as there was no propaganda issue like the reparations to blame for their misfortunes. This would have dreadful repercussions in the Second World War.

Meanwhile Raymond Poincaré, 'just short of sixty-seven years old, slightly rotund, his goatee beard whitened and his hair well receded'[428] became Prime Minister of France again in 1926. The Germans and the French Left had labelled the little man as a warmonger. The British public regarded him with huge suspicion, but the French people trusted him to stand up for the rights of their country.

Unfortunately, Montagu Norman still shared the British people's historic distrust of the French. He also believed that Britain was a world power, while Germany was only a regional European power, which had lost some of its land, (and a little of its coal), under the terms of the Versailles Treaty.[429] He did not realize that, besides lengthening the hours of work in the mines to ten hours above ground and eight and half hours below, real wages in the German mines had dropped to between fourteen and eighteen per cent below what the miners had received in 1913, making it almost impossible for the British coal mining industry to compete.

The story still circulates today in the American heartlands, that America paid Germany's war reparations during the Dawes Plan years between 1924 and 1929. 'Wall Street,' so the legend goes, 'made the loans to Germany so that Germany could pay reparations to France, which could then pay war debts to Britain and the US.'

This legend provides the basis for the present-day assertion that Germany was weak in the 1920s and needed America's money to pay the reparations. However, although Germany borrowed more and more money between 1924 and 1929, she paid very, little cash in reparations. In the main, she paid her reparations through exports rather than the cash which France so desperately needed.

Indeed, in 1927, Herr Dessauer of the German Centre Party, truthfully declared that 'the artificial stimulation of German exports caused by the Dawes Plan would, in the long run, do considerably harm to the rest of the world[430] because it gave German industry a solid base for export expansion. German goods were exported to France and Italy without charge in reparations, while the German exporters were repaid by their government out of indirect taxes on the railways, sugar etc. The French, Italians and Belgians would have much preferred cash. However, cash was not forthcoming. In contrast Germany was only too happy to provide 'deliveries in kind.'

After the French coal mines had been repaired, other products could be bought without charge and be credited to reparations receipts too. France and Italy did not want to import German products, but as they came free, they gradually came to rely on German engineering, particularly in the chemical and electrical engineering fields, where Germany had a lead in technology.[431]

In Britain, the situation was different. British reparations were received through a thirty per cent tariff on imports. Montagu Norman knew that the pound was too high and that wages would have to be lowered but he felt that Britain could compete with Germany with the thirty per cent tariff in place, but that proved not to be the case.

British industry did not have the profits to pay for the modernisation of its antiquated, machinery and the British miners had won the right to work for far shorter hours than the Germans worked. Although the tariff yielded a lot of reparations cash, especially during the miners' strike, the aim of German industrialist, Hugo Stinnes in 1923 was realised, that the British mining industry would be unable to compete with Germany.[432]

British workers had campaigned for a peace based on Woodrow Wilson's fourteen points and principles before the armistice was finally signed. A committee had been subsequently set up at the peace conference with a view to banning child labour and introducing the eight-hour working day world-wide.[433] The Sankey Report had even proposed a seven-hour day for Britain's 800,000 miners, being shortened to six in 1921 if circumstances allowed, but nothing concrete was ever written into the Treaty of Versailles.

In 1926, the British coal owners' desperate attempt to cut wages and lengthen coal mining hours to compete with German industry provoked a lengthy strike. However, even after it was over the British coal industry was never able to achieve anything like the cost reductions required to compete with the Ruhr.[434] By 1931, 432,000 miners, representing 41.6% of the workforce, would become unemployed.[435]

Montagu Norman soon became alarmed at Britain's penurious state. He complained to his 'friend' Schacht about Germany's high interest rates[436] which caused 'the continuous drain of gold from this market to Berlin.' He even dared to assert, 'Your German concerns borrow money in America (of which I do not think they have need).'[437]

His suspicions were correct. Short, fat and genial, German Foreign Minister, Gustav Stresemann, had decided that; 'The granting of a loan would give us an army of 300,000 people in America who would make propaganda for Germany because they would be interested in her welfare.'[438]

To further their interests, German heavy industry also developed cartels. IG Farben was founded in 1925 with the merger of six chemical companies, BASF, (27.4%), Bayer (27.4%), Hoechst and Chemische Fabrik Kalle (27.4%), Agfa (9.0%), Chemische Fabrik Griesheim-

Elektron (6.9%) and Chemische Fabrik Vorm. It had a market capitalisation of 1.4 billion Reichsmarks a workforce of 100,000 people. Its assets were claimed to be no more than two thirds the size of the American company, Du Pont. Nevertheless, 'there was no operation of chemical industry, which it could not undertake and no industrial combine in the world which it could not face or outface.'[439]

The Vereinigte Stahlwerke of Düsseldorf - United Steel - was founded in 1926 from a group of coal and steel companies. It included 151 coal mines, seventy-one coking plants, sixty-three blast furnaces, thirty-two Bessemer converters, 116 large open-hearth furnaces, rolling mills, railways, and port facilities. Enriched by selling coal to England during the miners' strike, it managed to attract funds for investment amounting to double the original total of the British Steel Corporation between 1927 and 1929.[440]

Krupps was a private concern, but it had been the largest company in Europe in 1900 and had made a fortune out of the First World War. Although it had reputedly made a loss in the war's aftermath, it had been rich enough to clandestinely invest in armaments companies in Sweden and Holland by 1921. In 1926 it secretly established offices called Koch and Kienzle on the top floor of one of the best located offices in Berlin. There Krupp's ordnance design team developed eight new types of heavy artillery, howitzers, and light field guns; a new, mobile 21-cm. mortar; and designs for tanks.[441] Nevertheless, to the outside world it seemed that the technologically innovative company was bent on a peaceful existence. In 1929 it produced a special stainless steel to clad the new prestigious art-deco Chrysler Centre in New York, which would retain the title of the highest building in the world for eleven months until the Empire State Building took the crown.

American financial advisors did not like cartels. However, they had a duty to look after their customers. They felt that their clients were safe investing in huge German companies, especially after Germany signed the Treaty of Locarno in December 1925 and became a member of the League of Nations in 1926.[442]

Coal magnate Hugo Stinnes, who had forced the German miners to accept the ten-hour day in 1923, died soon afterwards. However, another coal magnate, 'Chimney baron', and former Pan-German, Emil Kirdorf, who had poured money into the Navy League before the war and supported the German army gaining massive extra territory during it, was very much alive but frustrated.

Kirdorf had supported former Pan-German President, Heinrich Claß's 'rightest' coup in 1926, which aimed to overthrow the government and make former Pan-German and ex-Chairman of Krupps, Alfred Hugenberg economic dictator of Germany. A Reich Regent would be placed in the supreme position instead of the German Chancellor, and Alfred Hugenberg would assume the vital economics ministry, but the coup failed.[443]

Nevertheless, despite the Pan-Germans failure to install Hugenberg as 'economic' dictator, the Right was becoming increasingly assertive in Germany. In 1927 General Wauchope, Chief of the British Section Military Inter-Allied Commission of Control in Berlin, asserted, worriedly, 'The greatest loss which Germany suffered (in her Great Inflation) was the ruin of her middle classes. If her 'natural leaders' are now to be found in the present party of the Right, Germany may again become a danger. It is common knowledge that great numbers of factories could be rapidly reorganized, as in 1914-15, for the production of war material if the government wished. Many are so overbuilt at present that they could produce a large military as well as a large commercial output.'[444]

Emil Kirdorf heard Hitler speak in 1927. He was so impressed that he arranged to meet him in Munich. Kirdorf's only anxiety was that Hitler's more socialist supporters like Gregor Strasser had talked about the need to redistribute wealth, so he suggested that Hitler write a pamphlet for private distribution amongst Germany's leading industrialists to reassure them that he supported private enterprise and was opposed to any real transformation of Germany's economic and social structure. Hitler agreed and his *Road to Resurgence* was published in the summer of 1927.[445]

Meanwhile the Americans became anxious at the extent of their loans to Germany, and of Germany's inexhaustible requests for more. President of the Reichstag, Dr. Schacht blamed the German cities for wasting America's money. They were accused of throwing the money away on 'swimming pools, parks, libraries and playgrounds, although the cities bitterly complained that the charge was not true.'446

Indeed, later research would reveal that the German cities were far more parsimonious than Britain's cities.447 In reality, much of the American money had been used to rationalize German industry and some had been used for more secret nefarious purposes, like developing weapons.448 However, Americans were in danger of lending Germany so much cash that if, in more straitened economic times, a stark choice arrived between Germany repaying American loans or paying reparations to the Allies, they would insist that the repayment of their loans came first.

Many, indeed, were beginning to believe German propaganda that Germany had been wrongly charged with responsibility for the First World War in the first place. The Centre for the Causes of the War continued to be showered with funds, 23,000 marks in 1924-5, 34,000 in 1926 and a massive 84,000 by 1929-30.449 Soon the German programme of disinformation about the causes of the First World War started to bear fruit.

The Committee of German Associations, or ADV, had been formed by the Pan German League in 1921 to spread the word of Germany's innocence of causing the First World War through seminars, conventions, exhibitions, and rallies. In 1925 it was provided with 500,000 marks so that it could establish contacts with foreigners. One of its constituent bodies, the Wirtschaftspolitische Gesellschaft, had some 500 foreign correspondents and was read by British and American politicians.

Special care was lavished upon American historians. Harvard historian Sidney Bradshaw Fay placed the blame on Serbia and America's bogey, Russia, for the war. Two hundred and fifty books were bought and distributed free through German embassies and Fay was asked to write numerous articles.

Henry Elmer Barnes' *The Genesis of the World War* (1929) was particularly influential in America because it was the first book based on the available primary sources (specially selected for him by the German Foreign Ministry).

During the First World War Barnes had been a strong supporter of the Allies. Afterwards, he was given access to the sources in *Die Grosse Politik*. He was impressed. In the 1920s, he dramatically altered his opinion and portrayed France and Russia as the aggressors in 1914. As he was Professor at Columbia University his words carried weight. In 1925 he wrote: 'If we can but understand how totally and terribly, we were 'taken in' between 1914 and 1918 by the salesmen of this most unholy and idealistic world conflict, we shall be better prepared to be on our guard against the seductive lies and deceptions which will be put forward by similar groups when urging the necessity of another world catastrophe in order to 'crush militarism' (and) 'make the world safe for democracy.'[450]

His book was translated free into other languages, and he was asked to write numerous articles. At least one generation of American university students was raised on the outlook of historians such as Sidney B Fay and Harry E Barnes - and Harry E Barnes later became a prominent isolationist during the Second World War.

Germany employed a different tack in Britain, the country which liked to pride itself in its open-mindedness. In 1928, 5,000 copies of Hermann Lutz's *An Appeal for British Fair Play* were sent to the Great and the Good in Britain. This declared that Article 231 of the Treaty of Versailles, and Mr. Clemenceau in particular, had lied when he declared, that 'Germany alone among the nations was prepared for a great war.' In his *Appeal for British Fair Play* Mr Lutz wrote: 'We firmly contend that the verdict is, in its gross partiality untrue. Yet the Treaty of Versailles, a punitive peace almost unparalleled in history, which continuously poisons the life of the European Peoples and contains numerous germs of new wars, is based on it.'

Many people in Britain must have done much soul-searching after Hermann Lutz's heart-rending words. Those on the Left had drunk in the German Nationalists *Poincaré-la-guerre* propaganda of the early 1920s. France was after all Britain's historic enemy and Poincaré had 'invaded' Germany in 1923.

Nevertheless, the German Nationalists had changed the storyline in their own country. Although Lutz had appealed to 'British fair play' in assessing the causes of the war in 1914, stressing the responsibility of Russia and France for the conflict, teachers back home had decided to label Britain as the guilty country, which had caused all the bloodshed.

Five hundred thousand copies of *Merkblatt der Kriegsschuldfrage* (Catechism of the War Guilt Question) were printed which declared: 'The Policy of England under the guidance of King Edward VIII had sought to win over the two 'hereditary enemies of Britain France and Russia, in order to annihilate the new German rival. The first aims of British policy were the destruction of German trade and of the German Navy and Mercantile Marine – not only under Edward VII, but also under his successor and the responsible statesmen of his reign.'

Children were also taught in schools about Britain's responsibility for the war. I. C. Andrä's *Erzählungen aus der Weltgeschichte*, told its readers: The one aim of his (Edward VII's) ambition was to unite the enemies of Germany, and to encircle her. ... in the midst of his poisonous and perfidious activities Edward died.... But the evil he had initiated lived after him; all that was lacking were the final touches of armament, and the pretext for commencing hostilities.'[451]

A particularly evil book, *Lebensgut, ein Lesebuch für deutsche Mädchen*, which translated means *A Treasury for German Girls* was introduced into 600 schools in 1927. It quoted a 'truly disgusting' passage from the novelist Gustav Frenssen: 'At last the greed and vengeance of England was satisfied, and for the seventh time in the course of history, she withdrew, swollen and glutted with the blood and misery of Europe.'[452]

Not unnaturally, on the 8th March 1929, every German university and high school would send a delegate to the sixth University Congress at Munich, just as the Young Plan talks on the war reparations were about to begin. Their resolution would state: 'As the result of impartial historical investigation it has been shown that Germany is not guilty in the sense of the Treaty of Versailles, and no person earnestly desirous of discovering the truth can close his mind to the weight of this evidence. As a result, all the conclusions which have this Treaty for premise become invalid.'[453]

Meanwhile Hitler ranted against the immorality of 'American' capitalism declaring: 'We are enemies of today's capitalistic economic system for the exploitation of the economically weak ... and we are determined to destroy this system under all conditions.'

Hitler's words were addressed to the embittered German middle-classes on fixed incomes, who had been robbed of their savings in 1923. Yet the German middle classes had no conception of the wealth of their own heavy industrialists. These men were not frittering away their spare cash on personal consumption but were busy rationalizing their industries at home[454] and constructing armaments factories abroad.

Besides Krupp's many armaments plants, Fokker had a factory in Holland, Dornier, one in Russia, at Kronstadt, and another on the German shores of Lake Constance, a third on the opposite shore at Altenheim and another in Holland. Junkers had established itself in Turkey, at Eskisehir, with the firm of Rohrbach, which specialized in mounting machine-gun turrets, light cannon, and bomb racks on bombers. Heinkel was based in Sweden where it produced bombers and fighters, and U-boats were built by German engineers at Vigo.[455]

In 1926 the Allied Control Commission left Essen, where the firm of Krupp had been based since 1811. In 1927 Koch and Kienzle was dissolved, and the firm itself entered a new period of *schwarze production* in Germany. Work was stepped up on self-propelled guns, tanks, torpedo compressed-air containers, ship propellers, periscopes, aeroplane crankshafts, armour plate, devices for remote control of naval fire, and primitive rocket design. ... It also began the manufacture of tanks on a limited scale.'[456]

Cooperation between the German and Russian armed forces also flourished. An agreement had been concluded to build an aviation school in Lipetsk, to complement the existing military school, and to set up a tank school at Kazan. In the spring of 1927 the German chemical expert, Auer, led a delegation to view the joint Soviet and German mustard gas trials at Orenburg.[457]

Accountants across the seas and oceans in Britain and America were unaware of these massive armaments expenditures and fretted at the German government's continued current account deficits. But that did not mean that the country itself was running out of cash. Erich Eyck, who was a Social Democrat representative in the Reichstag, would later write, 'In order to be able to make expenditures which would remain hidden from the Entente, the (Defence) ministry presented false budgets to the Reichstag. The correct figures were shown only to representatives of the Reichstag's Committee, who 'out of patriotic sentiment, collaborated.'[458]

France was closer, and therefore more alarmed by Germany's secret armaments build-up than Britain and America. The French government still feared another German invasion. In 1927, on the tenth anniversary of America's intervention in the First World War, French Foreign Minister, Aristide Briand, asked America for a bilateral security pact but he was merely offered the Kellogg-Briand Pact which solemnly voted to 'Outlaw War.' Faced with this nebulous offer, France decided that she had no option but to build the Maginot Line of fortifications 'armed with cannons, mortars and machine guns' to protect her country in a concrete fashion from the threat of another German invasion. Unfortunately, however, for political and economic reasons, it did not include the area opposite the Ardennes Forest in neutral Belgium.

Meanwhile, despite the large amount of American money lent to Germany between 1924 and 1929, Germany preferred to deluge her neighbours with exports rather than using America's funds to pay France reparations in cash.

France was swamped with increasingly unwelcome German exports in the form of 'deliveries in kind' but starved of the 'actual cash' with which to start paying her war debts to America, which she had promised to start paying in 1929.[459]

CHAPTER SEVEN

The 1929 Wall Street Crash

It has been claimed that the Wall Street Crash was caused by the failures of the capitalist system. However, there was another more sinister reason which has never been investigated properly, that it could have been engineered by powerful forces in Germany to renege on the reparations and start Hitler on the road to power.

When the German people went to the polls in 1928, they recoiled from the avowed enemy of the Weimar Republic, the DNVP party, which still hankered after more 'living space in Eastern Europe' and planned to build a 'pocket battleship.' Many had voted for the German 'Nationalists' or DNVP in the previous election because the pain of Germany's Great Inflation had made them yearn for the pre-war era when the monarchy held sway. However, by the end of the 1920s they were happy with democracy and wanted no more wars. The DNVP's vote dropped by a third from 6.2 million to less than 4.4. Worryingly, the Communists vote rose to 3.2 million. Nevertheless, the vast majority voted for the Social Democrats who increased their share of the vote to 9.1 million and formed the country's first socialist coalition government.

The iron ore magnates of the Ruhr locked out their 225,000 workers for four weeks rather than allow the new socialist coalition to shorten the working week and allow an increase in wages, while German cash fled the Fatherland before the threat of heavier taxation. Dr. Schacht, who seemingly had performed such miracles in stabilizing the mark after Germany's Great Inflation, assured Parker Gilbert that he would force the Socialists to behave responsibly if America gave Germany a new, less onerous deal over the reparations.

Meanwhile sinister former Pan German, Alfred Hugenberg, became leader of the anti-democratic DNVP party in the Reichstag. Now known as the 'Randolph Hearst of Germany' because of his vast publishing empire, he was determined not to let Socialism take root in his country. The German people had turned to extremist parties, like Hitler's and the DNVP, in the last dark days of the Great Inflation of 1923, and Hugenberg was confident that he could also persuade them to reject democracy altogether if hard times came again.

The *New York Times*[460] reported how Hugenberg was going to achieve his aim, 'Herr Hugenberg offers his fellow Nationalists the panacea of dictatorship. He favours monarchism and Hohenzollern legitimism, indeed, but he believes that the restoration of the imperial throne can only be gained through the preliminary creation of a dictatorial regime akin to Premier Mussolini's in Italy. He is convinced, moreover, that this step can be taken legally, or at least without a violent upheaval, simply by expanding and strengthening the German President's constitutional right to dissolve Parliament and appoint a dictator if the country seems to warrant it.'

There were only two problems for Hugenberg; first he had to find a likely candidate to become dictator, and second, he had to create the sort of dire economic conditions which would persuade the German people to vote for him. It appears that, after the publication of Hitler's pamphlet *Road to Resurgence*, Hugenberg decided that Hitler would be the man for the job.

Hitler had not been completely out of the public eye since his attempted Putsch in 1923. On 21st March 1927, a band of 600 Nazi Brown Shirts had beaten up a group of Communists in eastern Berlin; then they had marched into the centre of the city, attacking anyone who looked Jewish. The authorities responded by banning Nazi activity in Berlin for a year.[461] Yet, although Hitler was treated as a freak by most of the German population, 800,000 people still voted for him in the 1928 elections.

Hitler had many attributes which appealed to Hugenberg: he was a natural orator, had been a corporal in the German army, was an Austrian, which would come in handy if Germany invaded Austria, and had similar sentiments to the Pan-Germans, even if his policy of sterilization, euthanasia and eventually extermination against the Bolsheviks and Jews, was a little extreme. He had been a 'drummer' for the Nationalist cause since the early 1920s, and Hugenberg's newspapers had praised his eloquence. He also had a valuable power base with his

800,000 votes. Soon he would become part of the inner circle of Hugenberg's anti-Young Plan Committee and would be featured regularly on Hugenberg's powerful media outlets.[462]

By the end of the 1920s the Americans become worried that the 1924 Dawes Plan had given an immense artificial stimulus to Germany's exports, [463] while producing very little 'actual cash' reparations to help France pay her war debts to America.[464] They knew that Germany could pay a sizeable sum as her national income in 1929 amounted to the handsome total of 75,900,000,000 gold marks or £3,800,000,000, and the monthly increase in German savings deposits had leapt from 103 million marks in 1925 to 8nearly 210 million marks (£10 million) in 1928.[465]

Whereas the US had a national debt $16,931,197,748 or £3,483,785,545, (at the par rate of 4.86 dollars to the £) Germany only had a national debt of 8,971.7 million reichsmarks in 1929 or £439,143.2 million (at the par rate of 20.43 reichsmarks to £)[466] and a record amount of gold in the Reichsbank.[467] She was also a member of the League of Nations, and a compliant socialist coalition government had come to power. It seemed an ideal moment to put a long-term arrangement for the payment of the reparations into place. The payments were envisaged to be paid in cash and treated like an ordinary bond.

Unfortunately, the economic comparison between the period before the 1929 crash and the period before the 1873 crash is startling. By returning to the Gold Standard in the 1920s, Europe and America had in effect adopted a large new currency, just like Bismarck had in 1870. The huge amount of German money arriving in America to escape from the socialist coalition in Germany would create a 'bubble' just like the 'bubble' of money that appeared after Bismarck extorted a huge indemnity from France in 1871. As there were no sound investments abroad at a reasonable price, foolish speculation would be indulged in. Then interest rates would rise, and money became scarce, followed by a panic and a stock market collapse as happened in 1873.

Dr. Schacht was very, excited by the prospect of changing the basis on which the reparations were paid. He had long prepared the ground to take Germany's former foes for a ride. His primary objective was to get France's control of German finances removed. He wrote to Stresemann on 28th September 1928, 'The psychological moment has now come to strike for everything. Almost more important than the sum at stake is the opportunity to regain our absolute international freedom. Every r8emnant of obligations, controls, and unresolved questions must disappear.'[468]

Ultimately, in a single currency, a powerful nation can affect all the other nations in its orbit. It is interesting to note that the rises and falls of the American stock market in 1929 almost exactly mirrored Germany's brinkmanship over the Young Plan negotiations.

In May 1928, the German Social Democrats victory at the polls precipitated an exodus of cash by nervous right-wing investors. In September 1928, the Allies decided to open negotiations on a new reparations' deal for Germany which they called the Young Plan. President of the Reichsbank, Dr Schacht, and head of United Steel, Dr Vögler, were the German negotiators of the Young Plan. The Allied representatives were two Americans, Dr. Owen Young and Mr. J. P. Morgan.

Like Schacht, Hugenberg was excited at the prospects for propaganda which the negotiations provided. Indeed, he and the 'Nationalists' viewed the prospect of the Young Plan negotiations 'as a golden opportunity to rally the masses and install a dictatorship. In their view a campaign against paying reparations could transcend party lines and entice millions of non-voters to unite in condemnation of the republic.'[469]

A flood of German cash arrived on Wall Street in the autumn of 1928 to influence the negotiations. Cash from other countries soon followed, excited by the rising stock market. Germany's gold holdings on 7th January 1929 stood at the magnificent total of 2,729,345,000 marks, (£136,467,250) the highest in the Reichsbank's history.[470] All seemed set for securing a reparations' deal favourable to all.

Preliminaries for the new agreement on the payments started on 11th February and finished on 18th February while Wall Street soared, inspiring confidence in the American negotiators that they could soon wrap up the deal. However, the American Press soon became uncomfortable with the way that their stock market was behaving.

On 2nd March 1929, the *New York Times* commented: 'There were times yesterday when even Wall Street began to think that the stock market was running absolutely wild.'

On 4th March 1929 the same newspaper 2sympathized with the new President Hoover on the eve of his inauguration: 'He is hardly likely to have watched with pleasure the tightening of credit under the strain of the speculative market's requisitions, until money rates now prevailing are such as have never been equalled in any new administration.'

On 7th March, alarmed financier, Paul Warburg, who knew Germany well,[471] warned that control of the cumbersome US Federal Reserve Board had passed into the hands of stock exchange operators 'who have now for many months governed the flow of money, not only in the United States but in the principal parts of the world.'

We do not know if Warburg suspected that German stock exchange pundits were playing the market, but he cautioned: 'The banking system of the United States today is tossing about without her helm being under the control of her pilots. Its aftermath is likely to be a depression involving the whole country.'[472]

Handsome new President Herbert Hoover was a mining engineer by training, who had come to power because of his efficiency in distributing American food in Europe after the war. He had been upset with the terms of the Treaty of Versailles. At daybreak on 7th May 1919, he had met up with Keynes and General Smuts. Keynes wrote to his mother: 'The Peace is outrageous and impossible and can bring nothing but misfortune.'[473] Hoover was similarly upset. But Keynes Smuts and Hoover had been wrong in 1919 in believing that the economic strictures of the Treaty of Versailles would cripple the German economy, and would have been even more astonished to hear that Hugenberg's DNVP had just passed an aggressive resolution which stated simply: 'We hate the present form of the German state with all our hearts because it denies to us the hope ... of gaining necessary living-space in Eastern Europe.' [474]

On 25th March the second stage of the Young Plan negotiations began, even though there appeared to be a gaping hole in the German budget. The deficit had been created because Alfred Hugenberg's DNVP refused to finance the Unemployment Insurance Bill, which it had been instrumental in bringing into law a couple of years earlier.[475] The DNVP's bill had only covered 1,100,000 workers, far less than was needed even for an average winter.[476] An extra million people had been thrown out of work in the recent icy weather but the DNVP had refused to vote funds to cover their unemployment.

Stresemann's expressed his bitterness at the DNVP's tactics: 'They wish ... to leave all responsibility to the Social Democrats; and they think of the joys of being in the 'nationalistic' opposition, where they *can let fly with all the phrases that they learned from the Stahlhelm and Hugenberg.* ... You know me well enough to know that I cannot go along with such a crowd.'[477] The fracas was bound to upset potential American investors because under the terms of the Young Plan, it was envisaged that commercial transfers would only be protected for up to one year, after which reparations payments would regain seniority.[478]

Many Americans had never heard of Hugenberg, the former supremo of Krupps, who was now a media titan, as well as leader of Germany's second largest party. However, that would soon change as Hugenberg sent a much-publicized letter to prominent right-wing American businessmen and politicians, informing them that the ocean of money that they had lent to Germany since 1924 had benefited only socialism, not business. Germany, Hugenberg stated, needed a generous settlement to prevent her from sliding into 'Bolshevism.'

Dr. Schacht felt very, confident. In April, the stock market slumped after he declared that Germany could only pay a paltry sum in reparations and asserted that even that amount was dependent on the return of the Saar and Upper Silesia to Germany. A *New York Times* reporter declared that his offer was 'outrageous' and gold flooded out of Germany.

The Reichsbank had held a record amount of gold in January 1929 before the start of the reparations' negotiations.[479] However, in the spring of 1929 Germany's loss of gold was not attributed to the weakness of the

German economy but to a negotiating ploy by Dr Schacht.⁴⁸⁰

Germany's gold reserves had stood at 2,729,345,000 marks, in January 1929, the largest total in her history. However, as the Reichsbank put no restrictions on gold leaving the country, 745,000,000 marks, or £35,714,286 had vanished by mid-April.

During the last days of April, the mark slipped to its lowest level since 1924 bringing a chill to all those Americans who had poured money into German bonds since the mark's stabilization so Germany took the opportunity to raise her interest rates by a full one per cent, triggering immediate rises in Vienna Warsaw and Hungary, before rises in Bucharest in May, Brussels in June, Belgrade in July and New York in August.

Over the very last April weekend the Young Plan was agreed between the German and American negotiators without the Allies being asked to participate. Under the terms agreed Germany was allowed to pay less cash in reparations than Britain and her dominions owed America in war debts.

History does not relate why the anxious American negotiators did not insist that Germany covered Britain and her dominions payments. German Minister for Economics, Julius Curtius, had no charisma but he was a good negotiator. He said scornfully: If 1.65 billion marks (82.5 million approx.) did not exceed Germany's productive capacity who could seriously argue that 300 million (£15 million approx.) more would break its back?'⁴⁸¹ Yet it was the vexed question of who would pay this relatively small extra amount, which would provide a great opportunity for Hjalmar Schacht later in the year.

The decision to accept a more onerous financial load was especially difficult for Britain because a general election was looming on 30th May. Britain was prepared to accept some sacrifice on her own behalf but not on behalf of her dominions. The Labour Party had scored its one and only success in the polls in 1923 on the back of high unemployment and anti-French sentiment during Germany's Great Inflation and Shadow Chancellor, Philip Snowden, had already criticized Balfour's expansive gesture, under which Britain cancelled some £3,400 million war debts, exclusive of interest, owed to her, and announced that she would only collect enough to pay the £850,000,000 in war debts owed to America.

History is divided on whether Snowden had been a pacifist in the First World War. In the early 1920s, German propaganda, supported by the extreme Left in France, had accused Raymond Poincaré of being the warmonger in 1914. Then Poincaré had appeared to cause Germany's Great Inflation in 1923 with his rapacious reparations demands. Yet now the small rotund man, with his goatee beard was Prime Minister of France again. In 1929 British unemployment was still painfully high, and anti-French sentiment over the reparations had not diminished. On 30th May the Labour Party won the British elections.

The leader of the Labour Party, Ramsay MacDonald, was tall and handsome, with piercing brown eyes and wavy grey hair. His intellectual power and 'nervous electric' energy had done much to create his Party. Unfortunately, in 1929, he did not regard Germany as a danger to Europe. Indeed, the impeccably dressed erstwhile opponent of Britain's participation in the Great War, was so opposed to what he considered as France's 'purely militarist' mentality, that he stated in 1929 that he regarded France as the 'peace problem of Europe.'

Wall Street was relieved that an agreement over the Young Plan had been reached. Yet, its joy was premature. Germany seemed in disarray. In previous years German Social Democrats and Communists had marched side by side but now the Communists declared that the Social Democrats were their greatest enemies. Seven people were killed and more than a hundred wounded in the May Day celebrations. Middle class Germans were aghast, and, as no exchange controls had been put in place, money flooded out of the country and bank deposits contracted by an astonishing five per cent between the end of March and the end of May.[482]

Then, on 24th May, Albert Vögler, General Director of Germany's largest steel works, *Vererinigte Stahlwerke*, (and future funder of the Nazis), resigned from the Young Plan negotiations after going to a banquet at Gustav Krupp's forbidding palace in Essen.

Georg Bernhard, editor in chief of the *Vossiche Zeitung* wrote disgustedly: 'These circles know quite well that, hard as the Paris agreements would be for the German nation to bear, the relief that they would involve for the German budget would be used for the restitution of ordered economic conditions in Germany ... that is also the deeper reason for the fresh attempts by working on Dr Vögler to blow the plan to pieces at the last moment.'

After this hitch in the negotiations, the Allied negotiators reluctantly agreed to remove all the untrusting controls over German finances, which France had successfully imposed to ensure the payment of the reparations during the Dawes Plan years.

It was decided that a new bank called the Bank for International Settlements (BIS) would be brought into existence to administer the reparations payments. Although the key architects of the bank would be Bank of England governor, Montagu Norman, as well President of the Reichsbank, Hjalmar Schacht, Hjalmar Schacht would in the future call the Bank for International Settlements, 'my' bank.[483]

There was only one other outstanding issue before the Young Plan was agreed. The *New York Times* explained the history of the matter: '... When they occupied Belgium (in 1914) the Germans removed all the Belgian gold and money and 'planted' marks in the banks in place of Belgian currency. Neither the facts nor the justice of the Belgian claim for restitution has ever been denied by Berlin. ... Yet for one reason or another a settlement has always been postponed ... Emile Francqui, chief Belgian delegate ... has gone so far as to accuse Dr Schacht of having been party to the wholesale pillage of the Belgian banks when he was on von Bissing's staff during the occupation, and such an accusation has envenomed the already delicate question.' But in the end the delegates decided that they would have to sign the Young Plan without agreement on Belgium's claim.

It was an older Raymond Poincaré, weary and sick, who pleaded for the ratification of the Young Plan by France's parliament. The arrival of a socialist government in power in Germany had impressed the democratic Frenchman. Yet Poincaré was no dewy-eyed idealist. He secured the private assurance that the payment of France's enormous war debts to the US, ($6,847,105 including interest), was conditional on Germany continuing to pay reparations to France.[484] Then he set about persuading his reluctant parliament to accept the agreement. He summoned up all his strength and gave one of the best speeches of his career. On 21st July, the Young Plan was ratified by the French parliament by just eight votes.

It was a time of rapprochement between France and Germany. French Foreign Minister, Aristide Briand, proposed the idea of a Federation of European States based on solidarity and the pursuit of mutual economic prosperity. A similar idea was put forward by Stresemann's friend, Dr. Koch-Weser, leader of the Democratic Party, who wrote a book called *Deutschlands Aussenpolitik in der Nachkriegszeit 1919-29*, in which he advocated what he called the formation of 'a United States of Europe,' which would open extensive sources of raw materials to German industry on the one hand, and would provide markets and an unrestricted field of activity to the enterprise of Germany's abounding and capable population on the other.' His aim was 'to be achieved by a gradual series of agreements, and to lead ultimately to much closer economic and political co-operation throughout the world.'

It was an ambition that powerful Germany, with the help of friendly America, could very, likely have achieved over the passage of a great many years but the anti-democratic forces in Germany were in a hurry. The German people had voted for a socialist government in 1928; the British had voted for a socialist government in 1929. The German Right wanted to destroy socialism and democracy and return to war and was prepared to manipulate economic events to secure its aim.[485]

Wall Street soared again as the Hague Conference convened to iron out the final issues of the Young Plan reparations agreement. Britain's new Chancellor, Edward Snowden, was still incensed that Britain and her dominions were being asked to pay more in war debts to America than they received in reparations from Germany. Convinced that Germany was weak, he sympathized with Germany's resistance to paying high reparations and his age-old prejudice against Britain's historic enemy France resurfaced. He called France's interpretation of the Balfour note 'ridiculous and grotesque' while the equally hostile French Minister of Finance, Henri Cheron, muttered to his associates, 'There sits the man who burned Joan of Arc!' Finally, Snowden threatened a walkout if his demands were not met.

The German delegation remained on the side-lines while their former enemies fought between themselves over who should pay a little more, to pay for the war, so that they could pay a little bit less. But eventually they offered, unsolicited, to pay more reparations than the terms agreed, to accommodate the British. They had only one condition, that the occupation troops would leave the Rhineland the following year, five years ahead of schedule. The Allies agreed. It was decided that Britain was to receive an extra £2,100,000 a year more than envisaged under the original Young Plan scheme and the Italian state railways would buy one million tons of British coal for the next three years.[486] Wall Street soared.

The sunlight streamed in from the North Sea onto the balcony of the hotel where Stresemann lay close to death, as French Foreign Minister Aristide Briand came personally to tell him that the Allies had agreed to remove their troops from the Rhine. Briand hoped for reconciliation with his former foe. Paul Schmidt, Stresemann's interpreter, recorded that 'unforgettable afternoon.' 'And now, at this moment, both looked forward to a new age when France and Germany would truly become good neighbours.[487] Alas, that was not to be.

On 31st August, the Young Plan was agreed at The Hague. Under its terms the capital sum was to be reduced to approximately £1,900 (38,000 million gold marks) and German payments were to begin with a reduced payment of £52 million (1,041 million gold marks) and eventually reach a maximum annual payment of approximately, £127,516[488] 2,352 million gold marks)

To put the demands in context, Britain had a national debt of £7,621 million in 1929 (which required £369 million a year to service), whereas Germany's national debt merely stood at 8,971.7 million reichsmarks (£429,143).[489] Half of Germany's reparations would come from the budget and the remaining £32.5 million a year from her highly profitable railways.[490] Germany was also to receive a loan of £60 million (1,200 million gold marks) to get the new arrangement off to a good start. It sounded an exceptionally good deal. Although the German Reichstag had yet to ratify the agreement, Dr. Schacht won acceptance that its implementation should be retrospectively effective from Sunday 1st September.

Wall Street had shot up until the final details of the Young Plan were agreed. Five days later, on Thursday 5th September, the *New York Times* recorded a sudden downturn on Wall Street on the 4th, commenting on its decline,

'The most obvious explanation ... would be that the pace of advancing prices during the past three weeks has been ... so regardless of the money market position, as to inspire a growing sense of caution even among convinced speculators for the rise.'

When the market continued to slide the editor of the *New York Times* consoled its readers:

'The money market is guarded against old-time panics, both by the country's accumulation of gold and by its fund of available foreign credits.' But the 'foreign credits' started to disappear, and money soon became scarce and tight. In September, the financial empire of the fraudulent British financier, Clarence Hatry, collapsed with large losses.

In the 1930s some pundits would blame Hatry for the Wall Street crash but there was another explanation. Germany had been buying gold in quantity from London since June, triggering purchases by France and other countries.[491] On 8th August the New York Federal Reserve had felt it necessary to raise American interest rates to six percent, which put further pressure on Britain.

On September 25th, *The Times* commented: 'An event of much more importance than the Hatry affair ... was the further loss of gold reported by the Bank of England. Withdrawals on this scale are unprecedented, and it is as well to remember that the present gold reserve is nearly £16,000,000 below the level recommended after the Great War.'[492]

After Britain had returned to the Gold Standard in April 1925, *The Times* had reported: 'This means that the Bank of England must use the weapon of the rate in the event of a persistent export of gold.'[493]

In view of the persistent export of gold in the summer and autumn of 1929, Governor of the Bank of England, Montagu Norman, had no option but to raise interest rates at the end of September 1929.

Montagu Norman would be blamed for the 1929 stock market crash because he raised interest rates at this critical time. The removal of the German funds from the

American stock market would also have had an impact on the market. On 2nd October Dr Hilferding, the German Finance Minister, promised to enact legislation to counteract the previous high tax on moderate incomes, which was supposed to have 'encouraged capital flight to abroad.' The German money started to leave Wall Street.

But it was not only tight money, and the departure of German cash which caused anxiety on Wall Street, a prominent politician also had influence on market sentiment. Machiavellian, bespectacled Alfred Hugenberg, had already sent a letter to prominent Americans in the spring with a plea for a generous new reparations' agreement to 'save Germany from Bolshevism.'

Yet, after the Americans listened to Hugenberg's warnings, and gave generous terms to Germany under the Young Plan reparations agreement, Hugenberg produced a pernicious petition, backed by the army veterans' association, the Stahlhelm, and all his own 500 newsppers, and put the minority leader, Adolph Hitler, in a prominent position on the petition's committee.

The predicted success of Hugenberg's petition would give Hitler enormous publicity and have a dire effect on the American stock market.

The first paragraph of Hugenberg's petition stated that Germany was utterly blameless of starting the First World War, blaming Britain for being the evil genius behind it. The second and third paragraphs instructed the government to make an official protest 'against the war guilt lie' and to reject the Young Plan and the entire policy of reparations, while the final paragraph proposed that any minister, including the President, who supported treaties like the Young Plan and even the Treaty of Versailles, should be tried for treason.

The leader of the Democratic Party, Dr. Koch-Weser immediately sought out Stresemann, in an effort to unite 'all groups which oppose the misdirection of nationalistic feeling.'[494]

Stresemann was acutely conscious of the threat Hugenberg posed to the German nation. One of the last acts of his life was to get the executive of his People's Party, the DVP, to pass a clear resolution opposing Hugenberg's petition. But he could do no more. His biographer, Antonia Vallentin, described Stresemann at Geneva:

'A marked man stood there in the shadow of death. His suit flapped about his shrunken figure ... His breathing came so hard that his sudden coughing often drowned out his words ... One could almost hear the fevered beating of his heart.' One week later he was dead.

On 13th October 1929 the German socialist coalition government felt itself sufficiently threatened by Hugenberg's propaganda campaign to issue an official proclamation stating that his petition was a 'monstrous attempt to incite the German people against the government and to annihilate the ten-year good-will policy of the republic with Germany's former enemies.'

On 17th October 1929, counting on Hugenberg's petition began. It was scheduled to take two weeks. The *New York Times* commented: '...no other post-war political issue has contained an equal amount of mischief in its make-up.' It also believed that Hugenberg would gain the necessary four million votes to trigger a national referendum on his petition because he could count on Hitler's 800,000 votes, and those of other extremist parties, if some of his party's 4.4 million faithful fell by the wayside.

On 18th October, the *New York Times* again predicted that Hugenberg and Hitler's petition would succeed because it had reopened the 'war guilt' issue.

On 21st October 1929 'perpendicular' falls were recorded on the American stock market: 'The outstanding feature of the past week's Berlin money market was the rapid descent of the dollar exchange in favour of the mark.' The newspaper complained bitterly, 'Although these withdrawals have increased the supply of money in the Berlin market, money rates have remained high.'

The Swedish match king, Ivar Kreuger, had reached an agreement through which he would lend the German government $125,000,0000 to help cover the initial instalment of the Young Plan agreement, in return for receiving a monopoly on the German match industry. It had been said that Kreuger would be able to take care of a large percentage of this loan without resource to the American market.

However, on the evening of 23rd October, 'formidable advertisements announced subscription rights in a new offering of certificates in Kreuger and Toll. Now it seemed that the Americans, themselves, were being asked to pay even the first instalment of the Young Plan payments This was too much for Wall Street.

On 24th October 1929 Wall Street collapsed, and 19,226,400 shares were sold. The stock market was hit by a devastating crash as it became apparent that not only America's war debts were at risk from Hugenberg's rejection of reparations payments but also that Hugenberg and his new friend, Hitler, were capable of defaulting on all America's loans. The paper loss in October and November 1929 ($26,078,000,000) was equal to the entire wartime increase in the American national debt.

It has been asserted that Germany suffered severely from the Americans withdrawing their money from their country after the crash. The substantial Beamtenbank collapsed leaving scores of unhappy creditors. When the German electrical giant AEG was hit by a cash-flow crisis and was forced to sell part of its business to American concerns, the Siemens finance chief complained bitterly that the 'whole world belongs to the Americans.'

Yet former Young Plan negotiator, Albert Vögler's principal objection to the Young Plan seems to have been that it would facilitate Americans grabbing control of German companies.[495]

Denunciations of 'Yankee' penetration of Continental production continued to echo down to the end of 1930. Meanwhile, most of the German money that had been on Wall Street was not sent back to Germany but was lodged in Switzerland and gold-rich France.[496]

The American stock market continued to plunge until the national referendum on Hugenberg's petition was turned down by the German people on 22nd December. Then the Allies and America breathed a sigh of relief. America remained firm in her belief that she could trust Germany. Wall Street staged a rally in the spring of 1930 in the conviction that the German socialist coalition government would ratify the Young Plan and that the reparations would continue to be paid.

In July 1929, *The Economist* had declared that German trade was forging ahead despite the 'almost complete stoppage of the inflow of foreign capital' and predicted a 'favourable ...balance of payments of hardly less than 4 milliards of marks.'[497] (nearly £200 million) for the year so they knew that the demands were reasonable.

On 12th March 1930 American faith seemed to be justified when Germany ratified the Young Plan. However, on 30th March the socialist coalition resigned en-bloc after President Hindenburg intimated it was time for it to depart. Nevertheless, Wall Street continued its upward path for another month.

On 12th April 1930, the *New York Times* wrote enthusiastically 'One of the most significant commentaries on the current securities market ... is that the demand for our securities from foreign sources continues unabated. The magnet of the New York stock exchange is attracting investors throughout the world.'

Yet, it seemed that foreign investors were more fickle than American investors, or perhaps they objected to Republican talk of 'rushing' a new tariff bill through Congress. The market paused mid-April. Then it started to fall. By 29th April, the *New York Times* had to relate of 'unrelieved selling pressure ... The widest break in the year to date.'

Most Americans could not conceive that it was their friends the Germans who were taking them for a ride. Britain was widely blamed for America's misfortunes. In 1919 President Woodrow Wilson had told an astonished British official at a reception at Buckingham Palace during the peace conference: 'You must not speak of us who come over here, as cousins, still less as brothers; we are neither.' Likewise, in 1929, Woodrow Wilson's former aide, President Hoover, and the American people refused to accept that their German 'friends' had caused their country such a devastating loss.

CHAPTER EIGHT

The Pan-Germans pave the way for Hitler and War

It has often been said that Americans woke up in October 1929 with a massive hangover from the heady party days of the late 1920s. They could not understand why everything had gone so drastically wrong. So why did it? The reason is that they thought that they could put their trust in the democratic German people in the 1920s, but it was the Prussian Pan-Germans, who now called themselves the Nationalists, who were now in control, determined to tear up the Treaty of Versailles and impoverish America so that she would not interfere when they returned to war.

The machinations of Hugenberg's fellow Pan-German, Gustav Krupp, in Russia were about to cause a major agricultural depression, which would come to be known as 'the dust bowl' in America. Meanwhile Hugenberg, had plunged a dagger into American hearts with his petition to try the President of the Republic for treason before the Wall Street crash. Then he and his friends were ready to turn their attention to the German Social Democrats back home, who maintained that the country should pay her war reparations and achieve her aim of securing 'a place in the sun' through cooperation with the international community.

The Social Democrats came under fire immediately. There was a yawning gap in the nation's finances because Alfred Hugenberg's DNVP, had refused to vote funds for the country's Unemployment Insurance Act in the spring of 1929. In December Hugenberg declared that the Social Democrat coalition's plan to raise a loan to cover the deficit was the 'last desperate act of a political system which has turned into a runaway pump.' Head of the Reichsbank, Dr Schacht, in whose probity so many Americans believed, sharpened the attack.

Schacht asserted that the socialist coalition had accepted alterations to the recently negotiated Young Plan reparations agreement, which he would never have accepted; moreover that it had failed to carry out vital reforms to the nation's finances.[498] Efficient, moderate General Gröner described the Social Democrat Finance Minister, Rudolf Hilferding, as 'stuffy' but 'a really decent fellow' and 'a great financial pundit.' Nevertheless, Hilferding was forced to depart. After Hitler came to power Jewish Herr Hilferding would escape from Germany, but he would not evade the Gestapo's clutches. In the Second World War he would be found dead in his cell in the Gestapo dungeon of La Santé, in Paris.

Although the 1929 Young Plan report had declared that the new Young Plan Reparations agreement 'makes possible an immediate resumption of the tax reduction programme',[499] Schacht said that taxes must go up not down! Indeed, he asserted that a huge pot of gold must be created to restore confidence and ensure the payment of the war reparations.[500]

In March 1930 Heinrich Brüning was installed as German Chancellor. He was no fan of Hugenberg or Hitler but a fervent enemy of the Treaty of Versailles and an ardent admirer of President, Paul von Hindenburg, who retained his perfect military posture until his dying days.

The aged ex-Field Marshall, who the Allies had originally intended to indict after the First World War, had kept a low profile since becoming President in 1925. However, after the signing of the Young Plan, he began to exert his authority. He wanted a cabinet which was prepared to use Article 48 of the Weimar Constitution to rule the country, enabling him to sign emergency bills into law without the consent of the Reichstag.

Sober balding workaholic Brüning had distinguished himself during the war, wining the Iron Cross, First Class, while commanding a machine gun company. He was trusted both by shop floor and management and had consciously postponed marriage feeling that 'whoever dedicates himself to service to humanity and the public good should not ... start a family.'[501] He was a perfect employee for the ex-Chief of Staff of the German army and now President of Germany, Paul von Hindenburg.

On 30th June 1930, after the Allied troops were withdrawn from the Rhineland under the terms of the Young Plan, Hindenburg forced the socialist authorities in Prussia to revoke their ban on Germany's ex-war veterans' organization, the Stahlhelm, which had supported Hugenberg's petition in 1929 and now boasted a membership of over 500,000.

The Stahlhelm then marched through the Rhineland in an ugly display of force, with their flag, the hated imperial standard of the Prussian monarchy, black and white with an iron cross in the left corner and the Hohenzollern eagle flying in the centre, prominently displayed. Their march provoked intense anger in France, but this was ignored by the German press, which merely used the occasion to call for the return of the Saarland.[502]

Devoted ex-soldier, and financial expert, Heinrich Brüning, was an advocate of 'austerity.' Soon to be nicknamed *Hungerkanzler* he reassured foreign bankers that his purpose was to return Germany to 'sound money' after the alleged excesses of the former socialist administration. However, he disclosed to his friends in the unions that his real purpose was to rid Germany of war reparations and debt.[503]

Brüning looked upon the German citizens as soldiers, who must suffer so that Germany could regain her place 'in the sun'. So, he kicked off with a poll tax, increased taxation, and reductions in expenditure. He also raised the tariff on wheat to twice that prevailing on world markets to protect his farmers from the imminent deluge of low-cost Soviet wheat onto world markets.[504]

The bewildered German people, faced with higher food prices and taxes, were angry about paying the war reparations, which industry had formerly paid. Their teachers had told them that Germany was not even liable to pay reparations because Great Britain had been the evil genius behind the war. And they were angry about the Wall Street crash which had had repercussions in Germany as well. So, when the elections arrived, they turned to Adolf Hitler who had fought against the reparations imposts when he was on Hugenberg's Freedom of the Enslavement of the German People committee the previous year.

Hugenberg himself blurred the distinction between his powerful DNVD party and the Nazi's NSADP during the lead-up to the elections by asserting that the DNVP now shared the same 'outlook towards religion' and about 'Jewry' as the Nazis.[505] He knew also knew that Germans were terrified of Communism. So, he stated that Hitler was not a communist, nor even a socialist telling his followers,

'Throughout the country we have to build up a strong, powerful, national anti-Marxist party. As uncomfortable as it is to me that the National Socialist movement has developed, we must still take it (and the Nazi party's strongly anti-communist attitude) into account.'[506]

As a result of Hugenberg's reassuring words many former supporters of the DNVP voted for Hitler when the elections were held in September 1930, while Hugenberg himself concentrated on campaigning against the territorial aspects of the Treaty of Versailles. Sir Horace Rumbold noted with alarm in his report to Foreign Secretary, Arthur Henderson: 'It may now indeed be said that the first electoral campaign which has taken place in Germany, without the shadow of the Rhineland occupation, has brought out into the open, through one party or another, all that Germany hopes for and intends to strive for in the field of external affairs,'[507]

Hitler scored a huge success at the polls in 1930 while the *New York Times* observed chillingly:

'In some quarters fears are expressed over the possibility of Adolph Hitler and Dr. Alfred Hugenberg combining to form a party of revenge.'

Whilst Hugenberg had been creating mayhem on the American stock exchange in 1929, his former employer and fellow Pan German, Gustav Krupp, had been busy in the Soviet Union. Gustav Krupp's greatest nightmare had been for the communists to gain power in Germany.

The German communists' aim was to control the 'means of production.' They had also secured a substantial increase in their vote in the 1930 elections, winning 4.6 million votes and seventy-seven parliamentary delegates.

Gustav Krupp felt that socialism was the slippery slope towards communism and was determined that neither socialists nor communists would grab hold of his business, which had taken generations of his family to build up, (and was arguably now the biggest company in Europe). So, he had an idea. In 1928 the Bolsheviks were nearly bankrupt. The Soviet 'economy had almost no reserves at its disposal, either financial or material' [508] so Krupp sensed an opportunity. He would help Stalin for his own evil ends.

Small, sallow, pock-marked Joseph Stalin had been born with gangly legs, a shrivelled left arm and darting yellow eyes. He had made his reputation by robbing banks and extorting money from factory owners to provide funds for the Bolsheviks. However, he was a master tactician and after Lenin's death had gradually been able to out-manoeuvre all his rivals. He proceeded, step by step, lulling his victims into a false sense of security before delivering the fatal blow. The execution would be swift, but the planning process could never be rushed. An embrace from him was often the prelude to a sudden fall. By 1928 the man who would later be called 'Genghis Khan with a telephone' not only had chilling power over his own party in the Soviet Union but also over the Communist party in Germany.

Stalin had outraged the international community by supporting the Chinese revolutionary government, which was waging war against the Peking government. This prompted overseas investors to shun the Soviet Union. Stalin had only ninety-two tanks in his possession and his country was nearly bankrupt[509] so he turned to the German former armaments' manufacturer, Krupp, for help. The Soviet newspaper, *Izvestia* commentated 'the western policy of Germany has not opened any possibilities for overcoming the Versailles system ... The development of relations with the Soviet Union is the only area of Germany's foreign policy that opens political as well as economic possibilities for her...' Nevertheless, the negotiations were long and tortuous.

Eventually Krupp agreed to help Stalin create giant farms like his own 50,000-hectare concession in the North Caucasus. This would enable Stalin to sell wheat abroad to pay for the modernization of his armaments industry and the heavy industrial base to support it without relying on his kulak farmers - but Krupp had two conditions, firstly that he and his German industrial friends had to be paid in hard currency, and secondly that even if the Communists were engaged in bloody warfare against the Nazis on the German streets, they must always vote with Hugenberg's DNVP and Hitler's National Socialists in the

Reichstag instead of with their former friends, the Social Democrats.

Krupp's terms were a bitter pill for Stalin but eventually he capitulated. On 28th August 1928 the Russian Foreign Office issued a statement to the German government stating that it wished to 'renew negotiations, as long as journalists are not involved' and on 1st September 1928 the Soviets used the cloak of universality to denounce the German Social Democrat Party, declaring: 'Have our relationships with the Social Democrats changed or not? ... Does this imply any practical conclusions? Yes, it does...'[510]

The deal with what the Soviets called 'The Union of Industrialists in Germany' was signed in December 1928.[511] Gustav Krupp agreed to help Stalin create giant farms like his own 50,000 hectare holding in the North Caucasus,[512] and to modernize Stalin's antiquated industrial and armaments base, while Stalin undertook to pay for his goods in hard currency and ensure that even if the German Communists were engaged in bloody warfare against the Nazis on the German streets, they would always vote with Hugenberg's DNVP and Hitler's National Socialists in the Reichstag. [513] Meanwhile, in the summer of 1928 a commission arrived in the North Caucasus to determine the location of the new state farms. About 130,000 hectares was allocated to become one huge state farm named Gigant (or Giant).

Stalin became a valued customer of Germany's between the years 1929 to 1933, buying not only anti-tank guns, howitzers, firing mechanisms and all kinds of munitions,[514] and the heavy engineering plants to modernize the Soviet Union's antiquated industrial infrastructure. Indeed, by 1931 over fifty per cent of all Stalin's imports came from Germany.[515]

Inevitably the most significant contract was concluded with Krupp on 17th June 1929. Under this agreement Krupp agreed to provide technical know-how to some of the largest enterprises in the Soviet Union – Barrkad, Zlatoustovskii, Krasnyi, Potilovets, Krasnow Sormovo, and Elektrostal. His help led to a significant improvement in steel casting in open-hearth furnaces (including those needed for military production of carbide and specialized steel).[516] Gustav Krupp had produced some of the finest steel in the world but now the Soviets were learning the secrets. The production of quality steel 'was one of the major achievements of Soviet industrialisation'[517] but neither the German public nor the Americans guessed that the professedly anti-Bolshevik German heavy industrialists were succouring the hated communist regime.

In return for Krupp's help Stalin maintained his immense hold over the German Communist Party, pressuring it to vote for Hitler's NSDAP and Hugenberg's DNVP in the Reichstag instead of with its comrades on left, the Social Democrats. In June 1929, October 1929 and July 1930 the Communists faithfully voted with Hitler's NSDAP and Hugenberg's DNVP. In the September 1930 elections, they alleged that the 'treacherous, corrupt' Social Democrats were 'the conscious agents of French and Polish imperialism' because they supported paying war reparations.[518] In the spring of 1931, after Stalin's personal intervention, the Communists reluctantly joined forces with Hugenberg's DNVP and Hitler's National Socialists to support the dissolution of the last bastion of democracy in Germany, the Prussian state Landtag (parliament).[519]

Krupp's deal succoured Stalin's regime. It enabled Stalin to dispense with his kulak peasants and produce quantities of wheat for export to pay for his goods in hard currency.[520] Stalin had always hated the kulaks and was happy to find a means of getting rid of them. After the heads of the households were shot, their dependents were crammed into 'death trains' headed for the 'icy North.' Meanwhile while Russians and Ukrainians starved, the Soviet Union's precious wheat travelled in trains and ships across the Atlantic Ocean to the unsuspecting continent of North America, where it was sold in 1930 and 1931 at 'slave labour' prices on the world's already overprovided wheat markets.

The effect on the US farming economy was devastating. Suddenly, America's wheat production became totally uneconomic. Farmers tried to expand their production to make up for the fall in prices, but prices were even lower in 1931 than in 1930 and production withered in the exhausted ground. Drought compounded the continuing disaster. 'Winds whipped across the plains, raising billowing clouds of dust.' The dust contained the topsoil holding the nutrients that fertile crops needed was blown away. Marginal land was soon semi-permanently depleted. Banks that supported agriculture went bankrupt up and down the country. For many farmers, and those who were dependent upon them, it was worse than being wounded in a war. Thousands of gaunt, unemployed ex-farm labourers descended on the cities in search of work and food, but America could not blame Stalin for the low price because he had labelled his success in selling his wheat at such low prices 'A triumph of Communism over Capitalism!' So, the farmers themselves were blamed for their misfortunes.

Meanwhile Stalin invited westerners, including prominent Britons, to witness for themselves the achievements of his economy. George Bernard Shaw was one of many who were excited with what they saw. He had been dismayed by the 1929 Wall Street Crash and the subsequent rises in unemployment throughout western Europe afterwards. In contrast, everyone he saw in the Soviet Union seemed to be in work. Shaw declared: 'If this great communistic experiment spreads over the whole world, we shall have a new era in history...'[521]

American liberals had also become disillusioned with President Woodrow Wilson and the defects of capitalism after the Wall Street crash. They were excited by what they felt was the solidarity and purpose of the Soviet Union. Even though over millions of people would die of starvation in the Soviet famine of 1932, blissfully ignorant American pacifist, Sherwood Eddy, wrote 'Russia has achieved what has hitherto been known only at rare periods of history, the experience of almost an entire people living under a unified philosophy of life' resulting in 'a flood of joyous and strenuous activity.'[522]

Prominent Americans could not conceive that it was their friend Germany who had helped Stalin destroy their wheat market, but they were aghast at Hitler's electoral success in 1930. Worried about the fate of their loans,[523] they turned to the one German they had put their trust in in recent times, former Reichsbank President, Hjalmar Schacht.

Dry, bespectacled Schacht did not reassure them when he spoke at a dinner discussion with John Foster Dulles at the Foreign Policy Association in New York. On the contrary, firstly he promised another crisis over the reparations, and secondly, he declared that now that the Allies had withdrawn their troops from the Rhine, there was nothing Americans could do about it.

At the discussion after the speeches, George Sylvester Viereck, who had edited the Prussian-sponsored weekly magazine, *The Fatherland*, during the First World War, asked Dr. Schacht whether Germany should pay 'one cent of the reparations, whether or not she is able to do so, since the obligation to pay reparations is based upon a document that grows from fraud, corruption and trickery?'

Dr Schacht did not directly answer the question, but it was obvious that he also felt that the reparations were not only onerous, but that Germany had been wrongly charged in the first place. Americans had put their trust in Schacht. In fact, they believed that he was a miracle-worker. Schacht had stabilized the German economy after her Great Inflation. In October 1930 he gave twenty-eight handsomely paid speeches for the American Institute of International Education and an extended interview to the American press in which he declared: 'If the German people are going to starve, there are going to be many more Hitlers.[524] Sentiment hardened round the idea that a terrible injustice had been done to Germany through the treaty Americans had declined to ratify, the Treaty of Versailles.

Meanwhile, in Germany Chancellor Brüning had been labelled with the nickname *Hungerkanzler* – starvation Chancellor - because of his callous cuts to the German people's standard of living. Nevertheless, he continued with his policy of 'austerity.' Between 1930 and 1932 budget cuts would reduce the central government's expenditure by over twenty per cent, throwing millions out of work and putting deflationary pressure on the whole of Europe.[525]

Some tightening of the ship may have been in order, to safeguard money for paying reparations and debt. The former armaments makers needed to be taxed to prevent them from secretly manufacturing weapons of war. Yet, Brüning's action was draconian. Germany's national debt in 1930 stood at a mere 10,375.1 million reichsmarks, or £507,836 (at par rate of 20.43 to £). This represented a fraction of Britain's national debt of £7,584 million on which Britain was paying an annual charge of £355 million a year.[526]

Brüning should have had no problem paying both reparations and debts and providing a reasonable standard of living for his countrymen. Nevertheless, the former soldier, without a wife and desperately hungry children pleading by his side, regarded his population as soldiers, who must suffer so that the country could become great again. Consequently, he hiked unemployment insurance premiums to six per cent and slashed salaries for members of parliament, the civil service, the Reichswehr and the railways. This led to salary reductions everywhere. On 24th January 1931, confronted by an angry crowd he merely replied that 'ardour in financial and economic matters' was vital as this is the only way to reduce the 'tribute burden' of the reparations.[527]

The German people were suffering but the German economy remained strong. In its review of the Leipzig Trade Fair on 4th April 1931, *The Economist* revealed how German industry had diverted all its production into exports, revealing: 'In pre-war days, when Germany was a lending and investing country, it was estimated that about ten per cent of the total production was exported. ... But according to recent investigations by the Institute for Konjunkturforschung, the share that export bears to total sales varies as a rule between twenty and fifty per cent.' ... 'These figures reveal the gradual conquest by German industry of foreign markets.'

America had slapped on a tariff on all imports in 1930 primarily in response to Japanese import penetration and increasing German competition.[528] Britain was the largest exporter to America at this time, but she had a roughly equal export and import trade with America, while France had half the number of exports to imports.

Naturally, therefore, Britain and France regarded the tariff against their goods as deeply unfair. And it did little to help America. Japan was the second largest exporter but took practically nothing in return, while German manufacturers immediately reduced wages to retain and increase their exports.[529] While the quantity of world trade remained stationary in 1930 Germany's share doubled. In 1931 Germany would become the world's leading export country.[530]

Meanwhile, within Germany's political and economic circles, the concept of international cooperation and the open market system of trading began to recede, and the former Pan-German idea of closed-bloc region called *Mitteleuropa* resurfaced. Carl Duisberg, head of the IG Farben chemicals trust and former internationalist, formulated his vision in March 1931:

'Out of the small national economic space, the strong industrial states and the agrarian states looking for markets push towards greater international economic spaces ... This tendency was started by the United States ... (but) also in Europe this aim of the regional economic space seems to be gradually taking shape. ... Only a uniform economic bloc from Bordeaux to Sofia is going to give Europe the spine which it needs to retain its importance in the world.'[531]

With the inclusion of Bordeaux, Carl Duisberg seemed to be including France in his pan-European vision. However, that same month, Brüning abruptly announced a customs union with Austria, in direct contravention with the terms of the Treaty of Versailles.

The French were horrified that Germany and Austria had so little respect for the Treaty of Versailles. They withdrew their short-term loans from Austria to persuade her to abandon the plan. As Austria paid no attention to their pressure, depositors started queuing up outside Austria's beleaguered Kreditanstalt bank. Germany then said that her banks were under pressure too, additional increases in taxes were published, and Chancellor Brüning came hotfoot to London to tell the British of his country's plight.

During Brüning's visit to England, Governor of the Bank of England, Montagu Norman, advised by his old friend, Hjalmar Schacht, declared that the crisis affecting the Kreditanstalt Bank was threatening the financial security of the Austrian nation and that all south-east Europe was on the brink of collapse.[532] One-week later Britain tried to rescue the Kreditanstalt bank, although by doing so it risked its own financial equilibrium.

The French were not impressed. Aware that the German industrialists had just given Stalin a substantial loan in April,[533] they argued that Germany was not poor but recalcitrant.

The ceremonial launching of the pocket-battleship, *Deutschland* in May, with 56,000 people in attendance, was a further cause for alarm. It was a potentially threatening vessel, as its 11-inch guns had a greater range and firing power than its British counterparts. The French tried to persuade Germany to abandon her plans to build a second pocket battleship. Yet the only crumb of comfort that they received was that 'credits for a third battle cruiser will not, at this juncture, be allocated.'[534]

Yet the financial situation in Germany in June 1931 seemed to get increasingly dire. Soon the panic spread to German savers. On 7th December 1929, *The Economist* had estimated that German national savings had reached the handsome total of £1 billion[535] but since that time they appeared to have evaporated. Gold and foreign exchange flooded out of Germany and panic reigned.

On 20th June, President Herbert Hoover of America, who had fed the starving German people after the war, generously offered Europe a one-year moratorium on the payment of reparations and war debts.

The French remained cynical. They were worried that once the reparations were suspended, they would never be re-imposed. For them, the real issue was how to 'maintain security against an increasingly restive neighbour which was stronger in terms of both population and economic capacity. Sooner or later, this would translate into military superiority. At this point, the reparations were France's only instrument to delay Germany's domination.'[536] At last, on 6th July they agreed to Hoover's proposal.

Unfortunately, as no foreign exchange controls had been imposed in the interim, German money had continued to quit the supposedly 'sinking ship.'

On 3rd July, Nordwolle, one of Germany's largest textile concerns, had collapsed. Unfortunately, its collapse affected the finances of the Danat Bank. The Danat Bank's failure caused a run on all the German banks and savings institutes, which had been starved of funds by the Reichsbank.

Many German industrialists were annoyed. They did not think that their country was in such a desperate state and if it was, they wanted to help. On 7th July, a thousand of Germany's larger businesses declared themselves ready to guarantee losses by the gold discount bank of up to 500 million Reichsmarks.[537]

The industrialists were right that their country was basically a powerful state. It was later discovered that the Danat Bank's collapse originated not from insolvency but from an order from government.[538] Nevertheless, its action was a calamity for German savers and caused consternation abroad, so America decided to help.

On 21st July, a conference was called in London at which the German government managed to secure agreement to a 'Standstill' of the repayment of most of the 'banking credits in Germany expressed in foreign currency' for a six-month period. Before asking for the 'Standstill' Germany had repaid billions of marks of short-term loans. Between July and December Germany would repay between another 1 to 1.5 billion of its short-term loans, reducing the country's foreign indebtedness by almost a third but America would whistle in the wind for the rest.

In 1919 Keynes had described the German negotiator at the Versailles peace conference, Dr Melchior, as 'exquisitely clean, very well and neatly dressed' and almost professed himself 'in love with him.'[539] Now Dr Melchior was entrusted with telling America and the Allies, in the nicest possible way, that Germany was reneging on her debts. Yet Melchior was a man of probity. He remarked disgustedly to his colleague Hans Schäffer, 'What we have just experienced is the destruction of the capitalistic system. Yet the system depends on the strictest observation of the rules. This is the first time I have had to refuse to fulfil an obligation ... simply because the state required me to sign. The capitalist system in Germany will not survive such a deviation from its rules. For the deviations will constantly increase, and the system will accordingly dissolve.'[540]

It was inevitable that Britain should choose this time to devalue her currency, while the world's attention was fixed on Germany's debacle. In 1925 Britain had been inveigled into going onto the Gold Standard at too high a rate. The decision was felt to be beneficial for the world economy at the time, yet it had merely brought Britain misery and unemployment. Norman was hoping that President Hoover's moratorium 'on all debts arising from the war', would soon be made permanent. In the meantime, although Britain had asked her workers to take yet more pay cuts, her exports were shrinking, and she was finding it impossible to compete on world markets. Indeed, after Germany's banking collapse, a run was immediately launched against sterling.

On 13th July 1931, the British released the Macmillan report, which asserted that Britain was failing her industrial base. The report precipitated a crisis. On 29th July, the Bank of England put its interest rate up 'only a point or two', which was deemed totally inadequate. That same day Montagu Norman, who suffered from permanent ill-health, collapsed during a meeting at the Treasury and disappeared, incognito, on a ship to Quebec. France and America offered funds to help the beleaguered country, but the money was belatedly and wastefully used by Norman's subordinates.

On 15th September, 500 Scottish sailors mutinied because of a pay cut. That was the final straw. On the 19th, Britain deserted the Gold Standard. Nearly two dozen other nations followed Britain's lead. [541] Two days later Montagu Norman's ship docked at Liverpool and on 28th September he was back at the Bank of England, allegedly 'utterly bowled over on discovering the terrible truth' that Britain had devalued while he had been away. [542] So, he escaped all censure for the crisis.

At first American opinion seemed sympathetic to Britain's action. J P Morgan declared the devaluation to be 'a hopeful and not a discouraging event.' Other bankers declined to give their names but were quoted as saying 'It was the correct move.' 'We had on our hands a patient who had to undergo an operation to save his life. ... now the operation is over, and we are feeling relieved.'[543]

However, then there was a terrible run against the dollar. Over the next five weeks European banks converted $750 million into gold, expecting that the United States would be the next to devalue. Naturally, as it had become an article of faith that Germany was poor, the French and the British were blamed for the disaster.

The run against the dollar came at a critical time of mounting US bank failures precipitated by the farming crisis. In early 1931, the Federal Reserve Bank of America had $4.7 billion in gold reserves. Nevertheless, like Germany, by law, every $100 in Federal Reserve notes had to be backed by at least $40 in gold, and the remaining $60 by prime commercial bills. So, although America was still sitting on a mountain of gold, American government paper was not allowed to be used to help in the crisis.544

America, like Germany, had decided upon a policy of 'sound money' so felt that she could not save the little banks, which had lent to her hard-pressed farmers, without experiencing an international loss of confidence in the dollar. Her exports had slumped from $5,373,456 in 1929 to $1,949,249 in 1932.545 Hoover's generous gesture in allowing a moratorium over the payment of war reparations and war debts was no longer affordable. Stalin's wheat had swamped world markets with wheat and created a huge hole in the American economy.

Initially, perhaps Krupp had believed that the German Junkers with their great estates would not be too affected by his agreement to help the Soviet Union's agriculture as Brüning had imposed a tariff before Stalin's wheat hit the German market. However, the volume of Soviet wheat was so huge, and its price so low, that it caused deep distress amongst German farmers too. On 34 7410 March 1931, Krupp was persuaded to give up his 50,000-hectare concession546 and Germany decided to lend Stalin the money to buy her armaments and the factories to construct them, rather than allowing him to destroy their agriculture.

Britain had seized the opportunity of the banking crisis to save her industry and lower her exchange rate against the dollar and the mark to a more tolerable level. Subsequently she slapped on Imperial Preference tariffs. Naturally, most members of Britain's empire followed Britain in lowering their exchange rates and as Britain's imperial preference was a blanket tariff, it discriminated against American agricultural produce too.

The Americans were outraged. They forgot that their industrial tariffs had been blanket tariffs, which had unfairly hit British industry. Around 10,000 American banks would go bankrupt between 1929 and 1933 and many of them serviced the farming sector.547 They would blame Britain and her Imperial Preference for their distress. Only Germany, they now believed, could be trusted as a bulwark against Communism, little realizing that Gustav Krupp had saved the mass murderer Stalin from bankruptcy by enabling him to grow and export his wheat.

On the face of it, German industry seemed to have been particularly hard hit by the Depression. By 1929 the German annual index of industrial production had soared to 117.3 in comparison to 1913 (=100); whereas Britain's industrial output had remained static, at 100.3. By 1931, however, statistics revealed that German industrial production had slumped to eighty-five per cent of pre-war levels (compared to Britain's eighty-two per cent).548

Nevertheless, the 1931 figure for Germany's industrial production might not have included her secret exports to the pariah state, the Soviet Union. *The Economic Transformation of the Soviet Union, 1913-1945* gives the return on her investment in Stalin's regime.549 The initial investment by Gustav Krupp had been repaid with the proceeds from Stalin's sale of wheat. The subsequent 600 million Reichsmarks in German credits provided between 1930 and 1932 produced 1,389 million Reichsmarks in German industrial exports, a very favourable return.550

After her banking crash in September 1931, Germany still had gold and foreign currency reserves in the Reichsbank to cover forty per cent of the value of the notes she had in circulation although they remained locked away from general circulation.551 The *New York Times* noted hopefully: 'It is held by many economists ... that the very large export surpluses now being realized every month in foreign trade will keep Germany on the direct and natural way to recovery.' 552

Unfortunately, the Americans did not realize that *hungerklanzler* Heinrich Brüning's aim was not to nurse Germany's recovery but to use depression and austerity to persuade American policy makers to free Germany from the constraints of the Treaty of Versailles and return to dictatorship under a Hohenzollern monarch.553

Hugenberg also hated democracy, but he wanted an entirely different sort of dictator to Hohenzollern monarch. He felt that a 'man of the people' like Adolph Hitler would be much more likely to win the hearts of the German population. And he had the support of the coal cartel, which included Gustav Krupp, Albert Vögler and Emil Kirdorf amongst its members and had placed a royalty on every ton of coal to finance the Nazi Party.554

So, Hugenberg had plenty of money to organize a rally to woo the middle classes at one of the few places where the wearing of Nazi uniforms had not been forbidden, the little mountain spa of Bad Harzburg. Bad Harzburg was festooned for the occasion with flags in the old imperial colours, and fourteen generals, three princes, Dr Schacht, the military veterans' association, the Stahlhelm, and the former Pan-German publicist Heinrich Claß attended.

The rally gave Hitler an opportunity to reassure the middle classes that he was not an upstart but a person they could trust. He declared repeatedly, 'We are protecting Germany and the rest of the world against Bolshevism.' These words were just what they wanted to hear.

The German middle classes, like the Americans, were terrified of Bolshevism. The press had relayed horrific stories of Soviet atrocities against the Russian kulaks of German extraction and of the desecration of the Russian Orthodox churches. Meanwhile, the good German Burghers were loaded with taxes and asked to pay reparations when they had been told that they were 'guiltless' of the First World War.

The War Guilt Section, supported financially by Hugenberg's Nationalists, had continued to censor and control government publications. A rival Parliamentary Committee, inaugurated by the Social Democrats, had also been set up after the First World War. It had chosen a German law Professor, named Hermann Kantorowicz, to undertake the task of deciding who was responsible for war in 1914. Kantorowicz had concluded that the Central Powers, Germany, and Austria were primarily to blame. However, Kantorowicz's report was judged so heretical that Stresemann had initially denied him publication in 1927.[555] In 1931 the Parliamentary Committee made its final report on the three volumes of documents. The War Guilt Section called upon an expert called Wilhelm Schauer to make his final recommendation about publication. In Schauer's view the report would provide Germany's former enemies with ammunition. So, the three volumes were never published and were subsequently lost.[556]

Germany was faced with huge unemployment because of *Hungerkanzler* Brüning's austerity policies. Yet the German government was in a better position to help the jobless than most of its neighbours because it had a social-welfare system unsurpassed anywhere except in Britain.[557] And the Right was consoled that the workers were no longer strong enough to stage a general strike to thwart a return to dictatorship.

The workers were weak, but the country was still powerful enough to support ailing industries. In 1931 and 1932 the Deutsche Bank continued to finance struggling car maker, Daimler-Benz, because its chairman, Emil Georg von Stauß, considered that Daimler-Benz's capacity for making war material was critical to the revival of Germany's armaments industry. BMW was also supported by the government, to guarantee Germany's ability for future military production.[558] Ex-soldier, Brüning, would himself confess his duplicity over the issues of reparations and disarmament in his memoirs, writing:

'to win ... three demands which seemed to contradict each other; elimination of reparations, disarmament of others, and rearmament for us ... I was now reaching a point where with one false move ... all the French propaganda could revive again ... and then the great two-year ... march (towards freeing the country from the reparations, returning to dictatorship and being legally allowed to re-arm), accomplished with endless sacrifice, would have been in vain.'

Brüning was an ex-soldier and a technocrat who had sworn allegiance to General Hindenburg. However, he wanted to accomplish his aims lawfully to keep American public opinion on side. In contrast Hugenberg and Hitler merely wanted to use the rule of law for the purpose of destroying it.

In May 1932 the Communists, the DNVP and Hitler's National Socialists proposed a motion of no confidence in Brüning's entire cabinet because he declined to dismiss General Gröner, who had refused to lift the ban on Hitler's paramilitary organization, the SA. Within one month of its eventually being lifted, ninety-nine people were killed and 1,125 wounded in sickening violence.[559] On 30th May Brüning announced his entire cabinet's resignation.

In June 1932, the Hoover moratorium on the payment of debts and reparations expired and there was another conference on the matter. As Germany had nearly 6,000,000 unemployed, she was offered ninety per cent off her reparations' payments. But that was still not enough for Hitler. On 31st July, elections were held. Hitler gained a huge increase in votes. In 1928 Hugenberg had declared that he believed that the creation of a dictatorial regime akin Premier Mussolini's in Italy could be achieved 'if the condition of the country seemed to warrant it.'[560] Subsequently Hugenberg had manipulated the German economy to create the sort of conditions where German people would vote for political change. But it took six million unemployed to persuade them to warm to Hitler.

In 1972 Imanuel Geiss in his 'Die manipulierte Kriegsschuldfrage' would maintain that Hitler's 'aggressive protestation of German innocence during the First World War and in its outbreak' won him many votes – but there were still many who voted against him. Indeed, if the Social Democrats and Communists had joined forces at the polls, their votes would have matched Hitler's. Yet Stalin's deal with Krupp was still in force so, 'At Moscow's order, the German Communist party still pronounced the Social Democrats 'enemy no.1.'[561]

Only a few months later Hitler achieved supreme power. Coincidentally, a new flight from the franc began.[562] The German money, which had been squatting in France, streamed back to Germany, while Hitler declared that his country would be paying no more reparations.

Former Pan-German, Gustav Krupp, who was said by witnesses to have been violently opposed to Hitler before Hitler became Chancellor, now became in the words of steel tycoon, Fritz Thyssen, 'a super Nazi.'[563] The company rapidly expanded to over 100,000 employees and in August 1933 the Nazi salute became compulsory in all Krupp's factories. Those who refused to use it were classified as work shy and sent to concentration camps for re-education. Huge portraits of the Führer hung in Gustav's forbidding mansion, Villa Hügel, and every administration office was linked to Gestapo headquarters so that any employee overheard 'sniping at the regime' could be sent there for questioning.[564]

Gustav contributed generously to Nazi propaganda in other countries too, designating members of his foreign sales force as members of the government's network. They estimated the industrial potential of possible enemies, including the United States, and forwarded their appreciation to Berlin.[565]

In 1935 General Morgan, who had been British Military Representative on the Inter-Allied Council in Germany between 1919 and 1923, was astonished to find on his visit to Germany, that 'the great armament factories' were 'working night and day in triple shifts.'[566]

The Americans had been horrified by Germany's unemployment before Hitler. They still felt genuine warmth towards the land of so many of their forefathers. Germany seemed to be in dire straits in 1932 – and they were in dire straits too. They could not quite understand what had happened to their wonderful country.

America in the 1920s had been fizzing with wealth and happiness. According to one historian, 'during the second half of the 1920s the United States, with about three per cent of the world's population, accounted for forty-six per cent of its total industrial output. During the same period, it produced seventy per cent of the world's oil and forty per cent of its coal.'[567] Yet by 1932 America looked like a country which had been struck by a hurricane. In his book *In the Time of the Americans* author David Fromkin described how the Depression hit America:

'Between a quarter and a third of the entire workforce lost their jobs. Fifteen million Americans were out looking for work. In their ranks were not only farmers and factory hands but also professionals who had thought of themselves as insulated from economic distress. People who only a couple of years before had been lawyers or civil engineers or bankers or architects wandered round in a daze, hopeless and defeated, wondering where to sleep or to get food.' Industrial production had halved since 1929 and nearly eighty per cent less homes were built.[568]

The Americans could not believe that the German hierarchy would throw their own citizens out of work in a propaganda exercise to persuade America to rid their country of the strictures of the Treaty of Versailles and allow them to return to dictatorship. They regarded the German people as their best friends and the German nation as a bastion against communism. Yet Krupp and his fellow industrialists had been enabling the Soviet regime to survive and grow, and many Germans considered Americans as a 'Kulturlose Herde.'[569] Hitler called America 'a deeply lazy country full of racial problems and social inequalities.' Many Germans believed the propaganda that

America had denied their army victory in 1918. In his book *Germany plots with the Kremlin* T. H. Tetens would write:

'The historic truth is that the German ruling class, industrialists, aristocrats, army officers and diplomats, have always viewed, with great apprehension, the United States as the chief antagonist and menace for Germany.'[570]

Hitler believed that America's intervention had denied Germany victory in the First World War. His aides continued to take concrete steps to impoverish America so that she would not interfere in any new war in Europe.

The first catastrophe for America had been Stalin's sale of wheat, which had plunged the whole world, but particularly America, into depression. As the Americans had no inkling who was responsible for the disastrous situation of their agriculture sector, they increasingly blamed Britain after she slapped on Imperial Preference to help her dominions Canada and Australia.

The second catastrophe was Hitler's refusal to pay any more reparations. In 1931 President Hoover had explicitly recognized the connection between the war debts owed to America and Germany's war reparations when he gave Germany and the Allies a moratorium on all debts payable from the war. Therefore, the British had been confidently expecting that America would agree to the Allied war debts being cancelled after Hitler reneged on them. Indeed, France would never have accepted the 1929 Young Plan Reparations agreement except on that basis. The restoration of France after the First World War had cost £830 million and she had received practically nothing in cash from Germany for its restoration. She was acutely worried by Hitler's arrival in power and was running out of money to complete the Maginot Line of fortifications.

Unfortunately, although Hitler was about to spend the enormous sum of 48,911 billion Reichsmarks on German rearmament in the seven years before the Second World War[571] the Allies were blamed for America's poverty through their refusal to repay their war debts after Hitler refused to pay any more reparations.

The Allies' war reparations' demands have always been regarded as extortionate, so it is worthwhile looking at how much Germany actually paid in actual cash in reparations. The headline figure was the modest sum of

£1,038,000,000. Yet as the Dawes and Young Plan loans had not been repaid only £938,000,000 was received by the Allies before the Second World War, most being credited being in the form of land, ships, coal, and exports rather than in actual cash. Nearly £400 million had been paid through exports between 1924 and 1929. However, the Czech economist G Borsky in his book on the reparations called *The Greatest Swindle in the World* estimated that the amount of actual cash that Germany had paid in total in reparations between 1919 and 1933, after deducting the proceeds of the Dawes and Young Plan loans, was £153 million net.[572]

Meanwhile the American historian Stephen A Schuker assessed that Germany had received a net inflow of funds since 1918 of 'no less than 17.75 milliard Reichsmarks (approximately £850 million) or 2.1% of national income for the whole period 1919-1931 and concluded: 'In price adjusted terms, this sum approached four times the total assistance that the United States government would provide to West Germany between 1948 to 1952 under the much-heralded Marshall Plan.' [573]

After another war, the Nazis would declare, 'Those dollar diplomats and cowboys are too untalented to cope with the problems of world politics.' In the 1930s the Americans complained that the British were robbers for not paying their war debts. But was that fair? If President Woodrow Wilson had not intervened at the end of September 1918 the German army on the Western Front would have eventually been crushed. Instead, America had thrown money at the problem, but it had made it even worse. President Wilson's aim had been to secure 'Peace without Victory' and that is what the pacifist President had managed to achieve.

In 1934 Hitler appointed Schacht to become Minister of Economics. After unlocking the door to the banks, which held the astonishing forty per cent cover for Germany's bank notes, Schacht decided on a policy of spending, but only by the state and the armaments manufacturers. He allocated so-called Mefo notes to the armaments manufacturers and encouraged them to massively expand their production, while he defrauded Germany's creditors. As his former friends in America held the most German loans, they were naturally the worst affected.

Once Germany had reneged on the reparations, it was easy to renege on other debts too. On 9th April 1934 Schacht told Germany's medium-term and long-term creditors, 'A moratorium seems inevitable,' declaring that it was unnecessary to call an international conference 'to establish the complete incapacity of Germany to make transfers ... since the facts are clear to everybody.'[574]

On 14th June 1934 he declared a moratorium not only on the Dawes and Young Plan loans, which had been offered to Germany as sweeteners to persuade her to accept the agreements but also on Germany's long-term and medium-term debts, the majority of which were owed to America.[575]

Germany had seemed to present a golden investment opportunity to Americans in the 1920s, with no debt and a compliant low-paid workforce. However, the loans could also have been viewed as a bribe to persuade Germany to comply with the terms of the Treaty of Versailles. Yet, no banker wanted to admit that he had squandered America's precious cash in a failed attempt to keep Germany as a peaceful democratic member of the international community. Neither did the banking community want other countries like Australia and Canada, who had faithfully paid their debts throughout the Great Depression, to follow Germany's path and default on their obligations. So, they stayed silent.

Unfortunately, American public opinion was by now convinced that Germany had been maltreated by the Allies at Versailles. American savers, who supported the Allies during the war, had lent France and Britain the money in the expectation that Germany would be defeated, and the money repaid. Yet, contrary to their wishes in the mid-term elections of 1918, Germany had been given an armistice. Then supposedly draconian war reparations, which they had never agreed to, had been imposed under the terms of the Treaty of Versailles, which they had never ratified. Finally impossible to pay reparations had been imposed and then the Allies had refused to pay their debts.

Amos J Peaslee (who would later become American Ambassador to Australia) in his memorandum called, GERMANY PAID NO REPARATIONS, wrote that 'American sentiment', in the early 1930s, '... was almost a unit in laying the blame for all the world's troubles on the

Versailles Treaty.'[576] Hundreds of American banks had gone bankrupt since Hoover had let the Allies off paying their war debts for a year between 1931 and 1932 and the Allies received the blame. The anti-British American newspaper mogul, Randolph Hearst's *New York American* declared of Britain's decision to abandon war debt payments: 'Someday this will be regarded as the most tragic mistake in England's history.'

Yet the Allies non-payment of war debts, and the German moratorium on her sovereign loans, was only the start of America's troubles. She had always regarded Germany as a Triple A customer. Therefore, she had a large balance of payments surplus with Germany and held forty per cent of Germany's long-term debt.[577] Unfortunately this made her uniquely vulnerable to economic assault if Germany wanted to keep her out of another war.

Cotton was America's chief export. Germany had been America's best customer since 1923. When Germany's imports of cotton halved in 1932 newspapers pointed out that if Hoover's moratorium on the payment of reparations was made permanent, it might be a small price to pay for the restoration of their market.[578] Yet although demands for reparations were abandoned in 1933, the American farmers' hopes for receiving a good price for their cotton were dashed.

Germany had decided that she needed her foreign exchange for rearmament so adopted a system of barter for imports. She therefore offered only German beer and wine in payment for America's quality cotton. American cotton growers were not amused. Since their government could not conjure up another large customer for their produce, they were faced with disaster. Handsome and infectiously self-confident new President, Franklin D Roosevelt, was landed with the problem. He instituted the American Adjustments Administration bureau, which paid landowners to leave land idle. Yet a vast expanse of 2.5 million hectares of cotton growing land had to be ploughed up and crops left to rot because of the loss of trade with Germany. Another 'dust bowl' had been created, this time in America's cotton-growing area.

The Allies and America were drifting farther and farther apart but Germany wanted to make sure that America stayed poor and isolated, so she decided to transfer her purchases of cotton to Brazil, where there were lots of Nazi sympathizers. Between 1933 and 1938 Germany doubled her share of cotton imports from Brazil. The Brazilian economy thrived, but an economy needs cash too and Germany only paid in compensation marks, which had to be spent on German goods. Brazil desperately wanted to buy German armaments but lacked the money to pay for them. So, in the end she decided to default on her American loans before signing a £8,280,000 armaments contract with Krupp in 1938.[579]

American unemployment fell between 1934 and 1937 but after this new blow it shot up again. Meanwhile the German propaganda machine poured money into the US to persuade the American people that their poverty was due to the Allies' failure to repay their war debts, and that they should stay out of a future European war.

In 1934, a leading Democrat named Samuel Untermyer asserted that Hitler's propaganda supremo, Joseph Goebbels, was spending $3,000,000,000 a year on propaganda, much of it being channelled through the German Embassy in Washington.[580] Retired Major General Smedley Butler even claimed that he had been asked to help create a fascist veteran's organization, and to use it in a *coup d'etat* to overthrow President Roosevelt.

George Sylvester Viereck, who had intimated that Germany was guiltless of starting the First World War at an important political dinner discussion with John Foster Dulles and Haljmar Schacht in 1931, became a prominent Nazi propagandist.

Viereck's mission was to encourage Americans to forgive and forget all the debts that Germany had defaulted on and to channel their anger for their subsequent poverty against the Allies instead. In 1934, he was temporarily discredited after admitting to the McCormack Committee that he had been engaged to promote Hitler's Germany. However, he had lots of good friends in high places. His 'Make Europe Pay War Debts Committee' would increasingly strike a chord with suffering Americans in the 1930s and 1940s.

Meanwhile flying ace, Charles Lindbergh, who had received world-wide acclaim for making the first non-stop flight from New York to Paris, was staying in pleasant but 'decrepit' England. He made friends with the Astors and the Clivedon set – some of whom were supporters of Nazi

Germany - and was disheartened that 'the country which produced the Industrial Revolution' had allowed so much of its aviation industry to rust.

In May 1936 he was asked by the American government to make a tour of the German aviation industry. He was received like royalty by Hermann Göring and allowed to fly a Junker, visit two Heinkel factories, and view the latest bombers and observation planes. The only programme that he complained of not catching a glimpse of was Germany's rocket development programme, which he had been told about in the 1920s.

Lindbergh and his wife Anne were completely taken in by the Nazis. Anne wrote to her mother, 'Hitler, I am beginning to feel, is a very great man,' while Charles expressed a sentiment which many right-wing Americans shared: 'Europe, and the entire world, is fortunate that a Nazi Germany lies at present, between Communistic Russia and a demoralised France.'[581]

Lindbergh was also invited to the Soviet Union by Stalin. Despite Stalin's efforts to impress him, his view of Russia was of a bleak regime, marked by secrecy and oppression. He would later write that the Soviet Union had become the most, evil empire on earth, an outlook was shared by many of those who ran American industry. They were relieved that Germany had adopted Fascism rather than Communism. What they did not realize was that both the tyrants, Hitler, and Stalin, had been nurtured by the same source.

Retail giants such as Woolworths had invested in outlets in Germany in the 1920s while chemical companies like DuPont shared patents with her. Companies such as Ford, and particularly General Motors after its purchase of Opel in 1929, were increasingly drawn into controversy when they were asked to make military trucks and 'tracked vehicles' after Hitler came to power. General Motors continued with its investment in Opel because the profits had to be reinvested in Germany. It was one of many American firms faced with a dilemma. It was not allowed to send capital home yet did not want to lose all its investments.[582] Eventually, after the war began, its indigenous management would be replaced by Nazis.

Charles Lindbergh was one of many who did not realize that that the German people's rise in wages between 1932 and 1936 was merely due to their having a longer working day,[583] nor grasp that the German aviation industry had been modernized with the vast sums of money that should have gone to pay Germany's debts. He had no idea that Hitler and his cohorts were criminals who had absconded with America's cash and were busy blaming their robbery on the Jews instead.

The Nazis realized that Lindberg's name was famous throughout the world and that he was a great expert on aviation. On 11th October 1937 he was invited to Germany again and allowed to see what sounded like a prototype for the earliest helicopter and became the first American to examine in detail the Messerschmitt 109, plans for the Messerschmitt 110, and the Dornier 17 aircraft. On 18th October 1938, he visited the Junkers engine factory at Magdeburg, and the assembly factory at Dessau.

Then one evening Lindberg was asked for dinner at the American Embassy. The dinner was apparently organized so that the American Ambassador could secure emigration visas for several high-ranking German/Jewish citizens. However, the occasion was highjacked by Hermann Göring who presented Lindbergh with a golden cross with four small swastikas 'by order of der Führer.'

Charles Lindbergh was pleased. He considered renting a house in Berlin. However, the very evening that he wrote to American Ambassador to Britain, Joseph Kennedy, saying, 'I am extremely anxious to learn more about Germany, and I believe that a few months spent in that country would be interesting from many standpoints' the Nazis staged a pogrom against the Jews. On *Kristallnacht*, as the infamous night became known, more than one hundred synagogues were burned, thousands of Jewish shops and houses were destroyed, and tens of thousands of Jewish people were arrested and carted off to concentration camps.[584]

The world was horrified. Lindbergh went home. However, Göring's efforts to woo him had paid off. Lindbergh would become an influential isolationist, drawing huge crowds to anti-war gatherings because of his name. Nevertheless, there was a silver lining for Britain. After Lindbergh had compared the British aircraft industry unfavourably with the German aircraft industry, Churchill threw money at the problem. The result was the Spitfire and the Hurricane.

Eventually, America also began with the massive modernization of her aircraft industry. But her resources had been appropriated by Hitler. By 1938 Hitler would be spending five times as much as Wilhelm II had spent on the armaments race before the First World War and the GDP at his command by 1939 was almost 60% greater than that available to the Kaiser.[585]

Unfortunately, the many Americans who had patriotically bought war bonds in the First World War, only for the Allies to refuse to carry on payments in the 1930s, continued to blame the Allies and the Jews for their poverty, instead of Hitler.

CHAPTER NINE

Germany and America in the Second World War

After Hitler came to power, former Pan-Germans, Heinrich Claß and Alfred Hugenberg joined Hitler's regime. Heinrich Claß, aged sixty-five, had used violent anti-Semitic rhetoric since 1912, met Hitler as early as 1918 and supported his putsch in 1923. Founder of the Pan German League, Alfred Hugenberg, aged sixty-seven, had given Hitler an all-important blast of publicity with his Freedom Bill in 1929 and encouraged his followers to vote for him in 1930. Claß would remain in Hitler's government until 1939, while Hugenberg initially became Hitler's Minister for Economics and Agriculture.

Hugenberg had never wanted to become dictator himself. A small rotund man, with an unattractive moustache, he was a pedestrian public speaker and knew that he lacked 'star' appeal. But he was a ruthless businessman and a consummate organizer who had always wanted to be Germany's 'economic dictator.' Claß's attempt to oust the elected government and launch a coup to install Hugenberg as economic dictator in 1926 had failed. In 1932 Hugenberg had outlined what he would do when he finally became 'economic dictator.'

'In haste because 'every clemency costs blood and time,' the bureaucracy and the police would be purged of hostile elements, strikes and opposition would be declared illegal, public opinion controlled and ring leaders and opposition parliamentarians would be taken into 'protective custody' with the help of paramilitary organizations.[586] Then he would put into action his ideas to help German farmers.

These ideas must have appealed to Hitler because on 29th January 1933 he offered Hugenberg four important economic portfolios in the Reich and Prussia. Hugenberg must have felt that he had achieved his ambition to become economic Tsar.[587]

However, Hugenberg was not Hitler's Minister of Economics and Agriculture for long. At the World Economic Conference on 16th June 1933, Hugenberg concluded his speech with the thesis that only 'two impartial steps' could make Germany solvent. One would be 'to give Germany a colonial empire again in Africa,' the other would be to 'open up to the 'nation without space' (*Volk ohne Raum*) areas in which it could provide space for the settlement of its vigorous race and construct great works of peace.'[588]

These words smacked of a renewed desire for warfare. The press revealed that Hugenberg had written a document revealing his ambition to colonise Russia.[589] Trusted Russian diplomat Maxim Litvinov also informed Stalin that Schacht had told a French diplomat that Germany intended to divide up Ukraine with Poland.[590] Britain and France were alarmed. Stalin halted his friendship with Germany and Hugenberg lost his job.

Like his friend, Claß, Hugenberg had branded Hitler as a 'classic example of megalomania ... uncontrollability imprudence and lack of judgement' in 1931.[591]

He was anxious, even then, that he might not be able to maintain his power over him. Events proved him right. Yet he did not completely lose his influence after he lost his parliamentary job. Although forced to relinquish his news agency, the Telegraph Union, he was able to keep his Scherl publishing company, which could be relied upon to take a Nazi view of events. His friends the 'Ludendorffians' even advocated Germany forging a closed-autarkic bloc that stretched beyond the German-speaking area into the Soviet Union up to the Urals.[592]

Hitler felt the same as the pre-First World War Prussian militarists after he came to power. Weary Britain and France, like America, had been weakened as a result of Germany's financial manoeuvres, and Hitler planned to spend all the money that he had stolen from his country's creditors on armaments.

France was much poorer than outsiders believed as the Germans had kept so much of their cash in French banks after 1929 rather than in Germany.[593] After Hitler became the Fuhrer in 1933, the German money in French banks had flooded back to Germany, leaving them even poorer. Hjalmar Schacht, in whom America had placed so much trust, became Hitler's Minister of Economics.

Schacht immediately adopted a fraudulent trading system, whereby goods were merely paid with unwanted German goods or devalued bonds. The result was that the German manufacturers ordered a multitude of French goods before the vote on whether the coal-rich Saar region (which had been allocated to France for fifteen years under the terms of the Versailles Treaty) should remain French territory or return to Germany. After the region had voted to return to Germany, Germany said that she had no cash to pay for the goods. Gradually all the countries trading with Germany had to adopt a barter system. Then Schacht had a new idea.

In 1936 Schacht instituted his so-called 'Drang nach Sudostern.' In this brilliantly conceived deception, he offered to pay the south-east European countries, Greece, Hungary, Yugoslavia, Rumania, and Bulgaria, thirty per cent above the world price for their agricultural produce. They were naturally delighted at such an opportunity and offered to underwrite the deal by advancing the money to the producers and waiting for Germany to repay them. Schacht's next move was to sell the commodities to Rotterdam or London, either at the ruling market price or even below it. His third step was to inform his south east European creditors that he was wholly unable to find the foreign exchange in the amounts required but that he was prepared to pay on his own terms in certain lines of manufactured goods – particularly armaments.[594] The weapons would be ready and waiting for Germany when their countries were occupied in the Second World War.

Aging Alfred Hugenberg had been expelled from office but there is no doubt that his ideas had been influential. Austria and Czechoslovakia were stepping-stones to Ukraine and Russia so one would presume that Hugenberg approved of Hitler's decision to invade them. He had also called for the 'annihilation' of the Polish population as long ago as 1899. Yet he should have been careful in his choice of vocabulary; Hitler was liable to take terms like 'annihilation' literally. The historian Ian Kershaw, in his study of Hitler called *Nemesis*, was horrified by brutality and oppression of the Polish people after Hitler's invasion, declaring: 'The treatment of the people of the newly conquered territory was unprecedented its modern forms of barbarism evoking, though in even more terrible fashion, the worst barbaric subjugations of bygone centuries.'[595]

In January 1940 Hermann Göring decreed that a million Poles, including women, were to be recruited to work in Germany, three quarters of them in agriculture. They were to be identified with the letter P, to be barred from all social contact with Germans and, also, have their wages slashed to twenty-five Reichsmarks a month. As there was resistance it was decided to break the backbone of the Polish people. The authorities started with a programme of political murders before adopting a more comprehensive system of genocide. Selective food rationing was also introduced. By the autumn of 1940, German people in Polish cities received 2,600 calories a day, the Poles 938, and the Jews 369. By the spring of 1941, the Wehrmacht was reporting incidents of Polish workers collapsing at their workbenches[596] but Hitler had given them a scapegoat to blame, the Jews, who died of hunger.

While Hitler indulged in a disgusting physical war in Europe, his propaganda chief, Joseph Goebbels, was waging a propaganda battle in America. During the First World War George Sylvester Viereck had published a paper called *The Fatherland* devoted to Germany's cause. Now Viereck successfully cultivated cordial relations with isolationist Senators and Congressmen who allowed him to use their offices as his base of operations on Capitol Hill. Viereck expanded the circulation of a sixteen-page newsletter called *Facts in Review* to 100,000 readers and managed to secure hundreds of thousands of copies of a speech by Senator Gerald Nye of Dakota for his 'Make Europe pay War Debts Committee.'

Through his newsletters Viereck rammed the message home to impoverished citizens and farmers throughout America, that it was the Allies' default on their war debts that had been responsible for their hardship and misery in the 1930s, not Germany's default on her reparations, her sovereign and commercial debts[597] and her trading obligations.

The German Embassy was also busy. It managed to send out mass mailings of anti-war postcards with Congressional Headings, in quantities of up to one million copies.[598] The German propaganda not only influenced

Americans of German heritage but also the Irish Americans.

Unlike the middle-class Germans who had come to America in the 19th century largely for ideological reason, the Irish, who were sent to America in 'coffin ships' for a new life after their dreadful famine, arrived penniless. They suffered severe privations in the northern and eastern urban centres where they settled. However, their numbers multiplied, and they gradually gained power, through rallying round their church, trade union membership and machine politics.'599 Nevertheless, many still blamed Britain for their hardships. In 1939 Terry Barry, one of the rivals for the IRA leadership, claimed that the German/American Bund, the main Nazi organisation in America, was bank-noting IRA leader, Sean Russell, to carry out bombing raids in Britain.600

Most Americans, however, were not violently anti-British. They were just impoverished and wanted to keep out of the war and so susceptible to German propaganda. In March 1940, the German Embassy in Washington published several documents to make it appear that Poland had attacked Germany before Hitler invaded. Roosevelt roundly dismissed the allegations as bogus, but they caused a huge amount of newspaper and radio coverage in the lead up to the Presidential elections.601 Roosevelt roundly dismissed the allegations as bogus, but they caused a huge amount of newspaper and radio coverage in the lead up to the Presidential elections.602

On 4th September 1940, the America First Committee was established to campaign for America to remain neutral and to avoid giving help to the Allies, including through Roosevelt's idea of 'Lend-lease.'

America First's chairman was the charismatic businessman Robert E Wood, who been a brigadier general and then Quartermaster General in the First World War and subsequently Vice President and ultimately Chairman of Sears Roebuck and Company. He had supported Roosevelt's New Deal and embraced Roosevelt's rearmament efforts. He had also backed Roosevelt's ambitious bid to build 50,000 planes in the next calendar year. However, he was determined to campaign against America becoming involved in the war in Europe and to oppose Roosevelt's 1940 election because he felt that impoverished America would get caught up in the war.

The America First Committee campaign against America joining the war was so influential that Roosevelt would secure a pledge from the Allies at the Casablanca conference in 1942 that America would insist on nothing less than 'unconditional surrender' at the end of the Second World War.[603] Nearly half of the America First's funding came from a few millionaires, such as Robert E Wood himself, the publisher, Joseph M Patterson of the *New York Daily News*, and Robert R McCormick of the *Chicago Tribune*. It also secured support from Democratic Senators like Burton K Wheeler of Montana and Republicans like Gerald P Nye of North Dakota and future Presidents, John F Kennedy and Gerald Ford.

Almost all Americans had shared America First's desire for American neutrality in 1939, but opinion began to change after the fall of France in 1940. Slowly Churchill managed to make progress in securing armaments from Germany. The terms of America's neutrality act meant that Britain had to pay cash, on the nail, for the weapons. However, Britain's cash rapidly ran out. So, the 2destroyers-for bases deal was devised. Britain handed over bases in Trinidad, Bermuda, and Newfoundland in return for fifty mothballed destroyers, only nine of which were operational by the end of 1940.

The America First Committee had opposed the Lend-Lease Bill, declaring that 'aid short of war' threatened to involve America in Europe's war. The Committee also backed Wendell Wilkie for President and asked the popular hero Charles Lindbergh to make fighting speeches to defend America's neutrality.

Hitler was also concerned to keep America out of the war and eager to invade his present ally Russia but first he wanted to deal with France and Britain.

France's ownership of the Longwy-Briey iron ore field made an invasion of France absolutely, essential given the necessity of 'iron' to make Germany's weapons. It was true that the Nazis had developed the vast low-grade iron ore deposits at Salzgitter. However, prominent Nazi, Albert Vögler, who had funded Hitler's 1932 electoral campaign with a donation of half a million Reichsmarks,[604] had announced in the First World War that Germany would fight for 'a further ten years' to retain Longwy Briey. Yet it had been returned to France in 1918. Recovering it in 1940 was a priority.

France did not want another invasion. Surrounded by predatory Fascists in Italy Spain and Germany, the French people had become poorer fearful and divided. She had tried to protect herself by creating the Maginot Line to protect her border with Germany but her borders with neutral Belgium and Luxembourg remained open to invasion by a country such as Hitler's Germany which did not respect international law.

After Germany's invasion of Norway and Denmark, the German guns roared into life again on 10th May 1940. The Belgian fortifications on the River Maas were seized and German Army Group B marched towards the Maas River. The bulk of the French army, backed up by the British Expeditionary Force, marched rapidly north. Yet their prompt action was a prelude to catastrophe. While the British and the French were hurrying north, Germany's Army Group A was hurrying west through the hilly, thickly wooded region in south-eastern Belgium called the Ardennes, towards the Maas bridges between Dinant and Sedan. At 8.30 pm on 20th May the advanced guard of the Second Panzer Division arrived at Abbeville, where the River Somme flowed into the sea. The entire Dutch and Belgian armies, the British Expeditionary Force and the pick of the French army were trapped between the German armies. Although 370,000 men from the British army escaped by boat from Dunkirk, it was an immense victory for Germany.[605]

The German army seized 314,878 French rifles, 5,017 artillery pieces, 3.9 million shells and 2,170 French tanks. It also seized 4,260 train engines and 140,000 wagons from France Belgium and Holland. The German firms who worked the Longwy-Briey iron ore fields in the First World War reclaimed control of the mines, although they had to share them with Hermann Göring who grabbed the de Wendel mining and steel conglomerate.[606] The Nazis also appropriated 81,000 tons of copper, plus substantial amounts of tin nickel petrol and oil,[607] plus great quantities of fish from Norway, dairy produce from Holland and Denmark and wheat from France. Hitler could look on his army's military success in Europe with satisfaction.

Former Pan-German, Heinrich Claß, had always wanted, 'by hook or by crook' to create a great Germanic-led bloc in Europe called *Mitteleuropa*. France, Belgium, Luxembourg, and the Netherlands all had important steel industries. They were also sophisticated manufacturers of cars, armaments, planes, electronic and consumer goods. Austria, Polish Silesia, the Czech Protectorate, and northern Italy also had important industrial centres. By 1940 the European bloc that Germany had defeated, or coerced into joining, would have a combined GDP greater than either the United States or the British Empire.

Success bred success. As news of Germany's victory against France was heard throughout Europe, Romania stopped her oil deliveries to Britain and delivered them to Germany instead. Mussolini altered his 1939 position and declared war on Britain and France. General Franco shifted Spain's attitude from neutrality to that of a 'non-combatant.' Even Switzerland made positive noises and allowed her high-precision tools and twenty-millimetre anti-aircraft guns to be sold exclusively to Germany.[608]

The creation of a European empire, or *Mitteleuropa*, had been the Pan German League's foremost ambition since before the First World War but it was not a bed of roses. In fact, it was a bed of thorns. Germany was an occupying force. She did not charge 'reparations' because the word was tainted. So, she decided to charge 'occupation costs' instead. Her principal victim, France, bore the heaviest load. The French maintained that the twenty million Reichsmarks per day demanded of them was enough to feed an army of eighteen million men. As France had no cash, she handed over her shares in Romania's oil industry, her interests in Mines de Bor in Yugoslavia, Europe's largest copper mine, etc., in payment. Cruellest of all, Germany continued with a twist to the barter economic system she had adopted in the 1930s. Young National Socialist civil servant Dr Gustav Schlotterer, explained how the Nazis used the system to defraud defeated Europe:

'Our tendency is to use sleight of hand, guilt and possibly violence to get the European states to sell their goods to Germany, but to leave their credits, when they build up, in Berlin.'

Exporters were encouraged to sell vital commodities to Germany but were paid not by the Germans but by their own governments, who had to raise taxes from their own citizens to pay their exporters. Germany did sell goods in return, at high profits, which could be credited against imports, but the gap between what western European countries sent to Germany and the goods they received in payment became larger and larger. By 1944 the French government was owed 8.5 billion Reichsmarks.

Germany had managed to appropriate a huge amount of French raw materials for free, and France would have to heap increasingly heavy taxes on her citizens to reimburse her unhappy producers. Meanwhile, although the 1,100,000 French who were forced to work in Germany were not paid slave wages like the Poles, they still received a third of the wages of Germany's allies, the Italians.[609]

It was no wonder that although the Germans at first behaved with strict propriety in the western European countries which they occupied, after a while they had to bring in the Gestapo. The men who had consented to act as Germany's tools, Quisling in Norway, Mussert in Holland, and Laval in France, became almost universally loathed.

The armistice with France was signed in the same railway carriage as the one in which the armistice after the First World War had been signed on 11th November 1918 and Hitler spent an afternoon sightseeing in Paris. He only had to polish off Britain now before turning his attention to Russia.

In the First World War the big economic associations were convinced that Germany could bring Britain to heel through unrestricted submarine warfare. They threatened to withdraw war finance unless the policy was adopted in 1917. Yet Germany's determination to use unrestricted submarine warfare finally persuaded President Woodrow Wilson to declare war against Germany on 2nd April 1917 and Hitler was worried that 'unrestricted submarine warfare' would draw the US into the Second World War too.

Germany was not allowed to own or build submarines after the First World War. However, Krupp had started designing submarines in the 1920s. So, in 1935, Hitler decided to build a new submarine force under the command of former First World War U-boat ace, Karl Dönitz. By the beginning of the Second World War Dönitz had sixty-five U-boats, with twenty-one at sea, ready for action.

Dönitz had a brilliant new way of using his U-boats – in Wolfpacks! Wolfpacks consisted of a pack of submarines, spread out across the ocean to detect enemy ships. When one spied a convoy, it reported its position and tailed it, with the other submarines regrouping ahead of the convoy. At a signal, preferably at night, the Wolfpack closed in, overwhelming the convoy's anti-submarine escort ships.

On 3rd September 1939, two days after Hitler invaded Poland,[610] head of the German fleet, Grand Admiral Raeder, called for unrestricted submarine warfare. On the same day, the British Liner, the *Athenia*, was torpedoed. However, it transpired that there were twenty-eight Americans among the 112 passengers who had lost their lives.[611]

Hitler was dismayed. He did not want history to repeat itself and America to become involved in his new war. He forbade attacks on all passenger ships, whatever their nationality. Admiral Raeder disagreed. He still advocated all-out submarine war against England, straight away, declaring: 'Even the threat of America's entry into the war ... must not give rise to any objections. The earlier and the more ruthlessly we commence ... the shorter the duration of the war.'[612]

On 4th November 1939 President Roosevelt announced America's neutrality and delineated 'combat zones' in the vicinity of Britain and France out of bounds to American ships. That gave the German submarines an area they could safely operate in. But Hitler was still worried about giving the US an excuse to declare war.

By the summer of 1940, the U-boats were a real threat to Britain. Between June 1940 and March 1941, the U-boats sank over two million tons of British shipping [613] and continued with their devastation until the Enigma cipher was broken. Winston Churchill, who had returned to his First World War position as First Lord of the Admiralty, would later disclose that 'the only thing that ever really frightened me during the war was the U-boat peril.' But Hitler did not give the production of U-boats priority at the start of the war. Instead, after the British turn down his offer of an Imperial partnership, he ordered the invasion of Britain to go ahead.[614]

It was lucky that Hitler's so-called 'Operation Sea Lion' involved a battle for the skies, and a sea crossing, before the Panzers could roll across Britain's green and pleasant land. But Hitler would have to move fast. Three days after General von Kleist secured his great victory against France, President Roosevelt proposed the construction of the world's largest military-industrial complex, capable of supplying the US with 50,000 aircraft a year, and available to Britain on lend lease.[615] Admiral Raeder consoled the Führer that the cost to Britain would be high. In his view the British Empire would not crumble but would have to submit to radical alterations, which would result in it giving America equal power.[616]

Hugenberg and the former Pan-Germans never contemplated the invasion of Britain and there were many arguments against it in 1940. For a start, the German navy had already been depleted in battle. The invasion of Norway had been expensive in shipping terms because the Oslo garrison destroyed Germany's newest heavy cruiser, the *Blücher*, and the Royal Navy wiped out ten modern destroyers carrying the German landing party to the Narvik fjords. Finally, the British torpedoed two heavy cruisers, the *Geisenau* and the *Scharnhorst* so Raeder dryly told Hitler that the invasion of Britain could only be contemplated after air superiority had been achieved.

Although the German air force had some wonderful fighters, like the Messerschmitt 109, many believed that the Luftwaffe needed a much larger and more powerful fleet of bombers and long-range fighter escorts to deal the killer blow. In July 1940, the Luftwaffe focused on bombing coastal shipping convoys and ports like Portsmouth; in August it concentrated on RAF airfields and attacking the hangars repairing the precious Spitfire and Hurricane planes. Finally, after an alleged Allied provocation, Hitler decided to bomb British cities, even managing to hit Buckingham Palace on 10th and 13th September. Yet by October Britain's days of fear and anguish were over. The Battle of Britain had been won by Britain's brave air force, helped by pilots from Poland, Czechoslovakia, New Zealand, Australia, Canada, South Africa and Belgium, and volunteers from neutral Ireland and America. The situation continued to be worrying but the threat of invasion faded.

Then Hitler concentrated on his plans for invading Russia, taking the precaution of concluding a Tripartite Pact with

Italy and Japan. He also encouraged the Japanese to invade Singapore, hoping that America's fear of Japan's predatory intentions would keep her preoccupied in the Pacific.[617]

Hitler's Tripartite Pact with Italy and Japan was soon enlarged to include Hungary, Romania, Slovakia, Bulgaria, Yugoslavia, (after a month lost in war), and Croatia. Finally, Hitler was ready for his grand scheme, the invasion of Russia.

Hitler has been condemned for his decision to invade Russia. He had such a large European empire in 1941 that people could not imagine why he wanted to venture further. Yet Hugenberg was obviously in favour of the invasion and if one looked at the First World War map of the German 'New Order' in the East in summer 1918, one could see why.

Although Germany had been tactful in not calling the areas, she had conquered in Russia in the First World War, 'Empire' to avoid upsetting President Woodrow Wilson, it was apparent that she had controlled a vast area by the autumn of 1918. She had called the Ukraine and the Crimea 'territories of closest economic involvement with Germany,' Poland and Lithuania, 'territories of direct German influence,' Estonia, Livonia and Georgia 'areas of German settlement' while and Rumania were officially termed 'territories of political and economic connection with Germany.' The Province of the Don Cossacks and the Kuban were named spheres of influence, with raw material bases demanded by Germany; finally, Azerbaijan and Armenia were said to be 'closely connected with the Central Powers.'[618] Nearly one million German soldiers were moved in to establish a direct military presence.[619]

This empire had been easy to snatch from the Bolsheviks in 1918. So, in theory the unloved Soviet Union should have been easy to invade again. This had certainly been Hitler's opinion.[620] But unknown to Hitler and the rest of the German people, German heavy industry had for a long time, been helping the modernization of the Bolshevik army. Former Pan German, Krupp, had persuaded the German government to cancel all Germany's wartime loans at Rapallo in 1922 so that the German army could train in Russia,[621] with the quid pro quo that the Prussian army would train the Soviet army too.

In 1928 Krupp had also undertaken to help Stalin modernize the Soviet army's equipment in return for political favours at home. Although Rheinmetall provided the Soviets with anti-tank guns, howitzers, and machine guns, the most significant contract was concluded with the firm of Krupp on 17th June 1929. This had led to a significant improvement in the steel casting needed for military production of carbide and specialized steel,[622] which could be used in the manufacture of tanks.

Industrial help had also come from America too. In the early 1930s, Stalin had erected a huge steel complex at Magnitogorsk behind the Ural Mountains, based on the one at Gary, Indiana. After Hitler came to power, and Hugenberg's aggressive remarks had dented Nazi/Soviet relations, Roosevelt recognized the Soviet Union, and by 1938, before the signature of the Nazi/Soviet pact, sixty per cent of all Soviet machinery and technology imports came from America. Even as early as 1939, therefore, Stalin had a modernized armaments sector and the heavy industrial base to support it.

Krupp had supported Stalin because he was a ruthless individual who could be relied upon to persuade the German Communists to vote with Hugenberg's DNVP and Hitler's NSDAP in the Reichstag. But it appeared that Hitler knew nothing of Krupp's assistance. He shared most Germans hatred of 'Bolshevism' and believed that the hapless citizens dwelling in the Soviet Union needed wiping from the face of the earth. In 1912 Pan German Heinrich Claß had written in his book, *If I were the Kaiser:* 'Since we have broached the question of evacuation (of native populations) in passing, so to speak, it is perhaps not out of order to speak of it publicly on occasion.'

In the Second World War, Hitler declared that Russia was populated by 'Untermensch' Slavs, ruled by 'Jewish Bolshevik' masters.' Through his invasion he hoped to kill two birds with one stone, slaughtering or enslaving most of the Russian population, and wiping out the Jews. Indeed, over a million Jews would be slaughtered even before the Final Solution massacres started.

Hitler called his plan to invade Russia 'Operation Barbarossa.' On 22nd June 1941, over four million soldiers of the Axis powers invaded the Soviet Union along a 2,900 km front. In July Hitler ordered Reichsmarschall

Hermann Göring to set in motion the process that culminated in the Final Solution of the Jewish question. Murdering millions of people was a tall order. But then Göring had an idea. In the year 2000 *Landeszentrum für politische Bildung Baden-Württemberg* would describe how handicapped Germans had been killed by Hitler's administration between 1939 and 1941 because they could not help the war effort:

'At first, some of the victims seemed to believe that it really was just a shower they were taking. Others began to resist and shout out ... after an interval, operatives in gas masks opened the doors. Terrible sights normally greeted them ... the operatives who attended to the crematorium, sometimes called burners, were also responsible for taking the corpses to the ovens ... patients with gold teeth had been identified by a cross against their names and these teeth were taken out and delivered to the administrators, to be melted down to fine gold.'

At last, on 3rd August 1941, Catholic Cardinal Clemens August Graf von Galen managed to stop the killings of the disabled German people, although he himself was kept under virtual house arrest until the end of the war and three of his priests were beheaded.[623] However Göring subsequently decided to use the gas ovens to kill the Jews instead and the appalling Holocaust began.

Hitler originally stated, in his Directive 34, that his aims in invading the Soviet Union were to take the Crimea, the Donets Basin, and the Caucasian oilfields. These aims were remarkably like Germany's ambitions in the First World War. However, after the German army's striking successes in the summer of 1941, the great tank general, Heinz Guderian, wanted to march to Moscow.

The Führer was reluctant to accept Guderian's plea for a march on Moscow. 'My generals,' he declared, 'know nothing about the economic aspects of the war.' Moscow had no war materials; it was Ukraine's iron ore, manganese and coal that were needed to prosecute the conflict, and Stalin was hastily moving his armour plate mill from Mariupol to beyond the Ural Mountains, although the fighting was still hundreds of miles away. The sprawling tube-rolling mill at Dneprpetrovsk was also being dismantled and 283 major industrial enterprises evacuated from Ukraine.

Yet, Guderian's superiors, Generals von Bock and Halder, put Guderian's proposal to march to Moscow to Field Marshall von Brauchitsch and Hitler surprised them by agreeing to fly to von Bock's headquarters at Novo-Borisov to discuss the way forward.

During the army's successful First World War invasion, it had never gone near Moscow, but it had traditionally been immensely powerful in Germany. Hitler interviewed Generals von Bock, Halder, and von Brauchitsch separately about the prospects for taking Moscow and changed his mind. The siege of Leningrad would start in September 1941 and the battle for Moscow started in October.[624]

The Abwehr had estimated that the Soviets had 200 combat-ready divisions at the start of the war and came in for criticism when the German army faltered. The number of Soviet divisions appeared much higher because Stalin had organized the home front into a paramilitary organization with thirty-six million members called Osoaviakhim, (thirty per cent of whom were women), whose specialities were harassment, night attacks and guerrilla activities. Loaded onto convoys without front-line training, they were taken to combat areas, tipped out and dispatched headlong against the superbly disciplined soldiers of the Wehrmacht. Machine-gun squads brought up the rear to prevent 'unauthorized withdrawals.' The resulting casualties were appalling. [625]

Hitler's Tripartite Pact with Italy and Japan had not intimidated Roosevelt. In fact, it had the opposite effect. In November 1940, after Roosevelt was re-elected for a third term, he immediately embarked on a massive expansion of his armaments programme. Germany's anti-Semitic embassy in Washington told the isolationists: 'As an exponent of Jewry ... Roosevelt wants England to go on fighting and to prolong the war ... until the armaments effort of the United States is fully in gear ...'[626]

Yet Roosevelt had made a measured response to the threat of war against his country. Although he reassured American fathers and mothers before his re-election for a third term by saying, 'I have said this before, but I shall say it again and again and again: Your boys are not going to be sent into any foreign war.'[627] His decision to vastly increase his armaments would be fully justified the following year.

In 1939 the Japanese Minister of Foreign Affairs, Yosuko Matsuyuki, had stated that the influence of American citizens of German origin was so strong in the US that it was most unlikely that America would go to war against Germany.[628] Indeed it was German-American farmers in states like Wisconsin Minnesota and North Dakota, which paradoxically had been hardest-hit by the deluge of Stalin's wheat in the Great Depression, who were most reluctant to send their boys away to fight against the land of their forefathers in the Second World War.

However, on 7th December 1941, Japan attacked Pearl Harbor. America was horrified by the raid. She speedily prepared for war with Japan – but did this mean that she had to go to war with her 'friend' Germany? Or indeed that the terms of the Tripartite Act necessitated Germany declaring war against her, when Japan had been the attacker, rather than the attacked?

Hitler's Foreign Minister, Joachim von Ribbentrop, was anxious.[629] The Tripartite Pact had been signed on 27th October 1940. Under Article 3, it declared, 'Japan Germany and Italy ... undertake to assist one another with all political, economic and military means if one of the Contracting Powers is attacked by a Power at present not involved.'

This seemed to let Germany off the hook as America had not attacked Japan. Japan had attacked America on her own initiative. In addition, the all-conquering German army had suffered a reverse. General Zhukov had launched Russia's counteroffensive, and on 5th December, General Guderian had written in his journal: The offensive on Moscow (has) failed. ... We underestimated the enemy's strength as well as his size and climate.' The German army was forced to retreat in the snow and bitter cold.

However, Hitler's mind was made up. He had an increasing hatred for America, and what was more dangerous, a tendency to drastically under-estimate her strength and power. On 11th December 1941, Hitler declared war on the United States. America decided that she would destroy Germany before defeating Japan.

In the postwar years Americans grew friendly to Germany and forgot about Hitler's wartime declaration of war, but Hitler's antagonism towards America was shared by many who had fought on the eastern front, in 1918, and had been convinced by Hugenberg's propaganda that Wilson had denied Germany victory in the First World War.

America had been impoverished in the 1930s because all her money had been stolen from her, but she possessed immense natural resources and an able and educated workforce. Presious cash had been flowing in from the Allies to purchase American planes and boats and armaments. Roosevelt had used the surplus to ready the nation for war. The America First Committee cancelled an anti-war speech by flying ace Charles Lindbergh and declared 'in view of recent critical developments' their full support for America's participation in the conflict.

In Operation Barbarossa the German forces had captured over three million Soviet prisoners of war, most of whom would be deliberately starved to death as part of Hitler's 'Hunger Plan' to diminish Eastern Europe's population.[630] Yet neither Leningrad nor Moscow would fall into German hands, and the carnage was only just beginning.

In 1942 the Axis powers launched a summer offensive to seize the oil fields of the Caucasus and to occupy the Kuban steppes. Gustav Krupp by that time had become senile. His son Alfried had taken control. Alfried Krupp had a hawk-like nose, sunken cheeks, and a sardonic mouth. His eyes were flat and faded, and his manner with strangers wary. He was a loner, but he had enormous self-control and presided over a vast slave empire.

It is not widely known that the Allied soldiers who became prisoners of war in the First World War had been treated like slaves. Some of the British prisoners of war in Germany were sent to Angersee, Mitau, Wainoden and Libau, where they had to suffer the rigours of a Russian winter. They were deliberately starved, denied food parcels and suffered from frostbite. Conditions for those imprisoned on the Western Front were equally bad, with guards using 'shocking barbarity.'[631] In 1925 the Geneva Convention came into force, which set a minimum standard for the Allied and American prisoners of war in the Second World War. Yet Hitler did not apply the same rules to the Soviet prisoners in the Second World War.

In 1942 Alfried Krupp attended a session of the Central Planning Board ... at which it was decided to impress 45,000 Russian civilians into the steel plants

Germany owned or had conquered, 120,000 prisoners of war and 6,000 civilians into the coal mines, and to set the medical standards for recruiting the Russian prisoners of war lower than those required of Germans employed in the coal mines. Alfried also had work for foreign saboteurs and Jews.[632] He was short of labour and thought that the 'Final Solution' was wasteful. He told the Führer that every party member favoured the liquidation of 'Jews, foreign saboteurs, anti-Nazi Germans, gypsies, criminals and anti-social elements' but he could see no reason why they should not contribute something to the Fatherland before they died.

After new arrivals had been issued with wooden clogs, Krupp blankets stamped with the three interlocking shields and the firm's prison uniforms ... the segregation began. Jews, at the bottom of the totem, wore yellow cloth tags, with the heads of the Jewish girls shaved to form grotesque designs. Russian slaves wore white initials SR, and the Poles were painted with a big P. Names were forbidden; individuals were known only by their numbers. They were put to work constructing a manufacturing plant for automatic weapons at Auschwitz.[633]

When the Russians were taken to Germany it was decreed that they must be strictly segregated from the German population, other foreign workers, and all prisoners of war. They were accommodated in closed camps from which they could only leave under armed guard, to go to their place of work. On 14th March 1942, the tool shop supervisor complained that the food of the Russians was so pitifully bad that they were getting weaker and weaker every day. He protested that with so little food they were not strong enough to tighten a turning part correctly and asserted that if care was not taken to change their feeding arrangements, 'their employment, and all the expense connected with it, would have been in vain.'[634]

Krupp was one of the few firms whose SS contract permitted it to make its own arrangements for feeding slaves, thus enabling it to cut its allotted four marks per diem payments to Himmler. I G Farben was also allowed to make its own arrangements, but Farben slaves were at least given the full ration, with supplementary meals provided for men assigned to heavy duty. Alfried ignored both the Führer and the army and the German population's call for better conditions for the Russians. At the

Nuremberg trials the eminent Washington attorney, Drexel A Sprecher, would declare that 'Alfried's exploitation of slave labour was worse than that of any other industrialist.'635

Unsurprisingly, by 1943, with the help of slave labour, Krupp sales would reach an all-time peak, surpassing the record year of 1939. ... 'Alfried was the king of the continent's greatest industrial empire ... no-one in Europe could challenge him; he held seven high offices in the government and the National Socialist Party, each of which entitled him to immediate access to Hitler. Indeed, the Führer even allowed Krupp to call his company 'a State within a State.'636

Things were not going so well on the battlefront, however. Neither Moscow nor Leningrad fell into German hands, and the Germans experienced a terrible defeat at Stalingrad. With the failure of the final large offensive at Kursk, the German army was on the retreat. The Eastern Front would cause ninety-five per cent of all the army's casualties between 1941 and 1944.

Germany was on the retreat on the Western Front as well. The Allies won a decisive victory at the second battle of El Alamein in the autumn of 1942 and in September 1943 they invaded the Italian mainland. Soon the American and Allied invasion of Normandy would commence. Then the Americans would attack Germany. This time the Americans would insist on the German army's 'unconditional surrender' if the Soviets did not get to Berlin first.

By 1943, Hugenberg could see the writing on the wall for Hitler, but all may not have been lost for Krupp and his friends. They had managed to turn President Woodrow Wilson's idea of 'peace without victory' after the First World War to their advantage and their use of 'slave' and indentured labour during the war had made them potentially far richer at the end the Second. Despite their shattered cities, they felt that there was still hope for the future.

On 10th October 1944, there was a meeting at the Rotes Haus, the famous old hotel in Strasbourg, which was in German hands. Among those present were representatives from Krupp, Rheinmetall, Volkswagen, and othermajor companies.

The SS Obergruppenführer, Dr. Scheid, who presided, outlined how the Nazi empire could survive defeat. He stated that all the industrial material in France should be evacuated to Germany immediately. From now on German industry should realize that the war could not be won and take steps in preparation for a post-war commercial campaign. Each industrialist should make contacts and alliances with foreign firms, but this should be done individually and without attracting any suspicion.

As examples Dr Scheid cited the fact that patents for stainless steel belonged to the Chemical Foundation Inc. and the Krupp company jointly. US Steel Corporation, Carnegie Illinois, American Steel and Wire, and National Tube ec., were thereby under an obligation to work with the Krupp concern. He also cited Zeiss Company, the Leisa Company and the Hamburg-American Line as firms which had been especially effective in protecting German interests abroad and gave their New York addresses to the industrialists.

The German industrialists were already increasing their patent registrations,[637] and placing their funds in neutral countries, (especially Spain), through the offices of the Basler Handelsbank and the Schweizer Kreditanstalt of Zuric. Dr. Scheid also stressed that the ground must be laid for borrowing considerable sums from foreign countries after the war.

Following this meeting a smaller pivotal meeting was held, presided over by Dr. Bosse of the German armaments industry, and attended by representatives from Krupp, Hecho and Rochling. At this meeting it was stated that, although the war was practically lost, the Nazi Party would continue fighting until a guarantee of the unity of Germany could be obtained.

One week later, on 18th October, Adolf Hitler officially announced the existence of the Volkssturm[638] comprising the elderly from all walks of life, those previously considered unfit for military service, former industrial workers, and teenagers. It was decided that each Nazi Party district leader, or Gauleiter, would be instructed to instil the Volkssturm with fanaticism. Newspapers would spread the word, not only of the Red Army's atrocities but also of atrocities committed by the Americans, (with their black troops portrayed as the culprits) and the members of the *Volkssturm's* fighting spirit would also be stiffened by the Hitler Youth and regular soldiers.

On 16th September Hitler had already declared that 'every block of houses in every German city, and every town, must become a fortress on which the enemy is either bled to death or in which its defences are buried beneath (the rubble) in man- to- man combat.'[639] By February 1945 even women and girls were conscripted to join and given instructions on the use of small-arms, bazookas, machine guns and hand grenades.[640]

The Volkssturm's losses were appalling. German military historian, Rüdiger Overmans, concluded that approximately 1.23 million German military personnel (including Volkssturm men, who suffered more than fifty per cent of the entire military losses) would die in the final four months of the war. Nevertheless, higher level Nazi politicians and corporate banking leaders and their children were not required to serve in the Volkssturm; nor were the offspring of leading industrialists like the Krupp family.[641]

Industrial representatives at the Red House were also told that they should increase post-war exports and prepare themselves to finance the Nazi Party, which would be forced to go underground. The government had accumulated large reserves from appropriating gold, raw materials, and foreign reserves and 'occupation costs' from invaded countries. From now until the end of the war it promised to allocate large sums to the industrialists so that they could establish secure post-war foundations in foreign countries.

The armaments factories were asked to create small high-tech research bureaux which could be absolutely, independent and have no known connection with the factory. They would receive plans and drawings of new weapons as well as documents which they would need to continue their research. They were to be established in large cities where they could be most successfully hidden, as well as in little villages near sources of hydro-electric power, where they could pretend to be studying the development of water resources.

The existence of these research institutes, producing rockets and bombs, was to be known only by a few in each industry, to avoid them falling into enemy hands.[642]

Unfortunately, for Hitler, his research units produced their results too late. On 13th June 1944, at Hitler's order, the first ten V-1 rockets were catapulted into the air with the aim of reaching London. Their fuel was designed to run out when they met their destination, then they would collapse and explode.

Their sudden arrival produced an alarming psychological effect. Hitler was delighted and ordered a massive increase in production. In total, 22,384 V-1s were launched but most failed to reach their target. Some were shot down by fighter planes and anti-aircraft fire. Others ran out of fuel. Fewer than 6,000 fell on Britain and they failed to cause the misery and despair which had been planned.[643]

The V-2 rocket was the world's first long-range guided missile. Twelve thousand forced labourers were reportedly killed in the effort to bring it into production. It had a range of 200 miles, was almost impossible to detect and would fall on its target at 4000 miles an hour. However, it was not ready to attack Paris and London until September 1944. When Germany collapsed, teams from the US, Britain and Russia would race to capture the key manufacturing sites.

In 1938 Göring had declared that he planned to construct rockets to launch against the 'arrogant people' in the United States. By January 1945, the A-9 had its maiden flight. It climbed vertically until it reached a speed of 2,700 miles per hour and an altitude of fifty miles. However, as it came back down through the upper atmosphere a wing tore off and it tumbled down to earth. Nevertheless, the technicians were delighted with its performance. All they needed was time and the rocket could be perfected and directed anywhere thousands of miles away. It was nicknamed 'American Rocket'[644] but there was no time to send it to the eastern seaboard of America.

Yet, the research that the Americans and the Russians were most interested in after the war was Germany's nuclear weapon development programme. In 2005 a book would be published by a German historian claiming that Germany tested a 'small atom bomb' in 1945. This claim was vehemently refuted in the press, but it was widely believed that 'during the last months of the war, a small group of scientists working in secret under the nuclear scientist Kurt Diebner, and with the strong support of the physicist Walter Gerlach, '... built and tested 'a nuclear device.'[645] Germany would exact a huge price from America for not allowing it to develop its own nuclear weapons in the coming years.

Meanwhile, Alfried Krupp managed to jettison his war bonds, and collect his outstanding debts from the Reich. Altogether 162,000,000,000 marks of what would become worthless paper[646] was sold off as Alfried squirrelled his cash abroad. Other industrialists were encouraged to do the same.

Sadly, with the ending of the war approaching, the unity of purpose between America and the Allies crumbled. In 1918 President Woodrow Wilson had not viewed the British as his cousins, nor believed that the British Empire was a force for peace in the world. So, he had advocated the principle of 'self-determination' for nations, believing that they could stand on their own two feet without being herded into old-fashioned empires.

Wilson's principle of 'self-determination' based on language has become the source for countless nations, large and small, to achieve their dream of statehood since that time. With the ending of the Second World War the Americans believed that Wilson's principle of 'self-determination' should be sacrosanct, which would lead to the demise of the Allied Empires.

The American isolationists also remembered that the British did not repay all their First World War debts and blamed them for their misery and unemployment in the 1930s. They did not realize that their friends and cousins in Germany had wilfully impoverished them in the Great Depression, and that millions of slave labourers from Russia, Ukraine, Poland, and all over Europe, had died in German concentration camps as well as six million Jews.

They also conveniently forgot that, had Wilson charged Germany indemnities in 1918, instead of trusting the Germans to pay reparations and wriggling out of them by pleading their innocence of starting the conflict, their war debts and their sovereign debts would have been paid, and Hitler would have been unable to spend 48,911 billion Reichsmarks on preparing for war.

Some Americans actively disliked the sanctimonious British and believed, like Harold Russell, (who would portray a vet who lost both hands in the war in the film *Best Years of our Lives*), that 'The Germans and Japs had nothing against us. They just wanted to fight the Limeys, (a derogative term for the British) and the Reds.' So, whereas in 1940 Admiral Raeder had envisaged Britain having to share her empire with America after the Second World War, with Britain as the junior partner, many Americans believed by 1945 that the British Empire was past its 'sell-by' date. It was high time that the British and other European empires were extinguished altogether under the principle of 'self-determination.'

The 'Prussians,' on the other hand, did believe in empires. That was why they had started two world wars, to achieve *Mitteleuropa* and Lebensraum. Despite the ravages brought about by Allied bombing, Germany could yet rise like a phoenix from the ashes if allowed to retain the coal-rich Ruhr. In 1942, Reich Minister for Economic Affairs, Walter Funk, (who would later be indicted at Nuremberg), had stated his ambition for a *Mitteleuropa*-type empire in Europe, declaring: 'Only on the foundation of such a European economic area can Europe really win the battle against Bolshevism and Americanism.'

However, many Americans started to worry more about the threat from Stalinist Russia, than about the embers of Nazi-ism in Hitler's Germany. Other influential American businessmen, whose trade was inextricably tied up with German industry in patents and licence accords, agreed.

In 1945, the Soviet army came crashing through the Berlin suburbs. The Russian soldiers were astonished at the wealth they saw there. The abandoned furniture, well stocked libraries, and pavements neatly planted with trees, begged the question as to why the German army had invaded 'impoverished downtrodden Russia'[647] in the first place. They responded with enthusiasm to Stalin's encouragement 'to rape and pillage' the country's former tormentors. Allegedly close to 100,000 German women were raped after the Russians invaded.[648] The German military/industrial leadership had been preparing to lay all the blame for the carnage and atrocities of the Second World War on Hitler alone, but now there was another monster to share the blame, Stalin.

CHAPTER TEN

Who Won the Peace after the Second World War?

In October 1918, at the end of the First World War, the *Boston Herald* pleaded for President Wilson to demand the German army's 'unconditional surrender', asserting; 'Unconditional surrender is not alone the sole course for us, but it is the best for our enemies. The German people and their rulers must trust to the magnanimity of the Allies. The hour of reckoning has come, and the reckoning cannot be a matter of bargain and sale.'

On 7th May 1945, at the end of the Second World War, America and the Allies secured the German army's 'unconditional surrender.' The Americans now felt that they could give Germany the sort of magnanimous peace that they believed the Allies failed to give at Versailles, but a lot of water had passed under the bridge since the *Boston Herald* made its plea for 'unconditional surrender' in 1918.

Germany had not been weak and the victim of injustice after the Treaty of Versailles, but strong and recalcitrant. Equipped with a powerful industrial base, propaganda, guile and ruthless economic manipulation, the German military/industrial clique had managed to reduce their enemies to poverty and live to fight another day. Adolf Hitler had elevated being 'German', and part of the 'Master Race', to the status of a religion and not only killed people on the battlefield but systematically tried to exterminate the Jewish race, and millions of Poles Russians and Gypsies too. Was there any hope for Germany after its soldiers were defeated in 1945?

Admiral Canaris, Chief of the Intelligence Division of the German High Command, termed the Abwehr, told his superiors in 1944, that there was still hope for Germany, even after a crushing military defeat because of the good will felt towards them amongst the previous isolationist Americans, who had campaigned against Germany joining the war. However, he also felt that Germany could come to an agreement with Russia, declaring: '... we must assume that the Slavs will do everything in order to retaliate against the harsh treatment that we have inflicted upon them. In spite of everything, no effort should be spared to stir up, through carefully directed propaganda, political animosity inside the Anglo-Saxon countries which would enrage the Soviets to such a degree that, as a consequence, they would welcome a chance to conclude a separate peace with Germany....

'In the event of a negotiated peace, or should we be defeated, Germany would have everything to gain – in the long run – by joining the East.'[649]

German heavy industry had a long association with the Bolsheviks. In 1918 the German leadership declared: 'The Bolsheviks are a very evil and antipathetic people. Nevertheless, politics have always been utilitarian and will be so for a long time.' In the 1920s Krupp had assisted Lenin's regime in return for Lenin allowing the German army to secretly train on the Russian steppes. In the 1930s he had helped Stalin modernize his economy and armaments system; Germany and the Soviet Union had also been partners between 1939 and 1941.

In the last desperate battles of the Second World War old men and boys had been dying in Hitler's *Volkssturm*, but the nation's industrial leaders remained confident about the future. The country remained the world's third strongest industrial power through its use of slave labour and the organized looting of occupied countries. It had also secreted vast sums abroad through bearer shares in holding companies, which could only be traced with immense difficulty.[650]

Germany had rescued industrial victory from military defeat after the First World War and hoped to do so again. A political deal with the Soviets was not a serious option but it could be used as a negotiating tool. Nevertheless, Admiral Canaris had thought that Germany could still secure a favourable deal with America, declaring: 'There is great fear in the USA of Bolshevism. The opposition against Roosevelt's alliance with Stalin grows constantly. Our chances for success are good, if we succeed to stir up influential circles against Roosevelt's policy of allying America with the Communists.... The campaign of hatred stirred up by Roosevelt ... against everything German has temporarily silenced the pro-German bloc in the U.S.A. However, there is every hope that this situation will be completely changed within a few months.' 651

President Roosevelt died on 12th April 1945. On 8th May new American President, Harry S Truman, had a very, special celebration for his birthday. VE Day was the public holiday to mark the 'unconditional surrender' of the Nazi forces in Germany. 8

By 11th May 1945, Otto A Friedrich, wartime Deputy Reich Plenipotentiary for Rubber, and soon to become an influential spokesman for West German industry, wrote confidently in his diary, 'the latent tension between Russia and the Western powers provides us with the opportunity to work our way up to the status of a new subject.' 652

In contrast to Roosevelt, who came from a wealthy, 2privileged background, Harry S Truman was a plain-speaking man from Independence, Missouri, who had spent much of his youth as a dirt-poor farmer on family land that was later repossessed by the bank. A snappy dresser, who always wore a double-breasted, light-coloured suit, he disliked the 'snobbery' of the smooth Ivy League officials ... particularly those from the Foreign Service, (who might have been more pro-British). He called them – 'the men in striped pants.'653

Unfortunately, the British were 'America's least trusted ally' after the Second World War. German publicist Viereck's assertion that Britain's non-payment of war debts had been responsible for the United States' penury in the Great Depression - rather than the ugly truth that it was Germany's determination to impoverish America by reneging on all her financial obligations – had caught the former isolationists' imagination.

The isolationists, including those of German ancestry who had sympathised with Germany during the war, embittered Irish/Americans who supported the Irish government's decision to bar the 4,983 Irish men who had fought with the British from receiving jobs and state pensions afterwards,654 also the many ordinary people who had lost their savings in Great Depression, blamed Britain for their subsequent misfortunes. This was not surprising as they had been told by the McCormick and Patterson press, 'and to a lesser extent by the Hearst newspapers, during the conflict, 'that America was fighting an unnecessary war against other white people on behalf of the ungrateful British and the un-American Jews.'[655] 8

The British would be made to pay their Second World War debts until the last penny was paid in 2006 while the isolationists even accused Roosevelt of manipulating America into the war by encouraging the Japanese to attack Pearl Harbor.[656]

William Shirer in his *Rise and Fall of the Third Reich* reveals that Japan's explosive attack need not necessarily have precipitated a full-scale war between Germany and America, finding a 'strong feeling in both Houses as well as in the Army and Navy that the country ought to concentrate its efforts on defeating Japan and not take on the additional burden of fighting Germany at the same time.'[657]

No-one seemed to have told them that it was that it was Hitler who had brought America into the war by declaring war against America. He would his cronies in 1942, 'It's a decayed country. ... My feelings against Americanism are feelings of hatred and deep repugnance.'

How far his sentiments were common to other Nazis is difficult to assess. It is certain that he shared many Germans belief that his country had been robbed of victory in 1918. He (and Japan) had also been fooled by America's poverty in the 1930s. Finally, he had fatally underestimated her fighting ability as well as her latent industrial and military might because of her army's failures at Meuse Argonne.

Unfortunately, the Americans were blissfully unaware of the measures that Germany had taken to bankrupt America in the 1930s, and seemingly even that she had declared war against America. They would heap blame on Britain for 'starving' the German people during Germany's great inflation after the war and Britain was ordered to pay her war debts until the bitter end in 2006. Lend-lease was also cancelled almost as soon as Truman came to power, with Britain's *Economist* lamenting 'to find that the result of losing at least a quarter of our national wealth in the common cause is to pay tribute for half a century to those who have been enriched by war.'[658]

In the autumn of 1945 John Maynard Keynes, who had been elevated to become a Lord, was sent to America to secure a loan for Britain. Lord Keynes insisted that withou8t help, and a lot of it, 'we have not a hope of escaping what might be considered, without exaggeration, a financial Dunkirk.'659

Keynes believed that he would be warmly welcomed in Washington, even though his impertinent and incorrect comments about President Woodrow Wilson being 'led by the nose' by British Prime Minister, Lloyd George, at the Versailles Conference660 had been bandied about in the 1920 American Presidential elections and grated on Americans ever since. Indeed, Keynes's statement that 'The poor President would be playing blind man's 'buff' at Versailles' could have been one of the reasons why the Americans had been so insistent on blaming the Allies rather than President Wilson for the defects of the Treaty.

Keynes asked for an interest free loan of $3.5 billion. However, he ultimately agreed to pay $3.75 billion at two per cent interest over fifty years, with the small print revealing that Britain must forgo its system of 'imperial preferences' which bound the Empire together to secure the money. Keynes also accepted that the repayment should be fixed in dollars, and that sterling must become a freely convertible currency within a year of the loan being agreed. Britain was aghast at the terms.

Lord Beaverbrook, a tough negotiator, who was Canadian by birth, and a firm believer in the Commonwealth, contended that Britain did not need the loan. He argued that Canada and the rest of the empire could provide the raw materials that Britain required and nearly caused a constitutional crisis between the House of Lords and the Commons over the issue.661

Another problem was Keynes' undertaking to repay in dollars. A nation at the centre of an empire like Britain could not wipe out its savers and indulge in a Great Inflation like Germany. However, every country had to have a little inflation after a Great War. It would have been much more sensible for Keynes to advise the socialist government to bow to the inevitable, and devalue the pound in 1945, instead of going cap in hand to America.662 As it was, there would soon be a 'run on the pound', leading to a thirty per cent devaluation of sterling in 1949. So, the American loan would ultimately become increasingly costly and lead to Britain losing her valuable ties with her empire.

Truman was acutely suspicious of Britain but looked forward to meeting Joseph Stalin, whose soldiers' valiant efforts, and enormous sacrifice of life, had driven the defeated German soldiers back to their homeland.

The Second World War had aged Stalin. At sixty-seven years old he looked shorter than his five feet four inches and had developed a paunch that was not entirely hidden by the baggy trousers and grey square-cut tunics that hung loosely around his body. He lost his temper more frequently and his formerly amber eyes lit up in a 'flash of menace and fury' when he heard something which displeased him. However, he still had a phenomenal memory and was a formidable negotiator. 663

Truman's meeting with Russia and Britain was a disappointment. Truman protested that 'Russia had no program except to take over the free part of Europe, (and) kill as many Germans as possible' while complaining that 'Britain wanted keep India, oil in Persia, the Suez Canal, and whatever else was floating loose.'

In contrast, Truman regarded himself as 'an innocent idealist ... who wanted free waterways, Danube-Rhine-Kiel Canal, Suez, Black Sea Straits, Panama, and a restoration of Germany ...' and other European and Asian states. 'But' he declared, 'a large number of agreements were reached with Stalin, only to be broken as soon as the unconscionable Russian Dictator returned to Moscow!'664

It would be easy for America to destroy the British Empire, although America would diminish her own power and influence in the process. However, Truman quickly discovered the threat that Stalin posed. By July 1945, Stalin effectively controlled the Baltic states; Poland, Czechoslovakia, Hungary, Bulgaria, and Romania, and was busy installing Communist regimes in his new Realm.

Although Stalin aimed to quell post-war internal dissent over the shattered state of post-war Russia by mass liquidations, if necessary, in the newly occupied countries he applied a softly, softly approach. In East Germany local mayors could be 'bourgeois' or Social Democrats, but their deputies must be 'loyal and report to the Communist Party' while in Poland he told the Premier, Gomulka, 'You must move towards Socialism not directly but in zigzags and roundabout ways.'665

On 10th May 1945 Truman signed the US occupation directive JCS. The integrity of the German

Reich would be respected, and states like Bavaria forced to stay glued to Prussia, but the US occupation forces were ordered to take 'no steps towards the economic rehabilitation of Germany.' However, sentiment soon altered. The Potsdam Conference agreed upon 'the elimination or control of all German industry that could be used for military production' but turned a deaf ear to France's plea that the Ruhr, which contained so many of Germany's immensely valuable industries, should be internationalized.

Although the Ruhr was only about fifteen miles wide by forty long, it contained almost all Germany's coal mines, also nearly all its iron and steel industries and a large proportion of its engineering plants, including Krupps at Essen. It had received massive waves of bombing during the war. Nevertheless, according to a visiting American economics professor I G Farben's three largest factories were 'almost untouched.' Due to the 'surprisingly good conditions' of the Krupp plants in the centre of ruined Essen and in the suburb of Borbeck, the professor also believed in the Krupp director's assertion that he could raise the steel production to two-thirds or more of Krupp's war production.'[666]

Coal was still the energy source of the age. Whoever owned coal could potentially become immensely wealthy. Germany had traditionally been one of the world's largest coal and coke exporters[667] but for now restrictions were placed upon coal production and distribution.

Stalin's retribution in the area his troops occupied in Eastern Germany was swift. Between 1945 and 1946 he took half a billion dollars-worth of factories and equipment from his zone as war reparations. The skilled technicians and managers of the plants were also taken to Russia. Under the Potsdam agreement Stalin was also allowed ten per cent of the war reparations taken from the Allies' zone in return for sending coal, wood, and food from the bread-basket areas of East Germany. However, in 1946 Stalin stopped delivering coal and agricultural goods to the West.[668] American opposition to him increased. In 1946, the American Joint Chiefs of Staff declared that 'the complete revival of German industry, particularly coal mining is now of primary importance to American security.'

After the war German coal production had plunged. West Germany and all the countries dependent on its coal in Western Europe were thrown into darkness; but now production was permitted to increase. Secretary of State, James F. Byrnes, who was accused by Truman of 'babying up to the Soviets'[669] reassured the West Germans: 'Our Security forces will probably have to remain in Germany for a long period. I want no misunderstanding. We will not shirk our duty. We are not withdrawing. We are here to stay.'[670]

Encouraged by this turn of events, German heavy industry spokesman Otto A Friedrich, raised the question as to whether it would not be better for Germany 'to come out openly *in favour* of the West's political aims and to clarify, slowly but determinedly, the preconditions of such an alliance, and to put demands accordingly.'[671]

The human tragedy of the war in Germany was immense; bombed-out cities, millions of homeless, sickness hunger and despair. Yet, William I Clayton had reported to the US Senate that there had been a 'flight of capital in anticipation of defeat' and that the Nazis 'have made strenuous efforts to move abroad assets of all kinds' while Senator Kilgore asserted darkly that Germany not only was the world's 'the third largest industrial economy', but also was 'better prepared to implement her plot for world conquest than she was at the end of the First World War.'[672] German industrial capacity was estimated to be eleven per cent higher in 1947 than in Hitler's Reich in 1936.[673] When German industry's funds were finally repatriated they could help restore power the country to greatness again.

Daimler-Benz, which employed thousands of slave labourers during the war, had been shattered by Allied bombing, but Volkswagen had suffered only surface damage and Krupp was poised to export household goods. In 1937 Volkswagen had the largest press shop in Europe and 2,700 of the finest specialized tools. Three Allied bombing raids against the strategically vulnerable Volkswagen plant at Wolfsburg had resulted in only superficial damage. A clever scheme in which the roof was deliberately damaged in non-essential areas to give the aerial appearance of destruction, deceived the Allies. With the help of British military engineers, it was soon in production again and allowed to become the sole supplier of vehicles to the occupation authorities.[674] Soon, however, the British were subject to odium in the German press.

In 1945, sixty-nine-year-old, wiry, Catholic Rhinelander Konrad Adenauer was asked by the Americans to resume his former Weimar Republic job as Burgomaster of the City of Cologne. A few months later he was dismissed by the British authorities. Sir John Barraclough, a Midlands industrialist who, as 'Brigadier Barraclough', did the actual sacking, revealed why:

The devastation in Cologne was almost indescribable. Public transport was non-existent. Electricity and gas supplies had broken down. The navigation channel of the Rhine, one of the main arteries of communication, was completely blocked. The sewers were open. Thousands of Germans were starving. Hundreds of thousands of refugees were moving on the roads. I arranged a meeting with Adenauer. We met in the office of the local commander in Cologne. ... Although I was impressed by his personality, I freely admit that I did not realize that I was face to face with a man who was to become one of Europe's leading politicians. ...I did my best to impress upon Adenauer the desperate urgency of the problems facing us and appealed to him to cooperate. His immediate reaction was to show me an album of drawings entitled 'The Cologne of the Future,' or something to that effect. Apparently, he thought it impracticable to rebuild the city on the existing site. His plan was to build a new Cologne outside the boundaries of the old city. We talked for the best part of two hours but made no progress. Surrounded by the chaos I have described here we had the senior p8aid administrative official with his head well in the clouds. With great reluctance, I decided that for the good of his own people he would have to go.'[675]

Maybe Dr. Adenauer knew that the German industrialists had millions secreted abroad, or perhaps sympathetic Americans had already offered help with rebuilding his shattered city [676] At all events, Adenauer made much of the iniquity of his removal from his position. He voiced his animosity towards the British, and to Social Democracy, and in no time at all he was made Chairman of the Conservative Christian Democratic Union, the second largest political party in Germany. The Americans were happy with Konrad Adenauer's political advancement.

Dr. Adenauer was a Conservative. There was not a whiff of Socialism about him. Meanwhile the 'Reds' seemed to be creeping up all over Europe. The American Republican Party not only objected to Britain's overseas empire, but also to the new British Labour Government's socialist policies at home.

The Labour Government had imaginative social welfare plans, including instituting a National Health Service. However, its ambition to nationalize the key industries of the post-war economy, such as the Bank of England, the fuel and power industries, inland transport, and iron and steel, brought horror into American hearts. They were frightened of 'Reds under the bed' at home and warm to 'der Alte,' (the old one), as Adenauer was affectionately called, with his resolute anti-socialist rhetoric and his firm stance against communism.

President Truman had been shocked by his meeting with Stalin. He consulted his Russian expert, George F Kennan.[677] George Kennan had investigated Stalin's great purge between 1936 and 1938 and believed that the only solution to prevent Stalin taking over the whole of Europe was to determine a demarcation line that the Soviets could not cross without risking war.

8On 12th March 1947 Truman made a pledge to support Greece and Turkey from falling into the Soviet sphere, stating that it was 'the policy of the United States to support free people who are resisting attempted subjugation by armed minorities or by outside persons.' In June 1947, Secretary of State George C Marshall proposed to widen America's assistance to give his so-called Marshall Plan money to all the devastated regions of Europe, the proviso being that they should use the funds to buy goods from America.[678]

The Marshall Plan was a brilliant concept to help the poor countries of Europe, without impoverishing the United States. America's goals were to rebuild war-devastated regions, remove trade barriers, modernize industry, and make Europe prosperous again.

One of America's gnawing anxieties had been to avoid the dreadful unemployment she suffered in the 1930s and to guarantee a trade surplus with the rest of the world. Every country benefitted from the Marshall Plan, but Britain was granted the greatest largesse. However, in practice the clause in the Marshall Plan that Britain should purchase her raw materials, (except oil), from the US was a further nail in the coffin of Britain's trade with her traditional suppliers in Canada and the Empire.

Twenty-six per cent of the Marshall Plan was allocated for Britain, eighteen per cent for France but West Germany had not been forgotten either. She was to receive sixteen per cent of the funds. However, General Marshall was frustrated. The ungrateful Germans were creating difficulties. He declared: '(German) recovery has been retarded by the fact that two years after the close of hostilities a peace settlement with Germany and Austria has not been agreed upon. ....'679 Otto A Friedrich and his friends in heavy industry had 'come out openly in favour of the West's political aims and (were putting) slowly but determinedly, the preconditions of such an alliance.'

Meanwhile inflation soared in Germany and the human toll of German misery mounted. Trainloads of penniless people fled from the communist zone to the West, clinging to the roofs of trains and between the carriages. Although Germany's breadbasket areas were in Soviet occupied Poland and East Germany, desperate people streamed to the Ruhr to seek work away from Communist oppression.

Faced with little food and stacks of extra mouths to feed, the British set the daily ration at 1,125 calories in their zone of occupation. They were lastingly castigated for their inhumanity in setting the daily food ration so low. In 1947 Europe had one of her vilest winters in a century. In the early months of the year, they were accused of reducing the German peoples' rations to between 700-800 calories per day for those not engaged in heavy labour. It was asserted that if the German population did not actually die of starvation on that amount of food, it would perish from disease and malnutrition.

The British had also had their meagre food rations slashed since the war ended. The average adult allowances for food had fallen to thirteen ounces of meat, one and a half ounces of cheese, six ounces of butter and margarine, plus one ounce of cooking fat, two pints of milk and one egg a week. However, stirred by the writings, amongst others, of left-wing publisher, Victor Gollancz, Britain dug into her empty pockets to buy extra food for Germany. Chancellor of the Exchequer, Hugh Dalton, was persuaded, extremely reluctantly, to spend £82 million to feed the starving German people but he declared of the gift: 'What we are doing amounts, essentially, to us paying reparations to the Germans.'680

Millions of Americans, from Quakers to trade unionists, also rose to the challenge to feed the German people. The first shipment contained 2.8 million packets of cheese, coffee, flour, sugar, cocoa, chocolate, and powdered milk but the situation was still dire. The currency reduced was to wastepaper in value while hundreds of thousands of people allegedly died from starvation and cold, including victims frozen to death in their beds.'681 West Germany was suffering from another Great Inflation similar to the one she had suffered in 1923. Mr. John Hynd, the British Minister responsible for Germany, later declared: 'It was a matter of days whether twenty-three million people were going to starve in the streets.'682

Eventually, Ludwig Erhard, the recently appointed director of economics of the Bizonal Economic Council, solved the problem. In June 1948, the worthless Reichsmark was removed and replaced by the Deutschmark. Suddenly people could buy delicacies that they had only dreamed of in the past three years. Bakeries produced and displayed delicious cakes, and masses of vegetables, butter and eggs appeared in the shops. More goodies appeared the next day and the next. Clothes and hardware, even silk stockings.683 It was a miracle! Or had it been contrived with the purpose of wiping out Germany's internal debts and to 'teach the German people how to work'?

In 1950, the Madrid Geo-Political Centre, (a Nazi think tank operating in exile after the war in Spain), revealed in its Secret Circular Letter that it sent to influential like-minded people all over the world, that the malnutrition and cold that the German people suffered in the Ruhr in 1947 was not due to the inhumanity of the British occupation authorities but was a deliberate ploy of the industrialists and their Nazi friends, stating: 'In order to bring the Americans back to reason ... we organized chaotic conditions in a thorough and systematic manner. ... The peasants were delivering next to nothing to the cities; no coal was brought up from the pits, the wheels of industry were not turning, the people came near to starvation; the monetary systems were disintegrating –

there was nothing for the Yankees to do but to give in and abandon the Potsdam programme.'684

To many this assertion may seem far-fetched. However, it has recently been discovered that Erhard had envisaged wiping out the currency as far back as 1943. He had been part of a panel of experts assembled on Hitler's orders by SS-Gruppenführer Otto Ohlendorf, at a time when the Nazis were already running out of money and kept going only by printing bank notes. After the war Erhard decided to implement the plan. In 1948, when the currency was finally reduced to wastepaper, private savers received an exchange rate of 15:1, while business assets were converted at 1:1. 'Thus, the cash savings of ordinary people were virtually destroyed but business capital was saved.'

After the stabilization of the currency, there was still widespread hardship in Germany. An American colonel criticised Chancellor Erhard for relaxing America's rationing system when there was still a 'widespread shortage of food.'

Erhard replied: 'But Colonel, I have not relaxed rationing, I have abolished it! Now, the only coupon people need is the Deutschmark. And they will work hard to get those Deutschmarks, just you wait and see.' The shop floor had been taught 'how to work in the same fashion as after Germany's Great Inflation in 1923 685

The adoption of the Deutschmark in June 1948 and the arrival of Marshall Aid a month later had far reaching results for the Soviet Union. Although Marshall Aid was available to all the devastated areas of Europe, Stalin was not happy for any his satellite states, which include Poland, Hungary, and Czechoslovakia, to receive it. Many people had believed that it was the Communist economic system, rather than the armaments and heavy industrial base that Germany and America had sold Stalin - and Stalin's giant will - that had enabled him to triumph over Hitler. He had promoted the benefits of communism to the rest of Europe and nations were warming towards it - but the small print disclosed that Marshall Aid would only be available to countries with an 'open-market capitalist system.' So, Stalin forbade Eastern bloc countries from accepting it.

Naturally, this made Stalin highly unpopular, especially in Czechoslovakia, where he had to resort to supporting a brutal *coup d'état* in 1948 to maintain order. The arrival of the Deutschmark was an even greater, permanent threat to his new empire. It had been blessed by the Americans. They had even printed the bank notes. The Deutschmark's arrival would mean a massive exodus of funds from the impoverished Soviet zone of Berlin to the American and Allied zones.

The day after the 18th of June announcement of the Deutschmark, Soviet guards halted all passenger trains and traffic on the autobahn to Berlin. On 22nd June, the Soviets announced that they would introduce a new currency in their areas of occupation in Germany, the Ostmark. On 25th June, the Soviets stopped supplying food and coal to the civilian population in the non-Soviet sectors of Berlin. The Americans declared: 'We are convinced that our remaining in Berlin is essential to our prestige in Germany and in Europe ... it has become a symbol of the American intent.' It was a brave decision. By 1948 there were only 31,000 American combat troops left in West Germany and only 8,973 American, 7,606 British and 6,100 French troops in West Berlin. Meanwhile the Soviets had one and half million troops surrounding the city.

America and the Allies decided to defy the blockade by flying food and coal into their beleaguered sector of Berlin. Aircrews from the Anglo-Saxon countries, America, Britain, Australia, Canada, New Zealand, and South Africa flew 200,000 flights in a year to Berlin. Eventually, Stalin gave in. The Soviet blockade was lifted a minute after midnight on 12th May 1949 and the trains started running again. The costs of the blockade were shared between America Germany and Britain.

America had won a great victory for the Deutschmark, for West Germany and for capitalism. West Berlin remained part of West Germany, 160 kilometres inside East Germany's borders. Between 1945 and 1946, the Western Allies, but primarily America, had contributed $700 million to their zones of occupation in West Germany.[686] Between 1948 and 1951, under the terms of the Marshall Plan, the United States gave about $13 billion to all the Western European countries. No-one in Western Europe should ever forget the assistance that America gave them after the Second World War.

In 1949 seventy-three-year-old Konrad Adenauer was elected Chancellor of Germany by one vote over Kurt Schumacher, his Social Democrat rival. The American leadership breathed a sigh of relief. Schumacher had excellent qualifications to become Chancellor of Germany. He had spent over ten years in Nazi concentration camps before and during the war, and had labelled the Communists, 'red-painted Nazis.' However, since the war he had campaigned against Allied and American propaganda to impose 'collective guilt' on the German people for the Nazi atrocities against the Jews,[687] advocating the nationalization of heavy industry, on the grounds that its funding had enabled the Nazis to achieve power. The Americans smelled a whiff of socialism about Schumacher's campaign, so they backed Adenauer instead.

Adenauer was a devoted Catholic and Rhinelander and was always impeccably dressed, despite his age. During the Second World War the Nazis had accused him of having formerly advocated separatism for the Rhineland and locked him up in a Gestapo prison, where he had to endure listening to the screams of those being tortured below. Eventually, Adenauer's soldier son managed to secure his release. Adenauer declared that there were two Germanys: 'the Germany which is fundamentally based on the Roman cultural inheritance, and the Germany of Prussia, which imposed its own will.'

In the years before Adenauer's election, he had made many memorable comments, including telling the British that the greatest mistake they had made was 'at the Congress of Vienna, when you foolishly put Prussia on the Rhine as a safeguard against France and another Napoleon', and that 'Prussianism in its turn culminated in National Socialism.' After he became Chancellor, his tone slightly changed because he had to represent all the people in his party, including the former Nationalists, (and Pan-Germans), who were in heavy industry, and those who were former Nazis.

After being imprisoned twice, Adenauer did not believe the post-war Nazis to be a serious threat despite his denazification law of 1951 pardoning 792,176 people, including 3,000 functionaries of the SA and SS, who had participated in deporting victims to prison camps, and 30,000 other Nazis sentenced for murder. One could not lock people up for ever. Besides, Adenauer concluded, there were able people, who he could use, among those indicted.

Adenauer had a simple formula for former Nazis whose services he wished to use in government. He was willing to have them in his administration, but it was made clear to them that if they crossed him, they could expect their case of denazification to be re-opened. Indeed, his aide, Hans Globke, had been largely responsible, in 1935, for the official commentary on the infamous Nuremberg Laws, which classified people as Jewish if they had three or four Jewish grandparents or Mischling, (mixed race), if they had one or two. The law prohibited the two groups from marrying a German and deprived them of German citizenship.

Globke was, however, exonerated at his denazification trial on the grounds of the 'administrative pressure' put on officials who were not members of the Nazi Party. Indeed, Adenauer denounced the denazification process on the grounds that it sought to punish all the millions of unfortunate Germans who had lived under the Nazi regime and were now Christian Democrat voters. He viewed the Nazis as a small criminal gang, who were now all conveniently dead, with the mass of their supporters being people whom Hitler had tricked into following him.

For this reason, Adenauer insisted that a Memorial Day should be set aside for the victims of National Socialism, provided that the Memorial Day included all the Germans killed by Allied bombing and the German soldiers fighting in the Wehrmacht and in the Waffen SS.

The only German soldiers that Adenauer failed to mention in his Memorial Day were the members of the country's 'Dad's Army', the Volkssturm, which consisted not only of the old, but former industrial workers, the very, young and the injured. The Volkssturm was raised in the last few months of the war, after the armaments' manufacturers had agreed that the military situation looked hopeless. They had suffered over 600,000 deaths but received no mention.

By 2013, the British historian Richard Overy, would revise down the figure of civilians killed by Allied bombing from 600,000 to 353,000, with *Der Spiegel* concluding that no more than 18,000 to 25,000 were killed at Dresden.[688] These were still huge numbers, compared to the roughly

43,000 initially killed by German bombing of British cities during the Blitz of 1940-1941.

Nevertheless, the Allies were certain that the Germans would have obliterated their own cities if they could. Indeed, many emaciated forced labourers and slaves were hung at the V 2 armaments camps at the Dora-Nordhausen-Mittelwerk complex as late as March 1945 for trying to thwart the Nazi's missile programme to destroy Allied cities. If Adenauer wanted to include the German military and Waffen SS killed by Allied bombing in his memorial, he should have included the Volksturm and the six million forced labourers and slaves who worked and died in the Nazi's huge factories and underground complexes during the war, and those who died trying to prevent the mass destruction of their own cities in Allied countries in the final days of the conflict.

Indeed, Adenauer's insistence on setting up a Memorial Day on his own terms, showed just how powerful West Germany had already become since the war. Largely pastoral East Germany may have been occupied by the Soviet Union, but West Germany had extinguished her internal debts, largely kept her coal, steel and chemical empire in the Ruhr and gone on the offensive. The Ruhr industrialists were now accompanying their protests, against paying war reparations, with a huge propaganda campaign against the Allied dismantling of West Germany's heavy machinery, declaring that the Allies' attempts to secure reparations were motivated by feelings of revenge such as had motivated the Allies after the Treaty of Versailles. [689] And they had friends in America too.

American historian Harry Elmer Barnes, whose history of the origins of the First World War called *The Genesis of War*, had become almost a bible in the 1930s had eventually decided historians had suppressed the fact that Hitler was the most 'reasonable' leader in the world in 1939 and that Britain was 'almost solely responsible for the outbreak of war on both the Eastern and Western Fronts.'[690] Besides expressing doubts about the holocaust, Barnes asserted that Churchill and Roosevelt caused the war in 1939 and declared that he could not recall any unprovoked invasion of France in modern times.

A lot of Barnes's material was self-published after 1945, but it gained much credence among the isolationists and the former leader of the America First Committee,

General Wood, considered commissioning Barnes to write another book.

Quieter but more influential than Barnes was George Kennan, who had been instrumental in helping formulate America's anti Soviet policy in 1947. According to the *New York Times*, Kennan had done 'post-graduate studies at the University of Heidelberg, the University of Berlin, the Oriental Seminary and the Hochschule für Politik in Berlin in the interwar period.[691] Kennan did not assert that Germany was guiltless of starting the First World War. However, in his book, *American Diplomacy* he was sympathetic to inter-war Germany. He forgot that the American people had wanted the total defeat of 'Prussian militarism' and the 'unconditional surrender' of the German troops in 1918, rather than Wilson's armistice, asserting,

'The Allies came to be interested only in a total victory over Germany: a victory of national humiliation, of annexations, of crushing reparations. They resented suggestions for an end of hostilities on any other basis.'

Nevertheless, he did acknowledge that Germany had been a predator, stating, 'The Germans wanted to retain military facilities in Belgium. They wanted to hold Belgium for the future in the status of a subordinate state. They wanted a slight increase in their own territory, for economic reasons, at the expense of France. ... 'Now plainly all this posed no easy problem for American statesmanship ... But none of this absolves us from looking coldly and critically at the nature of our national reaction to such a challenge.

Kennan stated that when Americans went to war in 1917, they were fighting for a better world, full of Wilson's principles of open markets and self-determination. But the Treaty of Versailles was 'forced upon the loser, a victor's terms imposed upon the vanquished, accepted in humiliation, under duress.'

Kennan's words carried enormous weight with the political establishment. The Soviet Union was a menace to the world, and the Allies seemed to be too weak to contain it. Meanwhile America's erstwhile friend, Germany, with whom Americans had had so many historical blood and cultural ties, could help. According to the 18th of November 1949 *US. News and World Report*, George Kennan, the American establishment's expert on Germany and Russia, had come to a novel decision. It declared:

'George Kennan, No. 1 brain Truster in the State Department, has a new idea that the U.S. had better put its faith in Germany, rather than France, as the bulwark against Russia. Mr. Kennan's view is that France never will regain her old position of leadership in Western Europe.'

Kennan's view fell on receptive ears in the State Department, already worried by the re-emergence of Nazism in the US and Latin America, and the way the former Nazis were appealing to Stalin's Russia to come to an agreement with West Germany.

On 17th November 1949, the *Buerger Zeitung* of Chicago published an 'Open Letter' to Stalin by the former Nazi and Black Front leader, Bruno Fricke, which stated: 'We Prussians have always been closely, associated with the Russians ... Socialist Germany and Communist Russia together are invincible and thus our alliance secures the peace of the world.'

An alliance between post-war Germany and the Soviet Union was unbelievable and horrific to the US, but Nazi Germany had conspired with Russia at Rapallo after the First World War and come to an agreement with her in 1939. America was already horrified by the spectre of communism and terrified of its appeal making inroads at home. Red-scare Senator McCarthy declared that there were eighty-one communists, or known security risks, in the Secretary of State's department alone, including a White House speech writer.[692] Americans were determined to take a strong stand against Communism at home and abroad and retain West Germany's friendship. Then the Korean War started.

Truman had ended the Second World War against Japan in August 1945, when he dropped atom bombs on Hiroshima and Nagasaki, but the spectre of Communism seemed to be spreading across Asia. Indeed, democratic South Korea was soon under threat from the communist North. North Korea like Germany had been jointly occupied by Russian and American troops after the Second World War while the war with Japan was still raging and the plan was to occupy the Japanese home islands.

Subsequently America and Russia had been able, without difficulty, to agree on the 38th parallel as the demarcation line between north and south, pending the creation of a single Korean government. The Russian and

American occupation troops were subsequently withdrawn. However, the country remained divided with the Republic of Korea in the South, supported by America by virtue of an election sponsored by the United Nations, whilst a Soviet-supported Democratic Republic of Korea ruled the North.

Neither of the Korean governments was happy with the situation. They both wanted control over the whole peninsula. One of the reasons that the Americans had withdrawn their troops from South Korea indeed, was the fear that South Korean President, Syngman Rhee, might drag them into a personal adventure against the North. However, America's decision to withdraw its troops may have given Rhee's North Korean counterpart Kim Il-Sung the wrong signal, that America would allow North Korea to grab the South without intervening.

Stalin had a vast European empire and huge armed forces, but his country was ravaged by war, and he had no money. A war in the East would remove the pressure against him in Europe. Kim Il-Sung was told that according to information coming from the United States ...' the prevailing mood is not to interfere' and the green light was given to Kim to invade. Kim Il-sung boasted: 'The attack will be swift, and the war will be over in three days.'[693]

President Truman was not keen on becoming militarily involved in South Korea, but John Foster Dulles was eager, and the reputation of the United Nations was involved. On 19th June, Dulles reassured the South Korean parliament: 'You are not alone. You will never be alone, so long as you continue to play worthily your part in the great design of human freedom.' But his words did not deter the North Koreans. On 25th June they invaded South Korea and the Korean War began.[694]

By November, the Americans thought that they had won the war. However, China's Communist leader, Mao Zedong, had other ideas. He wanted Stalin to give him the sort of military and heavy industrial base that German heavy industry had given Stalin during the Great Depression and was prepared to expend the lives of millions of Chinese in Korea to force a reluctant Stalin into providing it.[695]

As the Korean War became increasingly desperate the powerful German Ruhr industrialists, who controlled the best coal in Europe, and had put millions abroad before the end of the war, sensed an opportunity to secure better peace terms from the anxious Americans.

Indeed, it was not only the Ruhr's coal, steel, machinery, and chemicals that America was desperately short of; McCloy wanted thousands of German troops to help hold the line against Communism in Europe. Konrad Adenauer was quick off the mark. On 29th August 1950, without even consulting his Cabinet colleagues, he declared his readiness, 'in the event of the formation of an international West European army to make a contribution in the shape of a German contingent.'[696]

America was confronted by war in Korea and Stalin in Western Europe. Weak Britain had already pledged help for Korea. France was fractious and exhausted. There was only one strong Conservative country that America considered she could rely on to defend Europe, West Germany.

The French were aghast at the thought of German rearmament. Nevertheless, Secretary of State, Dean Acheson, told France's foreign minister, Robert Schuman, bluntly that if France wanted American troops to remain on French soil the U.S. government had 'to have an answer now to the possible use of German forces in Europe.' And the French had to accept 'the whole package.'[697]

The Nazi editor of the Madrid Circular Letter realised the strength of the German position. It posed the question; 'How should Germany proceed diplomatically in the present situation? ... 'We have to undo the shame of the judgements motivated by revenge (Nuremberg War Crimes Trial, etc.) which the victors executed on the military and civic leaders of the Third Reich. The offerings which the Americans could make in this respect would cost them nothing. ... But there is a difference between mere promises and such commitments as would bind us irrevocably. ... Those dollar-diplomats and cowboys are too untalented to cope with the problem of world politics. The struggle against American bossing of Europe will become Germany's main task in the future.'[698]

So, the West German negotiators demanded a quid pro quo for providing an army, that America let the leaders of heavy industry out of prison and commute the death sentence on SS war criminals.

The issue of the SS war criminals was the one that hit the headlines. At the end of 1950 more than two dozen men were still in the death cells in Germany, waiting for a decision on their fate. They consisted of the SS unit which had committed the notorious Malmédy massacre of eighty American prisoners of war in 1944, and the commanding officers of the various SS special task forces who had carried out the brutal mass executions of several hundred thousand Jews, Poles and Gypsies in the occupied East in 1940 and 1941. A huge petition was organized against imposing the death penalty for the SS murderers. Thousands of letters and telegrams arrived from all over the world pleading for their lives. The Christian Aid committee in Munich, which contained leading churchmen and politicians, flooded the High Commissioner's office with telegrams and petitions imploring that he let the 'red jackets' off the death sentence. At the same time McCloy's 'mail became heavy with threats against his life and that of his family.

'On 9th January 1951 High Commissioner McCloy received a delegation from the President of the Bundestag, Dr Hermann Ehlers, and other prominent dignitaries representing each of the political parties. They told a no-doubt astonished McCloy that West Germany had abolished the death penalty and 'they want no more blood spilling in Germany'.[699] She had decided to become a pacifist country. By the end of January 1951, Commissioner McCloy gave in to their pressure. He commuted the sentences of all but seven SS special task force officers, leaving the fate of Oswald Pohl, Otto Ohlendorf, Erich Naumann, Werner Braune, Pnaul Blobel, and the Dachau SS guards Georg Schallermair and Hans-Theodor Schmidt undecided.

Meanwhile, while the Press was concentrating on the SS criminals, several immensely powerful Ruhr magnates, who had employed thousands of slave labourers, also had their prison sentences reviewed without fanfare, and were quietly released from custody in small groups. At the end of the first week in January 1951, America allowed all the IG Farben personnel who had been convicted of responsibility for their employees' beatings, starvation, abuse, and murder of inmates, at Buna-Werke, Fürstengrube, Auschwitz and elsewhere, out of prison.

Former board member, Fritz ter Meer, who would later become Chairman of the supervisory board of Bayer again, told reporters as he walked out a free man, 'Now they have Korea on their hands the Americans are a lot more friendly.'

On Saturday 3rd February 1951, Alfried Krupp led twenty-eight other freed prisoners, including four former generals, out of jail. But the news had got out. Alfried heard 'a great shout' and discovered that he had 'become a national idol.'700 He would soon be privately acknowledged as the richest man in the European Economic Community.

The industrialist Friedrich Flick, who was convicted as a war criminal for plundering the Jews' factories in Germany and Eastern Europe, and of 'enthusiastically' using slave labour at Daimler-Benz and in other parts of his huge armaments combine, was also released in 1950. Much of his property was returned to him, including his thirty-nine per cent in Daimler-Benz. VW and Daimler-Benz received the warm breath of government and banking support to start manufacturing again. They lost no time in entering into a variety of patent, research and marketing and sales agreements with other core manufacturers to protect themselves and their partners from competitive American subsidiaries.701 The Americans had wanted to get the wheels of German industry turning again - but it came at a price.

In September 1951, Minister of Transport, Dr Seebohm, addressed a mass meeting of the Sudeten Germans at Suttgart, denouncing the 'monstrous crime the victors ... committed against Germany, Europe and the whole world.' In 1952, ten per cent of West Germans thought that Hitler was the greatest statesman of the century, and in 1953 thirteen per cent said that they would welcome a return of the Nazi Party. Indeed, a Nazi plot to overthrow the Bonn Republic was discovered. Its leader, Dr Werner Naumann, was with Hitler during the final days in the Berlin bunker, and was the person designated by Hitler in his will to succeed Dr Goebbels as Propaganda Minister. Among those arrested with him were Paul Zimmerman, former SS General and official of the concentration camp branch of the SS and Dr Heinrich Haselmeyer, head of the National Socialist Student League, and Hitler's 'expert on race and sterilization.'702

Worryingly, the plot also appeared to have had international backers and been instigated by a vast, well-resourced, Nazi network reaching from Düsseldorf to Cairo, Madrid, Buenos Aires, and Malmö in Sweden.[703] The evidence about the conspiracy was compelling but the plot was hushed up. The Americans did not want it to be publicized when West Germany was the lynch pin in their fight against Communism in Europe, while the injurious Korean War was dragging on in Asia.

West Germany realized the gnawing anxiety of the Americans that, even after the carnage of the Second World War, Germany might link up with Stalin. On 6th March 1952 one of the leading magnates of the Ruhr told the Swiss newspaper, *Wochen Zeitung*: 'Germany's prospects in the East are far more attractive than those in the West. ... Stalin is willing to pay a high price for German neutrality ... Seven years after unconditional surrender Germany holds most of the trump cards for the international poker game in her hands.'

This provoked an outstanding offer from Stalin. On 10th March 1952 in a Note addressed to the Three Western Powers, Stalin offered the West Germans 'German unification on the basis of free, elections, a new German Wehrmacht, fully armed, the decontrolling of Germany's war potential, and the return of Germany's Nazis and Wehrmacht officers to public life.'[704]

The West German people were thrilled.

On 16th May 1952, the industrialists weekly, *Der Fortschritt*, in its article called 'Courage Towards a Rapallo,' exulted:

'Never before has the world political situation been so favourable for Germany as it is today. ... It is not for nothing that both power blocs concentrate their efforts on Germany in order to dominate it politically and economically. Therein lies our chance and our obligation. Our economy has to be kept independent from both sides. ... This is the way that leads towards sovereignty and equality which finally eliminate all those clauses which were imposed upon us as a result of the lost war. ... While integration with the West restricts our industry to markets where we are subjected to a cut-throat competition, the Eastern bloc offers us markets where countless millions are hungry for our industrial goods. Here (in the East) is Germany's market. ..... Thirty years ago, on 16th April 1922 there were courageous men, who, in Rapallo, through direct Russo-German negotiations brought a great turning point in Germany's post-war policy. ... The situation in present day Germany should exhort our leading statesmen to show courage .... courage towards a new Rapallo.'

The Soviet offer had an electrifying effect on the West German people, who had been denied contact with relatives and friends in the East. It was also a bombshell for America. She decided to give West Germany a massive bribe to stay within the Atlantic Alliance.

Under the terms of the 1953 London Debt Agreement, Germany's pre-and post-war debts were slashed by 62.6%. Germany's pre-war debt amounted to 22.6 bn marks including interest. Her post-war debt was estimated at 16.2 billion. In the agreement signed in London on 27th February 1953 these sums were reduced to 7.5 billion and 7 billion, respectively. To make quite sure that West Germany could repay the remaining amount, she was given special terms for repayment. Firstly, West Germany did not automatically have to pay her debts if she was not prospering. To the astonishment of the historian and political scientist, Éric Toussaint, she was also allowed to pay her debts in her national currency. Although other Marshall Aid recipients had to buy American goods with Marshall Aid cash, West Germany was largely allowed to manufacture the goods herself and then sell them abroad to achieve a positive trade balance, a major blow to British, French and American exporters, who up till now had furnished over forty per cent of West Germany's imports.

Germany was also allowed to monetize the debt or to print money to pay it if necessary. Thirdly, she was given extra funds by America to keep her sweet, with at least 200 million dollars added from 1954 to 1961. She was also guaranteed low interest rates for repayment

But the largest concession that America gave to Germany under the terms of the London Debt Agreement concerned the payment of Germany's Second World War reparations. The payment of the reparations to those whose countries had been mutilated in the Second World War was abandoned until the distant day that when Germany might re-unified. [705]

In order to placate the many unhappy nations which had been 'raped and plundered' during the Second World War and were likely never to receive recompense for the terrible wrongs done to their countries, it was decided that charging reparations was counterproductive and merely led to wars. In consequence, the legend which Americans now firmly, believed, that the Allies cruel reparations charged under the terms of the Treaty of Versailles had led to Hitler and the Second World War, became doctrine world-wide.

France was in a desperately weak position. She had been invaded three times, in part because of the iron ore fields that she possessed. So French Foreign Minister Robert Schuman swallowed the legend that we all 'slithered' into war in 1914 and pushed his idea of a European Coal and Steel Community, as the only way forward for France's economic survival.

Originally France had a different idea. Civil servant Jean Monnet, came up with a scheme to turn the area spanned by the German coalfields east of the Rhine into an international state, supervised by America and France. When this was rejected, Monnet wrote to Schuman that the only solution was 'through the creation of a federation of the West.'

Schuman's aim was to make war between European Member states impossible by creating a single market. No longer would Germany have to invade France to secure the iron ore from Longwy-Briey. France would also have peaceful access to German coal without having to send her troops into Germany. Schuman and Monnet were credited with the concept of the European Economic Community, which has grown into the European Union.

Adenauer's first choice to handle the negotiations for the Schuman Plan was the banker, Hermann Abs, who spoke fluent Dutch French and English. However, Hermann Abs had not only been on the board of Deutsche Bank throughout the war, but also on the supervisory board of I G Farben, which had built its largest ever plant, at the cost of twenty-five thousand deaths, near the death camp at Auschwitz. So, Adenauer decided instead to use a Professor of Law called Walter Hallstein to draw up the Schuman Plan with Frenchman, Jean Monnet.

In 1942, the Germans had toyed with the concept of a European Economic Community, with Germany running the show. Reich Minister for Economic Affairs, Walter Funk, had declared: 'Seen this way, the creation of a European economic area that is immune to Europhobic influences, and relies on the cooperation of its people, also represents an act of European self-determination.' Dr. Philip Beisiegel, director of Hitler's Labour Ministry, seconded Funk's view, declaring:

'The European Economic Community is in no way yet a sure fact, rather a political aim ... We have to differentiate between the present needs under the circumstances of war and those of a peaceful order, which will look very, different from the wartime organization.'

Indeed, the Madrid Circular Letter intimated that the Germans and Americans had already discussed the project, declaring: 'These considerations resulted in a plan first formulated secretly in Washington and later openly discussed, aiming at the creation of a united Europe as a bulwark against Russia with the proviso that a strengthened and rearmed Germany be incorporated in such an organization.'

One would imagine, therefore, that West Germany would have been keen on Schuman's plan. Yet West Germany drove a hard bargain over sharing her resources with France, Italy, and the Benelux countries. Schuman also planned to create the world's first international anti-cartel agency so that a firm like Krupp would not be able to create a 'state within a state' in Europe. The German chemical industry responded with a thunder of opposition, alleging that the anti-Farben fanatics in Frankfurt and Washington had struck a new blow at Germany. IG Farben's many prominent American supporters also rose in a swarm to support Germany and the company.

Nevertheless, Schuman's idea of an anti-cartel agency appealed to America. She fervently believed in open markets. Before the Second World War Germany had operated a highly cartelised industrial economy. Then she became more and more of an autarkic regime, deeply inimical to the Americans. Indeed, the opinion of Professor Berghahn in his book '*Quest for an economic Empire*'

'leaving aside Hitler's racist ideology and the power-political dimensions of the world conflict, the (Second World) war had amounted to a gigantic struggle between two diametrically opposed views on how to organize the future world market: Closed Blocs versus the Open Door.'

Luckily, America won the battle for the 'Open Door' in the 1950s and her economic policy brought prosperity to the world. West Germany decided to turn her back on Stalin and The European Economic Community was born.

It was a huge blow for the West German people for their country to remain divided when re-unification had seemed so tantalisingly close. However, the West German industrialists were already trading with Stalin. Indeed by 1959 West Germany would become the Soviet Union's premier western trading partner[706] so her industrialists knew just how weak her economy was. The country had an enormous army and Stalin's legacy kept everyone in check. Yet sooner or later there would be another opportunity for reunification. Meanwhile West Germany had been given the opportunity to dominate Western Europe, if not the western world, and the Allies' reparations demands would, seemingly in perpetuity, be castigated as being responsible for Hitler and the Second World War.

How West Germany achieved German Reunification

'Die Stunde null', zero hour. That is what the Germans called it. Everything was to start afresh from the moment peace was declared. In fact, zero hour, more accurately could be said to have begun after the start of the Korean War. According to Frederick the Great's maxim 'Money is like a sorcerer's wand.' Without it one could do nothing. With it one could invade one's neighbour's territory or secure the return of one's own. The task of reunifying Germany would take forty years.

In 1950 the authors of the Madrid Circular Letter declared: 'The Americans have lost the peace, the Cold War and their entire future but they are not yet aware of it.' That may not have been a fair comment, but it deserved scrutiny, if only because of its anti-American rhetoric at a time when Americans believed that West Germany was their best friend. America was appeasing Germany by throwing money at her, in the same fashion as in the 1920s. Meanwhile the German industrial hierarchy was trading with the Soviet Union, while calling on America and NATO to defend their country against Communism.

Some seventy per cent of the German people were opposed to any rearmament. Yet Adenauer was determined that West Germany should rearm and the Americans, faced with the Korean War, were desperate for them to rearm too.

In 1950, French Prime Minister, René Pleven, proposed reluctantly that the European Defence Community (EDC) should be formed from the armies of Italy France and the Benelux countries, with the addition of a contingent from Germany. The French people were unhappy at the thought of the EDC in any shape or form if it meant German rearmament. Nevertheless, Adenauer gained a new friend to support him. In January 1953, the a8rch enemy of Communism, John Foster Dulles, became US Secretary of State. The stage was set for the Cold War.

Dulles had a rigid mind-set. After the First World War he clung to Keynes's 1919 view that the Treaty of Versailles would 'reduce Germany to servitude' and was still busy lending Germany money to make amends even after Hitler came to power.

After the Second World War Dulles's moral outbursts were against Communism. Stalin had conducted a nuclear bomb test in 1949. Adenauer announced that the US deployment of nuclear weapons in West Germany was essential for her defence. Only a few days' later people were astonished to see 280 mm nuclear-capable cannons 'make their journey down the Rhine amidst a fanfare of publicity.'[707]

Adenauer also pushed for the European Defence Community to be ratified. At a NATO council meeting on 14th December 1953, Dulles stated that if the French parliament did not ratify the EDC the United States would 'face an agonising reappraisal of its foreign policy.'

Dulles's words infuriated the French press. In August 1954, the French National Assembly voted against allowing the motion to ratify the European Defence Community onto its agenda. That killed the EDC.[708] Adenauer later complained in his memoirs, 'In France, in Britain, everyone was pressing for disarmament while we in the Federal Republic stood for rearming.' Yet Adenauer could depend on America while Dulles was Secretary of State.

Aggressive monster, Stalin, died in 1953 but he left his henchmen behind. Despite the Soviets being over-extended financially, having an industrial base a third of the size of America's, a faltering agricultural sector and a struggle in keeping up with the arms race, Dulles maintained that 'Soviet military threats and subversive efforts created an intolerable sense of insecurity.'[709]

No-one could disagree with those sentiments, especially not Adenauer. He was eager and able to help in a concrete way by rearming, and his country had the resources. When the German mark was stabilized in 1948 the Americans had allowed it to be fixed at a very advantageous level against other currencies. It was soon apparent that it was seriously undervalued. In the couple of years since the 1953 elections the economy had grown at an average of over seven per cent a year and by 1955 the balance of payments surplus would be a whopping DM 3.07 billion. To those with inside knowledge Germany seemed already to have won the Second World War but there was still a huge chunk of the Fatherland, torn away by Stalin in the East, which needed to be reunited with West Germany, either by chatting up the Soviets, or else by using America. Adenauer favoured using America.

America was desperate for West Germany to join NATO. In April 1949, the first NATO Secretary General, Lord Ismay, had defined NATO's aims as being 'to keep the Russians out, the Americans in, and the Germans down.'

Yet 'the Germans' were no longer 'down.' In fact, they seemed to have the upper hand. So, securing West Germany's acquiescence to becoming part of NATO meant more arduous negotiations and a final new concession by America and her Allies, which would come back to haunt them.

Although West Germany promised 'never to have recourse to force to achieve the reunification of Germany,' she extracted a pledge from the Western Allies that 'the achievement through peaceful means of a fully free and unified Germany remains a fundamental (NATO) goal.'[710] On that condition she finally joined NATO on 9th May 1955.

The significance of the deal would soon become apparent. West Germany promised not to use force (and nuclear weapons) to secure reunification herself but expected America to threaten to use force and nuclear weapons on her behalf.

The achievement through peaceful means of a fully free and united Germany' would soon mean a huge build-up of nuclear weapons in America and the Soviet Union, which would cost America a fortune and cause anxiety to the whole world.

Adenauer was happy in December 1956 when a NATO military committee stipulated that there should be twelve West German divisions on the Western Front, all equipped for nuclear warfare.[711] Although Adenauer told the pacifist German people that he favoured arms control and disarmament negotiations, it was soon apparent that he was intent on securing nuclear weapons for the Bundeswehr.

After a French devaluation, the European Economic Community developed successfully. West German industry pursued her traditional path of subsidising the European Economic Community's agriculture in order to sell her industrial goods. Her initiative was tremendously successful and provided the basis for a lasting friendship. Small French farmers flourished with just a few cows and Italian hills were clothed with olives. Wine producers were also encouraged to multiply their production, while an outlet for their wine was found in the former beer drinking countries of Britain and Northern Europe. Tariffs were lowered throughout the EEC, but each country continued to run its own economy. All was roses in the European Economic Community.

Adenauer's main preoccupation, however, was still with East Germany. He asked Walter Hallstein to draw up what became known as the Hallstein Doctrine. This asserted that West Germany had the exclusive right to represent, not just West Germany, but the entire German nation and that there would be 'serious consequences' for any state that recognized East Germany. This was a threat to the Soviet Union.

New Soviet President Nikita Khrushchev had started life as a poorly educated peasant. Blustering, yet aggressively insecure, he was appalled by the carnage that nuclear weapons could create but equally determined not to divulge the information to the Americans, claiming that he was turning out missiles 'like sausages' when there were far fewer than he asserted and he lacked the warheads to send them to their destinations.[712]

In November 1958 the Soviets proclaimed that all Soviet rights and duties in East Berlin were being handed over to the East Germans and therefore that the Allied troops should be withdrawn. Khrushchev told the Polish leader, Wladyslaw Gomulka, 'There will be tensions, of course' but 'war will not result from this.' His aim was to achieve the international recognition of East Germany (GDR).On 10th January 1959, Khrushchev followed up his note with a proposal to all the countries that had fought Germany in the Second World War, suggesting a peace conference to discuss the solution of the two German states, accompanied by a draft peace treaty, to be signed by both states or a confederation, offering Germany to be united as a neutral country.

Dulles was dying of cancer, but he was keen to call Khrushchev's bluff; yet Adenauer could not secure Britain or France's cooperation for a hard line.[713] At last, in May 1959, the conference that Khrushchev had been working for occurred with a delegation from East Germany (GDR).

To Khrushchev this constituted de facto recognition of East Germany, but he had achieved recognition only just in time. The Soviet Union was impoverished. It could not give East Germans the quality of life that West German citizens had come to expect. In July 1961 30,000 refugees poured into West Berlin.

In early August 1961 new President John F Kennedy reflected, 'Khrushchev is losing East Germany. He cannot let that happen. If East Germany goes, so will Poland and all Eastern Europe. He will do something to stop the flow of refugees. Perhaps a wall.' His prophecy was correct. In the early hours of Sunday 13th August 1961 East German workers erected the barbed wire barricade that was the precursor to the Berlin Wall.

There was no doubt that the Soviet economy was faltering. Adenauer's strategy of building up Western military strength until the Soviet Union either collapsed or negotiated over the future of East Germany on his terms had so nearly worked – yet the strategy was no longer tenable. The Wall was there, East Germany was being recognized as a country and, now that Dulles was dead, Adenauer could no longer count on the US threatening to bomb it into submission. Khrushchev had secured a success.

Moreover, although the Soviet economy was ailing, and Khrushchev's droves of missiles a fiction, his engineers had made an improved anti-aircraft missile. On 1st May 1960, it was used to shoot down a U-2 espionage flight and capture the pilot, Francis Gary Powers, which alarmed public opinion in Europe and America. In 1962 Khrushchev agreed to Cuba's request to place nuclear missiles in Cuba in response to America's Bay of Pigs invasion and America's Jupiter missiles which could hit the Soviet Union in Italy and Turkey.

Eventually, after a stand-off the Cuban missiles were removed, and the US secretly agreed to dismantle the Jupiter missiles in Italy and Turkey. A hotline was installed between the White House and the Kremlin and relationships between America and Russia improved.

However, the wider public in Germany the rest of Europe and America was not aware of this. They were not only alarmed by the threat of Communism but also of a Soviet-inspired nuclear war.

Adenauer was a strong man. He wanted to control negotiations with the Soviet Union. He warned his Minister for Foreign Affairs, Heinrich von Brentano, in 1955, 'I keep in my hands, the leadership in European affairs, affairs with the United States and the Soviet Union.' But occasionally Adenauer's ministers stepped out of line. His Defence Secretary, Franz Josef Strauss, was a heavyweight from Bavaria with unlimited ambitions.

In 1962, Strauss successfully sued the editor of the newspaper *Der Spiegel*, Rudolf Augstein, for libel over the newspaper's allegation that he was a threat to democracy, his lust for power was inexhaustible, and that he was planning a nuclear war. The editor of *Der Spiegel* spent 103 days in prison but eventually Strauss had to resign, complaining that he had been treated like a 'Jew who had dared appear at a Nazi Party convention.'

The idea that European nations owed a measure of reparation to West Germany for asserting that she was responsible for the First World War and for burdening her with unfair and onerous reparations after the Treaty of Versailles, had helped reconcile the nations of Europe with their former foe. European friendship blossomed in the new environment. Then German Professor, Fritz Fischer's book called *Griff nach der Weltmacht* (Grasp at World Power) in German, and *Germany's Aims in the First World War* in English, was published, threatening to destroy their spirit of solidarity. In his introduction to the book Hajo Holborn of Yale University wrote:

'Through long labour he (Fischer) has collected from archives in West and East Germany and Austria a tremendous range of unpublished material ... proving beyond any reasonable doubt that the Chancellor, Bethmann-Hollweg, was determined to use the Austro-Serbian conflict to break the 'encirclement' of Germany ... at any price, even that of a great war.'

Fischer's book caused uproar in West Germany but elsewhere reaction was muted. The European Economic Community was reliant on German funds to keep it marching forward and America wanted West Germany to keep protecting the world against Communism. Both in Europe and America, the German people and her leadership were now regarded as good friends and neighbours.

Yet Fischer's *Germany's Aims in the First World War* raised some awkward questions. How did Germany get away with causing so much misery and bloodshed in the First World War? Was her economy truthfully as weak as she made out in the 1920s, when her coal mining industry was massacring the British coal mining industry? Or could she have been too strong for the Allies to be able to enforce the terms of the Treaty of Versailles without American ratification of the Versailles Treaty and American troops on the ground? Could she, in fact, have caused the 1929 Wall Street Crash and been responsible for the Great Depression?

America and the Allies decided to sweep the issue under the carpet. Meanwhile West Germany was biding her time and subsidising the EEC. She knew that the person who paid the piper ultimately called the tune. She also realized that if – and when – the Berlin Wall came tumbling down, not only East Germany, but the whole of Eastern Europe would fall under her sphere of influence.

In 1963 Adenauer finally resigned at the ripe old age of eighty-seven. In October, his former Minister for Economics, Ludwig Erhard, became Chancellor of West Germany. Heavy-jowled, cigar-smoking Ludwig Erhard was not fooled by Khrushchev's attempt to put nuclear missiles on Cuba after America's abortive attempt to destroy Fidel Castro's regime. The German industrialists had told Erhard of Russia's threadbare existence behind the Iron Curtain. The Soviet Union had a powerful military machine, but in every other area its economy was weakening, and it was running out of cash. As he drove through Berlin with Mayor Willy Brandt, Erhard asked the astonished Social Democrat leader, how much 'would it really cost for Russia to concede the GDR to us?'

Cool economist, Ludwig Erhard amplified his scheme. West Germany would deliver industrial plant and equipment for the development of Siberia in exchange for a 'phased programme' involving 'the Wall, reunification, self-determination and freedom for Germany.' He also told American diplomats about his plan, but they did not believe that Russia would accept it.

Erhard was not to be deterred. He went to a barbeque at President Lyndon B Johnson's Texas ranch at Christmas in 1963. Johnson related: 'Erhard was all over me. He was ready to go in the barn and milk my cows if he could find the teats.' But Johnson was not prepared to meet Khrushchev, and in the meantime the British, French, Italians and Japanese provided the Soviets with cheap loans.[714] They did not like the Soviet regime, but they had become accustomed to, and even happy with the Berlin Wall, which restricted the clout of their powerful West German neighbour.

By the mid-1960s the West German Air Force was permitted to train with the US Seventeenth Air Force in handling arming and delivering nuclear weapons. Erhard believed that he could use America's nuclear arsenal to force the ailing Soviet Union to the negotiating table, or even hopefully to collapse the whole Soviet edifice in Eastern Europe.

In 1963 West Germany reputedly offered two billion dollars towards the creation of a five-billion-dollar multilateral nuclear force to confront the Soviet Union.[715] The Russians protested, asserting that the money would allow West Germany to wield undue influence over America's nuclear weapons policy.[716] A frustrated Erhard told the Bundestag on 10th November 1965:

'We have repeatedly made it known that we do not desire national control of nuclear weapons. We should, however, not be kept out of any nuclear participation simply because we are a divided country. The partition of Germany is an injustice. It must not be augmented by another injustice by making it more difficult for us – rendering substantial contributions to the Western Alliance – to defend ourselves against the threat from the East.'

Neither the European people nor the Americans realized the threat behind these words. West Germany was asserting that America must keep her nuclear arsenal in Western Europe the equivalent size to the Soviet Union's, otherwise West Germany's promise only to use nuclear power for peaceful means was no longer binding.[717]

American experts obviously believed that West Germany had the capability of producing a nuclear device in the 1960s because an atom bomb had already been made in Germany before the end of the Second World War.

In 2005 Mark Weber in the magazine *Nova* would declare of the device: 'At best this would have been far less destructive than the atomic bombs dropped on Japan. Rather, it is an example of scientists trying to make any sort of bomb they could in order to help stave off defeat.'[718] Other authors, however, asserted that Germany's atom bomb programme was much more advanced but that it lacked an effective delivery system to send it to America.[719]

According to the American Colonel Howard, A Buechner and the German army doctor, Kapitan Bernhart, (now a US Citizen), the A-10 rocket was called the 'Hammer of Thor' and nicknamed the 'American Rocket' since it was intended to be fired at major cities in the US, such as Washington, Boston, New York and Philadelphia and he declared that four test rockets had already been launched by the end of the war.[720]

Thousands of half-starved slave labourers had worked on producing the V-1 and V-2 rockets in the Harz Mountains. Perhaps they worked on the Hammer of Thor too and grew anxious about its ability to reach its targets because over a hundred were accused of sabotage in March 1945 and strung up to hang in front of their workmates in the final weeks of the war.

Just a little time later Himmler gave the directive that that the slaves working in the Dora/Nordhausen complex of concentration camps should be herded into one of the subterranean factories and gassed, but there was not enough time to carry out the order. The Americans arrived and found about 5,000 corpses in varying states of decomposition. Nevertheless, 1,000 of the starving slave labourers, their filthy prison uniforms hanging 'loosely on their shrunken bodies,' were rescued from the stinking decomposing scene of carnage.[721]

Some of the scientists working on the nuclear programme were also saved, de-briefed and employed by the Americans, others were taken to an uncertain fate in Russia and sixty-two were murdered by the SS. Nevertheless, America knew that Germany had enough knowledge to make good her threat to produce an atom bomb by the 1960s and to send it to its chosen destination in Russia (or America!).

West Germany eventually signed the Nuclear Non-Proliferation Treaty with the international community on the understanding that she could export nuclear energy for peaceful use, even if not allowed to produce nuclear weapons herself. She did, however, reiterate at the eighteen-nation disarmament committee meeting in Geneva in May 1967: 'Those who are the first to contribute have the right to expect the community of nations to rectify any resultant one sidedness.'

By 1967 the Deutschmark was declared to be the world's most 'stable' currency – a euphemism for saying that it was the strongest. The next month a grand coalition was formed under Germany's new President, Kurt Georg Kiesinger.

Suave, good-looking Kiesinger was a controversial figure because of his Nazi past. He had spent the war in the propaganda section of the Nazi Foreign Ministry, rising quickly to become the department's connection with Joseph Goebbel's Ministry. After the war Kiesinger was interned briefly before being released. In 1951 he became a member of the CDU executive board. In 1967 he became Chancellor of West Germany.

West Germany had maintained a confrontational attitude towards the Soviet Union, but her hard line had had no effect in achieving her aim of reunification. Indeed, in 1968, when Czechoslovak leader, Alexander Dubcek, tried to loosen the reins of power and give more freedom to the Czech people, East Germany, Poland and Hungary had supported the Soviet Union's action in sending tanks into Prague.

Meanwhile a young French woman called Beate Klarsfeld attracted public attention world-wide when she appeared in the Berlin Convention Hall and shouted out 'Nazi Kiesinger' and slapped him in the face. Later she said in explanation: 'Kiesinger and his colleagues are turning Germany into a revengeful, expansionist nation that ignores the consequence of world war and demands atomic weapons. So long as Kiesinger and his accomplices remain in power all the people who suffered under Nazism ... will have good reason to be wary of the Germany governed from Bonn.'[722]

Her gesture had a wide impact. A new approach had to be tried. The Russian economy was ailing. West Germany decided to try and woo the Soviets, instead of planning to bomb them into submission. In 1969 Kiesinger slipped out of the picture to be replaced by charismatic left-winger, Willy Brandt.

The frugal son of a single parent, Brandt had had to flee from the Nazis during the war. In 1946 he returned to Germany as Governor of Berlin. He also wanted the removal of Berlin's barbed wire entangled Wall dividing East and West Germany and believed in a conciliatory approach.

Brandt's arrival in power gave a fillip to left-wing movements everywhere. Thousands of British university students embraced Communist ideology while in Germany the Baader-Meinhof gang was born. Peace-loving Brandt would forge lasting relationships with his Soviet colleagues, but his mission was to secure political concessions from the Soviet Union through economic help.

The Deutschmark had been stabilized at too low a level after the Second World War. The world was awash with West German exports. Deutsche Bank Chairman Hermann Abs campaigned stridently against the revaluation of the Deutschmark but after Brandt became Chancellor, he allowed it to be revalued by a hefty amount against the dollar. The country seemed to have secured two major concessions for revaluing its currency, permission to construct a pipeline to the Soviet Union to meet its energy requirements, and finance so that German industry could help modernize Brazil.

America had been fighting Communism in Korea and Vietnam, and her economy was flagging. Although the 'Reds' in Russia were her greatest bogeys, it was difficult for her to refuse a plea from her close friends in West Germany. So although Adenauer had been an ardent supporter of the NATO decision to ban the sale of large-bore pipelines which could be used to transport Soviet oil and gas to the West in the early 1960s, a massive new pipeline deal was signed on 28th April 1969, through which Germany would receive fifty-two billion cubic metres of gas over twenty years in return for providing Russia with the pipelines. Germany did not actually need the gas at this time but the deal led to increased trade and a rapid thaw in political relations. Brandt secured Four-Power access to Berlin and increased human contact between the two sides of the city. However, even though the investment possibilities in Russia and Eastern Europe were exciting, revaluing the Deutschmark would make German exports more expensive so she was offered another sweetener, loans to facilitate her business investments in Brazil.

American investors had shunned lending money to Brazil because Brazil had reneged on her American debts in the 1930s and was governed by a repressive military dictatorship. This had led to widespread disturbances on the streets in the 1960s and to the kidnap of the US Ambassador, Charles Burke Elbrick.

'Then, quite suddenly', Professor Stephen A Shuker, remarked in 1988 in his book *American 'Reparations' to Germany 1919-1933, Implications for the Third World Debt crisis*, 'the climate of investment opinion changes.'[723]

American loans poured into Brazil to facilitate German investment in the country. One of the Brazilian Generals, Ernesto Geisel, was of German extraction. He would soon become President. West German investment in Brazil soared. In the 1970s, the city of Sao Paolo received the highest level of German investment in any one city in the world, including in West Germany.[724]

British companies were wary of investing in Brazil because of the unhappy labour situation but German heavy industry was prepared to deal resolutely with shop floor defiance. 'Soon after the elections (in 1974) more than two hundred workers at Volkswagen' were 'put into jail at one time.' There were also 'innumerable imprisonments', mainly of metal workers, at Mercedes, Phillips, and other factories in São Bernadino and São Caetano. However, Josef Rust, Chairman of Volkswagen's supervisory board, expressed his satisfaction that his company had chosen Brazil for expansion, boasting: 'the returns to the parent company are frightening.'[725] His company agreed to increase exports from its Brazilian operations from thirteen million dollars to 400 million dollars. The Brazilian government was overjoyed.

The British and Americans at home were impressed that the West German economy seemed to be riding out the recession in Europe so well. They were filled with admiration for their erstwhile foe, whose people seemed ever more peace-loving. Nevertheless, West Germany's heavy industrialists and politicians appeared to be less worried about world peace than their electorate. In the mid-1970s a German firm signed an agreement with Brazil for the purchase of up to eight nuclear reactors and plants to enrich and reprocess nuclear fuels,[726] with the 'hot breath' of governmental support.

The Americans were dismayed as Brazil had not signed the nuclear non-proliferation treaty. They argued that West Germany should have prevented the countries she sold enrichment or reprocessing plants to from making weapons from the plutonium produced. However, the German industrialists reply was that the International Atomic Energy Agency safeguards were all that could be hoped for.[727] They reiterated their view the following year, declaring that if countries really wanted the nuclear bomb, they would get it anyway.[728]

West Germany's intransigence over the nuclear plants she sold in Latin America upset new American President, Jimmy Carter. The American people wanted the nuclear arms race scaled down after the Vietnam War. However, there was a hawkish lobby among the American military. West German politicians were also more bellicose than was popularly supposed.

Carter was bitterly condemned by German right-wingers for his decision not to proceed with the production of neutron weapons. Adenauer's former Defence Minister, Franz Josef Strauss, who had lost his job in 1962 after the left-wing newspaper *Der Spiegel* alleged that he was 'planning a nuclear war'[729] declared:

'Doubts about the US capacity to lead are not only permitted but are unfortunately justified. ... - When the federal (American) government finally pulled itself together enough to approve this weapon, the American President withdrew. In my knowledge of American history since the Second World War this is the first time an American President has openly and recognizably bowed to a Russian Czar.'[730]

Social Democrat politician, Helmut Schmidt, now replaced Willy Brandt as Chancellor. 'The firm jaw, the intense grey eyes, the sudden brilliant almost voracious smile' quickly won Schmidt a newspaper vote as 'Germany's No 1 Sexy Man'[731]. However, Schmidt was deceitful.

When Schmidt was first elected to the Bundestag he had campaigned against nuclear weapons, but he soon lost his idealism. Even though German industry must have known of the weak state of the Russian economy, Schmidt soon expressed his disapproval of meagre American plans for upgrading the US's conventional and nuclear forces to defend West Germany to his NATO colleagues 'with the apparent course of events it suggests concerning 'limited nuclear options.'[732]

After Russia deployed a modern highly accurate missile called the SS20 Schmidt argued that Soviet missile technology had advanced to such an extent that it would be easy for the Russians to knock out essential strategic targets in Europe.

The Americans had overrated the Soviet Union's economic strength owing to its presence in poor African countries like Ethiopia Angola and Mozambique[733]so Schmidt's arguments for the modernization of America's nuclear weapons eventually prevailed as he revealed in his memoirs:

'In the summer of 1977 disagreements as to the proper response to Soviet SS20s were added to our other differences of opinion (with the US) ... My efforts had only slight results, (the opinion of American National Advisor, Zbigniew Brzezinski was that) ... should the Soviet Union ever threaten the Federal Republic with SS20s, the United States, using her strategic nuclear weapons, would be in a position to counter the threat. ... At the outset Carter agreed with his security advisor - Fifteen months later, however, there was quite a different outcome. They (the Americans) realized that what we call the 'grey zone' could not be neglected.'

The Carter administration eventually accepted the report of a working group of NATO members, which concluded that new intermediate-range nuclear weapons targeted against the Soviet Union would make it crystal clear to the Soviets that an isolated attack on Western Europe would be met by retaliation from American weapons aimed at Russia's heart. These new weapons were not to be viewed as a counterweight to the SS20, but as a qualitatively new type of deterrent with its own rationale.[734]

During this period, the West German people were pacifists. The rapprochement between the German people and their eastern neighbour was deepening. They would have been appalled if they had realized that their government was pushing America to modernize her nuclear weapons to defend their country. They did not want any more nuclear power plants in Germany, let alone nuclear weapons. On 23rd February 1975 30,000 people occupied the earthworks near the tiny hamlet of Wyhl, near the wine growing district of Kaiserstuhl in south-west Germany, where planning permission had been granted to build a nuclear reactor.

Schmidt therefore decided that if any nation was to appear bellicose it had to be the US, not West Germany. At a closed meeting on 31st January 1979 Schmidt's divided cabinet eventually agreed that any decision to deploy new intermediate-range nuclear forces had to be taken by the American President alone and that Bonn would not seek even partial control of any new warheads capable of striking the Soviet Union.[735]

Was it West German arguments within NATO that caused America to change her mind about deploying new nuclear weapons or did the Brazilian nuclear reactor order play a part in decision? If so, the West Germans continued to use the sale of their nuclear technology to Brazil as a bargaining chip right up to the time that the Americans decided to go ahead with their seemingly crazy new nuclear weapons programme.

The Russians looked as though they wanted détente. Their country was in an appalling state. However, in May 1979, one month before Russia agreed to the important SALT II nuclear arms limitation accord, the Brazilians expressed a desire to export their nuclear technology.

Nucleonics Week quickly reassured its readers that the West Germans continued to have control over the transfer of technology and decision-making in the Brazil-West German nuclear reactor deal, four years after it had been agreed.[736]

Nucleonics Week repeated the message with greater unease, on 30th August 1979, when it carried the headline on its front page: 'Brazil pot boils as German hold on nuclear technology is revealed.'

Finally, in November 1979, *Nucleonics Week* revealed that after Iraq's Industry Minister, Hassan Aliyin, visited Brazil in August, the President of Brazil's state nuclear agency, Nuclebras, Paulo Noguiera Batista, flew to Baghdad in September to sign a 'protocol' for nuclear co-operation between the two countries.[737]

Germany also seemed about to clinch a nuclear reactor deal with Argentina without adequate safeguards.[738]

Perhaps it was the prospect of Brazil (and Argentina) exporting technology that could be used to furnish countries like Iraq with nuclear bombs that finally persuaded Americans that West Germany, and NATO's pleas about her defence could not be ignored. At any rate, in 1979, America decided on a massive new arms race, despite the fact that the Soviets had just signed the SALT II arms limitation agreement, and that the Soviet economy was in its worst state since the Second World War.[739] By 1981 Russian life expectancy would be declining, 'an unprecedented phenomenon in an advanced industrial society.'[740]

American public opinion stiffened against the Soviet Union in the autumn of 1979 after it was revealed that some 3,000 Soviet troops were still stationed in Cuba.

In December 1979 NATO decided to deploy 572 new INF warheads, whilst simultaneously proposing new negotiations with the Soviets to limit their forces. [741] The Soviet invasion of Afghanistan at the end of December 1979[742] further worsened US-Soviet relations. President Reagan was more than happy to continue the nuclear arms modernization programme, which Carter had begun.

Meanwhile the West German public were horrified at the prospect of a possible nuclear war over their country and public alarm intensified over the potential contamination from the use of nuclear energy. So West Germany decided to lessen the pace of her industrial expenditure in Brazil.

The cost of the arms race would eventually cause the Soviet Union's collapse. It was also costly for America. And soon a new headache was added to the cost of producing new nuclear weapons to confront the Soviet Union – Brazil's reluctance to pay her debts. In 1984 Brazilian Finance Minister, Ernane Galvêas declared: 'We're not going to pay off our debt, the bankers know it, the official institutions know it, and the governments know it.'

Brazil had defaulted on her debts in the 1930s. In 1987 Brazil was the world's largest coffee and sugar exporter, the seventh largest steel producer and the ninth largest car producer, yet in February of that year she declared a moratorium on the payment of interest on her

$101 billion debt, most of it owed to American banks. On 19th October Wall Street collapsed. Nearly a quarter of the value of American stocks was wiped out. The *New York Times* wrote a banner headline 'Does 1987 Equal 1929?'

America did not blame the crash on the Brazilian default as she did not want other countries to follow Brazil's lead in reneging on their debts so the responsibility for the stock market's collapse in 1987 was laid upon 'mechanical, price-insensitive selling by a (small) number of institutions employing portfolio insurance strategies and a small number of mutual fund groups reacting to redemptions.'

Other reasons given were a breakdown of the New York Stock Exchange's automated transaction system and the lack of 'circuit breakers' which might have prevented the sell-off on the options and futures markets. [743]

And the stock market soon recovered. However, many people at home and abroad remembered the market's nasty fall, and blamed greed and American capitalism for the debacle.

On 12th November 1988, the fiftieth anniversary of the Kristallnacht Pogrom, Speaker of the West German Bundestag, Herr Philipp Jenninger, former aide to Franz Josef Strauss, and close friend of Chancellor Kohl, gave a speech lauding Hitler's triumphs in the 1930s. He said:

'From mass misery there was something like prosperity for the widest sections (of the population). Instead of desperation and hopelessness, optimism and self-confidence reigned. Did not Hitler just make reality what was just a promise under Wilhelm II – that is to bring wonderful times for the Germans? ...

'And as far as the Jews were concerned: hadn't they in the past measured themselves for roles that did not suit them? Didn't they finally have to accept restrictions? Didn't they perhaps, even deserve to be shown their place? And above all: Apart from wild exaggerations which were not to be taken seriously, didn't basic points of the propaganda reflect one's own speculations and convictions?'[744]

Herr Jenninger was sacked for his offensive words. Yet he and his friends must have been pleased. The American financial world had taken a battering and the Soviet Union's whole economic structure was about to collapse.

On 9th November 1989, the Berlin Wall crumbled, just a year after Philip Jenninger's speech. By goading America and the Soviet Union into an ever more expensive arms race, Germany had succeeded in securing Adenauer and Erhard's goal of German reunification without bloodshed. It was a monumental achievement. But Germany had played for high stakes and frightened the whole world. Did her actions bode well for the future?

CHAPTER TWELVE

Germany and the Lehman Brothers Crash

Western European leaders were ecstatic in public when the Berlin Wall fell, but privately they were dismayed. Germany had twice tried to grab a huge empire stretching from the Atlantic to the Urals, at the cost of millions of dead and wounded. Although not a shot had been fired to secure the fall of the Berlin Wall, many quaked at what might lie ahead. German Neo-Nazis paraded in the streets of Berlin and France's Socialist President, Francois Mitterrand, was gripped by a paroxysm of fear. He warned Mrs Thatcher that unification would result in Germany gaining more influence than Hitler ever had, and urged her to publicly, oppose heavy-weight German Chancellor Kohl's plans for immediate reunification.

At a personal level Helmut Kohl and Margaret Thatcher had not had the warmest of relationships. Kohl complained that Thatcher took exception to him serving her his favourite dish of pig's stomach with sausage and sauerkraut, while she was vexed that he excused himself quickly from their meeting, only to be spotted 'scoffing cream cakes in a nearby teashop'[745]

Thatcher's plea for a five-year transition period, with a lower exchange rate for East Germany before the two Germanys united, fell on stony ground. Chancellor Kohl brushed the idea aside and the East Germans supported him. Although they had a large and stable economy, they had been under the control of the Stasi. The Stasi was one of the largest secret-services the world had ever known, with links to Russia's KGB. Kohl offered East Germans freedom democracy and the D-mark. East Germany was delighted to be incorporated into a new reunited Germany.

After any honeymoon, however, adjustments are often necessary. For East Germans, the adjustments were particularly hard to cope with. They went on holiday with their precious new D-marks, only to find that their employers had gone bankrupt when they returned. The D-mark was too expensive an exchange rate for East Germany's industries, especially after Germany's hike in interest rates. The area soon became an industrial desert, with depopulation and huge levels of unemployment. Former Bundesbank official, Horst Bockelmann, later commented: 'It was not a surprise that the East German economy should collapse. If you wanted to ruin an economy that was the way to do it.'

Britain was also taken for a ride in 1990. Most British people shared the East Germans' joy at the fall of the Berlin Wall and supported Britain entering the Exchange Rate Mechanism (ERM), which meant that the pound would float within a narrow range of the D-mark. Margaret Thatcher's objections against the ERM were swept aside and her Secretary of State for Environment, Nicholas Ridley, was sent packing after he declared: 'Economic and Monetary Union is a German racket, designed to take over the whole of Europe.' In next to no time Thatcher went too.

Unfortunately, joining the ERM proved to be a disaster for Britain. The Bundesbank urgently needed to attract funds to pay unemployment benefits to pay for the unemployment benefits of all the formerly fully employed East German citizens who had returned from holiday to an industrial scrap heap. So, she decided to raise interest rates to unprecedented levels.

The Bundesbank's high interest rates had a devastating effect on Britain, which had to raise interest rates still higher to preserve funds at home, putting a terrible pressure on mortgages and businesses. On 16th September 1992, faced with a crippled economy and massive speculation, Britain bowed out of the ERM on the day that became known as 'Black Wednesday.'

The rise in German interest rates – to 9% - after reunification also had disastrous repercussions in Yugoslavia. The Communist Federation of Yugoslavia was once a powerful country but had decayed ever since President Tito's demise. German high interest rates had squeezed funds from the whole of Europe, bringing the Yugoslavian economy almost to breaking point. Many considered that the Balkan bloodshed in the 1990s was exclusively due to Serbian General Milosevic and his henchmen's murderous excesses, but it seemed that there was another side to the story.

After the fall of the Berlin Wall the Communist system was discredited everywhere. Hopefully, Yugoslavia would soon abandon Communism too. Time was what was needed at this difficult economic juncture. Yet the Croatians were in a hurry to desert the sinking ship and set up their own republic. And they had a powerful ally, Germany.

The Croatian ruling party declared Croatia's sovereignty on 22nd December 1990, six months after the collapse of the Berlin Wall. It asserted that the Croats aspired to democracy, western values, and free-market culture, in contrast to the Serbs, whom they depicted as old-fashioned barbaric Communists. This excited the press, especially in America. Yugoslavia was the last bastion of Communism in Eastern Europe. The Serbs were destined to become the sole villains of the Balkan tragedy.

On 25th June 1991, the Slovenian and Croatian parliaments declared their independence from Yugoslavia. German Minister of Foreign Affairs Hans Dietrich Genscher supported their claim with his American counterpart, James Baker.

Slovenia, which comprised some 2 million inhabitants, had never been an entirely independent nation before. Croatia, with a population of nearly 5 million, had been a puppet state under Hitler. The anxiety of the international community was that if a single region left the Republic of Yugoslavia, the country which had taken years recover after the deaths of 1,700,000 people in the Second World War, would collapse with more bloodshed.

On 9-10th December 1991, the European Council gathered for a crucial meeting at Maastricht to agree a treaty for the future development of the European Community. Before the meeting members were eleven to one in favour of maintaining Yugoslavia's unity. However, at four in the morning, after heated discussions on European security and a common policy on foreign affairs, Germany managed to force the EEC into recognizing Croatia and Slovenia's independence.

Aged pro-Serb French General Pierre Marie Gallois would later allege that the dismemberment of Yugoslavia had been planned by Germany, even before President Tito's death in 1980.

In the 1970s Gallois had been the French representative at informal, two-day international seminars, presided over by German Defence Minister, Franz Joseph Strauss. Gallois declared that it was at these seminars that Germany sought to gain acceptance for the proposal that Yugoslavia was already 'inanimate' and that its structure should be altered after Tito's death.

General Gallois would also allege that Germany's purpose was to reward Croats and Muslims, who had supported her during the Second World War, and retaliate against Serbia, which had held up precious German divisions from joining the attacks on Russia.

The bloodshed between Croatia and Serbia during the Second World War had been atrocious with the Serbs claiming that over a million of its soldiers and citizens had lost their lives.

Britain's Lord Carrington, who had been asked to preside over a Peace Conference on Yugoslavia in 1991, condemned Helmut Kohl for 'thoughtlessly' pushing Croatia and Slovenia's independence and warned that his action would lead to Bosnia demanding independence too, 'which would mean a civil war in Bosnia.'[746]

Yet, on 6th April 1992, coincidentally the fiftieth anniversary of Hitler's invasion of Yugoslavia, America and the European Community recognized the independence of Bosnia-Herzegovina.[747] In August that year, at a meeting to try to halt the fighting in Bosnia, a frustrated Lord Carrington asserted that the European Community 'should be held in large part responsible 'for the bloodshed in the region.'[748] However, NATO saw the conflict as a fight for democracy against Communism and threw its might against the Serbs, who then behaved in a most heinous manner.

America could count herself as a winner in the Balkan conflict because Communism was vanquished. Yet Germany was the overall victor. Croatia Slovenia and Bosnia-Herzegovina are all now aspirant members of the European Union and certain to vote with Germany on crucial issues. Historical maps also revealed a striking resemblance between the zones of Germany's current political and economic dominance in the region and those of the Holy Roman Empire.[749]

With the fall of the Berlin Wall, the Allies and America expected the payment of the rest of the Second World War reparations, which were due under the terms of the 1953 London Agreement, but President Kohl declared that the costs of reunification were huge, and his pockets were empty. Those to whom Second World War reparations were due, found themselves in the same position as Germany's First World War creditors in the early 1920s. Germany was large and powerful; if she chose not to pay there was little that they could do to exact payment.

In 2000, in a test case, the Greek High Court obliged Germany to pay twenty-eight million euros in compensation for the massacre at the village of Distomo on 10th June 1944, when a total of 218 men, women and children were raped and killed in revenge for a partisan attack. Yet the German Federal Constitution Court ruled in 2006 that Germany did not have to pay compensation to individuals seeking damages over war crimes. Except for compensation paid to forced labourers, no more Second World War reparations have been paid.

In 1990 President Mitterrand had been alarmed at the fall of the Berlin Wall. Germany's high interest rates were hurting the French economy too.

The German newspaper *Der Spiegel* would later accuse Mitterrand of having forced an unwilling Germany to abandon the D-mark and adopt the euro as his price for agreeing to German reunification.

Yet in some ways the decision was forced on Mitterand. By 1992, the French economy, like Britain's and that of the former Yugoslavia, was bleeding from being tied to the D-mark. 'We may have the nuclear bomb, but the Germans have the deutsche mark' protested the officials at the Elysee Palace as they watched their economy going into a tailspin.[750]

However, they were desperate not to quit the European Community. Their hope was that if all the countries, including Italy, Portugal and Ireland and Greece, adopted the euro it would be a weaker currency.

Mitterrand was subsequently bitterly criticized for forcing the German people to abandon their beloved D-Mark. However, German Finance Minister, Theo Weigel, insisted that the adoption of a single currency had always been Germany's ambition. And what better time could Germany have to negotiate than when her interest rates were at unprecedented levels? Former Bundesbank President Karl Otto Pöhl later said: 'I was convinced that we would have to wait at least a hundred years for the euro' – but the French and the Italians were already pleading for Germany to adopt it!

Chancellor Kohl gave his view that the adoption of the euro would be a 'castle in the air' without political and fiscal union. He also knew that the German people would also be diametrically opposed to losing their beloved D-mark. It was ominous that the arduous task was nevertheless adopted; Bismarck had succeeded in his unification of twenty-six exceedingly diverse states in the 1870s, so the deed was possible. However, times were different in the 1870s. Bismarck had been fortuitously aided by a stock market crash!

Kohl was right about the German people's dislike for relinquishing the D-mark. The plans for the euro created uproar in Germany. Both the best-selling *Bild-Zeiting* newspaper and the up-market *Der Spiegel* voiced the German people's alarm at the thought of any institution except the Bundesbank being in control of their currency.

The Bundesbank had a special place in the German peoples' hearts because of its claim to have preserved the value of the D-mark after Germany's Great Inflation of 1923. Heartrending pictures of little old ladies carrying baskets of worthless marks continued to terrify the German people with the thought that another Great Inflation could reoccur in the future. 'Never again' was the Bundesbank's rallying cry (even though Germany had presided over two more hyper-inflations, one in 1948 and the other in East Germany in 1990).[751]

Therefore, the Bundesbank prescribed the strictest criteria for aspiring members of the euro, the annual deficit for member countries should not exceed three per cent except in exceptional circumstances and governmental debt should not exceed sixty per cent of GDP. Watching from the side lines, Karl Otto Pöhl concluded that the French and Italians were ready to agree to almost anything to escape the grip of the D-mark. They even accepted that the new European Central Bank would be situated in Frankfurt, that all the future euro zone banks would be independent, and that the ECB would become a 'virtual' clone of the Bundesbank.

Meanwhile Chancellor Kohl decided to give massive financial assistance to France to enable her to stay in the ERM. There were strings attached, however, one of which was that a 40,000 strong French and German speaking military force was to be formed – out of the control of NATO.[752]

As the 1990s continued, and the arrival of the euro drew near, French worries about Germany's predatory ambitions eased. The costs of unifying the two Germanys seemed to be throttling the German economy. Britain's *The Economist* magazine even labelled Germany the 'sick man of Europe' after the euro was instituted (virtually) in 1999.

On 1st January 2002, the euro coins appeared, accompanied by fireworks champagne and Beethoven's 'Ode to Joy.' German Chancellor, Gerhard Schröder declared: 'We are witnessing the dawn of an age that the people of Europe have dreamed of for,'[753] but the German people remained sceptical.

Indeed, there was no joy for them at all in the first few years after the arrival of the euro. Soon over four million German people were out of work. It is no wonder that Katina Barysch also called her 2004 article for the Centre for European Reform, 'Germany the sick man of Europe?'

Katina Barysch's title however included a question mark. Although Germany had breached the sacred Maastricht criteria with a deficit of more than three per cent of GNP, she had become the world's largest exporter, with a hundred-billion-euro trade surplus. The only blot on the landscape was her huge unemployment rate of nearly ten per cent of the population, which would rise to a whopping twelve per cent in February 2005.[754]

One reason why German unemployment was so high was because there was no money in the country. People did not trust the euro, so they had put their money abroad. Yet when the money arrived in less profitable countries, there were fewer viable options for investment.

Former American President Bill Clinton could speak conversational German, as he had studied it at university. He had felt a kindred spirit with the German people after reunification, and stated, '*Amerika steht an Ihrer Seite jetzt und für immer*' (America stands at your side, now and for ever) to an audience of 50,000 people at the Brandenburg Gates in Berlin. Everyone knew that there would be a flight of some cash until the reluctant Germans got used to the euro. The tantalising question was whether Clinton had been asked if presently thriving America was ready to accept some German funk money before the euro gained acceptance at home.

In September 1999, the *New York Times* reported that the Clinton Administration was pushing for more lending to low, and moderate-income borrowers so that they could share in the American dream. The idea was that people would only have to put a few dollars down to buy a house and then repay when the house went up in value.

Exporters like a low value for their currency so that they can maximise sales. Therefore, China had bought hundreds of billions of dollars of U.S. Treasuries to prevent the value of the Yuan soaring and her exports becoming less competitive. This had forced down Treasury yields and made a lot of easy money available. The sub-prime market grew.

In 2004 the Federal Reserve raised her interest rates because of the cost of the Iraq conflict. Interest rates rose from 1.25% to 2.25% in December 2004. Meanwhile the National Public Radio Correspondent asserted that there was 'a giant pool of money', which was seeking a supply of relatively safe, income generating investments in the US. However, sub-prime mortgages in America represented only ten per cent of all mortgages up till 2004.

According to the Bank for International Settlements, Germany lent almost one and a half trillion dollars to Greece, Ireland, Spain Portugal, and Italy before the Lehman Brothers crash. Such was Germany's prestige after reunification, that everywhere her money arrived, cash from other sources came too.

Indeed, after the German banks put twenty-one billion dollars into Icelandic banks, UK investors, including pension funds and hospitals, could not resist putting thirty billion dollars into Iceland as well.

The biggest business of all was the 'round tripping' of dollars between America and Europe. Cheap money was raised in America and exported to banks in Europe, who subsequently reinvested it in the US.[755] Unfortunately, when the money arrived back in America it was attracted by the subprime market. Soon subprime mortgages swelled to twenty per cent of all American mortgages. Meanwhile interest rates swelled from 2.5% in February 2005 to 4.24% in December 2005.

How much of the 'giant pool of foreign money' that arrived in America was German was hard to assess but it was clear that 'wherever parties were taking place, German banks were supplying the drinks.'[756] In 2006 the euro was strong, but the dollar was weak and the cost of creating peace in Iraq was high. This was unfortunate because the European Central Bank had started to inch up its interest rates. It raised them by a quarter of a per cent five times in 2006. American interest rates now stood at 5.25% and ECB interest rates at 3.50%. If the European Central Bank would merely keep its interest rates on hold in 2007 it could allow the American authorities a breathing space to restore order to its sub-prime market. On 14th March 2007 New Century Financial Corporation, the second-biggest subprime mortgage lender in the US, was de-listed by the New York Stock Exchange and the Federal Reserve predicted that the next move in interest rates would be down.

Meanwhile in Europe, Germany had closed her home market and squeezed wages since the arrival of the euro. By 2007, the German 'general government' deficit had disappeared. Nevertheless, the German government decided to cut corporation tax and give other advantages to industry, and to raise VAT by three per cent to pay for them. Naturally, company bosses were asked by their workers for money in compensation. I G Metall boss Jürgen Peters declared: 'Order books are full, and profits are surging, so they can't fob off workers with cheap pay.'[757]

Yet, after wage increases of 4.1% were agreed with Germany's most powerful union, I G Metall, dark-haired heavyweight President of the Bundesbank Axel Weber, insisted that European Central Bank's governor Jean-Claude Trichet, must raise interest rates throughout the euro-zone to curb German inflation.

Statistics later revealed that German wages actually fell in real terms between the years 2000 and 2007.[758] France's bank chief, Christian Noyer, declared flatly: 'There is no concern that (Eurozone) inflation will get out of hand.'[759] while President Sarkozy complained bitterly that the euro was already so high in relation to the dollar and the Chinese yuan that it was ruining French competitiveness. Yet, such was the power of the

Bundesbank that Axel Weber managed to push the European Central Bank to raise rates for the entire euro area to 3.75% in June 2007, and 4.0% in July.

In the 1990s the rises in Germany's interest rates had adversely affected Britain's attempt to remain in the ERM and ultimately caused 'Black Wednesday' when she crashed out of the system. In July 2007, the ECB's rises in interest rates had an unfortunate impact on Germany's friend, America. The investment bank, Bear Stearns announced the bankruptcy and liquidation of two large hedge funds that had used leverage to invest in Collateralized Debt Obligations backed by sub-prime mortgage loans.[760]

German Finance Minister, Peer Steinbrück, seemed not to worry about Bear Stern's difficulties or the flood of cash into the euro, declaring that he 'loved the strong euro.' On the other hand, French President, Nicolas Sarkozy was distraught. 'When the dollar loses thirty-three per cent of its value against the euro, how can our industries retain competitiveness?' Sarkozy complained.[761]

On 6th August the tenth largest retail mortgage lender in the US, the American Home Mortgage Investment Corporation, filed for bankruptcy.

Subsequently, understandably, the French bank BNP Paribas announced that it was suspending withdrawals on two of its funds that were heavily invested in the US sub-prime market. Unfortunately, its decision hit Britain's Northern Rock Bank.

Northern Rock, a profitable and solvent bank, had relied for much of its borrowing on the wholesale markets which had previously seemed to have so much money to spare. Now the wholesale money vanished and there was a gaping hole in its finances. The press got wind of this drastic development, there was a run on the bank and dreadful pictures were shown in the media of thousands of desperate people queuing up to retrieve their savings. The following Monday the government stepped in to guarantee all Northern Rock's deposits.[762] Banks in America and Europe were going bankrupt and French industry was bleeding from the euro's high value.

Trichet offered European banks a huge injection of liquidity and then firmly blamed the Fed and the Bank of England for the banking crisis.

But there was an imminent crisis in the European Union too. On 23rd September 2007 France's President Nicolas Sarkozy renewed his pressure on the ECB to reduce rates. He declared that the ECB should take note of the American Federal Reserve's decision to cut interest rates by a whole point from 5.25% to 4.75%, while his aide, Henri Guaino, declared in an interview in *Le Parisien* 'We cannot sit with crossed arms and stay silent in the face of this absurdity.'

Unfortunately, ECB Governor, Jean-Claude Trichet resisted Sarkozy's plea. Trichet declared that European inflation was at a six-year high because of high prices for food and energy and said that the ECB would not hesitate to raise rates again if inflation rose above three per cent.[763] He was supported by German Chancellor, Angela Merkel, who declared that she would block any attempts to try and impinge on the ECB's independence.[764] That ended Sarkozy's intervention on the matter.

This was regrettable as it appears that it was largely a rise in 'energy' prices, which had caused the rise in European inflation. Oil was priced in dollars. When the ECB raised interest rates, the dollar lost thirty-three per cent in value and the oil price rose an equal amount to compensate oil exporters for their loss of income. Therefore, the rises in the ECB's interest rates were essentially adding to European inflation by leading to an increase in the value of oil.

Nevertheless, in October 2007, Bundesbank Chairman Axel Weber declared that German inflation was still rampant and that Eurozone interest rates would have to rise at least once more to curb it. Traders believed that he would be able to enforce his view in ECB summits despite President Sarkozy's opposition and the damage that the high rate for the euro was doing to France's industry. They hedged their bets accordingly.[765]

In November, the European Central Bank held interest rates at four per cent while beleaguered ECB President, Jean-Claude Trichet, declared that the Eurozone's present 2.6% inflation was caused by a spike in oil and food prices and would subside the following year. He was irate at the traders who had transferred their funds to the euro, calling its ten per cent rise against the dollar 'brutal.' Nevertheless, Bundesbank President Axel Weber was still worried about German inflation and traders believed that he had the clout to force the ECB to raise interest rates again, if he deemed it necessary.[766]

On 8th December 2007, under the heading *ECB hawks snub pleas for rate cut – and call for a rise*, *Daily Telegraph* reporter, Ambrose Evans-Pritchard, revealed that the German ECB council members, Bundesbank chief, Axel Weber and ECB chief economist, Jürgen Stark were calling for an interest rate increase, despite the dangers of a slump. Nevertheless, 'After an exchange of words' the ECB managed to keep rates at the same level. This was lucky as property prices in Southern Europe and Ireland were tumbling and Spain's current account deficit had reached the 'staggering' total of nine per cent of GDP with a huge total of unsold property from the housing bubble.

Yet it was not only Southern Europe which was suffering; Deutsche Bank was also in dire trouble. Thomas Mayer, Deutsche Bank's chief economist, declared that the ECB must cut rates immediately, regardless of inflation, saying 'This could go beyond just a normal recession' while American bank, Morgan Stanley, issued a full recession alert for the US economy, warning of a sharp slowdown in business and a 'perfect storm' for consumers as the housing slump spread.

The alarmed American government decided to act. On 11th December 'the US, supported by the ECB ($20 bn) and the Swiss National Bank ($ 4 bn) offered liquidity to European banks caught 'in the sub-prime mess.'

It 'was declared that 'part of the problem before had been that the Federal Reserve Bank and the ECB in August had lacked 'swap' arrangements.' However, *Daily Telegraph* financial journalist Evans-Pritchard commented drily, 'There is a real danger that this may not work. Both the Fed and the ECB have injected a lot of liquidity before, but the banks are hoarding it.'

American interest rates were drastically slashed in the spring of 2008 to prevent an international banking crisis and terrible distress in the American housing market.

From 4.25% on 11th December. they crashed to two per cent on 30th April. A friendly ECB would have reduced rates in tandem, and this would have lowered the oil price too. Unfortunately, the ECB did not reduce rates, so the oil producers continued to raise their prices to protect their income. Meanwhile, Bear Stearns agreed to be acquired by

J P Morgan Chase & Co in the hope of staving off bankruptcy and the New York banking industry teetered on the edge of disaster.

The price of oil had fallen to $60 a barrel in the early part of 2007 before rising steeply to $90 a barrel in October 2007. On 2nd January 2008, the price for light crude hit $100 a barrel. On 18th April it reached $119.90. On 6th June it rose $11 in twenty-four hours shocked by a rumour of an Israeli attack on Iran. Iranian Oil Minister Gholam-Hossein Nozari declared stoutly that world markets were saturated with oil, and the Saudis promised to increased production. However, on 27th June prices touched $141.71 a barrel for August delivery amid Libya's threat to cut output and the OPEC's President's prediction that prices would rise to $170 by the autumn.[767] On 27th June 2008 it reached $147 a barrel for August

In July 2008, the European Central Bank decided to raise interest rates again on the grounds that inflation had risen well above the sacred level of three per cent. Excluding the spike in the price of oil, alcohol, food and tobacco, euro zone inflation was only two per cent in June 2008[768] but the oil price had pushed it over four per cent. EU interest rates were raised to 4.25% as against the two per cent prevailing in America. Money fled from the US. Two months later the global financial services firm Lehman Brothers collapsed, threatening the collapse of the western world's banking system.

Many people had worried that China would 'pull the plug' in 2008, removing her funds from America, and causing a disastrous crash and millions of unemployed. However, the Chinese did not cause the crash. Indeed, Beijing's holdings of US securities actually rose from $922 billion in June 2007 to $1,464 billion in 2009.[769] So, if China did not 'pull the plug,' could the ECB have been the culprit, egged on by its strongest nation, Germany?

The German newspapers were quick to blame America. *Die Welt* declared: 'Greed and stupidity have plunged the market into chaos ... Any economics student in his first semester could have concluded that the American economic model is not tenable.' While *Die Zeit* posed the question: 'Is finance-capitalism finished? And predicted the 'end of world domination by the Anglo-Saxon finance industry.'

German odium was especially directed at the American hedge funds, many of which had performed in a particularly unattractively greedy and destructive manner. In 2005, President of the German Financial Supervisory Authority, Jochen Sanio, had gone as far as to declare that hedge funds were the 'black holes of the world financial system' and the *Süddeutsche Zeitung* warned that they could trigger another LTMC-size disaster, which would 'threaten the entire financial system of the globe.' After the Lehman crash, Reuters reported that German Chancellor Angela Merkel had indirectly criticized the United States and Britain for thwarting her government's attempts to tighten controls on financial markets before the crash, under the heading 'I told you so.'

Undoubtedly the hedge funds, and other financial instruments, made a bad situation much worse at a critical time. Traders behaved in a most irresponsible way but there was no way that they alone could have caused such an immense catastrophe.

Hedge funds affect individuals and companies but rises in interest rates affect continents. Germany's high interest rates in 1929 had precipitated rises in the whole of Eastern Europe, America, and Britain before the 1929 stock market crash. Germany should have admitted her mistake in pushing the ECB to raise interest rates in 2007 and 2008 when lower ECB interest rates could have averted the tragedy.

In his book *Adults in the Room* (2017) former Greek Finance Minister, Yanis Varoufakis, revealed how wrong Angela Merkel was to blame America when her own banks had behaved so irresponsibly: 'In 2008, as banks in Wall Street and the City of London crumbled, Angela Merkel was still fostering her image as the tight-fisted, financially prudent Iron Chancellor. Pointing a moralising finger at the Anglosphere's profligate bankers, she made headlines in a speech she gave in Stuttgart when she suggested that America's bankers should have consulted a Swabian housewife, who would have taught them a thing or two about managing their finances.'

'Imagine her horror when, shortly afterwards, she received a barrage of anxious phone calls from her finance ministry, her central bank, her own economic advisers, all of them conveying an unfathomable message: Chancellor, our banks are bust too! To keep the ATMs going, we need an injection of 406 billion euros of those Swabian housewives' money – by yesterday! The federal parliament in Berlin known as the Bundestag, conveyed to her dumbfounded parliamentarians the bad news and left with the requested cheque. At least it's done, she must have thought. Except that it wasn't. A few months later another barrage of phone-calls demanded a similar number of billions for the same banks.'

'Why did Deutsche Bank, and the other Frankfurt-based banks ... need more? Because the 406 billion euros was barely enough to cover their trades in US-based toxic derivatives. It was not enough to cover what they had lent to the governments of Italy, Ireland, Greece, Spain and Italy – a total of 477 billion euros.'

In 2009 the *Economic Intelligence Unit Survey* expressed surprise that 'the German banking system has been 'among the worst affected anywhere ... despite the absence of high price inflation and credit growth.' But luckily it appeared that America had saved Germany from disaster. Economic historian Adam Tooze in his article, *The Secret History of the Banking Crisis* in *Prospect Magazine* reveals how the Federal Reserve helped *Deutsche Bank*, Germany's largest bank:

'Even before the Lehman crash, in December 2007, the Federal Reserve Bank instituted 'swap lines' of currencies to save the western world's banking system from collapse. In 2008 they were expanded. For the inner European core, plus Japan, they were made unrestricted in volume. The sums of liquidity were huge. All told, the Fed would make swap line loans of a total of $10 trillion to the ECB, the Bank of England, the National Bank of Switzerland, and other major banking centres. The maximum balance outstanding was $583 billion in December 2008, when they accounted for one-quarter of the Fed's balance sheet.' ... 'The Swap lines were central bank to central bank. But who did they really help? The reality, as all those involved understood, was that the Fed was providing preferential access to liquidity not to the 'euro area' or 'the 'Swiss economy, as a whole, but to Deutsche Bank and Credit Suisse.'

Every crash is associated with criminals and foolish speculators. The Federal Reserve Bank blamed itself for the 2008 debacle. However, although the financial journalist Michael Lewis censured 'extremely smart traders inside Wall Street investment banks' for devising 'deeply unfair complicated bets,' and then for sending sales forces abroad to find 'some idiot' who would take 'the other side of those bets' he revealed that 'a wildly disproportionate number of those idiots were in Germany.'[770]

It appears that Michael Lewis's assertion was true. The European Banks, encouraged by Germany's eagerness to invest, ultimately turned out to be deeper involved than their US counterparts.[771]

Nevertheless, the German press succeeded in blaming what it called 'the American economic model' and 'Anglo-Saxon capitalism' for the Lehman debacle.

On 7th February 2009 the German authorities decided that 'austerity' was to be the new policy. The government and Länder would adopt new rules compelling them to eliminate their budget deficits by 2020.[772] Naturally they lost no time in calling upon the entire European Union to abandon frivolity and return to the economic policy of 'sound money.'

Their appeal initially found favour internationally. People remembered Mr Micawber's famous caution in Charles Dickens' *David Copperfield* that 'happiness depends on living within your income' and were full of censure of America for causing the Lehman crash, and for the profligate countries of Southern Europe, who had taken advantage of Germany's largesse.

Nevertheless, America's *Bloomberg* newspaper disagreed that the Southern Europeans were the only irresponsible nations. In writing about the Greek crisis on 23rd May 2012 *Bloomberg*'s editors wrote under the catchy heading, *Hey Germany: You got a Bailout Too* 'Irresponsible borrowers can't exist without irresponsible lenders. Germany's banks were Greece's enablers ... According to the Bank for International Settlements, by December 2009 German banks had amassed claims of $704 billion on the so-called PIGS – Portugal, Italy, Ireland, Greece, and Spain, much more than the German banks' aggregate capital. In other words, they lent more than they could afford.'

'Indeed, when the crisis began German banks had thirty per cent of all the loans made to these countries public and private sectors, representing over fifteen per cent of the size of the German economy.'[773] Yet now they wanted the money that they had lent Southern Europe to be repaid.

Unfortunately, it was almost impossible for the southern European countries to starve their home economies and repay their loans because Germany had grabbed their home market, and their economies were in a tailspin. In consequence huge numbers of people became unemployed.

In 1930 Chancellor Heinrich Brüning had told the trade unions that he was going to adopt a policy of 'austerity' to persuade America to abandon charging reparations and let Germany return to dictatorship under a Hohenzollern king.

American economist, Paul Krugman, became increasingly suspicious of Germany's austerity policy after the Lehman crisis.

In his book, published in 2012 called *End this Depression Now*, Krugman declared: 'While modern conventional wisdom links the rise of Hitler to the German hyperinflation of 1923, what actually brought him to power was the German depression of the early 1930s, a depression that was even more severe than that in the rest of Europe, thanks to the deflationary policies of Chancellor Heinrich Brüning.'[774]

As a matter of fact, the German banks escaped almost scot-free from their Greek adventure. *Bloomberg* revealed:

'When the German banks pulled money out of Greece, the other national central banks of the euro area collectively offset the outflow with loans to the Greek central bank. These loans appeared on the balance sheet of the Bundesbank, Germany's central bank, as claims on the rest of the euro area. This mechanism, designed to keep the currency area's accounts in balance, made it easier for the German banks to exit their positions ... In short, over the last couple of years, much of the risk sitting on German banks' balance sheets shifted to the taxpayers of the entire currency union.'

Was the German policy of 'austerity' after Lehman crash imposed because the government cared about the savings of the German people and felt that 'austerity' was the best way to preserve what was left of them? Or was austerity adopted to help her consolidate her hold over southern Europe? If the latter was so, the results are encouraging. In his article, *The Bank that nearly broke Europe* (August 2018) Adam Tooze revealed how austerity helped Germany achieve control over the states of southern Europe.

'When the Eurozone governments took steps towards fiscal discipline, (ECB President) Trichet backed them up in the market. When they appeared to be backsliding, he ... let the markets rip. ...' 'And when market pressure was not enough ... he issued *instructions* to the governments of Ireland, Spain and Italy, demanding spending cuts, tax increases and changes to labour laws that reached deep into their internal affairs.'

Tooze continued 'Was Trichet driven to do all this by the Germans? .... The evidence certainly suggests that he was constrained by the German members of his board. Jürgen Stark, his chief economist, is widely blamed for the extraordinary decisions both to raise (interest) rates in 2008 and then again in 2011.'

Now the euro area has a system to ensure European stability. It is called Target 2. If there is a new crisis in southern Europe and people put their money in German Bonds, the Bundesbank merely transfers the cash to the ECB, which sends the money back to their countries. The same is true if they buy German goods. This ensures a large home market for German goods, even at zero profit.

It is a gilded cage, which affects both sides. The southern European states are trapped in German austerity and never seem to recover their former prosperity, while German savers are denied the profits of their labours. By 2016 former central bank governor Alan Greenspan assessed the amount of money that Germany had lent the ECB under the terms of Target 2 at 7,800 billion euros,[775] while the German autobahns aged, and their motorway bridges needed repair.

Yet Germany had succeeded in creating a single currency for the EU, which former Chancellor had called 'A castle in the air' and the euro has become one of the world's most powerful currencies, a remarkable achievement.

Moreover, it has been accomplished with a far shorter depression than occurred after Bismarck adopted the gold standard in the 1870s, let alone in the Great Depression before Hitler, thanks to the intervention of Paul Krugman.

CHAPTER 13

War in Ukraine

In 1996, German historian, Volker R Berghahn remarked that although Germany had twice attempted to grab a formal empire by force, stretching from the Atlantic coast to Russia's Ural Mountains and beyond, she found herself after her reunification on the verge of acquiring a similar empire in Europe without a shot being fired.

Nevertheless, although 'not a shot' had been fired by West Germany before her reunification, the German government had managed to persuade the Americans to use NATO to threaten the use of war on her behalf in the 1970s and America's subsequent 'Star War' nuclear programme had achieved the magnificent result of the ailing Soviet Union's collapse.

Reunified Germany now set her sights on gaining more power and influence in the European Union. France seemed able to tie up Germany's ambitions in red tape in Brussels, so Germany sought reliable friends who would support her interests through thick and thin, initially by insisting on the EU's support for Croatia and Slovenia declaring their independence from Yugoslavia so that they could become EU members.

The war which decimated Yugoslavia, cost 140,000 lives and 4 trillion dollars, mostly paid by America but Croatia and Slovenia are now fully fledged members of the EU.

Now war has been raging in Ukraine. As America is tiring of paying the costs, it is worthwhile the re-examining the evidence as to how it began.

Russia's neighbour Ukraine is a huge, young, impecunious country, which nevertheless is rich in raw materials and has, in the past has been prominent in Germany's territorial ambitions.

In the First World War, after Germany had concluded the rapacious Treaty of Brest-Litovsk, her triumphant army surrounded Ukraine's parliament on 28th April 1918 and asked the government to surrender. Two days later Germany took control of Ukraine and decided that heavy industry, under such famous names as Krupp, would organise Ukraine's coal, iron ore, manganese, electrical and chemical industries, with the agricultural sector restructured so that its precious Black Earth could produce food for the Reich.

The industrialists were so excited by Ukraine's treasures, their ambition was for Ukraine to be sealed off from what they termed 'Great Russia' and 'any third power,' and for her economic system to be aligned to Germany's.'[776]

Germany had to abandon Ukraine in November 1918 but the country's long-cherished concept of *Mitteleuropa*, a central European political and economic confederation, which would give the German industrialists a wider home market for their goods remained. When the Nazis gained power in the 1930s it came back into favour. What was now termed *Großraumwirtchaft* came increasingly to mean a closed-bloc autarkic economy, stretching as far as Russia's Ural Mountains.

The Ukrainian people suffered dreadfully in the Second World War. Some four million soldiers died, with Eastern Ukrainians fighting on Russia's side and Western Ukraine fighting for the Nazis.

After the Second World War America helped to finance what has since become the European Union with the aim of preserving peace in Western Europe. The rapprochement between France and Germany has been its great achievement and many more countries have applied to join the EU - but at the edge of Europe it faces competition.

The principal hindrance to the EU's eastern expansion is Russia. Russia and Germany were on friendly terms after the Soviet Union's collapse. Eventually the Russian economy stabilised and began to grow again. However, Russia was still regarded as weak and a 'pushover' by many outsiders, including in the United States, because of the Soviet Union's dramatic downfall.

In 1990 American Secretary of State, James Baker, had given the President of Russia, Mikhail Gorbachev, the assurance that if he removed his troops from East Germany, the Allies military organization NATO would not move 'one inch eastward.'

Ukraine had declared herself an independent and neutral state in 1991. Yet soon NATO moved East to include the Czech Republic, Hungary, and Poland.

NATO's move eastwards alarmed former US diplomat and Russian expert George Kennan, who had had a profound influence on American opinion in the aftermath of the Second World War. He declared 'I think the Russians will gradually react quite adversely and it will affect their polices. ... it is a tragic mistake.'

Reporter David Frost wanted to know whether new Russian President Vladimir Putin regarded NATO as a threat. Putin was careful to reply 'Russia is part of European culture. I cannot imagine my country in isolation from Europe and from the so-called, as we so often say, civilised world. So, I find it difficult to envisage NATO as an enemy. It seems to me that ... even posing the question is damaging.'[ii]

The European Union was also moving eastwards. It is possible that Putin regarded both as a threat. At all events he decided to establish an association like the EU, called the Eurasian Economic Union, or EAEU which would steadily grow in power and influence. Meanwhile NATO's eastern expansion continued, with Bulgaria, Estonia, Latvia, Lithuania, Romania, Slovakia, and Slovenia being admitted in 2004.

NATO was getting closer and closer to Russia's borders. Missiles were placed on the soil of member countries, and they all seemed to be pointing at Moscow. Yet, while former President Yeltsin had 'gnashed his teeth' against the first wave of entrants, impotent new President Putin had offered little active resistance to the second, and in 2007 bullish American Vice President Dick Cheney felt confident enough to offer Georgia and Ukraine a Membership Action Plan (MAP) as a preparation for membership.[iii]

A horrified American Ambassador to Russia, William J Burns, told his superiors,

'I have yet to find anyone (in Russia) who views Ukraine in NATO as anything other than a direct challenge to Russian interests. ... At this stage, a MAP offer would be seen not as a technical step along a long road toward membership, but as throwing down the strategic gauntlet.'

Indeed, Burns was so alarmed at the thought of America offering Ukraine the prospect of entering NATO that he decided to risk losing his job by adding, 'I can conceive of no grand package that would allow the Russians to swallow this pill quietly.'[iv]

France and Germany were also against the idea at the time as they were planning the construction of the Nord Stream I pipeline to bring Russian gas to Europe. [v] As a result, when the communiqué was issued at NATO's Bucharest summit in April 2008, it did not mention the Membership Action Plan (MAP) but declared in Angela Merkel and American Secretary of State, Condoleezza Rice's name: 'We agreed today that Ukraine and Georgia will become members of NATO.'[vi]

Merkel later wrote in her memoirs that she had been against giving MAP to Ukraine at that time but that she could foresee Ukraine and Georgia eventually entering NATO, so put her name to the statement. However, she recalls that for Putin it was 'a declaration of war.'

At the final press conference of his presidency, Putin spelt out his hostility towards 'the further eastwards expansion of NATO, the establishment of military infrastructure on the territories of the new members… (and) plans to deploy elements of the strategic antimissile defence from the United States to Europe.'[vii] The West had spread its tentacles far enough and must come no further.

Putin had regarded Georgian President Mikheil Saakashvili of Georgia as a puppet of the United States. Saakashvili had led the Rose Revolution which had ousted the former pro-Russian Georgian President and improved the Georgian economy. However, he was impulsive. He had successfully forced one semi-independent area of Georgia to submit to central authority and was now aching to bring the other semi-independent regions of South Ossetia and Abkhazia neighbouring Russia to heel.

Putin was cold and careful. He was not going to initiate anything, but had warned Ambassador Burns more than once, 'If Saakashvili uses force in South Ossetia … I will have no alternative to recognising South Ossetia and Abkhazia and responding with force.'

Unfortunately, after the less dynamic Dmitry Medvedev became Russia's President, Saakashvili felt that he could disregard Putin's warning. On 8th August Saakashvili launched an artillery barrage against South Ossetia's principal city, Tskhinvali. Unfortunately, although Putin was no longer President, he was the power behind the throne. Russian troops poured over the border, bombed Georgia's capital city Tbilisi, and the Russian state recognized the independence of the tiny states of South Ossetia and Abkhazia.

Putin had originally responded to NATO and the EU's expansion by expanding his Eurasian Economic Union. By 2012 it comprised Russia, Armenia, Belarus, Kazakhstan, and Kyrgyzstan and produced 20.7% of the world's natural gas, 14.6% of the world's oil, 18.6% of its sugar beet, 22% of its sunflower oil and a large amount of the world's wheat. It began to look an attractive organization to join. In contrast, the mighty European Union seemed weak as it was suffering from the austerity policy that had been adopted after the Lehman crash.

Although Ukrainian President Viktor Yanukovych had a murky past, his 2010 election victory had been judged fair by international monitors. He signed a new foreign policy document declaring Ukraine's neutrality and appointed Petro Poroshenko, one of the richest men in Europe, as his minister for trade and development.

Poroshenko was nicknamed 'the chocolate king' as he owned Ukraine's largest confectionary concern, the Roshen group, as well as two television channels and numerous other businesses. A large extremely forceful character, Poroshenko was eager for Ukraine to be a member of the EU. Yanukovych wanted to keep him on side.

Yanukovych came from Eastern Ukraine but decided to try to reach an association agreement with the EU. His object initially seems to have been for Ukraine to join both the EU and Russia's EAEU. Unfortunately, on 25th February 2013, José Manuel Barroso, the EU's president, made it clear that 'One country cannot at the same time be a member of a customs unions and be in a deep common free trade area of the European Union.'

Yet, Yanukovych still wanted to join the EU, as the EU had brought wealth and good governance to Ukraine's friends in Western Europe. Consequently, he signed an association agreement with the EU on Ukraine's behalf on 20th March 2013.

As an inducement to Ukraine to join, the EU had offered Ukraine $838 million in loans, but in return Ukraine had to agree to political, judicial, and financial reforms while the IMF heaped on the agony by demanding budget cuts and a rise in the price of gas. This looked unpalatable to the cash-strapped Ukrainian government so, eventually, America stepped in with a sweetener of $4 billion. Yet, America's generous action arrived too late. Yanukovych eventually decided on his country accepting oil-rich Russia's 'bribe' of $15 billion and one third off the price of gas.[viii]

With time and the offer of more money, corrupt but pragmatic Yanukovych might have reacted more positively to the European Union's offer to his country, but he felt that there was no way he could accept such a poor deal in 2013.[ix] However, many citizens in the western half of Ukraine had been longing to join their friends in Poland and the Czech Republic etc. who were working in western Europe.

Protests erupted against Ukraine joining Russia's EAEU. Although initially only 37% of the vast country supported joining the EU, [777] the numbers of protesters in Kyiv according to billionaire Petro Poroshenko, swelled from 2000 to 30,000 in just four hours, despite the freezing winter. Thousands more followed, braving the icy temperature; then subversives from abroad arrived. Soon they were said to be involved in the seizure of buildings of local authorities, the Interior Ministry, Security Service, military units, and ammunition depots.

'These are not just signs of terrorism, but concrete terrorist acts' declared the *Los Angeles Times* (19 02 2014). President Yanukovich was accused of using Russian snipers to quell the riots. Scores of policemen died, and hundreds of civilians too. Yanukovych fled and a pro EU government came to power.

Who was responsible for Ukraine's Maidan protests and the so-called 'Revolution of Dignity' which followed? It seems at first sight as though America was the prime force. In December 2013, when the Maidan protests were escalating into violence, Senator John McCain, who was standing beside boxer turned politician, Vitali Klitschko's brother, told the protesters: 'What we're trying to do is try to bring about a peaceful transition here, that ... would give the Ukrainian people ... a real society.'[x]

However, in his chapter on Russia in his recent book, *Prisoners of Geography* former diplomatic editor of *Sky News* Tim Marshall revealed that Germany shared responsibility, stating: 'The Germans and Americans had backed the opposition parties, with Berlin in particular, seeing former world boxing champion turned politician Vitali Klitschko as their man.'[xi]

Vitali Klitschko had won multiple world heavyweight boxing championships before he began his political career and was very popular in Germany. He claimed that 'Germany adopted me' and had a house in the country. Later, supported by, amongst others the Konrad Adenauer Foundation he became leader of the political party, Ukrainian Democratic Alliance for Reform (UDAR) and in 2012 the UDAR won 40 seats in the Ukrainian government. According to the magazine, *DER SPIEGEL*, Germany's target in Ukraine was to 'set up Klitschko purposefully as a new strong man ... in order to counter ... the Kremlin's growing influence.'

Klitschko became influential during the Maidan riots. Although he would be pipped at the post by Poroshenko for the presidency in May,[xii] he became the mayor of Kyiv, a powerful position, which he holds to this day.

One must conclude, therefore, that both Germany and America bore responsibility for the Maidan protests which led to the country's 'regime-change.' They would have had sympathy from many quarters. Most of the countries in western Europe had suffered from the Soviet Union's repression and wanted Ukraine to join. Nevertheless, the fact remains that Germany and America's so-called 'Revolution of Dignity' cost over 100 lives and had disastrous results.

Flushed with victory the interim pro EU government in Kyiv made stupid statements including its resolve to abolish the Russian language as Ukraine's official second language.[xiii] This inflamed all those in the East of Ukraine's vast country whose mother-tongue was Russian, including in Crimea.

Crimea was cherished by Russia because it was the home of Russia's warm water fleet. It had been part of Russia for 150 years before Ukrainian-born Soviet President Nikita Khrushchev gave it to Ukraine in 1951, believing that the two countries would be eternally united. Yet, after Ukraine became independent in 1991, the rupture between Ukraine and Russia widened, with members of the

Ukrainian parliament in Kyiv resorting to blows in 2012 over whether to renew the Russian fleet's lease.

Putin felt that Russia was in danger of losing his fleet's precious warm water port. After Yanukovych was undemocratically booted out of power in Kyiv, he decided to remedy the situation,[xiv] surreptitiously assembling his troops in Crimea and taking over the government buildings without bloodshed. Then he held a referendum on 16th March, asking Crimeans if they wanted 'a reunification with Russia as Federal Subjects of the Russian Federation.' The 82% of Crimea's population that were of Russian descent lined up to cast their votes and 97% of them said 'Yes'.

France's ex-President, Nicolas Sarkozy wanted to accept the vote as legitimate, but Angela Merkel declared that the presence of Russian troops rendered the vote invalid. Moreover, the German Council on Foreign Relations and NATO maintained that Russia's Black Sea Fleet in Crimea was the 'strategic backbone of projection of Russia's power, through the Bosphorus and into the Eastern Mediterranean and that its presence in Crimea was a threat to the stability of the region.'

Russia's absorption of Crimea upset America as well. Five days after the Crimean vote, America and the EU agreed a hefty set of sanctions against Russian individuals and corporations and expelled Russia from the powerful G8 international organisation.

The sanctions were to be the first of many. American Assistant Secretary of State for European Affairs, Victoria Nuland was livid. She did not seem to be aware that Putin was bound to react to the regime-change that America had just helped carry out in Kyiv. She also grossly underestimated Russia's economic strength and threatened Putin with the collapse of the Russian Federation.

The rouble dropped precipitously as she warned: 'Unless Putin changes course ... the current nationalistic fever will break in Russia.' 'When it does, it will give way to a sweaty and harsh reality.'[778]

Nevertheless, despite Nuland's threatening words, and the tough sanctions, Crimea's session from Ukraine spawned another independence movement in Eastern Ukraine, which would ultimately be supported by Russia.

Although the whole of the vast country of Ukraine had decided to leave the Soviet Union's sinking ship and vote for independence in 1991, the inhabitants of Luhansk and Donetsk, whose state capital is nearly as far from Kyiv as it is from Moscow, subsequently changed their minds. Before Ukraine's 'regime change' the Russian-speaking area in the East had higher wages than the rest of Ukraine and was a major exporter. Now Luhansk and Donetsk wanted to achieve, not unity with Russia, but 'self-determination' and independence like Croatia and Slovenia had been allowed to secure from the former country of Yugoslavia.

Unfortunately for Luhansk and Donetsk, powerful billionaire Petro Poroshenko had become Ukraine's President. His very first measure stated that, although every 'village, city, district and regional administration' in Ukraine would be given the right to determine its local language under the supervision of 'presidential representatives,' Ukrainian from now on would be the nation's only state language.

As Poroshenko's talk of 'presidential representatives' supervising the language that every village spoke, did not appeal to Russian-speaking Luhansk and Donetsk, Poroshenko asserted that 'fake' separatist referendums in the regions had to be prevented. He maintained that the separatists were 'terrorists' and that the only language that they understood was 'that of force' and so employed Arsen Avakov, an extremely able, unsavoury, and ruthless individual, who had managed to quell a separatist movement in Kharkov, to carry out his dictate.

Over thirty volunteer battalions of Ukrainian fighters were formed in 2014, many raised with the help of the Oligarchs like the billionaire Ihor Kolomoisky, who saw himself threatened with losing his assets in the region and reputedly spent £10 million on creating the Dnipro Battalion.

Damien Sharkov in his *Newsweek* article called *'Ukrainian Nationalist Volunteers committing ISIS-style war crimes'* revealed that that the Ukrainian volunteer Battalions used beatings and extortion in their campaign against the separatists from Luhansk and Donetsk. The war became increasingly bitter with thousands losing their lives on both sides. Russian military equipment increasingly found its way to the separatists and American equipment to Ukraine. However, the separatists lost any sympathy they might have received by accidently shooting down an airliner, killing 283 passengers and 15 crew.

In late August, after severe reverses the separatists received Russian help and dealt the Ukrainian forces a 'hammer blow'[779] which led to the Minsk protocol, signed by Ukraine, Russia and the OSCE. However, the war continued albeit with fewer casualties.

On 24th December 2014 Amnesty International charged the volunteer battalions with blocking food supplies from reaching the starving civilians. Nevertheless, the separatists with Russian help managed to turn the tide against the battalions supporting the government in Kyiv again and seized Donetsk airport.

German Foreign Minister, Frank-Walter Steinmeier, was a friend of pro-Russian former German Chancellor, Gerhard Schroeder. His government was about to sign the agreement with Russia over the Nord Stream II pipeline. He expressed his concern over the situation in Luhansk and Donetsk, and his government tasked him with achieving a compromise.

The so-called 2015 Minsk II accord between Ukraine and Russia, Germany, and France, envisaged leaving the whole of the nation of Ukraine intact, with only minor concessions. One concern to Kyiv was that the Luhansk and Donetsk separatists would be allowed to retain Russian as their first language. Another was that although they would remain within Ukraine's borders they would be allowed 'cross-border cooperation ... with districts of the Russian Federation' which could mean that they could continue to operate under Russia's economic system, rather than that of the EU. Crucially, also Russia would only have to return control of the border after the constitutional amendments had been agreed.

Ukrainian President Petro Poroshenko agreed to the Minsk II accord with Russia Germany and France in February 2015 and the scale of the conflict in the East subsided. Nevertheless, the extremists in Kyiv refused to endorse the Minsk II treaty, even though it had been agreed by their own President.

American Assistant Secretary of State for European Affairs, Victoria Nuland, had acknowledged that Germany and America's 'regime change' in Ukraine 2014 had necessitated using some 'very ugly colours.' These had given the neo-Nazis in Western Ukraine a boost in power.

In 2015 Petro Poroshenko argued that Stalin's Holodomor of the 1930s, in which about 4 million peasants died and the Nazi crimes of the 1940s were equally atrocious and decreed that the Organization of Ukrainian Nationalists (OUN) and the Ukrainian Insurgent Army (UPA) which had murdered countless Jews and Poles during the Second World War, should now be called the 'heroes of Ukraine.'

Ukraine became a more intolerant society and outsiders and the infirm were heckled. On 14th October 2018 the descendants of UPA and the OUN were joined by Nazis from the National Democratic Party of Germany's youth organization and the German neo-Nazi Third Path in celebrating 'Defender of Ukraine Day' to celebrate the Nazi victory in Ukraine in 1942. A Holocaust memorial in Ternopil was bombed, a Romani gypsy camp attacked and burnt, while hundreds rocked at a neo-Nazi concert clad in Swastikas.[780]

In the meantime, across the ocean in America, Donald Trump had become President in 2017. He struck a friendly attitude towards Putin and asserted that the Europeans (and especially Germany!) were freeloaders on America's defence industry. Moreover, he called upon them to pay their fair share towards NATO, airing the possibility that he might legally recognize Russia's occupation of Crimea.

Germany immediately called for the EU to establish its own army, and France upheld her move. This alarmed the American armaments establishment. If Europe had its own army, NATO would eventually be redundant in Europe and would lose its power and influence in the world. That would be a dreadful scenario. So, the US insisted that any proposed new European army should be 'complementary to' and not distracting from NATO but in return agreed that a new NATO headquarters separate from the normal command structure could be placed in Germany.

As a result of this negotiation, one could say that although the result of Donald Trump's initiative was to beef up NATO, it also enhanced Germany's power and influence in the organization.

The Americans then sought Germany's assistance in their campaign against China. Germany decided that although China was a valuable trading partner with around 200 billion euros in annual trade, a disengagement from the USA' would hit it harder, particularly in terms of 'security policy.'

'Security policy' was a euphemism for the supply of armaments, which America had supplied Germany with so liberally in the past. In return for Germany supporting America's campaign in the Pacific, Germany argued that America should help it secure her ambitions in Ukraine and Georgia. And that is what appears to have happened.

Soon the German rhetoric against Russia increased. Under pressure Russia was becoming decreasingly democratic, and Putin was murdering and imprisoning his opponents like the autocrats in Egypt, Iran, and Saudi Arabia. German newspapers also asserted that Russia was becoming a predator. The EU was under threat.

Already, in 2015, while the Minsk II agreement was being finalised, the *Frankfurter Allgemeine Zeitung*'s editor, Berthold Kohler asserted that 'NATO had to make clear to the Kremlin that any breach-of-area will be countered with a military response.'

In 2016 NATO agreed an armaments support package for Ukraine and staged a simulated attack on Poland with more than 30,000 troops. Germany did not supply any armaments (it had just signed the Nordstream II gas agreement) but it did approve of the EU sanctions against Russia being extended.

In 2018 German foreign Minister Heiko Maas concluded, 'We have reached the point, where we must clearly state that we are waiting for constructive contributions in the Skripal case, the annexation of Crimea, and the hacker attacks' while Defence Minister, Ursula von der Leyen, asserted, 'President Putin does not appreciate weakness. He must be dealt with from a position of determination and strength.'

That was billionaire Petro Poroshenko's outlook in Ukraine too. However, he would be charged with tax evasion and money laundering after he lost the 1919 presidential elections, and Volodymyr Zelensky swept to victory on the basis that he would be the new untarnished leader of Ukraine, who would secure peace in Luhansk and Donetsk and fight corruption.

Unfortunately, after Zelensky had announced that he had reached an agreement over Luhansk and Donetsk based on the one Russia had agreed at Minsk in 2015, Poroshenko joined a crowd of extremists in Kyiv screaming 'No to capitulation' even though he had put his signature to the original agreement in 2015 and the agreement would have kept the whole of Ukraine as one country.

Neo-Nazi leader of the Azov battalion, Andriy Biletsky, expressed his disgust at the peace agreement, accusing Zelensky of 'acting on behalf of the Kremlin and disrespecting the veterans who had fought against the separatists.'

A dejected Zelensky revealed to the German weekly magazine, *Spiegel*, 'As for Minsk as a whole, I told ... Angela Merkel that we will not be able to implement it.'

However, Merkel did not seem downcast and indeed in 2022 would astonishingly disclose that the Minsk accords had merely been signed in the first place to 'give Ukraine time' to get stronger and for NATO to increase its support against Russia. [xxv]

The citizens of Ukraine wanted to end the war in Luhansk and Donetsk, but neither the Oligarchs, nor Petro Poroshenko nor Mrs Merkel liked the peace agreement.

However, Germany had committed herself to full implementation of it and Merkel had agreed that contracts 'should be honoured' so she blamed Zelensky for its failure at the Paris summit in December 2019 because he insisted that the Ukrainian state must return to policing the border with Russia, before the elections in Luhansk and Donetsk had taken place, and not afterwards as internationally agreed. Zelensky finally decided 'NATO is the only way to win the war in Ukraine.'

Ukraine's aim to become a member of NATO had actually been written into the Ukrainian constitution before Zelensky had even became President. By early 2020, it was said to be on track to secure NATO Enhanced Opportunity Partner status and in December of that year Ukrainian defence Minister Andrii Taran, addressed the ambassadors and military attaches of NATO countries with the words: 'Please inform your capitals that we count on your full political and military support for such a decision (granting Ukraine MAP) at your next NATO summit in 2021.'

This was a worrying development as over ten years earlier, in February 2008 the American Ambassador to Russia, William J Burns, had warned:

'Ukraine's entry into NATO is the brightest of all red lines for the Russian elite (not just Putin). In more than two and half years of conversations with Russian players ... I have yet to find anyone who views Ukraine as anything other than a direct challenge to Russian interests.'

The trouble was that the Americans were wanting Germany to abandon the Nord Stream II pipeline - which would bring valuable cheap gas from Russia to Germany - and to help them in their campaign against China - and the Germans wanted reciprocity. A report called 'NATO 2030' declared that while Russia was 'by economic and social measures a declining power' it was 'likely to remain the chief threat facing NATO over the coming decade.' So, NATO tried to intimidate Russia through military manoeuvres.

In 2020, American B-52 bombers entered Ukrainian airspace for the first time and on 25th September they staged a mock attack on the Russian enclave of Kaliningrad where Russia had her Baltic fleet.

In March 2021 NATO began its Defender 21 Exercise in Europe with 28,000 multinational forces. It included Air Force and Navy participation and several smaller 'linked' exercises, some of which involved special airborne operations in Estonia, Bulgaria, and Romania.

'It's defensive in nature, focused on deterring aggression' said Pentagon Press Secretary John F Kirby, but Putin was in no doubt that it was aimed at Russia and moved 100,000 troops forward towards the Ukrainian border, declaring that Russia would be forced to react if her Red Lines were crossed – 'if necessary, with massive retaliation.'

Meanwhile the left-wing American on-line magazine *Counterpunch* recorded that Zelensky had pulled out of the next round of talks with Russia declaring: 'NATO is the only way to end the war in Donbas,' adding 'MAP will be a real signal for Russia.'

As a result, at the NATO summit which started on 31st May 2021, NATO Secretary-General Jens Stoltenberg decided to ignore Putin's red line declaring: 'It's up to Ukraine and the 30 NATO members to decide whether it aspires to be a member of the 'Alliance. Russia has no say in whether Ukraine shall be a member.' And NATO launched another naval exercise in the Black Sea as part of an exercise named Sea Breeze 2021.[xxxii]

Putin was determined that Ukraine should retain her neutral status. He reduced the number of the Russian troops at his border before he met American President Joe Biden and reiterated that changing Ukraine's status to become a member of NATO was a Red Line for his country.

Biden took him seriously. The American people were still decamping from Afghanistan and had no appetite another conflict.

The subsequent discussions between America and Russia were wide and seemingly constructive. It was agreed that a 'Strategic Stability Dialogue' would begin at ministerial level 'to lay the groundwork for future arms control and risk reduction measures.' Yet, the American government did not and indeed could not give Putin any cast-iron guarantees about NATO as the Europeans had the majority in the democratic organization and they seemed to be encouraging it to apply.

Unfortunately, Ambassador William J Burns had warned as long ago as 2008 that 'a MAP offer to Ukraine would be seen … as throwing down the strategic gauntlet.' He was right.

In December Putin muscled up a huge number of troops again and declared that NATO must give Russia 'reliable and long-term security guarantees' that would 'rule out any further eastward expansion of NATO and the deployment of weapons systems posing a threat to us in close proximity to the territory of the Russian Federation.' When he did not receive a satisfactory reply, he invaded.

Putin was a cold and careful individual. His Red Lines were sacrosanct. But he was also an opportunist. As his Red Line had been ignored by NATO, he felt that he had an excuse to rescue the separatists in Luhansk and Donetsk who had defied central government for eight years. Therefore, on 24th February 2022, he recognised the separatist states of Luhansk and Donetsk, began the siege of Mariupol and rolled his tanks up to Kyiv 500 miles away in Western Ukraine declaring that his invasion of Ukraine was 'a special military operation.'

The British were horrified. Whatever the provocation, the invasion of a peaceful country by another e country was detestable. Besides the British had signed the Budapest Memorandum in 1994, under which the United States, Britain and Russia had assured Ukraine that they would defend her territorial integrity.

A member of the US delegation in Budapest had denigrated the memorandum and Britain and America had not invoked it after Russia's take-over of Crimea. However, the attempted invasion of Kyiv was different. Putin himself had declared that the western part of Ukraine was 'really European.' So, Britain was proud of Boris Johnson's action in rushing to the defence of Kyiv, and Britain and America were the first to offer the Ukrainian people weapons to defend themselves.

The German reaction was quite different. The German people were ardent pacifists after the horrors of Hitler and the Second World War, so their seemingly equally pacifist government offered Ukrainians no weapons, just helmets to protect themselves. Germany's pacifist action had a huge impact abroad. Yet In 1979 the German government had deceived its electorate and the wider world over its action in pushing for the American Star Wars project, whilst appearing to be pacifist. In 2022 the same rule seems to have applied.

Whilst German Foreign Minister, Annalena Baerbock declared: 'We have woken up in a different world' and the German government pretended that the whole country was pacifist. Chancellor Olaf Scholz himself immediately approved, without fanfare, a shipment of 1,000 anti-tank and 500 surface to air missiles to Ukraine. Even more surprisingly, he allocated an astonishing 100 billion euros to raising the country's military expenditure to the more than 2% of GDP, which he had baulked over providing NATO with in 2018. Scholz also suspended the Nord Stream II gas pipeline project which was about to bring Russian gas to Germany.

Russia's Gazprom had born the bulk of the Nord Stream II gas pipe's investment costs, and Germany's neighbour Norway was happy to fill the gap with her gas. Wind power and renewables were also increasingly supplying Germany's energy needs, leading one to suspect that Nord Stream II had essentially been used as a bargaining chip to heap pressure on America.

The German press quickly reacted to the war by portraying the Russians as non-European ... spectres, ethnically – racially - hybrid, with war in their genetic code. The German people were warned that 'the next two years' would be 'very difficult', and they had to make sacrifices to win the war. Meanwhile the government decided to borrow 200 billion euros, while the Chancellor declared that the rest of the countries in the EU (who would be shut out of the market for raising money because of the immensity of German borrowing) could 'no longer afford' the privilege of 'national vetoes, for example, on foreign policy issues."

Putin's invasion of Kyiv horrified the world but luckily the Russian soldiers did not seem very successful and serious peace negotiations between Russia and Ukraine kicked off almost immediately. On 29th March the press reported that the initial negotiations had been successful.

'The Treaty ... would proclaim Ukraine as a permanently neutral, nonnuclear state which would renounce any intention to join military alliances or allow military bases or troops on its soil. The communiqué listed as possible guarantors the permanent members of the UN Security Council (which comprised of China France Russia, the UK and the US) along with Canada, Germany, Israel, Italy, Poland, and Turkey.'

The head of the Russian delegation, Vladimir Medinsky optimistically declared 'Yesterday, the Ukrainian side, for the first time fixed in written form its readiness to carry out a series of most important conditions for the building of future normal and good neighbour relations with Russia'

The question of Ukraine's membership of the EU was left open, but Russia had no objection to its accession in principle. Elections would be held in Donetsk and Luhansk, the areas would remain parts of Ukraine but allowed decentralisation as in the Minsk Agreement, and it was stated that Russia and Ukraine would 'peacefully resolve their dispute over Crimea' over the next 10 to 15 years.

This was huge break-through as Putin had formerly refused point-blank to talk about Crimea's status before, but the Russian negotiators had been over optimistic in thinking that the agreement was nearly signed and sealed.

Putin would blame British Prime Minister Boris Johnson for the talks' subsequent breakdown. Boris arrived in Kyiv on 9th April 2022 with a promise of £100 million of high-grade military equipment for Ukraine and the assertion that Britain and America were not ready to sign a peace agreement. He had felt deeply about the plight of the Ukrainians and obligated to help them under the terms of the Bucharest memorandum. However, he was little respected in Britain because of his failures during the Covid crisis and had even fewer friends in Europe because of Brexit.

Putin had always regarded Britain as America's pawn, indeed, after Boris, presumably with NATO's encouragement, had sent a destroyer into the disputed waters of Crimea in 2021, Putin reflected that no-one would have gone to war if he had blown the destroyer up.[xl] Nevertheless, he would blame Boris for the breakdown of the important Ukrainian peace negotiations in 2022.

America's reservations about the agreement were not surprising as Washington had not been consulted, even though the treaty as it stood would have obliged America to go to war if Russia invaded Ukraine again. The question is whether Boris had been solely Britain and America's envoy, sent to stiffen Zelensky in the negotiations, or whether he was the unofficial agent of Germany and NATO as well.

American Secretary of State, Antony Blinken declared, 'The strategy that we've put in place – massive support for Ukraine, massive pressure against Russia, solidarity with more than 30 countries engaged in these efforts – is having real results,' which leads one to believe that Boris was Germany and NATO's envoy too.

The Russian troops retreat after their invasion seemed to have given the wrong signal anyway. The mood hardened in Kyiv, especially after the news that nearly 500 people had been murdered in Bucha. The Ukrainian government refused to reduce the size of its armed forces from 250,000 to 85,000 and demanded Russia's retreat from the whole of Ukraine before it signed the treaty. The Ukrainian government's decision was a tragedy as it would have kept Ukraine intact, but it was not surprising as the leader of the Azov Battalion, Andriy Bilestsky – with the tacit support of Angela Merkel - had already reacted violently against a similar, albeit friendlier deal in 2019.

On 2nd May 2022, Oleksiy Danilov, Zelensky's Chair of the Ukrainian National Security and Defence Council declared proudly: 'A treaty with Russia is impossible – only capitulation can be accepted.' While in June 2022, former Ukrainian President Petro Poroshenko would tell Germany's *Deutsche Welle* that the 2015 Minsk II agreement with Russia, France and Germany, repeated by Zelinsky in 1919, had merely been a distraction for Kyiv to buy time to rebuild its own army.

American political scientist John J Mearsheimer who had written an article in 2014 called 'Why the Ukraine crisis is the West's fault,' blamed Russia's invasion of Ukraine on America's support for NATO's eastern expansion.

Yet America had not seemed eager to be become entangled in another war after its experience in Afghanistan. It realized all too well that if NATO became involved America would be picking up most of the Bill. However, many German/Americans identified with their historic German homeland and possessed a hatred of Russia. Some even felt that they should have been on Germany's side in its fight against Stalin in the Second World War.

Therefore, when President Biden described Putin as 'a war criminal, a murderous dictator (and) ... a butcher' it struck a chord. America decided that it would provide weapons for Ukraine, but not cluster bombs initially, nor long range missile systems that could reach beyond the range of the ones that Ukraine was currently using on the battlefield. It obviously hoped that the war would be over soon.

A year later, on 27th July 2023, Putin would declare that his forces had intentionally retreated from Northern and North-Western Ukraine after his invasion of Ukraine in February 2022, so that he could meet the conditions for his April peace accord with Ukraine. Whatever the truth of this, his army's untidy retreat had given NATO and America the disastrous impression that Russia was a soft touch. So, they were happy to support the Ukrainian soldiers.

Unfortunately, neither the Ukrainian soldiers nor America realised Putin's philosophy. 'If something happens,' he had maintained when he was very young, 'You should proceed from the fact that there is no retreat.'

On 20th May, Mariupol surrendered after devastating bloodshed. It was an omen of things to come. By the end of June American political scientist John S Mearsheimer noted that the 'Russian forces have conquered at least 20% of Ukrainian territory.'

Nevertheless, the Ukrainians launched a counteroffensive at the end of August 2022 and made some initial encouraging gains. Olaf Scholz promised Germany's support for Ukraine 'For as long as it takes,' and urged the 27 members of the EU to do the same, whilst calling for the EU to be enlarged to include Ukraine, Moldova and Georgia and for key EU issues to be decided by majority voting.

The Ukrainian population endured a cold winter in 2022/23, but Ukraine's success in its autumn offensive encouraged the Eastern European countries to turn to the EU.

By May 2023, Danish politician and EU Commissioner, Margrethe Vestager in 2023 was astonished by how the war had enabled the Commission to cut red tape and move closer to EU President Ursula von der Leyen's ambition for it to become a geopolitical force.' declaring,

'The EU has changed. There is no turning back. ... Our response to the invasion was by the hour at first ... but it is absolutely Europe's top priority, and we will stay supportive of Ukraine until the war is won' [xlv]

Yet the war ground on, despite the West providing the Leopard tanks, the F-16 fighter jets and the other powerful weapons that America and Germany had initially refused to give President Zelensky.

On 11th July 2023 Zelensky condemned NATOs unwillingness to offer Ukraine a timetable for membership as 'unprecedented and absurd.' His accusation had results. Despite NATO rules stating categorically that having 'no territorial disputes is a prerequisite for joining NATO,' Joe Biden declared that, although Ukraine needed to make further reforms and 'democratization' it would not need to complete the arduous 'Membership Action Plan,' which could last for years.

In September 2023 Putin signalled a serious willingness to freeze the frontline on existing lines and move to a ceasefire but his offer was rejected. Ukraine endured another cold dark winter.

On 4th March 2024 the German Bundeswehr decided that the way to win the war was to pulverize Russia itself with long range weapons.

Biden had put a veto on NATO countries using American missiles to strike inside Russia (except if Kharkiv was attacked). However, the Bundeswehr considered that 'ten or twenty' of Germany's Taurus missiles could destroy the vital Kerch bridge linking the Russian mainland and Crimea. The problem was that if Germany fired the missiles, it could signify that 'pacifist' Germany was at war with Russia because most of the Kerch bridge is on Russian territory. Public opinion in Germany would be horrified as its AfD party – 'the largest pro-Russian-far-right party in Europe' according to one observer - was militantly pacifist. So, the Bundeswehr had the bright idea of asking the British military advisors in Ukraine to do the job for them, which caused an upset at Westminster.

The British did not like Germany pretending to be pacifist and encouraging other countries to do her fighting for it. Nevertheless, Germany had a powerful influence within NATO. In May 2024 President Macron of France declared that he would allow French missiles to attack military facilities inside Russia, and in July Britain's new Prime Minister, Kier Starmer, declared that Britain would allow the 'defensive' use of her Storm Shadow missiles inside Russia too.

On May 24, 2024, Reuters disclosed that Putin was ready for more peace talks but declared that the negotiations should be based 'on the realities on the ground' and 'Not just upon the basis of what one side wants.'

In June Zelensky held a peace summit in Geneva. Putin was not invited and China refused to take part. Nevertheless, it was not a total failure for Zelensky as it was accepted that a portion of Russia's reserves of $280 billion, which had been frozen at the beginning of the war, could be used by Ukraine in her fight against Russia.

The looming crisis had been Ukraine's ability to continue the fight if the American funds - which had totalled the incredible sum of $175 billion to date - dried up and the EU's funds were not forthcoming. The EU's most powerful state, Germany, had forked out $37.2 billion, but popular opposition was mounting, with the pacifist anti-war AfD rising in the German opinion polls.

Nevertheless, the German government and the EU found an innovative way of continuing the war by taking money from the precious reserves, which Russia had placed in their safekeeping.

The first instalment was a modest amount of 1.5 billion euros. However, In October 2024 the European Parliament agreed that it could secure a 35 billion-euro-loan from future revenues out of Russia's $280 billion.

It is unclear whether Germany's assets were ever used in the fight against Hitler and the raid on Russia's would caution other countries from keeping their money in Europe in the future. Nevertheless, at the time, it seemed a neat solution.

Yet, Russia's economy was not collapsing despite the war and the draconian sanctions levied against it. True her trade surplus had fallen by nearly 70% to $87.68 in 2023 from an astonishing $289.89 in 2022.[xlix] Yet, the war was clearly not crushing the Russian economy, and it was winning the war on the ground.

The main reason for Putin's success seems to have been that over 100,000 Eastern Ukrainians were fighting on his side. Indeed, one could say that they were the backbone of the Russian army. Over 300,000 Eastern Ukrainians had died of malnutrition in Krupp's and other Nazi armaments factories during the Second World War. Their descendants believed Putin's assertion that the present war had been caused by the neo-Nazis in Western Ukraine and their supporters in Germany. They wanted to keep their ties with Russia and were determined to fight for them.

To rescue the Ukrainians, America allowed Ukraine the use of her Army Tactical Missile System within Russia. On 18th November a key air base defence system and an air base in Russia were hit by ATACMS missiles. Within days Russia struck back with an attack on Ukraine with an Oreshnik intermediate-range ballistic missile, capable of flying between 300 and 3400 miles. The six submunitions released by each warhead were unarmed but even so had a high kinetic energy estimated to deliver a destructive force equivalent to tons of explosives.[781] The war in Ukraine was getting really, dangerous. More than one observer was talking of a Third World War.

Yet, in October 2024, despite Ukraine's devastation and loss of life, and Putin's rooted objections, new NATO secretary-general Dutch politician Mark Rutte declared: 'Ukraine is closer to NATO than ever before. And will continue on this path, until you become a member of this alliance.'[782]

Some European members of NATO who will have to pay the tab for the long war which it will necessitate for Ukraine becoming a member of NATO over Russia's rooted objections, might have been surprised by Rutte's inflammatory comments. Some might even have privately argued that the Europeans should persuade Zelensky to be more open to a peace agreement which conceded losing a portion of his enormous country.

Ukraine is under Marshall Law, so its citizens do not have a say in whether its leadership should continue the war or talk about peace. However, polls last autumn revealed that 70% of Ukrainians believed that their government was using the war for personal gain and more than 57% supported immediate negotiations to end the war.

Although Zelensky continues to insist that Ukraine must return to its pre-war borders, other senior ministers in Kyiv have asserted 'We need to cut off the lost territories like a gangrenous limb … 'The gap between the political elite and the ordinary people who are losing this war couldn't be wider.' [783]

CHAPTER 14

Conclusions

After the Second World War, when Germany was defeated and divided, America let many prominent former 'Prussians' out of prison because she was faced with Stalin. Friendship grew between America and West Germany, and Hitler was blamed for all the horrors of the Second World War.

However, although anti-Semitism is now banished from reunited Germany, and America Germany and Britain are close friends, we do not want our affection for the pacifist German people to cloud our judgement about the aggressive and deceitful 'Prussians,' lest now that Germany is reunified, they start to return.

The Prussians originally came from the East. They were known for gathering huge armies and invading their neighbours. What they were less known for, was the deceit they employed, which helped them to grab their objectives without censure.

This book has started with 19th century Chancellor Otto von Bismarck as Bismarck created, albeit through war against supposed enemies, a unification of all the neighbouring different sized German-speaking kingdoms, principalities and republics that had previously been independent.

By force and guile, he succeeded in forging the new German Reich out of the former 26 Germanic kingdoms, republics and principalities, but his next task was to unite them. He adopted a Gold-backed currency which caused a collapse in the value of silver and a stock stock-market crash, which he blamed on Austria. In the ensuing depression he conjured up alarms that France and Russia were about to invade. This helped to unify his Reich, but led to an increase in militarism, and the armaments company Krupp becoming an enormous enterprise.

The book has re-examined the untidy ending of the First World War because its ending has led to so much propaganda about how it began. It has also led to an enduring loss of friendship between Britain and her closest ally America because of its aftermath. But first we must begin at the beginning.

After Bismarck died and Wilhelm II became Emperor of Germany, Krupps continued to thrive. The company's chairman, Gustav Krupp, secretly bank-noted the Pan-German League, which was dedicated to retaining the military/industrialist junta's power in Germany in the face of the rising tide of democracy. Soon its propaganda evolved into the promotion of war.

The opportunity to wage a major war arrived at a most auspicious time in 1914. The British were preoccupied with near civil war in Ireland, a prominent journalist had just been murdered by the ex-Prime Minister's wife in France, and the heir presumptive to the Austro-Hungarian throne, Archduke Franz Ferdinand, was assassinated in Serbia, which would ensure Austria's support.

Chancellor Bethmann Hollweg was a deceitful Prussian. He egged Austria into war against Serbia, even if the war threatened to become a wider European conflagration, whilst pretending to Britain all the while that he was striving to maintain peace. However, when at last he discovered that Britain would support France if Germany invaded, he decided that the odds were too onerous and tried to avert the conflict.

Nevertheless, the German army was responsible only to the Emperor Wilhelm II under Bismarck's constitution and so ignored Bethmann Hollweg's change of heart. After the Russian Tsar Nicholas II had ordered his army's 'general mobilisation' from the depths of his vast country, Germany declared the full force of responsibility (of the war) falls on Russia alone'[784]

The huge pacifist German Social Democratic party hated the repressive Tsar. It was satisfied that its country was waging a war of defence, and the British socialists agreed. Indeed, the rise of the British Labour Party into a national force could be said to have been due to its opposition to the First World War, especially after the bloodshed mounted.

Britain was unprepared for the conflict, but she could not tolerate a hostile Prussianized Germany on her doorstep, or France, losing the coal and iron, which made her as an industrial power.[785] France was fighting for her survival, and Britain was prepared to support her. But as with all wars of attrition, the bloodshed was appalling.

Many people know of the bloodshed and seemingly useless carnage on the western front in the First World War. Yet few even today seem to know of the extent of Germany's great victories in Ukraine and Russia after the Treaty of Brest Litovsk, including a supplementary treaty to extort an indemnity of 6 billion roubles in Gold and kind from the prostrate Russians in August 1918.

Yet while the German army in the East went from triumph to triumph, the German army in the West was on the verge of collapse.

President Wilson had trusted Germany's plea of innocence of starting the war and become increasingly annoyed by the high-handedness of the impecunious British during the conflict. Sickened by the American army's bloodshed at Meuse-Argonne, Wilson dreamed of a better world where war would have no place. Yet his offer of an armistice when the German army was at the point of collapse would prove disastrous.

Wilson had been certain that he was right in giving Germany an armistice until he met their negotiator at Versailles. Then he suddenly realised that he had made a terrible mistake.

He must have been only too aware that no foreign soldier had entered Germany, and that German industry remained unscathed in contrast to the devastation of France. Yet by now he had lost the affection of the American public. No-one would listen to his fears of the resurgent 'Prussians' anymore.

Wilson had ruled out asking Germany for indemnities. So, reparations were asked instead, on the basis that Germany had caused the war. The German government refused to pay cash in reparation, while using the low value of the Mark to eliminate the country's debts.

The British had not been invaded. They wanted to get the world economy moving again, so they came to accept the little white lie that Germany was too poor to pay.

However, the French people, faced with their country devastated and their coalmines destroyed, elected their former hardline President Raymond Poincaré to obtain the coal that was needed to light their homes and ignite their industry. When it was not forthcoming, Poincaré invaded Germany with a handful of men to secure it. His 'invasion' gave the German coal owners an excuse to completely trash their currency. After it became absolutely, worthless, they persuaded their destitute coal miners to return to working longer hours for low pay, enabling them to cripple Britain's coal industry after the German currency was stabilised.

The story still circulates today in the American heartlands, that America paid Germany's war reparations during the Dawes Plan years between 1924 and 1929. 'Wall Street,' so the legend goes, 'made the loans to Germany so that Germany could pay reparations to France, which could then pay war debts to Britain and the US.'

This inferred that Germany was too poor to pay to pay the reparations without help, which was very far from the truth.

The German economy was very strong in the mid-1920s, and the armaments makers were busy making weapons abroad, but the government refused to pay its reparations in cash as its academics now asserted the nation's innocence of starting the war in 1914. Abroad it was asserted that France and Russia were the culprits, but in German schools and universities the blame was pinned on Britain.

Around £400 million in reparations was extracted by Britain and France between 1924 and 1929 through a 30% British tariff on German goods and deliveries of coal etc to France. Yet France received so little in 'actual cash' that the Young Plan was devised in 1929, so that she could pay her war debts to America.

Meanwhile, worryingly, ex-supremo at Krupps, and now politician and newspaper mogul, Alfred Hugenberg, declared that Germany needed to return to dictatorship, but that, due to the rise of socialism, the new dictator should be a man of the people, rather than a Hohenzollern king. Equally alarmingly, Hugenberg declared that he thought the public would vote for dictatorship if times were hard enough.

The negotiations with Germany over the new Young Plan reparations agreement were tortuous. After a crisis Germany put up her interest rates, causing interest rate rises throughout Europe. At last, in August 1929, America raised her interest rates as well, followed by Britain in September.

Then, in October 1929, Alfred Hugenberg declared that Germany was guiltless of starting the First World War and that the President of Germany, Paul von Hindenburg, should be tried for treason for accepting to pay any reparations at all. Two weeks later the American stock market crashed.

Unfortunately, Germany then adopted a savage deflationary economic policy. New German Chancellor Heinrich Brüning lowered wages, raised taxes and imposed a poll tax, and a 'man of the people' called Adolf Hitler gained adherents at the polls. Meanwhile, Gustav Krupp, the head of Krupps great manufacturing company came to an agreement with Stalin.

There had been a disastrous famine in Russia in 1921. Gustav Krupp had subsequently taken a 50,000-hectare agricultural concession. In 1928 he promised to help Stalin expand his agricultural concessions, so that Stalin would not have to rely on his recalcitrant peasants; in return Stalin promised to force the German Communists to vote with the extreme Right rather than with their fellow socialists.

The deal would be fruitful for Stalin, and for the German industrialists and armaments makers too. German investment poured into Russia, giving Stalin a modernised industrial base and the armaments to go with it. Meanwhile the Russian people starved and the American and Canadian farmers and all those dependent on them, were made bankrupt.

In 1931, after a banking crisis in Austria, Germany also experienced a banking crisis, even though the *Financial Times* had recently commented on 'the gradual conquest by German industry of foreign markets.' Germany was given a one-year holiday on paying war reparations, and the Allies on paying their war debts too. Unfortunately, Britain instituted Imperial Preference to help the struggling farmers in Australia and Canada at the time, which stirred up animosity in America.

In 1932 the squeeze on the German economy continued. Nearly six million people became unemployed. Then Germany declared herself quite unable to resume payments of the reparations and Hitler swept to victory on the back of his successful fight against paying them.

Gustav Krupp had secretly been rearming since the early 1920s. Now his factories went into overtime.

Meanwhile Hitler's economic Tsar, Hjalmar Schacht, decided to impoverish the Europeans and Americans by placing large orders with their industries and then pleading poverty and refusing to pay.

The 'American people had put their faith in Germany's good will. They seethed with anger at the British, with their huge empire, their imperial preference, and their refusal to repay America's citizens for the loans they had lent them to help win the war. The Johnson Act was passed, forbidding any new loans to nations that had not repaid their First World War debts.

The trouble was that the British and the French were feeling abjectly poor in the 1930s. France said that she had only agreed to pay her war bonds so long as Germany paid her reparations. Britain did not have that assurance but felt the same way. Germany's deflation had hit the whole of Europe's economy and now the rabidly anti-Semitic dictator Hitler was defaulting on his debts and re-arming.

Nevertheless, America's economic situation was even worse than the Allies because so many Americans were of German extraction and therefore had traded more extensively with Germany.

America had been hit by Stalin's export of wheat at throw away prices in 1931; then by Germany's refusal to pay cash for her cotton crop, which created another 'dust bowl' in 1933. Subsequently Germany reneged on her reparations' payments, causing America the loss of her war debts. Germany also reneged on repaying the Dawes Plan and Young Plan loans and declared that a moratorium on the repayment of her medium and long-term loans was 'inevitable,' decimating their value.

The final insult was when she encouraged the Brazilian government to renege on its debts to America in 1937 so that it could buy Krupps armaments.

Had the Americans known about Germany's economic machinations, they would have realised that the 'Prussians' were deliberately trying to impoverish their country so that it would not interfere in another war. However, the 'Prussians' had spent millions of pounds on propaganda, and they were completely deceived by her tales of poverty and innocence.

After Hitler invaded Poland, a million Poles were sent to work in Germany. They were half starved and identified only with a letter P. Meanwhile, the German propaganda machine was still pumping out misinformation in America. In March 1940, the German Embassy in Washington published several documents to make it appear that Poland had attacked Germany before Hitler's invasion[786] and hundreds of thousands of copies of a speech by Senator Gerald Nye of Dakota for his 'Make Europe pay War Debts Committee' were circulated to embitter America against the Allies and persuade them to believe that their impoverishment had been the Allies fault.

Meanwhile, Hitler invaded France and threatened Britain. Then he embarked on his Russian invasion to secure the victory that, in his eyes and those of so many of the soldiers from the eastern front, had been snatched from them by President Wilson of America in 1918.

Before his re-election President Roosevelt had told Americans, 'I have said this before, but I shall say it again and again and again: Your boys are not going to be sent into any foreign war.'[787]

However, after he won the election, Roosevelt massively increased his investment in armaments. His action was timely because the Japanese decided to attack Pearl Harbour.

William Shirer in his *Rise and Fall of the Third Reich* reveals that Japan's explosive attack need not necessarily have precipitated a full-scale war between America and Germany, finding a 'strong feeling in both Houses (Congress and the Senate) as well as in the Army and Navy that the country ought to concentrate its efforts on defeating Japan and not take on the additional burden of fighting Germany at the same time.'[788]

The uncomfortable truth that the American isolationists would never confront was that Hitler then declared war against America.

Like many of his disciples who had fought on the victorious eastern front in the First World War, Hitler had drunk in the propaganda that the 'Prussian' army had been denied victory by President Wilson in 1918. He therefore had an enduring animosity towards America.

How many other Nazis, let alone the ordinary German people, supported Hitler's hostility is not known, but it is certain that Hitler grossly underestimated

America's military capability because of the American army's failures and pause in fighting at Meuse-Argonne.

Hitler also fatally misjudged Russia's military ability. On 5th December, six days before Hitler's declaration of war against America, General Guderian acknowledged in his journal: The offensive on Moscow (has) failed. ... We underestimated the enemy's strength as well as his size and climate.'

Yet, Hitler was still confident. He had forced some 12 million labourers to help him to produce the armaments to wage the war. Hundreds of thousands of Russians from Eastern Ukraine would die producing them. The punishment allotted to the Jews was even worse. Over six million were slaughtered. However, the profits for Krupps armaments concern reached an all-time high and he was allowed to call his company 'a State within a State.'[789]

Things were not going so well on the battlefront, however. Neither Moscow nor Leningrad fell into German hands. Soon the American and Allied invasion of Normandy would commence. Then the American army would reach German soil.

On 10th October 1944, there was a meeting of the foremost German industrialists at the Rotes Haus, in Strausberg. It was decided that the war was lost, and that Germany must ensure her future by secreting her money abroad and enforcing her patents.

At last, the Russian army reached Berlin. America and the Allies had won Second World War. Meanwhile, the Russian army behaved so badly in Berlin that American sympathies stretched towards the defeated Germans.

Admiral Canaris, head of German military intelligence, declared: 'The campaign of hatred stirred up by Roosevelt ... against everything German has temporarily silenced the pro-German bloc in the U.S.A. ... However, there is every hope that this situation will be completely changed within a few months.' [790]

Canaris was correct. Blissfully unaware of the steps that Germany had taken to bankrupt their country in the 1930s, the American isolationists reserved their wrath for the impoverished Allies who had refused to pay their war debts when they most needed them and then dragged America into another war against their German kith and kin.

Many American newspapers did not even seem to have told their readers that Hitler had declared war against America in 1941. Their line was that America had been fighting 'an unnecessary war against white people on behalf of the ungrateful British and the un-American Jews' - and their readers agreed.

It was not surprising that Lend-lease was cancelled almost as soon as Truman came to power, and that Britain would be made to pay her Second World War debts until the last penny was paid in 2006, even though the war had rescued America from poverty.

President Truman was shocked by his postwar meeting with Stalin. Truman's Russian expert, George F Kennan[791] believed that the only way to prevent the monstrous dictator taking over the whole of Europe was to determine a demarcation line that he could not cross without risking war.

In 1947, Secretary of State George C Marshall proposed the so-called Marshall Plan to help all the devastated regions of Europe, including West Germany.

Meanwhile West Germany was wracked with hyperinflation and the human toll of German misery mounted. Unhappy impoverished people from the East poured into the Rhineland and the hard-pressed British authorities were accused of reducing their rations to starvation levels. Eventually, the worthless currency was replaced by the Deutschmark and food flooded into the shops. However, as the 'starvation' was in the British sector the British received the odium for the misery which Germany's post-Second World War inflation had caused.

After another generation, we have a different view of Germany's Great Inflations after both the First and Second World Wars, realising that they were self-inflicted wounds to rid Germany of her insurmountable internal debts. After describing how the Reich finance ministry pumped out ever-rising quantities of Treasury Bills during the Second World War, the economic historian, David Marsh, wrote in his book *The Bundesbank, the Bank that rules Europe* in 1992, 'The massive quantities of debauched money flowing through the torn country were in fact already preparing the way for the next currency reform – and the 1948 birth of the D-Mark'[792]

America warmed to the Allies after their defence of Berlin against Stalin in 1948. However, Truman's advisor George Kennan's view of their inhumanity over their First World War reparations demands was still influential. Then America was confronted by War in Korea.

While America was preoccupied with Korea, with Britain at her side, there was only one strong Conservative country that America considered she could rely on to defend Europe against Stalin, West Germany. Therefore, faced with unpalatable options, she decided to let the former 'Prussian' industrialists like Alfried Krupp, and the directors of I G Farben out of prison so that they could stoke up their factories to provide war material for America.

This provoked an outstanding offer from Stalin. On 10th March 1952 in a Note addressed to the Three Western Powers, Stalin offered the West Germans 'German unification on the basis of free, elections, a new German Wehrmacht, fully armed, the decontrolling of Germany's war potential, and the return of Germany's SS and Wehrmacht officers to public life.'[793]

This was a bombshell for America. She decided to give West Germany a massive bribe to stay within the Atlantic Alliance.

Under the terms of the 1953 London Debt Agreement, West Germany's pre-and post-war debts were slashed, and she was given grants, an advantageous exchange rate and many other sweeteners, which would inevitably impact unfavourably on the Allies economies. [794]

At the same time, it was decided to adopt the legend everywhere, which had become dogma in America, that the cruel reparations that the Allies had charged under the terms of the Treaty of Versailles had led to Hitler and the Second World War.

France was in a desperately weak position. She had been invaded three times. Therefore, French Foreign Minister Robert Schuman came up with the idea of the European Coal and Steel Community, the pre-cursor of the European Economic Community and the European Union, with Germany as a member, as the only way forward.

Indeed, the European Economic Community was welcomed everywhere when it was first instituted. Deluged with propaganda in the 1930s 'British and French policymakers' in the historian Andrew Robert's words, had drawn 'the erroneous conclusion that it had been the

[Allies] encirclement policy towards Germany of 1904-7, the 'destabilizing' alliance system, the armaments race, faulty communications, secret diplomacy, staff talks and strategic plans which had caused the (1914) war.'[795] In those circumstances sentiment warmed to West Germany and the EEC seemed a wonderful idea for a brave new world.

In the early 1960s Professor Fritz Fischer of Hamburg University introduced a discordant tone when he published two major books, which exposed Germany's aggressive intentions before and during the First World War. However, his evidence was disregarded. Powerful West Germany had become everybody's friend, and she was felt to be a buttress of democracy against the Soviet Union.

America had been desperate for West Germany to become part of NATO in the early 1950s. Eventually Germany extracted a pledge for joining, that 'the achievement through peaceful means of a fully free and unified Germany remains a fundamental (NATO) goal.'[796]

The agreement's significance would soon become apparent. West Germany promised not to use nuclear weapons herself but expected America to threaten to use them on her behalf to unify her country.

In the 1970s ardently peace-loving Jimmy Carter became America's President. The Russian economy was weak, and Carter's advisors did not feel that the Soviet Union, even equipped with its latest missile, was a threat to Europe. However, West Germany's Chancellor, Helmut Schmidt disagreed.

Eventually, on Schmidt's initiative, the Carter administration accepted the report of a working group of NATO members, which concluded that new intermediate-range nuclear weapons targeted against the Soviet Union would make it crystal clear to the Soviets that an isolated attack on Western Europe would be met by retaliation from a qualitatively new type of deterrent with its own rationale.[797]

It is evident that Helmut Schmidt had managed to change Jimmy Carter's outlook because of his influence in NATO. However, he still managed to deceive his own electorate and the rest of the world of the threat that the Soviet Union posed.

During this period, the pacifist West Germans would have been appalled if they had realized that their government was pushing America to modernize her nuclear weapons. They did not want any more nuclear power plants in Germany, let alone nuclear weapons. So, Schmidt's influence in persuading NATO and America into adopting the so-called Star Wars program was kept completely hidden from them – and from the rest of the world.

Yet, the Soviet Union was in a much weaker state than outsiders imagined, and the stunning result of America's Star Wars program was the demise of the Soviet Union and the reunification of Germany.

German reunification was such a remarkable event that it was bound to have repercussions. The worry was whether the aggressive 'Prussians' would return to prominence.

The German government put its interest rates up to an unprecedented level despite President Bush declaring 'you've got deep pockets.' However, Chancellor Kohl had many uses for his money. Besides paying for the Russian troops to go home, he successfully campaigned for the East Germans to unite with their cousins in the West, promising them that they could have the treasured Deutschmark instead of their more, lowly valued Ost mark, even though it led to mass unemployment in the former East Germany.

Germany's high interest rates had distressing effects elsewhere too, in Britain, France and Yugoslavia. Britain crashed out of the ERM and France was only saved with an injection of cash, while Germany refused to agree to sign the Maastricht Treaty with the European Economic Community except if Croatia and Slovenia were allowed to become independent from the Communist state of Yugoslavia.

Slovenia had never been an independent nation before. Croatia had been a puppet state under Hitler and thousands of Serbs had died in her Concentration and Extermination Camp in the Second World War. Britain's Lord Carrington warned that giving them independence would lead to Bosnia's demand for independence, and bloodshed. He was right.

We have happily all passed the blame for the subsequent bloodshed in the former Yugoslavia onto Serbian President, Slobodan Milošević. Chancellor Kohl himself would later describe the fighting in Bosnia as 'a return to barbarity that very few of us would have thought possible.' Yet he himself must share the blame for initiating the carnage.

In the year 2000 a new currency, the Euro, was introduced for the EU - but the demise of the Deutschmark prompted a mass exodus of German money abroad.

Interest rates rose in America in December 2004 because of the costs of the Iraq war, and it was noted that 'a giant pool of money' was seeking safe, income generating investments in the US. Soon subprime mortgages swelled to twenty per cent of all American mortgages. By the autumn of 2006 America became alarmed and predicted an interest rate cut. However, the German government decided to give advantages to industry and an increase in wages and insisted that the ECB raise interest rates throughout the euro-zone to curb German inflation.

Statistics later revealed that German wages had fallen in real terms between the years 2000 and 2007.[798] Yet, the President of the Bundesbank Axel Weber managed to persuade the ECB to raise rates for the entire euro area again in July, luring money from the dollar to the Euro.

On 23rd September 2007 France's President Nicolas Sarkozy renewed his pressure on the ECB to reduce rates. Yet, ECB Governor, Jean-Claude Trichet stated that the bank would not hesitate to raise rates again if inflation rose above three per cent.[799]

On 8th December 2007, Axel Weber and ECB chief economist, Jürgen Stark were still calling for an interest rate rise, despite property prices in Ireland tumbling, Spain's current account deficit reaching the 'staggering' total of nine per cent of GDP, and the American bank, Morgan Stanley, issuing a full recession alert for the US economy.

American interest rates were drastically slashed to 2% in the spring of 2008. Nevertheless, the ECB decided to raise interest rates again to 4.25%. Two months later the global financial services firm Lehman Brothers collapsed, threatening the collapse of the western world's banking system.

Is it possible to introduce a huge new currency without a major economic upset? After all, there was a stock exchange collapse and international upset after Bismarck adopted Gold in 1873, and the 1929 stock market crash occurred after nations returned to the Gold Standard in the 1920s.

The striking similarity between the 1929 stock market crash and its aftermath and the Lehman banking crash of 2008 and its aftermath, was the effect of rising interest rates in an already tight money market in 1929 and 2007, and the deflationary policy that continued after the 1929 stock market crash, and again after the Lehman banking crash in 2008.

American economist, Paul Krugman, became increasingly suspicious of Germany's 'austerity' policy after the Lehman crisis. In his book, called *End this Depression Now*, he remarked 'What actually brought Hitler to power was the German depression of the early 1930s, a depression that was even more severe than that in the rest of Europe, thanks to the deflationary policies of Chancellor Heinrich Brüning"[800]

Yet, it seems that fiscal union rather than Germany's return to dictatorship was Germany's ambition in imposing 'austerity' after the Lehman crash.

In his article, *The Bank that nearly broke Europe* (August 2018) Adam Tooze revealed how austerity initially helped 'unify' Europe. Nevertheless, the Euro area now has a new economic system to ensure European stability, and the EU could be compared to Bismarck's Reich with a large measure of integration and a stable currency.

The ends in many people's eyes have justified the means. After all, Croatia and Slovenia are now treasured members of the EU, and the euro is one of the most valued currencies in the world. However, there is always some collateral damage. Many good businesses collapsed after the Lehman crash, 140,000 people died during the demise of Yugoslavia, and it seems that America has got tired of funding NATO for what it believes are essentially Europe's ambitions.

The question is whether Germany bore responsibility for NATO's disastrous decision to welcome Ukraine as a future member in 2021.

Although America pays most of the bills, NATO is a democratic organization, and America was busy removing its troops from Afghanistan when the decision to offer Ukraine membership was made.

In 1990 American Secretary of State, James Baker, had given the President of Russia, Mikhail Gorbachev, the assurance that if he removed his troops from East Germany, NATO would not move 'one inch eastward.' Yet NATO had subsequently moved hundreds of miles to the East.

When America and Germany offered Ukraine future membership of NATO in 2008, the horrified American Ambassador to Russia, (and later head of the CIA) William J Burns, told his superiors, 'I can conceive of no grand package that would allow the Russians to swallow this pill quietly.'[iv] Yet that is precisely what NATO did in 2021.

There was some pre-history to NATO's offer, which this book has explored. It all started when Ukraine chose to enter Russia's Eurasian Economic Union rather than become part of the EU. This led to a 'regime change' in Ukraine by Germany and America, anxious to have a pro EU government in Kyiv. However, their action did not have the full support of the Ukrainian people, especially in the South and the East.

Unfortunately, as Burns had predicted, Russia retaliated by grabbing Russian-populated Crimea and supporting the independence movements in Eastern Ukraine.

The Minsk Accord was agreed in 2015 after the forces supporting the Ukrainian government suffered a severe reverse against the Russian-aided separatists in Eastern Ukraine. That agreement would have meant Ukraine remaining intact, with Kyiv merely losing a measure of control over a portion of Luhansk and Donetsk, but the extremists in Kyiv rejected the agreement.

Four years later Volodymyr Zelensky was elected President on the promise that he would end the war in Eastern Ukraine. However, the peace terms that he agreed were still based on the Minsk Accord, and the extremists in Kyiv still opposed them.

In 2022 Angela Merkel would astonishingly disclose that she had merely signed the Minsk Accords in the first place to 'give Ukraine time' to get stronger and for NATO to increase its support against Russia.[xxv] After the extremists in Kyiv had turned them down in 2019 Zelensky decided that 'NATO is the only way to win the war in Ukraine'[xxvii]

NATO had helped Germany achieve her aim of reunification with the help of America's expenditure on 'Star Wars'.

NATO's billions had also achieved Germany's aim of the independence of Croatia and Slovenia, so we can speculate whether it was German influence which was ultimately responsible for NATO's decision to offer Ukraine membership in 2021.

In an extraordinary passage from her autobiography, Angela Merkel discloses that Putin had already told her, in 2008, that he regarded Ukraine becoming a member of NATO as a declaration of war, asserting 'You won't be chancellor forever, and then they'll become NATO members. And I'm going to prevent that.'

Yet Angela Merkel was still Chancellor in 2021 when NATO's offer of NATO membership was made to Ukraine.

At the outset of the war in Ukraine, in view of the pacifism of large sections of the German populace, deceitful German Chancellor Schulz merely offered helmets to the beleaguered Ukrainian people. However, at the same time as his pacifist gesture, he immediately approved, without fanfare, a shipment of 1,000 anti-tank and 500 surface to air missiles to Ukraine, while allocating 100 billion euros to raising the country's military expenditure to the more than 2% of GDP, which he had baulked over providing NATO with in 2018[xxxv] and borrowing a whopping 200 billion euros extra. [xxxvii]

The Russians and Ukrainians nearly reached a peace based on the Minsk agreement a month after Putin invaded. Russia's main demand, as always, was that Ukraine remained neutral and never joined NATO. However, Zelensky said that the security guarantees were insufficient and refused to reduce the size of his army and on 2nd May 2022, Oleksiy Danilov, Zelensky's Chair of the Ukrainian National Security and Defence Council declared proudly: 'A treaty with Russia is impossible – only capitulation can be accepted.'[xli]

In taking such a huge decision to take on Russia, Zelensky must have believed that NATO would always support him, even though it would be America who would be supplying most of the armaments for the fight, and Europe, which would enjoy most of the spoils.

Putin's attempt to invade Kyiv merited outright condemnation, but his defence of the eastern separatists is more understandable. Most eastern Ukrainians speak Russian as their first language, a considerable number have familial ties with Russia, their parents fought with Russia in the Second World War and over 100,00 are fighting on Russia's side against Zelensky's forces.

The trouble is that like the Ruhr in the First World War, eastern Ukraine is full of coal and iron and valuable raw-earth materials. The EU, which lacks raw-earth materials wishes to have it in its sphere, but Russia which has resources elsewhere, wants to retain it, as apart from ties of kinship, the iron and steel factories and armaments factories in eastern Ukraine are too close to Moscow to fall into 'unfriendly' hands.

So, the war has ground on, with the gratifying result for Germany that it increases and centralizes the power of the EU as the European nations rearm against Putin's purported plans to grab the whole of Europe.

In fact, the war in Ukraine has been fairly, static over the last three years but the weapons used on both sides have become more menacing, with the danger that the conflict could spill into a European war rising by the day.

President Trump refuses to go on spending billions in a never-ending war, which he felt could have been avoided in the first place if NATO had not offered Ukraine membership. He is trying to stop the fighting and to secure some of the spoils himself. He is accused of being pro Putin, even though he could be regarded as saving the Ukrainian army from defeat. Although the latest reports show the Ukrainian soldiers fighting valiantly, and achieving a spectacular drone attack on Russia's airfields, there have been previous accounts of desertions, while last December Colonel Laurence Wilkerson of the US army asserted: 'We need to face the truth. If Russia wanted to, it could occupy Odessa.'

So, Trump's ambition for an armistice is welcome even if it has many pitfalls, as happened with President Woodrow Wilson's armistice at the end of the First World War.

Hitler never forgot the German army's victory in Russia in the First World War. In 1941 his generals thwarted him from marching South to grab the Ukrainian resources and achieve a similar success in Russia at the start of the Second World War. The German people are pacifist and our close friends today. Yet the deceitful 'Prussian' leadership under Angela Merkel could have been accused of inciting NATO and the Ukrainian army to fight and win the war for Germany against Russia, which it lost in 1945.

Bibliography

AMERICAN DOCUMENTS
Dinner discussion between John Foster Dulles and Dr. Halmar Schacht 'The Young Plan in relation to the World Economy' 20 October 1930 at Foreign Policy Association, 18 East 41 St. New York
US Military Intelligence Report EW pa (1944)
Statement by William L Clayton, Assistant Secretary of State 25 June 1945
Report by Senator Kilgore to the Senate Affairs Committee on Germany's war potential 10 July 1945

BRITISH DOCUMENTS
Lloyd George Papers, House of Lords
Baldwin File, c/8 F/3/1
Churchill to Lloyd George, 7 July 1933 F/1/2/17
(*Report dated 11 July 1922*) referred to in Note on the German Chemical Industry and the possibility of its employment for the production of poisonous gases F/26/2 Q/8 (t28)

GERMAN DOCUMENTS
Directive issued by the Chief of the Intelligence Division of the German High Command, Admiral Walter Wilhelm Canaris is, 15 March 1944
Madrid Circular Letter 1950, Secret memorandum from the German Geo-political centre in Madrid (1950)

RUSSIAN DOCUMENTS
Central State Military Archive, Fischmann to Unchlicht, 29 April 1927
Foreign Policy Archives, Moscow, including *Protocol* 22 File 694 No 37, 21 March 1922 on negotiations for Krupp's 50,000-hectare agricultural concession with Krupp
No 701, 25 August 1928 and No 390 re: Communists regarding Social Democrats as Enemies

Ahamed, Liaquat, *Lords of Finance* (2009)
Akhtamazyan, A A, *New and Latest History,*
    No. 4. *Soviet and German economic relations between 1922 and 1932* (1988)
    No 5. *Military Co-operation between the USSR and Germany 1920-1933* (1990)
Alexander, Andrew, *America and the Imperialism of Ignorance,* (paper ed) (2012)
Annual Register 1888-1952
Augustein, Rudolf, *Konrad Adenauer* (1964)
Baker, J Ellis, *Woodrow Wilson Life and Letters,* vol 8 (Garden City, New York, 1939)
Bailey Catherine, *Black Diamonds*

Balderston, Theo, *The Origins and Causes of the German Economic Crisis, 1923-1931* (1993)
Bark, Dennis L, & Gress, David R, *A History of West Germany*
Vol, *From Shadow to Substance*
Vol, *Democracy and its Discontents, 1963-1988* 1989
Barker, J Ellis, *Foundations of Germany* (1916)
Barker, J Ellis, *Modern Germany* (1918)
Barnett, Correlli, *The Audit of War* (paper ed. 1996)
Berghahn, Volker R, *Imperial Germany 1871-1914* (1994)
    Resisting the Pax Americana? West German industry and the United States 1945-55 in M Ermath, *America and the Shaping of German Industry* (1993)
    American Big Business in Britain and Germany, (2015)
Bernhardi, General Friedrich von, *Germany and the next War* (1912)
Beyer John C & Stephen A Schneider, *Forced Labour under the German Reich,* parts 1 and 2
Blake, Robert, *The Private Papers of Douglas Haig*, (1952)
Blanke, David, *Panic of 1873*
Boemeke, Feldman and Glazer, *The Treaty of Versailles, a Reassessment after 75 Years* (2006)
Bookbinder, Paul, *The Weimar Republic, the Republic of the Reasonable* (1966)
Borsky, G, *The Greatest Swindle in the World, the Story of the German Reparations*, with a preface by Rt. Hon. Lord Vansittart (1942)
Boyce, Robert, *French Foreign and Domestic Policy, 1918-1940, the decline and fall of a great power* (1998)
Braim, Paul F, *The Test of Battle,* (1987)
Bresciani-Turroni, *The Economics of Inflation,* in ed. Capie, Forrest, *Major Inflations in History* (Edward Elgar 1991)
Burleigh, Michael, *The Third Reich, A New History* (paper ed 2001)
Burns, William J, *The Back Channel* (2019)
Butler, David Allen, *The Burden of Guilt, How Germany shattered the last few days of Peace, summer 1914* (2010)
Carr, J C and Walter Taplin, *British Steel Industry* (1962)
Carr, T W, *German and US involvement in the Balkans: A Careful Coincidence of National Policies?* (1995) (Presented at the Symposium on the Balkans War, Yugoslavia, Past and Present, Chicago, August 31-1,1995)
Chang, Jung and Jon Halliday, *Mao: The Unknown Story* (2005 paper ed)
Charap, Samuel, Timothy J Coltman, *Everyone Loses* (2017)
Chichering, Roger, *We Men who feel most German, a cultural study of the Pan German League, 1886-1914* (1984)
Clark, Christopher, *The Sleepwalkers: how Europe went to War in 1914* (p.ed.2013)
Clay, Sir Henry, *Lord Norman* (1957)
Claughton, Peter, *New Techniques, new sources, the British steel industry and its ore supply 1850-1950*

Class, Heinrich, *If I were the Kaiser*, Pamphlet quoted in Oxford Book of Fascism (2010)
Coleman, Major 1V, Michael le Cour-Little, Kerry D Vandell, S*ubprime Lending and the Housing Bubble, Tail Wags Dog?* (April 2008)
Conrad, Sebastian, *Globalisation and the nations in Imperial Germany* (2014)
Crowdy, Terry, *The Enemy Within, A History of Spies, Spymasters and Espionage* (2008)
Davies, Kenneth S, FDR, *Into the Storm, 1937-40* (1993)
Davies, R W, Mark Harrison, S G Wheatcroft, eds., *The Economic Transformation of the Soviet Union, 1913-1945,*
Dobbs, Michael, *Six Months in 1945, FDR, Stalin. Churchill and Truman, from World War
     to Cold War* (paper ed. 2013)
Justus D Doenecke and Mark A Stoler, *Debating Franklin D Roosevelt's Foreign Policies,* (2005)
Dulles, John W F, *Vargas of Brazil* (2012)
Dyck, Harvey L, *Weimar Germany and Soviet Russia* (1966)
Die Welt, Döpfner, *Wir mussen uns entscheiden* (03 05 2020)
Dorn Brose, Eric. *The Kaiser's Army* (2004)
DW, Bettina Marx, Nina Werkhauser, 0508 2014. Politics, Ben Knight 02 08 2018
Eichengreen, Barry, *Golden Fetters, The Gold Standard and the Great Depression,* (paper ed.1992)
Ermath, Michael, *America and the Shaping of German Society 1945-1955* (1994)
Evans, Richard J. *The Third Reich at War,* (2005)
Eyck, Erich, *Bismarck and the German Empire
     The Weimar Republic* vols.1 & 2 (translated by Harlen P
     Hansen and Robert G L Waite)
Faria. Miguel, *Cuba in revolution, escape from a Lost Paradise, 93-98* (2002)
Feldman, G D, *The Great Disorder, Politics, Economics and Society in the Great Inflation, 1914-1923* (1993)
Ferguson, Niall, *The Pity of War* (2009) *The War of the World,* 20th Century Conflict and the descent of the West (2006)
Fergusson, Adam, *When money dies, the nightmare of the Weimar Inflation* (p.ed.2015)
Fischer, Fritz, *Germany's Aims in the First World War* (translated by Hajo Holborn and James Joll (1968)
     War of Illusions, German Policies from 1911 to 1914
translated by Marion Jackson and Alan Bullock (1975)
     From Kaiserreich to Third Reich (1986)
Friedlander Saul, *Prelude to Downfall, Hitler and the United States, 1939-41*
Foerster, Friedrich Wilhelm, *Europe and the German Question* (1940)
Frankopan, Peter, *The Silk Roads, A New History of the World,* (2015)

Fromkin, David, *Europe's last summer, Why the world went to war in 1914* (2005)
    In the time of the Americans (1995)
Frye, Alton, *Nazi Germany and the American Hemisphere,* (2019)
Gaddis, John Lewis, *The Cold War.* (2007p.ed)
Gatske. Hans, W. *Germany and the US A Special Relationship* (1980)
Gerwath, Robert, *November 1918* (2020)
Georg, Friedrich, *Hitler Siegeswaffen Band 1; Luftwaffe und Marine Geheim Nuclearwaffen des Dritten Reich und ihre Traegersysteme* (2008) quoted in Henry Stevens *Hitler's supressed and still secret weapons*
Giangreco, D M, Griffin, Robert E, *Airbridge to Berlin, The Berlin Crisis of 1948, its origins and its aftermath* p.1988)
Goldhurst, Richard, *Pipe, Clay and Drill, John J Pershing, the classic American Soldier* (1977)
Haffner, Sebastien, *Failure of a Revolution* (1973)
Hanley, Brian (Lecturer, Institute of Irish Studies, University of Liverpool)
    (https://www.qub.ac.uk) 'Irish Republicanism and Nazi Germany.'
Harrison, Mark, and R W9 Davies, *The Economic transformation of the Soviet Union, 1915-1945* (1993)
Harrison Mark and R W Davies, *The Soviet Military-Economic Effort during the Second Five-Year Plan (1933-7)* in *Europe-Asia Studies, Vol 49, No 3, The Soviet-Military-*
    Economic effort during the Second five-year plan (1933-37) art.
Hawes, James, *The Shortest History of Germany* (2017)
Heffer, Simon, *Staring at God, Britain in the Great War,* (2019)
Herman, Arthur, *Joseph McCarthy,* (2000)
Herwig, Holger H, *Luxury Fleet, The Imperial German Navy, 1888-1918* (1987) *Clio deceived, The Campaign against article 231 of the Treaty of Versailles*
Hillgruber, Andreas, *Hitler's Strategie* (1965)
Hogan, Michael J, *The Marshall Plan, America, Britain and the reconstruction of Western Europe* (1998)
Hollander, Paul, *Political Pilgrims: Western Intellectuals in Search of the Good Society* (4th ed. 1998)
Huddleston, Sisley, *Poincaré, A Biographical Portrait* (1924)
Hubble, Nicolai (Southbank Research) *How the Euro Dies,* (2018)
James, Harold, *The German Slump, Politics and Economics, 1924-1936* (1986)
Journal of Economic Perspectives vol.28. no.1. (2014)
Jung Chang & Jon Halliday *Mao The Unknown Story* (2005)
Kantorowitz, Hermann, *The Spirit of British Policy and the myth of the Encirclement of Germany* (London 1931)
Kater, Michael H, *Hitler Youth* (2014)
Liam Kennedy, *The Conversation,* 06 09 2020, 'How Brexit is leading a resurgent Irish American influence in US politics.'

Keylor William R, *The Twentieth-Century World, An International History* (1992)

Kershaw, Ian, *Hitler 1889-1936, Hubris*, (1999) *Nemesis*, (p.ed. 2001)

Keynes, John Maynard, *The Memoirs, Dr. Melchior, A defeated Enemy, and My Early Beliefs* (1949)
    The Economic Consequences of the Peace (1919)

Kieger, J F V *Raymond Poincare* (1997)

Kitchen, Martin, *The Political Economy of Germany 1815-1914* (1978)
    A History of Modern Germany 1800-2000 (Dec 2005)

Klarsfeld, Beate, *Wherever they may be* (1975)

Knight-Patterson, W M, *Germany from defeat to Conquest* (1945)

Eberhard Kolb, *The Weimar Republic* (1988)

Krugman. Paul, *End this depression now* (2012)

Lee, Christopher, *Carrington, An Honourable Man* (2018)

Leopold, John A, *Alfred Hugenberg, The Radical Nationalist Campaign against the Weimar Republic* (1977)

Link, Authur S, *Woodrow Wilson, Revolution War and Peace* (p.ed.1979)

Lippert, W, *Economic Policy of Ostpolitik, The Origins of NA's energy dilemma* (Berghahn Books, 2010)

Lipstadt, Deborah, *Denying the Holocaust*, (1993)

Manchester, William, *The Arms of Krupp* (1968)

Mantoux, Etienne, *The Carthaginian Peace or the Economic Consequences of Mr Keynes* (1946)

Marks, Sally, 'Smoke and Mirrors' contribution of Boemeke, Feldman and Glazer (eds)
The Treaty of Versailles a reassessment after 75 years (2006)

Marsh, David, *The Bundesbank, The Bank that rules Europe* (1992)

Marshall, Tim, *Prisoner of Geography*, (2015)

Mason, Tim, *Social Policy in the Third Reich*, (1993)

Matthews, Owen, *Overreach*, (2022) Ukraine's *NATO fantasy, Spectator*, 19 10 2024

Merkel, Angela, *Freedom* (2024)

Millin, Sarah Gertrude, *General Smuts* vol 2 (1936)

Mombauer, Annika, *The Origins of the First World War* (2013) *The Origins of the First World War, Controversies and Consensus*, (2013)

Morgan, Brigadier General J H, *Assize of Arms, the Disarmament of Germany and her Rearmamement 1919-1939*

Muhaben, Joyce Marie, *Becoming Madam Chancellor, Angela Merkel and the Berlin Republic* (2017)

Münchau, Wolfgang, *Kaput, The End of a German Miracle* (2024)

Nash, Gary B, 'Wars averted, Chanak1922, Burma 1945-7, Berlin 1948' in *Journal of Strategic Studies* (1999)

Nekrich, Alexander, *Pariahs, 2Partners, and Predators, German Soviet relations 1922-1941* (1997)

Nelson, R, *Germans, Poland & Colonial Expansion to the East, 1850 through to the Present*, (2015)

Newman, A. M. *Economic Organization of the coal industry* (1933)

Overy, Richard, *The Bombers and the Bombed: Allied Air War over Europe 1944-1945*
Owen, Frank, *Tempestuous Journey* (1954)
Paine, Lauran, *The Abwehr, German Military Intelligence in World War Two* (1984)
Pakenham, Thomas, *Scramble for Africa* (p.ed)
Patch, William L Jnr, *Heinrich Brüning and the Dissolution of the Weimar Republic* (1988)
Piszkiewicz, Dennis, *The Nazi Racketeers, Dreams of Space and Crimes of War* (2007)
Plokhy, Serhii, *The Russo-Ukrainian War* (2023)
Pound and Harmsworth, *Northcliffe* (1999)
Guido Giacome Preparata, *Conjuring Hitler, How Britain and America made the Third Reich* (2006)
Reader, W J *Imperial Chemical Industries,* Vol. (London 1975)
Reich, Simon, 'Fascism and the Structure of Capitalism', in Volker R Berghahn, *Quest for Economic Empire* (1994)
Reid, Walter, *Douglas Haig, Architect of Victory* (2006)
Reiman, Michael, *The Birth of Stalinism: The USSR on the eve of the Second Revolution* (1987)
Rich and Fisher, *The Holstein Papers, 1v,* no 904 (available on internet)
    Ritschl, Albrecht, 'The German transfer problem 1920-1933, A Sovereign Debt Perspective,' in *European Review of History* (2012) vol.6 'Reparations, Deficits & Debt Default, The Great Depression in Germany, (2012)
Roberts, Andrew, *The Holy Fox, A Biography of Lord Halifax,* (2014)
Röhl, John, C G, *Kaiser Wilhelm II, A Concise Life* (2014) Goodbye to all that (again)?
    The Fischer Thesis, The new revisionism and the meaning of the First World War (available on the Internet), *Into the Abyss of War and Exile,* (2014)
Royal Institute of International Affairs, *Survey of International Affairs,* 1929, 1930, 1931, 1936, *papers*
Sarotte, M E *Not One Inch, America, Russia, and the making of Post-Cold war Stalemate* (2021)
Schacht, Hjalmar, *My first 76 years* (1955)
Scott Berg A, *Lindbergh* (1998)
Sebestyen, Victor, *1946, The Making of the Modern World,*
Shekhovtsov, Anton, *Kyiv Indeendent* I 02 2024
Schliemann, Peter-Uwe, *The Strategy of British and German investors in Brazil* (1981)
Schmidt, *Statist,* (1950)
Schröter, Harm D *'Europe in the Strategies of Germany's Electrical and Engineering Trusts, 1919-1939'* in Volker R Berghahn, *Quest for Economic Empire,*
Schuker, Stephen A, *The End of French Predominance in Europe: the financial crash of 1924 and the adoption of the Dawes Plan* (1976)
American 'Reparations' to Germany 1919-1933, Implications for the Third World

Debt Crisis (Princeton Studies in International Finance, No 61 (1988)
J M Keynes and the personal politics of Reparations (2014)
William L Shirer, *The Rise and Fall of the Third Reich,* (1991)
Short, Philip, *Putin his life and times,* (2021)
Skidddelsky, Lord Robert, *John Maynard Keynes,* vol 1, *Hopes Betrayed 1883-1926* (1983)
Smythe, Donald, *Pershing, General of the Armies,* (1986)
Snyder, Timothy, *Bloodlands: Europe between Hitler and Stalin* (2010)
Spaulding, Robert Mark, Jr., 'Recovering our position, West German Osthandel
Statesman's Yearbook 1933. Figs.
Straumann, Tobias, *Debt, Crisis and the Rise of Hitler,* (2019), Strategies of the 1950s' in Volker Berghahn *Quest for an Economic Empire*
Stevens, Henry, *Hitler's suppressed and still secret weapons, science and technology* (2007)
Stevenson, David, *With our backs to the Wall, Victory and defeat in 1918* (p.ed. 2012)
Steinberg, S H, *A Short History of Germany*, (Cambridge University Press) (1944)
Steinberg. Jonathan, *Bismarck, A Life* (2011)
Stone, Norman, *World War II, A Short History* (2014)
Swing, Raymond Gram, *Good Evening* (1964)
Tampke, Jürgen, *A Perfidious distortion of History, the Versailles Treaty and the rise of the Nazis* (2017)
Tarpley, Webster G. *British Financial Warfare: How the City of London created the Great Nazi Depression* (1996)
Tetens, T H, *Germany plots with the Kremlin* (1953) T H Tetens *New Germany and the old Nazis* (1962)
Terraine, John, *Douglas Haig, the educated Soldier* (1990)
Thayer, William Roscoe, *Theodore Roosevelt, An Intimate Biography* (1919)
Thyssen, Fritz, *I paid Hitler* (1941)
The Times Jan 20th 1912,5. Col 1., 02 12 2014,
Toland, J W, *Adolf Hitler* (1991)
Tooze, J Adam, *Statistics and the German State 1900-1945, the Making of Modern Knowledge,* (2001)
Wages of Destruction, the Making and Breaking of the Nazi Economy (2007)
Crashed (2018)
Townsend Hoopes, *The Devil and John Foster Dulles,* (1973)
Trachtenberg, Marc and Christopher Gehr. Article, *America, Europe and German rearmament 1950, critique of a myth* (2017)
Toussaint, Eric, *The Marshall Plan and the Debt Agreement on German Debt,* (2006)
Tuchman, Barbara, W, *The Zimmermann Telegram* (1959)
Turner, Henry Ashby Jr. *Hitler's Thirty Days to Power, Janaury 1933* (1996)
UN Doc ENDC/84 8 April 1963

Walker Mark, *Nazi Science Myth, Truth and the Atom Bomb* (p.ed)
Waterhouse, Michael, *Edwardian Requiem, A Life of Sir Edward Grey* (2001)
Watson, *Ring of Steel, Germany and Austria at War, 1914-1918* (1979)
Wertheimer, Mildred, S, *The Pan German League*
Wheeler-Bennett, *Brest-Litovsk, the forgotten Peace, March 1918* (1938)
Nemesis of Power, the German army in Politics, 1918-1945 (1954)
Williams, Charles, *Adenauer. The Father of the New Germany* (2001)
Willits, R Brian, 'The German American role in the fight for Irish freedom' Irish Times 9 12 1916
Yelton, David K, *Volt Steht Auf: 'The German Volkssturm and the Nazi Strategy, 1944-1945'* in *Journal of Military History* (2000)
Yoder, Amos, ‚The Ruhr Authority and the German Problem' in *The Review of Politics*
John Zametica, *Folly and Malice, The Hapsburg Empire, the Balkans and the start of World War I*, (2024)

NEWSPAPERS PERIODICALS and on-line news Agencies
Ap news 04 01 2025
Al Mayadeen Agencies, 8 12 2022, info from interview in *Zeit* newspaper, 08 02 2023   09 02 2023
Asia Times, Daniel Williams, 26 10 2023
BBC news, Transcript of Nuland-Pyatt call. Ass. Sec Victoria Nuland to US Ambassador to Ukraine, ' I don't think that Klitsch (Vitali Klitscho) should go into the government.'
Counterpunch 09 04 2021, '*NATO to stop Donbas War*'
Daily Mail 3 8 1923 reported Poincaré's speech: 'Germany ought to restore its credit, stabilise its currency, balance its budget and encourage its production. ... But Germany ... has ... disdained all advice'
Daily Mail, 26 01 2012
Daily Telegraph 18 05 2007 Ambrose Evans-Pritchard 'France and Germany clash over inflation as north-south divide widens', 12 07 2007, 'Sarkozy drafts fresh plans to hobble the ECB as euro nears $1.40, Ambrose Evans-Pritchard 09 11 2007 *Eurozone at Loggerheads over interest rates, Telegraph* 02 10 2008, Ambrose Evans-Pritchard, 'So much for tirades against American greed'
Economist 7 12 1929,   *Economist*, 13.7.29, *Economist* 10 July 1972.
Economist Intelligence Unit June 2008
Financial Times, 17.6.1930, *Financial Times* 21 07 2009, Wolfgang Münchau, 'Berlin waves a deficit hairshirt for us all'
Foreign Affairs, Dmitri Trenin, *What Putin really wants in Ukraine*, 12 12 2021
German-Foreign-Policy.com 18 12 2016, 02 12 2021, *Red Lines*
Guardian 3 February 2005

Nucleonics Week, 20.12.1975. *Nucleonics Week,* 16.11.1976, *Nucleonics Week,* 1.1.1976, *Nucleonics Week,* 10.2.1977, *Nucleonics Week,* 31.5.1979,
Prospect Magazine, 14 07 2017, Adam Tooze, 'The Secret History of the Banking Crisis'
New York Times, 12 12 1918, *New York Times, New York Times* 03 02 1920, *New York Times,* 1.2.1920, *New York Times,* 18th January 1923, 26 02 1924, *New York Times* 15 7 1928, *New York Times,* 21 4 1929, *New York Times,* 18 08 1930, *New York Times* 09 28 1931, *New York Times,* 26 09 1931, *New York Times* 22 09 1931, *New York Times* 18 May 1963, *New York Times* 21 08 2011 Gordon Brown *The Euro Zone's Cure starts with Germany, New York Times* 23 12 2023*Anton Trolanovksi,* Adam Entous, Julian Barnes, *Putin quietly signals he is open to a cease fire in Ukraine, Reuters* 23 09 2007, Francois Murphy and Jon Boyle, *Trichet brushes off French Criticism of ECB*
Spectator 19 02 2014, John Laughland, *Ukraine, It's not about Europe versus Russia, articles by Owen Matthews*
Solidarity Eric Toussaint, 15th March 2019, 'Why the 1953 cancellation of German debt won't be reproduced for Greece and Developing Countries.'
Der Spiegel 10 04 2011, *Der Spiegel* 09 30 2010 'Was the deutsche Mark Sacrificed for Reunification?'
Sun & New York Herald 24 01 1920, 08 02 1920,
The Times, Jan 20th 1912 (5) 27 06 1929 reported £3,414,000 gold bought by Germany over two days, *The Times* 25 09 1929, *The Times* 20 04 1925, *Times* 24 January 1931, *The Times, 19 06 1933* 14a.
Die Welt 7 02 09

Index

Abs, Hermann, 258
Acheson, Dean, 253
Adenauer, Konrad, 4, 241-242, 247-249, 253, 258, 261-267
    background and Congress of Vienna, 247
    omits Volkssturm from War Commemoration, 248-9
    rearmament, 253, 261-262
    and Hallstein Doctrine, 264
    rebukes Franz Josef Strauss, 266
American isolationists and America First,
    205, 212-214, 235-235
Angell, Norman, 72
Avakov, Arsen, 305
Anton, Prince, 13
Asquith, Henry, 50, 73, 89-90
Baerbock, Annalena, 312
Baker, James, 298
Baldwin, Stanley, 144
Balfour, Captain Arthur James, 29,
Balfour, Arthur Prime Minister, 171, 174
Ballin, Albert, 102
Barnes, Henry Elmer, American historian, 160-161, 249-250
Barraclough, Sir John, 241
Barroso, José Manuel, 301
Baruch, Bernard, 144, 148
    1923, 'Unless compelled to pay some fixed tax in reparations 'Germany will conquer the world industrially', 148
Beaverbrook, Lord, 237
Beazley, Raymond, American historian, 148
Beisiegel, Philip, 259
Berchtold, Count, 42, 56, 60
Berghahn, Volker R, German historian, 1, 259, 297
    Hitler's economic aim, 259
Bernhardi, General Friedrich von, 38-39
Bernstorff, Ambassador to US, Heinrich von,
    told to turn down Wilson's peace initiative, Feb 1916, 87
    fraudulent Dec 1916 peace initiative, 91

Bethmann Hollweg, Chancellor Theo von, 39, 41, 46, 49, 53, 76, 78, 96
    excluded from military's talks in 2012, 42
    and Prussian Lieutenant Forstner, 46
    promises Austria-Hungary 'entire might' against Serbia, 56
    deceives the British, 63-64
    says Russia must take blame for war, 65-66, 71-72
    offers Turkey deal in war, 64
    reveals war aims to British ambassador, 67
    Britain's reply prompts him to try to evert war, 68-69
    army takes independent action, 69
    asks for indemnity from Britain, 73-75
    his extensive war aims after war begins, 80-81
    fraudulent Dec 1916 peace initiative, 91-92
    advises to concentrate of defeating Russia, 94
Biden, President, Joe, 311, 315-317
Biletsky, Andriy, 309
Bismarck, Chancellor Otto von, 8-11
    war against Denmark, 8
    war against Austria, 9-11
    war against France, 12-17
    adopts Gold as currency, 18-20
    and the Jews, 22
    and the army, 20-21, 25
    accidents, health, pensions insurance, 22-24
    and Russia, 24, 25
Blinken, Antony, 314
Bock, General von, 223
Bockelmann, Horst, 280
Bonar Law, 75
Borsky G., 202
Bosse, Dr, 228
Brandt, Willy, 267, 271, 273
Brauchitsch, Field Marshall, 223
Briand, Aristide, 139, 164, 174
Briey **Iron** basin, 44, 48, 79, 81, 88, 214

in 1917 magnate Vögler would declare, 'to obtain Briey we would fight for another ten years,' 48
   'will ensure Germany's dominance on the world market,' 81
   'an absurdity' to have the iron in France and coal in Germany, 88
Brockdorff-Rantzau, Count, 95, 128-129
Brüning, Chancellor Heinrich, 182-183, 189-191, 196, 295, 324, 333
   austerity measures between 1930 and 1932, 183, 189
   arrives in London to plead for reparations moratorium, 191
   imposes tariff before Russian wheat arrives, 195
   refuses to sack General Gröner, 198
Brusilov, General, 87, 95
Bülow, Bernard von, 31
Burns, William J, 299
Caillaux, Joseph, and wife, Henriette, 54-55, 58, 66
Calmette, Gaston, 56
Canaris, Admiral, 233-235,
Carrington, Lord, 282, 331
Carter, President Jimmy, 273-274, 276, 330
Chelius, Philipp Oscar von, 65-66
Cheron, Henri, 174
Cheney, Dick, 299
Churchill, Winston, 59, 97, 154-155, 214, 218
   horrified by Austria's ultimatum to Serbia, 59
   reveals French mutinies in spring of 2017, 97
   advised to return to Gold Standard at high rate, 154-155
   alarmed by U-Boat challenge, 218
Claß, Heinrich, 35, 80, 97, 197, 215
   publicist for Pan German League, 35-38
   war aims, 79 imprisoned for trying to publish them, 84
   blames Jews for loss of war, 117, 130
   coup to make Hugenberg economic dictator fails, 159
   joins Hitler's government, 209
   and WW2 ambitions, 215-216

   believes in ethnic cleansing, 221
Clemenceau, Georges, 123, 140,
   October 1918, complains American troops 'merely unused', 109
Clinton, President Bill, 285-286
Coal, 24, 48, 81, 88, 100, 132, 134, 143, 146, 157
   iron in France and Coal in Germany 'an absurdity', 132
   retreating German army makes 220 French mines unworkable, 121
   easy to incite Poincaré to invade… just cut off the coal supply! 143
   British coal miners cannot compete with German miners' long hours and low wages, 157
   post-World War II still the major energy source, 239
Crowe, Sir Eyre, 62, 70
Cunliffe, Lord, 125
Curtius, Julius, 171
Danilov, Olesky, 315
Dawes Plan reparations agreement, 154, 154, 201, 323,
   given 'transfer protection,' 150
   France puts inspectors into Germany treasury, 151
   DNVP refuses to accept Dawes Plan without extra loans, 150-151, 153
   Schacht sets up gold-backed discount bank for loans, 152
   reparations paid by export rather than America's cash, 156
Delbrück, Clemens, von, 39, 82
Delcassé, French Foreign Minister Théophile, 31
Dewey, Admiral George, 30
Diebner, Kurt, nuclear scientist, 231
Dönitz, Carl, 217-218
Dubcek, Alexander, 270
Duisberg, Carl, 191
Dulles, John Foster, 262, 265
   Wilson's negotiator before Versailles Treaty, 1255
   at dinner discussion with Schacht in 1930, 188
   and the Korean War, 252
   presses for European Defence Community, 262

348

strong anti-Communist stance, 265
Ebert, Friedrich, 96, 137,
  as President 1918, accepts army's terms, 120
  found guilty of treason, 149
Elbrick, Charles Burke, 272
Erhard, Chancellor Ludwig, 244, 245, 267-268, 278
  envisages wiping out currency in 1943, 245
Erzberger, Erhard, 96, 138
Eyck, Erich, German historian, 163
Falkenhayn, General Eric von, 65, 70, 82, 83, 86, 89-90, 93, 142
Favre, Jules, French Republican leader, 16itte
Fay, Sidney Bradshaw, American historian, 160
Fellner, Fritz, German historian, 56
Fischer, Fritz, German historian, 1, 53. 266-267
Flick, Friedrich, industrialist, 255
Foch, Marshall Ferdinand, 107,
  bitterly criticised for accepting armistice, 114,
  'this is not a peace. It is an armistice for 20 years', 130
Frederick the Great, maxims and example, 4, 8, 11, 15, 51, 117
Frederick VII of Denmark, 8
Frederick William I, 3
Frederick IV, 3
French, Sir John, 83
Frost, David, British reporter, 299
Funk, Walter, Hitler's Minister for Economic Affairs, 259-259
Galen, Cardinal Grav von, 222
Gallois, General Pierre Marie, 281-282
Geiss, Imanuel, historian, 199
Genscher, Hans Dietrich, 281
Gerlach, Walter, physicist, 231
Globke, Hans, 248
Goebbels, Joseph, 205
Gold reserves, 121, 154-155, 168, 176,
  Germany's gold reserves double by 1918, 121
  British gold goes to Germany after return to gold standard, 157
  Germany's gold reserves January 1929, 168
  Britain's loss of gold in 1929, 176
Gollancz, Victor, 243

Gomulka, Wladyslaw, Polish Premier, 264
Göring, Hermann, 206
Gorbachev, Mikhail, 298, 334
Goschen, Sir William, 65-67
Grey, Sir Edward, 42,
  1912 warned against giving Austria 'blank cheque', 42-43
  1914 said Austria must retract 'impossible demands', 59
  slow and inadequate replies from Germany, 60,
  told that Germany would be waging war against France, 66-67
  meeting with American journalist to avert war, 73-75
Gröner, General Wilhelm, 119-120, 182, 198
Haig, Field Marshall Douglas, 97-98, 103-5, 111-114, 127
  at Passchendaele, 1917, 97-98
  at Passchendaele, 1918, 103
  German army in his sector 'completely breaking', 104-105
  Loses confidence in American army, agrees to armistice, 111-114
  with allied armies disbanded, Haig says peace in jeopardy, 127
Haldane, Viscount, 40-41, 50
Halder, General Franz, 223
Hallstein, Walter, 258, 264
Hamid II, Abdul, 30
Harding, President Warren G, 133
Hatry, Clarence, 176
Helphland, Alexander, (also called Parvus) 95
Hearst, Randolph, 165, 204, 236
Herwig, Holger H, historian, 134
Hitler, Adolf, 1, 142, 162-63, 178, 182, 196, 201-209, 214-219, 324-328
  becomes 'drummer' for Nationalist cause, 132
  his Putsch prevents Bavarian 1923 independence, 145
  writes article supporting private enterprise, 159
  newspaper magnate, Alfred Hugenberg, warms to, 166
  on petition to try President for treason against the Young Plan, 177
  supported by Hugenberg press in 1930, 184

349

negative attitude to Americans, 201
   spends $3 million dollars on propaganda in US, 205
   chooses Hugenberg in administration, 209
   reasons for invading Russia, 220
   declares war on America, 224-225
   'It's a decayed country..' 236
Hoffmann, General on the eastern front, 100
Hohenlohe, Prince Gottfried, 49, 81,
Holleben, Dr. Theodore, German ambassador to US, 29-30
Hoover, President Herbert, 128, 169, 180, 192-3, 195. 198, 201, 204
Hötzendorf, Conrad von, Austro-Hungarian Chief of Staff, 53
House, Col., 87, 103, 105, 119
   gives Allies Wilson's ultimatum to accept armistice, 112
Hoyos, Count, 56
Hugenberg, Alfred, 211, 219, 138
   becomes leader of Krupp's armament industry, 32-33
   supports campaign for increase in army, 38
   responsibility of Krupp and Hugenberg for war in 1914, 76-77
   wants to pitch public war aims high, 83
   buys Schell publishers to promote war aims, 85 -86
   supports pro war Fatherland Party, 97
   promotes 'national opposition' to Weimar Republic, 131
   attacks 'War Guilt' clause, 134
   coup to make him 'economic dictator' fails, 159
   believes dictatorship possible if times are hard, 166
   sends widely publicised letter to Americans, 170
   petition against Young Plan affects stock market, 178-179
   asserts that he and the Nazis are equally anti-Jewish, 183-184
   and Bad Harzburg Rally, 196-197
   sacked by Hitler but keeps newspapers, 209

Isabella of Spain, 13,
Jagow, Gottlieb von, German Foreign Minister, 49, 70, 88, 92
   'It is important that we should appear to have been provoked', 44
   asked to precipitate a preventative war, 49
   '.. that gives us the *casus foederis*', 57
   'It will be your task ...to prevent ... an offer of mediation', 87-89
Jenninger, Philipp, 277
Johnson, Boris, 312, 314
Johnson, Lyndon B, 268
Joseph, Franz, Emperor, 10, 56
Kapp, Wolfgang, 131
Kahr, Gustav Ritter von, 145
Kantorowich, German historian, 197
Keim, General August von, 39
Kennan, George F, 250
   advocates demarcation line against Soviets in 1947, 241
   advises supporting Germany as bulwark against Russia, 250
Kennedy, John F, 214, 265
Kennedy, Joseph, 207
Keynes, John Maynard, 121-123, 147
   'starvation' propaganda, 121
   his book's disastrous effect in US, 129
   his book's disastrous effect in Germany, 130
   denounces Clemenceau for Carthaginian Peace, 139-140
   prediction of German starvation seems to come true in 1923, 147
   fights against high return to Gold Standard, 154-155
   seeks loan from America after Second World War. 236-238
Kiderlen-Wächter, German Foreign Secretary, 34, 42
Kiesinger, Chancellor Kurt Georg, 270
Kilgore, Senator, on state of German economy after WW2, 240
Kim-Il Sung, North Korean leader, 252
Kirby. John F, Pentagon Press Secretary, 310
Kirdorf, Emil, coal magnate, 33, 89, 158-159, 196
   suggests Hitler writes pamphlet for industrialists, 159
Kitchener, Field Marshall, Herbert, 86

Klarsfelt, Beate, 270
Kleist, General von, 219
Klitschko, Vitali, Mayor of Kyiv, 303
Koch-Wesser, Dr., leader of German Democratic Party, 174, 177
Kohl, Helmut, German Chancellor, 277, 331
    reunification and D-Mark for East Germans, 279
    'thoughtlessly' pushes Croatian and Slovenian independence, 282
    no money for World War II reparations, 283
    the euro, a 'castle in the air' without political and fiscal union, 284
Klotz, Louis-Lucien, French Minister of Finance, 122-123, 125
Kluck, General von, 79
Kreuger, Ivor, Swedish match king, 178-179
Krugman, Paul, American economist, 295
Krupp, Alfred, 7, 12, 21-24
Krupp, Fritz, son of founder, 27, 28
    supporter of Pan-German League, 32
Krupp, Gustav, 79, 102, 140, 195-196, 199-200, 221 225, 234, 324
    secret member of Pan German League 32
    ruthless attitude to business, 33
    supports Hugenberg's expansionist aims, 38
    power over Wilhelm II, 55-56
    big Bertha guns enable army to invade France, 76-77
    war aims, 80
    postwar making weapons abroad, 140, with others, 163
    agriculture, gold and train deal in Russia. 140-142
    starts *schwarz production* of weapons in Germany, 163
    deal with Stalin, for a political favour, 184-187
    made to give up agricultural concession, loan instead, 195
    Brazil signs deal to buy Krupp's armaments, 205
    had started designing submarines in the 1920s, 217
    and help with steel for Stalin's tanks, 221

Krupp, Alfried, 225, 227-228, 259
    gives prison labourers less to eat than I G Farben, 225-226
    allowed to call company, 'a state within a state', 227
    children of industrialists not obliged to join Volkssturm, 229
Khruschchev, Nikita, Profile and Berlin Wall, 264-265
Kühlmann, Richard von, diplomat dealing with Russia, 89-99
    phrase 'self-determination' used 'to get for ourselves ... whatever territories we absolutely needed.' 98
Lenin Vladimir, 99-101. 125,
    agrees to topple Russian gov. if Germany promises 'no annexations and no indemnities', 94-95
    overthrows government, 98
    deceived over 'no annexations and no indemnities' 99-100
    faced with starvation turns to Krupp for help, 141-142
Leopold, Prince, 13-14
Leopold, King of Belgium, 31
Lerchenfeld, Count, 72
Lewin, General Harry, 123
Lewis, Michael, 294
Leyen, Ursula von der, 316
Lichnowsky, Prince Karl von, Ambassador to London, 39, 59-60
    'such policy is comprehensible only if war was our aim, not otherwise.' 60
Liggett, Major General, 109
Lindbergh, Charles, 205-207, 214Litvinov, Maxim, 210
Liggett, Major General, 109
Lindbergh Charles, 201-203, 209
Litvinov Maxim, 205
Lloyd George, 34, 87, 90, 140,
    offers Germany generous peace initiative, May 1916, 87,
    assumes office as Prime Minister, 90,
    denies France security of German gold in reparations, 122-123
    and Treaty of Rapallo, 140
Loans to Germany, approx. £850m between 1919-31, 202
Ludendorff, General Erich von, 84, 95, 106-107, Ludendorffians, 210

occupies Crimea, April 1918, campaigns for German colonists, 101,
  Spring 1918 offensive on western front, 106-107,
  reinforces Meuse-Argonne at the expense of defences in Flanders, 108
  attempted coup with Hitler stops Bavarian independence, 145
Lutz, Hermann, German civil servant and propagandist, 161
Maas, Heiko. German Foreign Minister, 308
Macdonald, Ramsay, 82, 172
McCain, Senator John, 302
Max, Prince, 117, 119
Mantey, Eberhard von, 29
Marshall, George C, and plan, 242-243
Mao Zydong, 252,
Mayer, Deutsche Bank chief economist, 290
McCloy, John J, 253-254
Mearsheimer, John J, 315
Medinsky, Vladimir, 313
Medvedev, Dmitry, 296
Melchior, Dr. Carl, 193
Meer Fritz Ter, German industrialist, quote, 249
Merkel, Chancellor Angela, 292, 300, 304
  criticises US and Britain for Lehman crash, 292
  2008 statement Ukraine would become NATO member, 300
  declares the referendum in Crimea illegal, 304
  'Says that Minsk accord had merely been to enable NATO to get stronger', 309
Michaelis, Chancellor, 96
Milosevic, Slobodan, 281
Mitterand, President François, 283
Moltke, General Helmuth von, 51, 61, 70-71
  'to wait any longer diminishes our chances' 51
  'We hope to be finished with France in six weeks ...' 61
Monnet, Claude, 258,
Morgan, Brigadier-General, 121, 200
Moreau, Émile, Governor of the Bank of France, 155

On friendship between Norman and Schacht, 155
Müller, Admiral Georg von, 42
Nuland, Victoria, 304
Nozari, Gholam Hossein, 291
Napoleon III, 13-16
Nicholas II, Tzar, 66, 71,
  '.. these measures do not mean war', 71
Nivelle, General Robert, 97
Northcliffe, Viscount, 85-86, 127
Norman, Montagu, Governor of the Bank of England, 152, 191
  pressure from Germany to return to Gold Standard, 152
  bribe from America to return to Gold Standard, 153
  and Bank for International Settlements, 173
  raises interest rates in September 1929, 176
  devaluation, 193-194
Noyer, Christian, Governor of the Bank of France, 287
Nye, Senator Gerald P, 212, 214
Overy, Richard, historian, 248
Pan-German League, 32, 39
  founder, Alfred Hugenberg of Krupps armaments company, 32
  supports grabbing parts of Morocco, 33-34
  wants European customs area, secured by force, if necessary, 35
  funds campaign protesting innocence of starting 1914 war, 160
Payer, von, Vice Chancellor, 102
Peaslee, Amos J, 203
Pershing General, 97-98
  in command at battles of St. Mihael and Meuse Argonne, 107
  relieved of his post and important railway junction not shelled, 109
  says victory imminent, armistice could lead to another war, 114
Pleven French Prime Minister, Rene, 261
Pöhl, Karl Otto, 284
Poincaré, President Raymond, 61, 139, 155,
  orders the repatriation of German money, 149,

352

puts financial controls over German treasury, 151,
    agrees to Young Plan reparations agreement, 173
Poroshenko, Petro, 301,
    agrees to Minsk II Accord, extremists in Kyiv turn it down, 305,
    argues that Stalin and Nazis equal, pro-Nazi marches follow, 307
    protests against signing a Minsk II-like peace accord in 2019, 309
Prim, General, 14
Putin, Vladimir, 299, 296-297, 303-304, 307-308, 311
    talks to David Frost about Europe and NATO, 299
    regards 2008 offer of NATO to Ukraine as 'declaration of war' 300
    and Georgia, 300-301
    and Crimea, 303-304
    and Donald Trump in 2017, 307
    2021 threatens to respond if Red Line over NATO is crossed, 310
    and Boris Johnson, 314
    peace initiatives, 2022, 2023 and 2024, 313, 316, 317
Raeder, Admiral Erich, 218, 232,
Rathenau, Walter, 138
Reagan, President Ronald, 276
Reparations, in cash,by 1921, none, 135,
    in kind, by 1921, approx. £400 m, (including ships, trains, etc.,)
    in cash, by 1924, £80 million, 151
    in cash by 1929, nearly £400m, with tariffs and 'in kind,' 202
    summary of total reps paid, 201-202
Rhee, Syngman, South Korean President, 252
Ribbentrop Joachim von, 224
Robinson, Geoffrey, (later known as Geoffrey Dawson) 85,
Röhl, Professor John, 43
Roon, General Albert von, 5, 7
Roosevelt, President Theodore, 29-30, 92, 111
Roosevelt, President Franklin D, 204, 213, 234-235, 326
Russell, Sean, IRA leader, 213,

Rutte, Mark, Secretary General of NATO, 319
Saakashvili, Mikheil, 300
Salisbury, Lord, 26-27
Sanders, General, Liman von, 30, 60
    by Dec 2013 Turkish army virtually under his control, 50
Sanio, Jochen, President of German Supervisory Authority, 292
Sarkozy, former French President Nicolas, 289, 304
Schacht, President of Reichsbank, Hjalmar, 151-153, 168, 170, 173, 181-2,
    re: Young Plan, 'every remnant of obligations ... must disappear', 168
    declares payment dependent on return of Saar etc., to Germany, 170
    regards Bank of International Settlements as 'my bank', 173
    becomes Hitler's Minister for Economics, 202
    fraudulent 1930s economic schemes, 211
Scheid, Dr. SS Obergruppenführer, 1944 directive, 228,
Scherl, August, newspaper concern, 85-86
Schlieffen, General Alfred von, 29, 31
Schotterer, Dr Gustav, World War II occupation extortion, 216
Schmidt, President Helmut, 273-275
Schmidt, Paul, 175
Scholz, President Olav, 312, 316
Schröder, President Gerhard, 285, 306
Schuman, Robert, 258-259
Shirer, William, historian, 236, 326
Schumacher, Kurt, Social Democrat politician, 247
Seebohm, Dr, 255
Shuker, Stephen A, American historian, 202, 272
Smedley Butler, General, 205
Snowden, Philip, 147, 171-2, 174
Sprecher, Drexel, A, Nuremberg Attorney, 221,
Starmer, Kier, 317
Stalin, Joseph, 1, 239, 252, 262
    nearly bankrupt, saved by Krupp's offer, 185
    industrial and military help, 186, 221

wheat exported while peasants expelled, 187-188
Steinmeier, President of Germany, Frank-Walter, 306
Stieber, Wilhelm, Bismarck's spy, 9-10, 12-13, 16-17
Steinbrück, Peer, German Finance Minister, 288
Stinnes, Hugo, coal magnate, 33, 81, 89, 102, 158
    and 8 hour working day, 139, 144,
    return to 10 hour working day, 146-147
Stoltenberg, Jens, 310
Stresemann, Gustav, 138, 150, 157, 168, 170, 174-175, 178
    resolution People's Party opposed Hugenberg's petition, 177
Strauss, Franz Josef, 266, 274, 277, 282
    threat to democracy, 266
    advocates nuclear weapon modernisation, 274
    supports Herr Jenninger's pro Hitler's speech, 277
    asserts Yugoslavia 'inanimate' supports altering status, 282
Strong, Benjamin, 153-154
Sumner, Viscount, 125
Swing, Raymond Gram, American journalist, 73-74, 88
Tampke, Jürgen, historian, 130
Taran, Andreii, 309
Thatcher, Margaret, 279
Thysssen, August, 33, 48, 81,
Thyssen, Fritz, 144, 198
Tripitz, Alfred von, 28-29, 40, 42-43, 80, 97, 98,
Tisza, Count Stephen, 56
Tooze, Adam, 293
Treitschke, Heinrich von, 39
Trichet, Jean Claude, 287-289
Trotsky, Leon, 98-100
Truman, Harry S, 235-236, 238, 241-242, 251, 252, 328-329
Trump, President Donald, 307, 336
Tschirchky, Heinrich von, 54, 57, 62, 64, 68
Untermyer, Samuel, 205
Varoufakis, Janis, 292
Vestager, Margarethe, 316
Viereck, George Sylvester, 189, 205, 212, 236
Viktor, Archduke Ludwig, 20
Viviani, René, 58, 61, 66, 70
Vögler, Dr. Albert, 48, 138, 168, 172-3, 179, 196, 214
Weigel, Theo, 284
Waldersee, Alfred, 14
Warburg, Max, 51, 135, 169
War Guilt, 162, 177
    Bethmann Hollweg, Russia must be blamed for coming war, 64-66, 71
    Dec. 1914, he accuses Britain and Russia of starting war, 82
    inter-war historian, Barnes, blames Russia and France for war, 161
    German children taught that Britain started 1914 War, 162
    Britain the evil genius behind the First World War, 177
    Petition to call President a traitor for accepting the 'war guilt lie,' 177
    Social democrats' investigation blames Germany and Austria, 197
Wauchope, General Andrew, 159
Weber, Axel, 287-290
Webb, Beatrice, Sidney, 40, 41, 50
Wellington, Duke of, 4
Wenninger, General von, 42
Wilhelm I, King, Emperor, 5, 7, 13, 14, 17, 25
Wilhelm II, Emperor, 26-29, 40-43, 56-57, 63-64
Willert, Arthur, 127
Wilson, President Woodrow, 72, 81, 83, 85, 89-93, 98-99, 102-104. 109-121, 124-129, 133, 138, 144, 148, 153, 180, 188, 202, 207, 220, 224, 237, 250, 322, 326, 336, 342, 352-356
    his spring 1916 peace feeler ignored by Germany, 88
    Germany's Dec 1916 'peace initiative' a disappointment, 92
    deceived by German talk of 'no annexations, no indemnities' 98-99
    Germany's decision to seek peace through the 'idealist' Wilson, 102
    prejudiced against Allies, 103
    pressured Allies to accept armistice, rather than military victory, 112

       against charging 'indemnities'
       so reparations charged, 124
       changes his mind about
       German war guilt, 128-129
       on the necessity of insisting on
       adequate reparations, 148
Wilhelmina, Queen of the Netherlands, 31
Wolf, Julius, 35
Wood, Robert E, 213, 214, 250
Yanukovych, Viktor, 301, 302, 304
Yeltsin, President Boris, 299
Young Plan, 162, 167-8, 172, 201-203, 323-325
       German economic strength, 167
       Financial details of, 172
Zelensky, Volodymyr, 308-310, 314-316, 319, 334-336
Zimmerman, Arthur, 34, 92-93, 98
Zhukov, General, 224

References

[1] Frederick the Great 'Political Testament' 1752, quoted in J Ellis Barker *Foundations of Germany* (1916), 37.
[2] Frederick the Great 'Political Testament' 1752, quoted in J Ellis Barker *Foundations of Germany* (1916), 33.
[3] Late Deputy Adjutant-General J. H. Morgan, *Assize of Arms, The Disarmament of Germany, and her Rearmament 1919-1939* vol.1. (1945), 101.
[4] J. H. Morgan, *Assize of Arms* vol.1.101
[5] J. H. Morgan, *Assize of Arms* vol.1. 97-98.
[6] S H Steinberg, *A Short History of Germany* (Cambridge University Press, 1944), 207.
[7] Willam Manchester, *The Arms of Krupp, 1587*-1968 (1968, paper ed.2003), 99.
[8] Frederick the Great 'Political Testament' 1752, quoted in J Ellis Barker *Foundations of Germany* (1916) 88.
[9] S H Steinberg, *A Short History of Germany* (Cambridge University Press 1944), 216.
[10] S H Steinberg, *A Short History of Germany* 217.
[11] *The Chancellor's Spy,* 97-101
[12] *The Chancellor's Spy,* 102
[13] *The Chancellor's Spy,* 103-104
[14] S H Steinberg, *A Short History of Germany* 217.
[15] Frederick the Great 'Political Testament' 1752, quoted in J Ellis Barker *Foundations of Germany* (1916), 99
[16] *The Chancellor's Spy,* 117-118
[17] *The Chancellor's Spy,* 126
[18] *The Chancellor's Spy,* 133
[19] *The Chancellor's Spy,* 134-5
[20] *The Chancellor's Spy,* 136
[21] Jonathan Steinberg, *Bismarck, A Life* (Oxford University Press, 2011, paper ed.2012),285-286.
[22] Jonathan Steinberg, *Bismarck, A Life,* 287.
[23] *The Chancellor's Spy,* 140
[24] *The Chancellor's Spy,* 141
[25] Wilhelm Stieber *The Chancellor's Spy* 216-217
[26] Wilhelm Stieber *The Chancellor's Spy* 204
[27] S H Steinberg, *A Short History of Germany,* 231
[28] Wikepedia *German Gold Mark*
[29] Jonathan Steinberg, *Bismarck, A Life,* 330
[30] Martin Kitchen, *The Political Economy of Germany, 1815-1914,* (Montreal, 1978), 132.
[31] Jonathan Steinberg, *Bismarck, A Life,* 330.
[32] National (American) History Education Clearing House.org *The Panic of 1873*

[33] Martin Kitchen, *The Political Economy of Germany, 1815-1914*, 139.
[34] E Eyck *Bismarck and the German Empire* 205
[35] Jonathan Steinberg, *Bismarck, A Life*, 334-335.
[36] Jonathan Steinberg, *Bismarck, A Life*, 330.
[37] James Hawes *The Shortest History of Germany* (paper ed) 118-119
[38] Erich Eyck, *Bismarck and the German Empire*, (1950) 200
[39] Erich Eyck, *Bismarck and the German Empire*, 219
[40] S H Steinberg, *A Short History of Germany* (1944), 221.
[41] Martin Kitchin, *The Political Economy of Germany, 1815-1914*, 170-171.
[42] Frank Owen, *Tempestuous Journey* (1954) 133. British unemployment fluctuated between 3 and 5%. 'In Germany between 7 and 30 per cent.'
[43] Martin Kitchen, *The Political Economy of Germany, 1815-1914*, 178.
[44] Martin Kitchen, *The Political Economy of Germany, 1815-1914*, 252.
[45] Description of coal pollution from Catherine Bailey *Black Diamonds* 71
[46] Volker R Berghahn, *Imperial Germany 1871-1914*, (1994) 58, 302
[47] Quoted in James Hawes, *The Shortest History of Germany*, 126
[48] Martin Kitchen, *A History of Modern Germany 1800-2000* (2006), 207.
[49] Erich Eyck, *Bismarck and the German Empire* (1945) 294-5
[50] *Annual Register 1888* 268
[51] J Ellis Barker, *Modern Germany* (1919) 377
[52] Martin Kitchen, *The Political Economy of Germany, 1815-1915*, 196.
[53] S H Steinberg, *A Short History of Germany*, (1944), 235.
[54] Thomas Pakenham, *Scramble for Africa*, (paper ed.200-213.
[55] Mildred S Wertheimer, *The Pan German League 1890-1914*, 27, from Bismarck, *Gedanken und Erinnerungen*, vol iii (1919) 147
[56] Eric Dorn Brose (2004), *The Kaiser's Army*, 120
[57] Holger H Herwig, *Luxury Fleet, The Imperial Germany Navy, 1888-1919*, 40
[58] W Manchester, *Arms of Krupp*, (paper ed.), 224-225.
[59] Henning Sietz, 8 May 2002, *Die Zeit* on line, 'In New York wird die größte Panik ausbrechen: Wie Kaiser Wilhelm II die USA wit einem Militärschlag niederzwingen wollte' Also reported in *The Guardian, Daily Telegraph, American Heritage* etc. Also Holger H Herwig, (1970) 'Naval Operations Plans between Germany and the United States of America 1898-1913: A Study of Strategic Planning in the Age of Imperialism' 5-52
[60] Hans W Gatske, *Germany and the United States: A Special Relationship*, 31

[61] Seitz, Henning (8 May 2002) 'In New York wird die größte Panik ausbrechen: Wie Kaiser Wilhehlm II die USA mit einem Militärschlag niederzwingen
[62] William Roscoe Thayer, *Theodore Roosevelt,* (1919) XIV, *The President and the Kaiser*
[63] Sietz, Henning (8 May 2002) 'In New York wird die größte Panik ausbrechen: Wie Kaiser Wilhehlm II die USA mit einem Militärschlag niederzwingen.
[64] William Roscoe Thayer (1859-1923) XIV *Theodore Roosevelt* (1919) *The President and the Kaiser* (Bartleby.com)
[65] Notes by Hans Adolf con Bülow, 30 December 1904, printed in Rich and Fisher, *The Holstein Papers, 1v,* no 904. enclosure
[66] John C G Röhl, *Into the Abyss of War and Exile,* 310f.
[67] Martin Kitchen, *A History of Modern Germany, 1800-2000,* 193
[68] John C G Röhl, *Kaiser Wilhelm, II,* 88-89
[69] William Manchester, *Arms of Krupp,* 248-249.
[70] William Manchester, *The Arms of Krupp,* 243
[71] Sebastien Conrad, *Globilisation and the Nation in Imperial Germany,* 175
[72] Leopold, *Alfred Hugenberg,* 31.
[73] Leopold, *Alfred Hugenberg,* 4.
[74] William Manchester *The Arms of Krupp,* 279.
[75] Roger Chichering, *We men who feel most German, A Cultural Study of the Pan German League, 1886-1914,* 228
[76] Fritz Fischer *Germany's Aims in the 1st World War,* (paper ed.), 13.
[77] Volker R Berghahn, *Imperial Germany,* 1871-1914, Table 17, page 303 4,762,312 to 5,321,400 marks a year (20.43 to £)
[78] *The Times* Jan 20th 1912,5. Col 1. See also Roger Chichering, *We men who feel most German,*263-267
[79] Roger Chichering, *We men who feel most German, A Cultural Study of the Pan German League, 1886-1914,* 265, ADB (1911),57-8, ADB (1912), 406-7, *Strom,* 209.
[80] Claβ's pamphlet sold over 50,000 copies and asserted that the only response to Britain's intervention was hatred. Chichering, 293, ADB (1911), 257-8, 298-9.
[81] Fritz Fischer, *War of Illusions,* (with a foreword by Sir Alan Bullock, 1975),86.
[82] Roger Chichering, *We men who feel most German,* 263-266
[83] Volker Berghahn, *Quest for Economic Empire,* 8
[84] Roger Chichering *We men who feel most German* (1984) 79
[85] Heinrich Claβ, *Wenn ich der Kaiser wär.* (translation on Internet. Forum Wereldoorlog Forum Index. Personen.)
[86] Henry Ashby Turner Jr, *Hitler's Thirty Days to Power: January 1933* (1996) 137
[87] William Manchester *The Arms of Krupp* 16
[88] General Friedrich von Bernhardi *Germany and the Next War,* (1912), V

[89] General Friedrich von Bernhardi *Germany and the Next War* (1912), 39
[90] Fritz Fischer, *War of Illusions*, 263-265.
[91] Roger Chichering, *We men who feel most German*, 283.
[92] Fritz Fischer, *War of Illusions*, 105-108.
[93] In *We Men who feel most German* Chichering comments that Claß lied in his memoirs about the extent of the industrialists' support.173
[94] Fritz Fischer, *Germany's Aims in the First World War*, (paper ed), 36
[95] Niall Ferguson, *The Pity of War* (paper ed. 1999), 122-123.
[96] Walter Reid, *Architect of Victory, Douglas Haig* (2006), 140
[97] Fritz Fischer, *War of Illusions*, 210.
[98] Christopher Clark, *The Sleepwalkers*, (paper ed. 2013),109.
[99] Fritz Fischer, *War of Illusions, German Politics from 1911 to 1914* (1975), 156
[100] Fritz Fischer, *War of Illusions, German Politics from 1911 to 1914* (1975), 157-158, OU, 4, No. 4954, Szögyény to Berchtold, 22.11.12; No. 4571, Archduke Franz-Ferdinand to Berchtold, 22.11.12; cf. also Hugo Hantsch, *Graf Berchtold*, 350
[101] David Fromkin, *Europe's Last Summer* (paperback 2004) 90
[102] John C G Röhl, 'Goodbye to all that (again)? The Fisher thesis, the new revisionism and the meaning of the First World War' lecture at the University of Sussex 6 11 2014 (reprinted on the Internet)
[103] John Zametica, *Folly and Malice*, 642
[104] Fritz Fischer, *War of Illusions*, 212
[105] Fritz Fischer, *War of Illusions*, 190-192
[106] Sisley Huddleston, *Poincaré, A Biographical Portrait* (1924), 38
[107] Christopher Clark, *The Sleepwalkers* (paper ed.), 486
[108] Roger Chichering, *We Men who feel most German,* Kiderlen revealed the suppressed passage to the Reichstag's budget commission, 260
[109] Christopher Clark, *The Sleepwalkers* (paper ed.), 440, 518, 'The French Army' *The Times*, 14 July 1914.
[110] *Annual Register 1913,* 318-320
[111] Brigadier-General J H Morgan, *Assize of Arms,* 95
[112] *Annual Register 1914,* 306
[113] Brigadier-General Morgan, *Assize of Arms,* 94
[114] Fritz Fischer *Germany's Aims in the First World War* (paperback ed) 47
[115] Zametica, *Folly and Malice,* 564
[116] Martin Kitchen, *The Political Economy of Germany 1815-1914*, 278
[117] Fritz Fischer *War of Illusions* 325, 326
[118] Fischer, *War of Illusions*, 427-8 Treaty signed 30 12 1913, 9 02 1914 Russia received loan of 665 million francs, June 1914

the Duma voted the money for the big army bill. Became law in July
[119] Fritz Fischer *War of Illusions*, 444
[120] J. F. V. Keiger, *Raymond Poincaré*, 157
[121] Fritz Fischer, *Germany's Aims in the First World War*, 50, Also Pogge-v. Strandmann and Imanuel Geiss, *Die Erforderlichkeit des Unmöglichen, Hamburger Studien zur neuren Geschichte, No 2. (Frankfurt, 1965) 66*
[122] Fritz Fischer, *Germany's Aims in the First World War*, 37, Conrad, *Aus Meiner Dienstzeit*, III, 674.
[123] Fritz Fischer *War of Illusions* 427-428
[124] Niall Ferguson, *The Pity of War*, 23
[125] Fritz Fischer *War of Illusions* 372 quoted from Conrad *Aus meiner Dienst* 626
[126] Niall Ferguson, *Pity of War*, 100, Geiss, Docs. 3, 4.
[127] Niall Ferguson, *Pity of War*, 100, quoted from M M W, Max Warburg papers, 'Jahresbericht 1914', pp.1f; Warburg, *Aus meinem Aufzeichnungen*, p.29.
[128] Fritz Fischer *War of Illusions*, 448
[129] Fritz Fischer *War of Illusions*, 453, DHW, No.6, 20.3.14, p.112
[130] Fritz Fischer, War of Illusions, (1975) 412
[131] Michael Waterhouse, *Edwardian Requiem*, 324
[132] Fritz Fischer, Germany's Aims in the First World War, (1967) (paperback ed) 55
[133] W. Manchester, *The Arms of Krupp* 1587-1968, (1969) 288, 317, 318
[134] W. Manchester, *The Arms of Krupp*, 318
[135] Zametica, *Folly and Malice*, 546-547, *DSPKS*, vol. 7/2, no.415, telegram Pašilić, 14 July 1914
[136] DSPKS, vol 7/2 no.415, telegram Pašlić, 18 July 1914, Zametica, *Folly and Malice*, 547
[137] Fritz Fischer, *Germany's Aims in the First World War*, (paperback ed) 53, DD, No,49, Tschirschky to Bethmann-Hollweg
[138] Fritz Fischer, *Germany's Aims in the First World War*, 56
[139] Fritz Fischer, *Germany's Aims in the First World War*, 58, DD, I. No.34a (1927ed) Tschirschky to Chancellor, July 11, marked out by Bethmann-Hollweg, July 12th. Cf. also Schoen, Bavarian Chargé d'Affairs, to Hertling, July 18. *DD*, IV, App IV, No.2. Zimmermann's account of demands of the Austrian Note, *DD*, 1, no.49, Tschirschky to Chancellor, July 14
[140] *Germany's Aims*, 56
[141] *Germany's Aims*, 58, Letter from Szögyény to Berchtold, July12
[142] *Arms of Krupp*, 312-13
[143] *Arms of Krupp*, 318
[144] *Germany's Aims*, 60, DD, I, No. 72, cf. n.23
[145] William Manchester, *The Arms of Krupp*, 328

[146] *Germany's Aims,* 64, D. tel., I, No 67, Jagow to Wedel, (Minister *a latere* to the Emperor) July 18; id., No. 80, Wedel to Foreign Ministry, July 19, also n.4. to no.80
[147] *Germany's Aims,* 62, For Jagow's letter to Tschirschkyn, id,I., No 61
[148] *Germany's Aims,* 64, Id., 82, Müller to Jagow
[149] Simon Heffer, *Staring at God,* (2019) 8, 21
[150] *Germany's Aims,* 61, note 2, Jagow writes: 'Let Austria postpone presenting the note by one hour, to make certain that the Frenchmen have left.'
[151] David Fromkin, *Europe's Last Summer,* 191
[152] *Edwardian Requiem,* 293, 296
[153] *Edwardian Requiem,*293
[154] *Germany's Aims,* 65, Id., No. 157, Lichnowsky to Foreign Ministry, No.164, Jagow to Lichnowsky, July 25; No 171, Jagow to Lichnowsky, July 25
[155] *Europe's Last Summer,* 195
[156] Norman Stone, *A Short World War II history* 2013 (paper-back ed) xiv
[157] *War of Illusions,* 427
[158] *Germany's Aims,* 66,
[159] Annika Mombauer, *The Origins of the First World War,* 16
[160] *Germany's Aims,* 67
[161] *Germany's Aims,* 66, Id., Bethmann-Hollweg to Lichnowsky, July 26
[162] Sisley Huddleston, *Poincaré,* extract from Poincaré's *Les Origins de la Guerre* 63-64
[163] *Germany's Aims,* 68, *DD,* II, No. 376, Jagow to Minister in Brussels, July 29. The demand was addressed in Moltke's draft to the Belgian government; it was recast by Stumm and given the form of a communication from Jagow to the minister, who was to wait for special instructions before presenting it (no.375) Cf. also Albertini, op.cit., p.487, also on 26 July, when Moltke returned from Carlsbad.
[164] *Germany's Aims,* 37
[165] Butler, David Allen, *The Burden of Guilt, How Germany shattered the Last Days of Peace, Summer 1914,* 103
[166] Sir Eyre Crowe, memo to Sir Edward Grey, 27th July 1914
[167] Simon Heffer, *Staring at God,* (2019), 18, 36
[168] *Germany's Aims,* 68, This was also the opinion of the acting French Foreign Minister, Bienvenu-Martin; *Doc, Fr.,* III, II, No 20 (circular instructions by Bethmann-Hollweg., no.2),
[169] *Germany's Aims,* 69, Id., I, No.257, Tschischky to Foreign Ministry, July 27, Bethmann-Hollweg transmits contents of Lichnowsky's telegram No 238 to h, No. 277
[170] *Germany's Aims,* 70 Id., I, No.272, Bethmann-Hollwg to Tschirschky, (author's italics); with last sentence cf. No 258, Lichnowsky to Foreign Ministry, July 27

171 *Germany's Aims*, 71 Text of British telegram
172 *Germany's Aims*, 71 Id., No 278, Bethmann- Hollweg to Lichnowsky, July 27
173 *Germany's Aims*, 71 *PD*, II, No.293, Emperor to Jagow, July 28; cf. also the Emperor's marginal notes at the end of the Serbian answer to the Austrian Ultimatum, *DD*, I, No.271 (author's italics)
174 *Germany's Aims*, 65, Emperor's Minutes on Lichnowsky's dispatch informing him of Grey's attempt at mediation, Id., No.121, July 23.
175 *War of Illusions*, 487-8
176 *Germany's Aims*, 72, Id., II, No.323. Chancellor to Tschirschky, (author's italics)
177 *Germany's Aims*, 84, *DD*, II, No.320, Chancellor to Wangenheim; Id. Nos, 405 and 411, Wangenheim to Foreign Ministry
178 *Germany's Aims*, 73, *DD*, II, No.307; *DD*, I, No.214, Jagow to Chargéd'Affaires in Bucharest.
179 *Germany's Aims*, 74, Id., No.323, cf. 72
180 Akin A Soyoye *World War I Introduction*, 14
181 *Germany's Aims*, 75-top of 76. Interviews with the generals, Cf. also Albertini, op. cit., pp.490 ff., n. 1. To p.491, DD, !V, Annexe !Va. No.2. 1917 ed.; cf. also Hanz v. Zwehl, *Erich von Falkenhayn, General der Infanterie,* Berlin, 1926, pp.56 ff. The demand to allow the German armies through Belgium had been drafted on 26th July.
182 *Germany's Aims*, 76
183 *War of Illusions, 491* 29
184 Poincaré, *Les Origines de la Guerre,* reproduced in Sisley Huddleston, *Poincaré,* A biographical Portrait, (1924), 65
185 *Germany's Aims*, 79, Id., No. 380, Bethmann to Pourtalès, July 29 No 385, id. To Tschirschky July 29
186 *Germany's Aims,* 77, *DD*, II, No.373. Chancellor's notes for his interview with Goschen; cf. also Goschen's report to Grey, checked for accuracy by Bethmann-Hollweg, *BD*, XI, No. 293. Jagow's draft for the declaration to Goschen originally included an offer of a naval agreement in return for assurance of Britain's neutrality in the crisis at issue; this offer, however, had to be cancelled owing to objections by the Emperor. Cf. Albertini,op.cit. pp.506 ff
187 Spartacus Educational, Edward Grey
188 *War of Illusions,* 137
189 *Germany's Aims,* 47
190 *Germany's Aims,* 78, *DD*, II, No.368, Lichnowsky to Foreign Ministry, July 29. Only three days before Jagow had confidently told Jules Cambon, who thought that Britain would intervene immediately: 'You have your information re ours; we have ours.

We are certain of British neutrality.' *DD,* II, No.395, Chancellor to Tschirschky, sent at 2.55 am

191 *Germany's Aims,* 78-79, Telegrams to Tschirschky at 3.0 am. *DD,* II. No.395, Chancellor to Tschirschky, five minutes late one to Vienna. Id., No.396, id. To id., These two documents, together with Bethmann's address to the Prussian Ministry of State on the afternoon of July 30th are used to show the 'absolutely desperate efforts' made by Bethmann-Hollweg to make Vienna retreat.

192 *Germany's Aims,* 82, Id., No, 399; Chancellor communicates to Emperor Pourtalès despatch of July 29 (No 343) (arr.2.52 pm) Both were handed to the Emperor at 7. Am on July 30 and returned by him the same day with his minutes on the covering letter.

193 *Germany's Aims,* 83, Marginal notes on Lichnowsky's despatch (cf.n.87) and Pourtalès report, No.401, July 30

194 *Germany's Aims,* 85, Conrad, op. cit.,pp151ff. Tel. Captain Fleischmann to Moltke, cf Ritter, op, cit.pp.319ff., cf. Wegerer, op.cit.,II.pp.113ff.; *DD,*II, No.410, Pourtalès to Foreign Ministry, July 30

195 *Germany's Aims,* 83

196 *Germany's Aims,*85

197 Simon Heffer, *Staring at God,* 52,57

198 *Annual Register,* 282

199 *Annual Register,* 282

200 *Aims of Germany,* 86

201 *Germany's Aims,* 84-86

202 *Germany's Aims,* 86

203 David Fromkin, *Europe's last Summer,* 238,240

204 Germany requested that Russia demobilize within the next 12 hours. Russia's refusal to do so was taken as a declaration of war against Germany. Many historians have since argued that Russia's general mobilization did not amount to a declaration of war

205 *Germany's Aims,* 86 DD,1V, Annexe !V, No. 27, Lerchenfeld to Hertling, July 31st private letter

206 *War of Illusions,* 504, Geiss, No 1001, Hammann to Ballin, 1.8.14

207 Niall Ferguson, *Pity of War,* 153

208 S H Steinberg, *Short History of Germany,* 254

209 Peter Frankopan, *The Silk Roads, A New History of the World,* 315

210 *The Times,* 1 August 1914

211 Simon Heffer, *Staring at God,* 43

212 Conservative and Unionist, 2,270,753, (271 seats) Liberal, 2,157,256, (272 seats) Irish Nationalists, 90,416 (81 seats) Labour 309,963 (56 seats)

213 Simon Heffer, *Staring at God,* 68

214 *Annual Register,* 168

215 *Germany's Aims*, 86
216 Simon Heffer, *Staring at God*, 67, taken from British Documents on the origins of the War, 1898-1914.
217 Simon Heffer, *Staring at God*, 76
218 Poincaré, *Au service*, Vol.IV, pp.482-3, quoted in J F V Keiger, *Raymond Poincaré* (1997), 181
219 J. F. V. Keiger, *Raymond Poincaré*, 182
220 Fischer, *War of Illusions*, 508-9
221 Niall Ferguson, *The War of the World*, 106-107
222 Roger Chichering, *We Men who feel most German*, 229.Willibald Gutsche, *Ausfsteig und fall eines Kaiserlichen Reichskanzlers ((1973)* 107, Paul Herre,,*Kronprinz Wilhelm: Seine Rolle in der deutschen Politik,* 38
223 Roger Chichering, *We Men who feel most German*, 228. The other major funder was the coal baron, Emil Kirdorf.
224 W. Manchester, *The Arms of Krupp*,284. In 1913 the Belgian Parliament had ordered heavy artillery from Krupps but it had never been delivered. 282
225 W. Manchester, *Arms of Krupp*, 287.
226 W. Manchester, *Arms of Krupp*, 284.
227 W. Manchester, *Arms of Krupp*, 289.
228 'Edgar Hartwig, Alldeutscher Verband, (ADV)' in Dieter Fricke, ed., *Die bürglichen Parteien in Deutschland* (Berlin, 1968), 1: 9-10
229 The extensive correspondence between Hugenberg and Class is in DZA Potsdam, Akten des Alldeutsche Verbandes (ADV), 179/1 Also Leopold, Hugenberg, 6
230 *Germany's Aims*, 104
231 *Germany's Aims*, 257
232 Martin Kitchen, *Political Economy of Germany 1815-1914* (1978) 278
233 *Germany's Aims in the First World War*, 257-259
234 Peter Claughton, *New techniques, new sources: The British Steel industry and its ore supply 1850-1950*
235 *Germany's Aims in the First World War*, 119
236 *The Times* 2 December 1914
237 *Germany's Aims in the First World War*, 331, account of interview preserved in the archives was first published by Jürgen Kuczynski, 1957
238 Leopold, *Alfred Hugenberg,*7, Class, *Wider den Strom,*326-55,
239 Leopold, *Alfred Hugenberg,* 7, Rohbraken, WP,18
240 James Hawes, *The Shortest History of Germany*, (paper-ed.), 138.
241 Leopold, *Alfred Hugenberg*, 8, The *Ausland* was established in 1914, the *Wirtschaft* in 1916 and the *Deutschland Gewerbehaus A.G.*, in 1917,
242 *Centralverband Deutscher Industrieller, Bund der Industriellen, und Bund der Landwirte, Deutscher Bauernbund, Reichsdeutscher*

Mittelstandverband, Christlische Deutscher Bauernvereinge, and the *Hansabund*
[243] R. Nelson, *Germans, Poland & Colonial Expansion to the East, 1850 through to the Present*, 80
[244] *Germany's Aims in the First World War*, 244
[245] *Germany's Aims in the First World War*, 532
[246] *Germany's Aims in the First World War*, 167-168
[247] Pound and Harmsworth, *Northcliffe*, 367
[248] Simon Heffer, *Staring at God*, 239
[249] J.M. McEwen, 'Northcliffe and Lloyd George at War, 1914-1918
[250] Alexander Watson, *Ring of Steel, Germany and Austria-Hungary at War, 1914-1918*, 330-331
[251] Fischer, *Germany's Aims the First World War*, 286, Also Müller, op.cit.,p.152
[252] *Germany's Aims in the First World War*, 288, taken from Id., pp.273 ff. also Birnbaum, op.cit
[253] Bernstorff, op. cit. pp.276 ff. Fischer, *Germany's Aims in the First World War*, 289
[254] Raymond Gram Swing, *Good Evening*, (1964) 107-109
[255] Leopold, *Alfred Hugenberg*, 10, the *Industriegesellschaft 1916 m.b.H*, the *Bodengesellschaft 1916* and the *Verkehrsgesellschaft 1916 m.b.H*
[256] Niall Ferguson, *The Pity of War*, (paper ed.), 263.
[257] Miles, W *Military Operations France and Belgium, 1916 Vol II: 2nd July to the End of the Battle of the Somme* (1992)
[258] Gilbert, III ©, III, 1542-43 quoted in Simon Heffer, *Staring at God*, 447
[259] Simon Heffer, *Staring at God*, 470
[260] R Brian Willits, 'The German-American role in fight for Irish Freedom' *Irish Times*, 9 12 2016
[261] Authur S Link, *Woodrow Wilson, Revolution War and Peace*, 52
[262] *Germany's Aims*, 92
[263] *Germany's Aims in the First World War*, 294
[264] Skiddelsky, *John Maynard Keynes,* vol 1, (paper-back ed) 335-336
[265] *Germany's Aims in the First World War*, 303
[266] Barbara W Tuchman, *The Zimmerman Telegram*, (1959) 162
[267] *Zimmermann Telgram*, 149
[268] *Zimmerman Telegram*, 146
[269] *Zimmerman Telegram*, 183
[270] Arthur S Link, *Woodrow Wilson, Revolution, war and Peace*, 55
[271] *Germany's Aims in the First World War*, 308
[272] *Zimmermann Telegram*, 185
[273] *Germany's Aims in the First World War*, 244
[274] John W Wheeler-Bennett, *Brest-Litovsk, the forgotten Peace, March 1918*, 16
[275] *Germany's Aims in the First World War,* 147-154

[276] *Germany's Aims in the First World War*, 278-9
[277] *Germany's Aims in the First World War*, 367
[278] *Germany's Aims in the First World War*, 383
[279] *Germany's Aims in the First World War*, 385
[280] *Germany's Aims in the First World War*, 391
[281] Alexander Watson, *Ring of Steel, Germany, and Austria-Hungary at War, 1914-1018*, 480
[282] *Germany's Aims in the First World War*, 396
[283] *Germany's Aims in the First World War*, 397
[284] Leopold, *Alfred Hugenberg*, 10,
[285] *Germany's Aims in the First World War*, 396-8
[286] *Germany's Aims in the First World War*, 404
[287] Paul Bookbinder, *Weimar Germany: The Republic of the Reasonable,* (1996), 222-223
[288] Quoted in Raymond 'Gram' Swing, *'Good Evening!'* 126, details also in C. R. M R. Crutwell, (1934) *A History of the Great War, 1914-1918*
[289] Simon Heffer, *Staring at God, Britain in the Great War*, 504
[290] Haig, 240, Stevenson II, 183, in Simon Heffer, *Staring at God*, 557
[291] R J Unstead, *A Century of Change*, 129, Quote taken from Siegfried Sassoon
[292] *Germany's Aims in the First World War*, 432
[293] *Germany's Aims in the First World War*, 493
[294] *Germany's Aims in the First World War*, 479
[295] *Germany's Aims in the First World War*, 500
[296] *Germany's Aims in the First World War*, 542
[297] *Germany's Aims in the First World War*, 483-5
[298] *Germany's Aims in the First World War*, 508, taken from Gottfried Mehnert, *Evangelische Kirche und Politik*, 64 ff
[299] *Germany's Aims in the First World War*, 507
[300] John A Leopold, *Alfred Hugenberg* (1977) 10-11
[301] Arthur S Link, *Revolution, War and Peace*, 86
[302] Fritz Fischer, *Germany's Aims in the First World War*, (p.ed), 538
[303] *Germany's Aims in the First World War*, 521
[304] *Germany's Aims in the First World War*, 535
[305] *Germany's Aims in the First World War*, 579
[306] John Terraine, author of *Douglas Haig the educated Soldier* estimated that Germany had over 500,000 troops on the victorious Eastern front in 1918, Niall Ferguson in *The Pity of War 1914-1918* estimated the number to be almost 1,000,000, 285
[307] Niall Ferguson, *The War of the World* (paper ed.), 131-133
[308] Fritz Fischer, *Germany's Aims in the First World War*, 631, 1d., pp.290 f.(from Ballin's noted of August 25-26 1918)
[309] Schwertfeger, op.cit., pp.242 ff., Fritz Fischer, 630

310 Ray Stannard Baker *Woodrow Wilson Life and Letters* vol 8. (1972)

311 His 14 points include open covenants, openly arrived at, freedom of the seas in war and peace, a free-minded and absolutely impartial adjustment of all colonial claims, a free Poland with access to the sea, the autonomy of all the nations making up the Austrian and the Turkish Empires, Germany to evacuate France and Belgium and its eastern empire, and a League of Nations.

312 *The Conversation* 06 08 2019, Liam Kennedy, 'How Brexit is leading a resurgent Irish American influence in US politics.'

313 Robert Gerwath, *November 1918*, (Oxford University Press, 2020) 26

314 *Current History,* November 1918, 214

315 Robert Gerwath, *November* 1918, 58. Also Nebelin, *Ludendorff,* 414-5

316 Simon Heffer, *Staring at God*, 711

317 Robert Gerwath, *November* 1918, 58-60, Zabecki, *German 1918 Offensives 139-73*, David Stevenson, *With our backs to the Wall: Victory and Defeat in 1918*, (2011) 67

318 Richard Goldhurst, Pipe, Clay & Drill *John J Pershing, the Classic American soldier*, 360

319 Paul F Braim, *The Test of Battle,* 96

320 Paul F Braim, *The Test of Battle,*122, Also Pershing, 2: 328

321 Combat Studies Institute, Battlebook, 12-A The battle of Montfacon, 51-52. 'The use of chemicals against the 79th (division) was not the deciding factor for the division's defeat. ... (Nevertheless, the 79th's) reaction to the conventional and chemical environments of the day should have been predicted by the leaders of the AEF.

322 MHI WWI Questionnaire: MHI Archives.

323 David Stevenson, *With our backs to the Wall, Victory and Defeat in 1918*, (paper ed.), 164

324 David Stevenson, *With our backs to the Wall, Victory and Defeat in 1918*, (paper ed. 2012), 254

325 Paul F Braim, *The Test of Battle,* 135

326 Etienne Mantoux *The Carthaginian Peace, or the Economic Consequences of Mr. Keynes* (1946), 91, f.1. *Die Industrie im besetzten Frankreich: bearbeitet im Auftrage des General-quartiermeisters*, München, 1916.

327 *New York Times* 12 12 1918

328 Ray Stannard Baker, *Woodrow Wilson, Life & Letters* (1939), 484

329 R S Baker, *Woodrow Wilson, Life and Letters,* vol. 8, 530-31

330 *Annual Register 1918* (taken from The Times newspaper) A committee was set up which recommended amongst other things, no employment under the age of 14, a weekly day of rest, and an 8 hour day.

[331] Smythe, *Pershing*, 233-234
[332] Blake, *Private Papers of Douglas Haig*, 334
[333] Blake, *Private Papers of Douglas Haig*, 329
[334] *The Papers of Woodrow Wilson*, 51, *1918*, 523-4
[335] Niall Ferguson, *The Pity of War*, 437
[336] Leopold, *Alfred Hugenberg*, 11
[337] J Ellis Barker, *The Foundations of Germany*, (1916), 101-2
[338] Fritz Fischer, *From Kaiserreich to Third Reich* (1986) 72
[339] See note 67, Leopold, *Alfred Hugenberg*, 12, See the Hugenberg-Vögler correspondence in AH Rohrbraken, M7
[340] Ray Stannard Baker *Woodrow Wilson Life and Letters 8,* (1939) 533,
[341] Sebastien Haffner, *Failure of a Revolution*, 72
[342] Sebastien Haffner, *Failure of a revolution*, 74-5
[343] David Fromkin. *In the time of the Americans* (1995) 200
[344] Wheeler-Bennet, *Nemesis of Power*, 25-31
[345] Brig. Gen. J.H. Morgan, *Assize of Arms* (1945) 182
[346] *New York Times*, 12 12 1918
[347] Quoted in Foerster, *Europe and the German Question*, 223-4
[348] *New York Times*, 26 02 1924
[349] *New York Times* 12 12 1918
[350] Germany's gold reserves had swelled from 1.25 billion gold marks in 1914 to 2.56 billion on Armistice Day 1918. *New York Times* 12.12.1918
[351] Sally Marks, 'Smoke and mirrors' in Boemeke, Feldman and Glazer (eds) *The Treaty of Versailles, A Reassessment after 75 years* 359
[352] J M Keynes, *Dr Melchior, A defeated Enemy* 61-2
[353] J H Morgan *Assize of Arms* (1945) 188
[354] J M Keynes, *Dr Melchior, A defeated Enemy* 30-31
[355] *Statesman's Yearbook 1923* France's population actually fell in 1919 while the German population increased.
[356] *New York Times*, 12 12 1918
[357] Skiddelsky, *J. M. Keynes*, vol.1, 364.
[358] Etienne Mantoux, *The Carthaginian Peace* (1946), 135-6
[359] Stephen Gross, 'Confidence and Gold: German War Finance, 1914-1918, in *Central European History*, (June 2009), 228, 238, 223
[360] Morgan, *Assize of Arms* 96
[361] Morgan, *Assize of Arms* 19
[362] J. Lee Thompson, *Northcliffe, Press Baron in Politics, 1865-1922* (London,2000), 317
[363] Address at St. Louis, E Mantoux *The Carthaginian Peace,* 59.
[364] Jürgen Tampke, *A Perfidious Distortion of History, The Versailles Peace Treaty, and the success of the Nazis*,210
[365] *Sun & New York Herald* 24.1.1920
[366] *Sun & New York Herald* 8.2.1920
[367] *Annual Register 1920* (Info. Taken from *The Times*) 177-8

368 John A Leopold, *Alfred Hugenberg, The Radical Campaign against the Weimar Republic* (New Haven Conn, and London, 1977) 10
369 Brigadier-General Morgan, *Assize of Arms* 19
370 Ian Kershaw *Hitler 1889-1936: Hubris* (1999) 101
371 *New York Times* 03 02 1920
372 E Eyck *History of the Weimar Republic* vol 1. 167
373 Guttman & Meehan, *The Great Inflation,* 112-3
374 *Lloyd George Papers,* Baldwin File. c/8 F/3/1/13
375 Eberhalb Kolb, *The Weimar Republic,* (1988)
376 *New York Times*, 1.2.1920
377 Niall Ferguson, *The Pity of War*, (paper ed.), 414
378 Erich Eyck *A History of the Weimar Republic* vol 1, 168
379 Kieger, *Raymond Poincaré*, 271, French Legation Bavaria to Quai d'Orsay, 5 April 1921
380 Holger H Herwig, 'Clio deceived, Patriotic Self-Censorship in Germany after the Great War' in Keith Wilson, F Holger H Herwig,'*Forging the Collective Memory, Government and International Historians through the Two World Wars*, 87
381 Holger H Herwig, 'Clio deceived, Patriotic Self-Censorship in Germany after the Great War,' 94
382 Figs. From G. Borsky, *The Greatest Swindle in the World* (1942) 45
383 Etienne Mantoux *The Carthaginian Peace, or the Economic Consequences of Mr. Keynes*, (1946), 137.
384 Etienne Mantoux *The Carthaginian Peace* 139
385 Adam Tooze, *The Deluge*, 426-427
386 Jürgen Tampke, *A Perfdious Distortion of History, the Versailles Peace Treaty and the success of the Nazis*, 91
387 J. V. F. Keiger, *Raymond Poincaré*, 291
388 William Manchester *The Arms of Krupp*, 389, Also Shirer, 282
389 William Manchester *The Arms of Krupp*, 351-354, Bofors quote, TWC IX 272-3, C-156; NIK-12294.
390 William Manchester *The Arms of Krupp*, 390
391 Raymond Gram Swing, *Good Evening*, 135-137
392 Terms laid down in a letter from Vladikavkaz to Lenin, 25 3 1922, *Foreign Policy Archives Moscow*
393 Adam Tooze, *The Deluge*, 427, information taken from A. Heywood, *Modernising Lenin's Russia: Economic Reconstruction, Foreign Trade and the Railways* (Cambridge 1999), 6
394 Alexander Watson, *Ring of Steel, Germany and Austria-Hungary at War 1914-1918*, 488-489.
395 Niall Ferguson *The Pity of War* 421
396 Fritz Thyssen, *I paid Hitler* 98
397 *New York Times*, 18th January 1923
398 *Daily Mail* 3 8 1923 reported Poincaré's speech: 'Germany ought to restore its credit, stabilise its currency, balance its

budget and encourage its production. ... But Germany ... has ... disdained all advice'
[399] *Smythe* Pershing, 233
[400] *Annual Register 1922* 79
[401] In 1922 Germany became the second largest shipbuilder in the world *Annual Register 1922* 92 Finance & Commerce
[402] Leopold, *Alfred Hugenberg*, 11-12
[403] Leopold, *Alfred Hugenberg*, 23, Also D Traub, 'Gerechtigkeit, *München-Augsburger Abdenzeitung,* 14 11 1923. Traub believed that Hitler had 'gone to piece' but remained irreplaceable as a drummer for the Nationalist cause. Author's note: There is an implication here that the Nazis were receiving some sort of support from the Hugenberg syndicate or industry.
[404] Kershaw *Hitler 1889-1936: Hubris* (paper-back ed, 1999), 248
[405] *The Times* 10 10 1923
[406] Adam Tooze, *The Deluge,* 426
[407] *New York Times* 8 11 1923
[408] G D Feldman, *The Great Disorder, Politics, Economics and Society in the German Inflation, 1914-1923* (1993) Table 49, 850
[409] Harold James *A German Identity* 126
[410] *The Times* 10 10 1923
[411] Annika Mombauer, *The Origins of the First World War, Controversies and Consensus,* 96
[412] Sarah Gertrude Millin *General Smuts* vol 2. 262
[413] *New York Times* 11 10 1923
[414] *New York Times* February 1924
[415] E. Eyck, *The Weimar Republic,* 300,307
[416] Albrecht Ritschl, 'The German Transfer Problem, 1920-1933, a Sovereign debt Perspective,' in *European Review of History,* vol.19. (2012), Issue 6
[417] Schuker, *American 'Reparations' to Germany,* 284-9
[418] *New York Times,* 17.5.24
[419] G Borsky, *The Greatest Swindle in the World, Table of Payments,* 45-6
[420] *Royal Institute Survey 1929*
[421] Hjalmar Schacht, *My First 76 Years,* (1955) 191-206
[422] (although Germany has, of course, given itself a get-out clause in the shape of transfer protection) see Stephen A Schuker, *American'Reparations' to Germany,* 87 'When the Germans accepted the Dawes Plan, they fully intended to ask for another reduction in reparations within three to four years. The outcome of London, by tying France's hands in the event of default, made it virtually certain that the next German bid for downward revisi.on would meet with success.'
[423] The American Federal Reserve agreed to consider certain trade bills, payable in the United States, as eligible for their open market purchases 'if Germany agreed to stabilise its currency on

the basis of a 'gold exchange' in effect'. *New York Times* 17 05 1924

[424] Liaquat Ahamed, *Lords of Finance*, 229

[425] *The Times* 20 04 1925 'the Bank of England must use the weapon of the rate in the event of a persistent export of gold'

[426] Liaquat Ahamed, *Lords of Finance*, 59

[427] Liaquat Ahamed. *Lords of Finance*, 234

[428] J. F. V. Keiger, *Raymond Poincaré*, 320

[429] In the autumn of 1923, the French and Belgian engineers tried to argue that the price of German coal was so cheap that it would undercut British coal, even after 20% had been given in reparations. But the industrialist Hugo Stinnes argued that although this was true for the consumer it was not true for the producer who could only take the 'pithead price into account in making his calculations'. *New York Times* 18 10 1923

[430] *Royal Institute of International Affairs Survey, 1929*, 126

[431] Harm G Schröter, '*Europe in the Strategies of Germany's Electrical and Engineering Trusts, 1919-1939*' in Volker R Berghahn, *Quest for Economic Empire*, 41

[432] J. W. Angell, *The Recovery of Germany* (1932). Committee on Foreign Relations, 320

[433] *Annual Register 1919*

[434] A M Newman *Economic Organisation of the British Coal Industry* (1934) Appendix A p.475. After the coal strike 'Most of the districts made arrangements on the basis of an eight hours working day: only Yorkshire, Nottinghamshire, Derbyshire and Kent agreed on a 7½ hour basis, whilst the North East introduced 7½ hours for hewers only'.

[435] Catherine Bailey *Black Diamonds* 274 Recollections of a miner from Sheffied

[436] 9% 1925, 6.5% 1926, 7% 1927, 6.5% until 25 April 1929, 7.5% from April 1929

[437] Clay, *Lord Norman*, 223

[438] Stresemann's Diary (1/591) G Borsky, *the Greatest Swindle in the World* 63

[439] W J Reader, *Imperial Chemical Industries*, Vol. (London 1975) 412

[440] Barnett, Correlli, *The Audit of War*, 92, Carr and Taplin, *British Steel Industry*, 410 1929 is a record year with coal output up in the Ruhr district by 23% and coke and briquette output up by 50% *Economist 18.1.30*

[441] W. Manchester, (paper ed. 350, TWC IX 76-7

[442] although the Bolsheviks paraded the fact that Germany had also signed a treaty with them, demonstrating the eternal friendship between the two formerly pariah states The treaty was signed on 24 April 1926, E Eyck, *History of the Weimar Republic*,2, ,61

[443] Leopold, *Alfred Hugenberg*, 31-32

[444] Adam Fergusson, *When money Dies* (2010) 246-247
[445] John Simpkin, *Spartacus Educational*. From an interview published in *Preussiche Zeitung* (1937)
[446] Erich Eyck, *The Weimar Republic, Vol II*, 120
[447] Theo Balderston, *The Origens and Causes of the German Economic Crisis, 1923-to May 1931* (1993)
[448] Erich Eyck, *A History of the Weimar Republic*, vol.2, 120, Bonn, *Neuer Plan*, 130
[449] Holger Herwig, *Clio Deceived, The Campaign against article 231 of the Treaty of Versailles*, 22
[450] Mombauer, Annika (2002) *The Origins of the First World War*, 87
[451] H Kantorowicz, *The Spirit of British Policy, and the myth of the encirclement of Germany*, 493
[452] H Kantorowicz, *The Spirit of British Policy, and the myth of the encirclement of Germany*, 491
[453] H Kantorowicz, *The Spirit of British Policy, and the myth of the encirclement of Germany*, 499-S500
[454] Erich Eyek, *History of the Weimar Republic II*, 120, also Bonn, *Neuer Plan*, 130
[455] W M Knight-Patterson *Germany from Defeat to Conquest* (1945) 400
[456] W. Manchester, *Arms of Krupp*, (paper ed.) 354-355, Haux, 138
[457] *Central State Military Archives, Moscow,* Taken from a report from Chief of the Chemical Department, Fischmann to the Deputy Minister of the Red Army, Unchlicht (29 April 1927)
[458] Eyck, *A History of the Weimar Republic*, vol.2., 144, Henry Bernhard, 'Seeckt und Stresemann,' *Deutsche Rundschau* May 1953, 471, Speidel, *'Reichswehr und Dote Armee,'* 22, n.1. NB.Erich Eyck was a German Social Democrat politician, who escaped to London and was given a desk at the London Library before World War II
[459] *Royal Institute of International Affairs, Survey, 1929.* The highest amount 38% was in 1929
[460] *New York Times* 15 7 1928
[461] Liaquat Ahamed *Lords of Finance* 282
[462] Tobias Straumann, *Debt, Crisis and the Rise of Hitler,* (2019), 41
[463] *Royal Institute of International Affairs, Survey 1929* and is harming world trade, 126
[464] *Royal Institute of International Affairs, Survey 1929* 116, at no time did actual cash transfers exceed 35.8% of Germany's total payments. 65 million, 2nd year, 876 million (20.43 £) fifth year. G Borsky, Of the total of 3,834 million gold marks entered by the Reparations' agent as 'payment in gold and foreign currency only 1,737 million was paid in cash (including the Dawes Loan). The remaining 1,510 was revenue from tariffs and deliveries in kind.

E Mantoux, *Carthaginian Peace*, from Reichs-Kredit-Gesellschaft, *Germany's Economic Development in the First Half of the Year, 1931*, 27 (20.86 to £)

[466] *Statesmans Year Book, 1933*

[467] *Statesmans Year Book, 1933*, 938 (comparisons of different nations currencies taken from *Annual Register 1929*, 74

[468] *Stresemann Papers,* 7439 Erich Eyck *The Weimar Republic* vol 2 175

[469] Leopold, *Alfred Hugenberg*, 56

[470] *New York Times* 26 09 1931

[471] Niall Ferguson, *The Pity of War*, (paper ed. 1999), 402

[472] *New York Times*, 8.3.1929

[473] David Fromkin *In the time of the Americans*, 276, 296-297,333

[474] Erich Eyck, *History of the Weimar Republic, Vol 2*, 167-8

[475] Erich Eyck, *History of the Weimar Republic, Vol 2*, 196,

[476] Erich Eyck, *History of the Weimar Republic, Vol 2*, 135

[477] Erich Eyck, *History of the Weimar Republic, vol. 2*, 197, Stresemann, *Vermâchtnis*, 434f

[478] Albrecht Ritschl, 'Reparations, Deficits & Debt Default, The Great Depression in Germany, 7.

[479] *New York Times,* 26 9 1931

[480] *New York Times,* 21 4 1929

[481] Erich Eyck, *History of the Weimar Republic*, vol. 2. 189, Curtius, *Young Plan*, 43.

[482] H James, *The German Slump* (1986) 284. For figures 298-300

[483] Adam Lebor, *The Tower of Basel*, xviii

[484] Borsky *The Greatest Swindle in the World* (1942) 60

[485] Eyck, *History of the Weimar Republic*, 2, 197

[486] *Royal Institute of International Affairs, Survey, 1930*, 504-5

[487] Schmidt, *Statist*, 183, Erich Eyck, *History of the Weimar Republic*, Vol. 2. 207

[488] Borsky, *The Greatest Swindle in the World*, 60

[489] *Statesman's Yearbook* 1933, Britain, 38, Germany, 938

[490] *Royal Institute of International Affairs Survey, 1929*, 155

[491] *The Times* 27 06 1929 reported £3,414,000 gold bought by Germany over two days. many's continued purchases thereafter prompted France and other countries to buy gold. Further heavy purchases in mid- September prompted the British government to put interest rates up. See howhitlercametopower.com

[492] *The Times* 25 09 1929

[493] *The Times* 20 04 1925

[494] Erich Eyck, *A History of the Weimar Republic*, vol.2, 212

[495] Leopold, *Alfred Hugenberg*, 58. A minority of disenchanted business leaders, such as Vögler, espoused a more radical approach. Fearful that the Young Plan would increase foreign interests in key German industries and undermine the national

independence of the state, they were determined to support crisis politics.

[496] Social Democrat Carl Severing in June 1930 estimated Germany's capital flight to Switzerland at 7 billion RM. The New York Times also said that it was going to Paris, despite its low interest rates.

[497] *Economist*, 13.7.29

[498] Erich Eyck *The Weimar Republic II*, 212

[499] Young Report, 22

[500] Erich Eyck *The Weimar Republic II*, 230-232

[501] Tobias Straumann, *1931, Debt, Crisis, and the rise of Hitler*, 51

[502] Documents on British Foreign Policy, (19300 1, 486.

[503] William L Patch Jnr, *Heinrich Brüning and the Dissolution of the Weimar Republic* (Cambridge University Press, 1996) 77

[504] Eyck, *A History of the Weimar Republic*, vol 2, 267

[505] John A Leopold, *Alfred Hugenberg*, 82,95

[506] John A Leopold, *Alfred Hugenberg*, 80, 83

[507] *New York Times*, 18 08 1930

[508] Michal Reiman, *the Birth of Stalinism*, 75, 'The national economy has almost no reserves at its disposal, either financial or material'

[509] Michael Reiman, *The Birth of Stalinism, The USSR on the eve of the Second Revolution* (1987), 37

[510] Foreign Policy Archives, Moscow, no. 390.

[511] Dyck, *Weimar Germany and Soviet Russia*, 147-8

[512] *Foreign Policy Archives, Moscow, Protocol 22. File 694. No 37*

[513] R W Davies, Mark Harrison, S G Wheatcroft, eds., *The Economic Transformation of the Soviet Union, 1913-1945*, 319, Table 52 gives Sources of Soviet Imports between 1921 and 1940. In 1931 over 50% of all Soviet imports came from Germany. 'The large new tractor factories under construction at Stalingrad, Khar'kov and Chelyanbinsk were designed for rapid conversaion to tank production.' 144

[514] Nekrich, *Pariahs, Partners and Predators*, 24, 61,

[515] A A Akhtamzyan, *New and Latest History* no 4, *Istoriya vtoroi mirovoi voinv*, vol 1, 270

[516] A. Nekrich, *Pariahs, Partners and Predators*, 24, 61

[517] Davies, Harrison, and Wheatcroft, (eds) *The Economic Transformation of the Soviet Union*, 150

[518] William L Patch Jnr, *Heinrich Brüning and the Dissolution of the Weimar Republic*, (1998) 103

[519] Erich Eyck, *The Weimar Republic Vol 11*, 332-3, 228, 314, 298, Hamilton, *Who Voted for Hitler*,278

[520] 1930 Documents on British Foreign Policy 2, 220-221

[521] Quoted from Shaw's *The Rationalization of Russia (1931)* in Niall Ferguson, *The War of the World*, 198-199

522 Quoted in Paul Holllander, *Political Pilgrims: Western Intellectuals in Search of the Good Society* (4th ed. 1998) and Arthur Herman, *Joseph McCartney*, (2000), 65
523 5 billion Reichsmarks in long term German bonds and 7 billion Reichsmarks in German short-term bonds
524 Tobias Straumann, *1931, Debt, Crisis, and the rise of Hitler*, 97, *New York Times*, 30 10 1930
525 Albrecht Ritschl, 'Reparations, Deficits, and Debt Default, the Great Depression in Germany,'18
526 *Statesman's Yearbook 1933*. Figs. For British national debt are on pages 38 and 39. The headline figure for 1930 was £7584 million. Interest payable £355 million. Details of German debt see page 938
527 *Times* 24 January 1931
528 Germany increased her exports to the US by 15% while taking 12% less in imports.
529 *Financial Times*, 17.6.1930
530 *Annual Register* 1931, p.189
531 Volker R Berghahn, *Quest for Economic Empire*, 16-17. Quote from R. Opitz, (ed) *Europastrategien*,581f.
532 *Royal Institute of International Affairs, Survey, 1931,* 32
533 *Royal Institute of International Affairs, Survey, 1936,* gives figures for the trade between the two countries. In 1931 German exports to USSR 762.7 million Reichsmarks. Imports from USSR 303.5 m Reichsmarks. In 1932 German exports to USSR 625.8 million Reichsmarks. Imports from USSR 207.9m Reichsmarks
534 Robert Boyce, *'Business as usual' in French Foreign and domestic policy, 1918-1940* (1998), 120
535 *Economist* 7 12 1929 (after the payment of reparations and subtracting the net increase in foreign indebtedness)
536 Tobias Straumann, *Debt, Crisis and the Rise of Hitler*, (2019), 174
537 *Annual Register 1931,* 186
538 *Annual Register 1931,*187
539 J M Keynes, *Two Memoirs*, 50
540 Carl Melchior to Hans Schäffer, State secretary to the Minister of Finance, Erich Eyck, *Weimar Republic, II,* 323-324
541 Eichengreen, *Golden Fetters,* 289
542 Guido Giacome Preparata, *Conjuring Hitler, How Britain and America made the Third Reich* (2006) 182-185
543 *New York Times* 22 09 1931
544 Liaquat Ahamed, *Lords of Finance* (hard-backed copy) 435-436
545 *Statesman's Yearbook,* 1933, United States finance, 458.
546 *Foreign Policy Archives,* Moscow. Ambassador Dirksen, 3rd March 1931, 'I fully support Brockdorff-Rantzau's view that the concessions rather hamper the bi-lateral relations and are not compensated by a corresponding beneft.'
547 Niall Ferguson, *The War of the World*, (paper ed.), 193.

548 Volker Berghahn, *American big business in Britain and Germany*, 214
549 Volker R Berghahn, *American Big Business in Britain and Germany*, 214
550 Robert Mark Spaulding, Jr 'Reconquering our Old Position,' in Volker R Berghahn, *American Big Business in Britain and Germany*, 126
551 40.1% September 26th 1931
552 *New York Times September 28, 1931*.
553 Eberhard Kolb, *The Weimar Republic* 181-184.
554 Report on Germany's war potential, July 28, 1945, given by Senator Kilgore of the Subcommittee on War Mobilisation, quoted in T H Tetens, *Germany plots with the Kremlin* 269
555 Annika Mombauer, *The Origins of the First World War, Controversies and Consensus*, 99
556 Annika Mombauer, *The Origins of the First World War, Controversies and Consensus*, 108-9
557 Stephen A Schuker, *American 'Reparations' to Germany*, 46
558 Simon Reich 'Fascism and the Structure of German capitalism' in Volker R Berghahn *Quest for Economic Empire* 83 & 87
559 Erich Eyck, *Weimar Republic, II*, 374, 409.
560 *New York Time*, 15 July 1928
561 Nekrich, *Pariahs, Partners, and Predators*, 64
562 Robert Boyce, 'Business as usual' in Robert Boyce (ed.), *French Foreign and Defence Policy, 1918-1940*, 125
563 William L Shirer, *The Rise and Fall of the Third Reich*, 145
564 William Manchester (paper ed.), 369-370.
565 William Manchester (paper ed.), 384-385.
566 General Morgan, Report of his speech in *International Affairs* published by Royal Institute of International *Affairs* (1936) vol xv, No1, pp.74-77
567 William R Keylor *The Twentieth-Century World, An International History* (1992) 133
568 David Fromkin, *In the time of the Americans*, 300
569 Gatske, *Germany and the United States, a special relationship* (1980), 97
570 T H Tetens, *Germany plots with the Kremlin*, 30
571 H James, *the German Slump*, The Schwerin on Krosigle-Overy figures represent a reliable minimum spent on rearmament.' 383
572 Borsky, *The Greatest Swindle in the World*, 11, He estimated cash payments to be £253 million, but took £100 million off because the Dawes and Young Plan loans were not repaid before the 2nd World War.
573 Stephen A Schuker This equates in price-adjusted terms, to 'four times the total assistance that the United States government will provide to West Germany from 1948 to 1952 under the

much-heralded Marshall Plan.' *American 'Reparations' to Germany*, 119
[574] *Survey of International Affairs 1934*, 37
[575] *Survey of International Affairs 1934*, 38
[576] 'GERMANY PAID NO REPARATIONS' letter between Amos J Peaslee of the American Courier Service and Admiral Sir Reginald Hall who directed British Naval Intelligence from 1914-1919, 4th January 1940
[577] *Survey of International Affairs 1934* 40*
[578] *Annual Register 1932*, 300, American exports of raw cotton had shrunk to 340 million dollars in 1932 compared with the average yearly exports of 611 million dollars for the previous five years.
[579] Dulles, *Vargas of Brazil*, 175'
[580] Alton Frye, *Nazi Germany and the American Hemisphere, 1933-1941*, 39
[581] A Scott Berg *Lindbergh* (1998) 357-362
[582] Simon Reich, 'Fascism and the Structure of German Capitalism, The Case of the Automobile Industry' in Volker R Berghahn, *Quest for Economic Empire* (1996), 80
[583] Tim Mason, *Social Policy in the Third Reich*, 133
[584] A Scott Berg, *Lindbergh* (1998) 377-379
[585] Adam Tooze, *The Deluge, The Great War and the Remaking of Global Order, 1916-1931* (paper ed.), 513
[586] John Leopold, *Alfred Hugenberg*, 130
[587] John Leopold, *Alfred Hugenberg*, 136
[588] Quoted in John Leopold, *Alfred Hugenberg*, 154
[589] *Annual Register* 1933, 186, *The Times, 19 06 1933* 14a. The incriminating text is alleged to be part of the notes of an undelivered speech.
[590] Mark Harrison and R W Davies, *The Soviet Military-Economic Effort during the Second Five-Year Plan (1933-7)* in *Europe-Asia Studies, Vol 49, No 3*, 369-406
[591] John Leopold, *Alfred Hugenberg*,99, DZA Potzdam. ADV.211, Class to Hugenberg, 21 04 1931
[592] Volker R. Berghahn, *Quest for Economic Empire*, 18
[593] Boyce,
[594] *Royal Institute of International Affairs*, Survey, 1936
[595] Ian Kershaw *Hitler Nemesis (paper-back ed)* 239
[596] Adam Tooze *Wages of Destruction*, 363-366
[597] G. Borsky, *The Greatest Swindle in the World*, 'The German *Statistisches Reichsamt* gives the following specification of the German foreign indebtedness

On July 31st, 1931,	Long-term debts marks	10,700 million gold
	Short-term debts	13,100
	Other foreign investments	5,900
	Total	29,700

Rate to £ 1929, 20.43

[598] Alton Frye *Nazi Germany and the American Hemisphere 1933-1941*, 160-161
[599] Liam Kennedy, *The Conversation*, 06 09 2020, 'How Brexit is leading a resurgent Irish American influence in US politics.'
[600] Brian Hanley, (Lecturer, Institute of Irish Studies, University of Liverpool) (https://www.qub.ac.uk) 'Irish Republicanism and Nazi Germany.'
[601] Frye Alton, *Nazi Germany and the American Hemisphere 1933-1941*, 132-133
[602] Frye Alton, *Nazi Germany and the American Hemisphere 1933-1941*, 132-133
[603] National Archives, Franklin D. Roosevelt Museum. Paul M Sparrow, director, 'The Casablanca Conference, Unconditional Surrender.'
[604] Heinrich Brüning, *Memoiren, 1918-1934* DVA, Suttgart 1970, S.531
[605] Adam Tooze *Wages of Destruction*, 368-9
[606] Adam Tooze, *Wages of Destruction*, 389
[607] Adam Tooze, *Wages of Destruction*, 385
[608] Adam Tooze, *Weapons of Destruction*, 382-3
[609] John C Beyer & Stephen A Schneider, *Forced Labour under the German Reich*, parts 1 and 2
[610] Raeder, memorandum, Sept 16, 1939, ND, D-804, ibid., 527.
[611] Saul Friedlander, *Prelude to Downfall*, 57
[612] Quoted in Saul Friedlander, *Prelude to Downfall, Hitler and the United States, 1939-41*, 60
[613] Adam Tooze *The Wages of Destruction* 399
[614] Adam Tooze, *Wages of Destruction*, 394
[615] Hillgruber, *Hitler's Strategy*, 159-162
[616] Saul Friedlnder *Prelude to Downfall, Hitler and the United States, 1939-41* 125
[617] Saul Friedlander *Prelude to Downfall, Hitler and the United States, 1939-1941* (1967) 200
[618] Fischer, *Germany's aims in the First World War*, 547 map.
[619] Wheeler-Bennett, *The Forgotten Peace* (1939)
[620] Shirer, *The Rise and Fall of the Third Reich* (paperback) 84 *Mein Kampf*: 'The giant empire in the East is ripe for collapse.'
[621] R.W. Davies, Mark Harrison, S G Wheatcroft, *The Economic Transformation of the Soviet Union, 1913-1945* (hard copy ed.), 145
[622] Alexandr Nekrich, *Pariahs, Partners, Predators, 1922-1941*, 24, 61
[623] James Hawes *The Shortest History of Germany*, (paper ed. 2018), 178-179
[624] Lauran Paine, *The Abwehr*, (1984), 157-166
[625] Lauran Paine, *The Abwehr*, 150

626 Tooze, *Wages of Destruction*, 395
627 Kenneth S Davies, *FDR: Into the Storm 1937-1940 (1993)*, 621
628 Saul Friedlander, *Prelude to Downfall*, 136,
629 John Toland, *Hitler,* (paper ed.), 695
630 Timothy Snyder (2010) *Bloodlands: Europe between Hitler and Stalin* 416
631 Brigadier-General Morgan, *Assize of Arms*, 261, Appendix 1V
632 W Manchester *The Arms of Krupp 1587-1968*, 465
633 W Manchester *The Arms of Krupp 1587-1968* 541
408 W Manchester *The Arms of Krupp 1587-1968*
635 W Manchester *The Arms of Krupp 1587-1968* 554,
636 W Manchester *The Arms of Krupp 1587-1968*, 513
637 30 March 1945, US State Dept. quoted in T H Tetens, *Germany plots with the Kremlin* 259
638 Burleigh, *The Third Reich: A New History*, (paper ed), 786
639 David K Yelton, *'Ein Volk Steht Auf,' The German Volksturm and the Nazi Strategy, 1944-45'* in *Journal of Military History* (2000), 1069
640 Michael H Kater, *Hitler Youth* (2004) 238
641 Wikepedia
642 US Military Intelligence report EW-Pa 128
643 Richard J. Evans, *The Third Reich at War*, 660-661, 673
644 Dennis Piszkiewicz, *The Nazi Rocketeers*, 176
645 Nova Science magazine, (Kid Zone) Mark Walker, *Nazis and the Bomb* 11 08 2006
646 W Manchester *The Arms of Krupp 1587-1968*, 635-7
647 Michael Dobbs, *Six Months in 1945* 190
648 Michael Dobbs, *Six Months in 1945* 198
649 This directive was issued Canaris on 15th March 1944, reproduced in T. H. Tetens, *Germany plots with the Kremlin* (1953), 233-235
650 William L Clayton to US Senate June 1945, Senator Kilgore report to Senate Military Affairs Committee, in T H Tetens, *Germany plots with the Kremlin*, 261, 267
651 Directive issued by the Chief of the Intelligence Division of the German High Command, Admiral Walter Wilhelm Canaris, on 15 03 1944.
652 Volker Berghahn, 'Resisting the Pax Americana?' in Michael Ermath *America and the Shaping of German Society, 1945-1955* 91-92
653 Victor Sebestyen, *1946, The Making of the Modern World*, 19-21
654 Daily Mail, 26 01 2012
655 Kathryn S Olmsted, *The Newspaper Axis*, 211
656 Justus D Doenecke and Mark A Stoler, *Debating Franklin D Roosevelt's Foreign Policies,* 147
657 William L Shirer, *The Rise and Fall of the Third Reich*, 894

[658] Quoted in Volker R Berghahn, *American Big Business in Britain and Germany*, 302
[659] Victor Sebastien *1946 The Making of the Modern World* (paperback) 73
[660] 'The President was not a hero or a prophet ... but a generously intentioned man, with many of the weaknesses of other human beings and lacking that dominating intellectual equipment which would have been necessary ... What chance could such a man have against Mt. Lloyd George's unerring, almost medium-like sensibility to everyone immediately around him...? John Maynard Keynes, *The Economic Consequences of the Peace*, quoted in Viereck's *American Monthly* 1920
[661] *New York Times, December 1945*
[662] *Wikepedia The Bretton Woods System Pegged Rates**
[663] Victor Sebastien, *1946, The Making of the Modern World*, 30
[664] Bark & Gress, *A History of West Germany, 1, From Shadow to Substance* 55-56
[665] Victor Sebestien, *1946 The Making of the Modern World*, 167
[666] Volker R Berghahn,
[667] Amos Yoder, 'The Ruhr Authority and the German Problem' in *The Review of Politics* Vol 17, No 3, 346
[668] Bark & Gress, *A History of West Germany, 1, From Shadow to Substance* 54
[669] Victor Sebestyen, *1946, The Making of the Modern World*, 192
[670] Bark & Gress, *A History of West Germany, 1, From Shadow to Substance* 178
[671] Volker Berghahn, 'Resisting the Pax Americana?' in Michael Ermath *America and the Shaping of German Society, 1945-1955*, 94
[672] From Senator Kilgore's report to the Senate Subcommittee, on War Mobilisation 10 07 1945, Statement by William L Clayton to the Subcommittee on Military Affairs, 25 06 1945
[673] Volker Berghahn, 'Resisting the Pax Americana?' in Michael Ermath *America and the Shaping of German Society, 1945-1955* 88
[674] Simon Reich, 'Fascism and the Structure of German Capitalism, The Case of the Automobile Industry' in Volker R Berghahn, *Quest for Economic Empire* (1996) 74-75
[675] Rudolf Augustein, *Konrad Adenauer*, 14-15 (reproduced from *Daily Express* 15 10 1963)
[676] T H Tetens, *Germany plots with the Kremlin* (1953) 182
[677] Victor Sebastyen, *1946 The Making of the Modern World*, (paperback ed), 91
[678] Michael J Hogan, *The Marshall Plan, America, Britain and the Reconstruction of Western Europe*, 415
[679] The 'Marshall Plan' speech at Harvard University, 5 June 1947 OECD
[680] Victor Sebastyen *1946, The Making of the Modern World* 68-72

[681] Bark & Gress, *A History of West Germany, 1, From Shadow to Substance* 131
[682] A Spy, *From Marks to Deutsche Marks*
[683] Bark & Gress, *A History of West* Germany, 1, *From Shadow to Substance* 201
[684] Secret Memorandum Captured German Foreign Office files show that from 1943 to 1944, diplomats in the Wilhelmstrasse felt sure that, if defeated, Germany would enjoy the protection of influential circles in the United States.
[685] James Hawes, *The Shortest History of Germany,* 192, 194
[686] Bark & Gress, *A History of West* Germany, 1, *From Shadow to Substance* 128-9
[687] Victor Sebestyen, *1946, The Making of the Modern World,* 48
[688] *Der Spiegel* 'How many died in the Bombing of Dresden?' 10 02 2008
[689] Michael Ermath *America and the Shaping of German Society 1945-1955* 89
[690] Deborah Lipstadt, *Denying the Holocaust,* 69
[691] 11th December 1949
[692] Arthur Herman, *Joseph McCarthy,* (2000), 113
[693] J L Gaddis (paper ed) *The Cold War* 40-42
[694] Townsend Hoopes, *The Devil and John Foster Dulles,* 92-97
[695] Jung Change & Jon Halliday *Mao The Unknown Story* (paper ed) 447-458
[696] Rudolf Augustein *Konrad Adenauer* 24-25
[697] Minutes of the foreign ministers' meeting, Sep 12-13, 1950. Quoted in Marc Trachtenberg and Christopher Gehrz *America, Europe, and German Rearmament, August –September 1950,*
[698] Madrid Circular letter, quoted in T H Tetens *Germany plots with the Kremlin,* 227-228
[699] T H Tetens *The New Germany and the Old Nazis* (1962) 206-207
[700] W Manchester *The Arms of Krupp* 759
[701] Simon Reich in 'Fascism and the Structure of German capitalism' in Volker R Berghahn *Quest for Economic Empire, European Strategies of German Big Business in the Twentieth Century,* 86
[702] Annual Register, *1953,* 209
[703] T H Tetens *New Germany and the old Nazis* (1962) 24-27
[704] T H Tetens, *Germany plots with the Kremlin,* (1953), 5
[705] Eric Toussaint, *Solidarity,* 15th March 2019, 'Why the 1953 cancellation of German debt won't be reproduced for Greece and Developing Countries.'
[706] Robert Mark Spaulding, Jr, Chapter 5, *Reconquering our old Position, West German Osthandel Strategies of the 1950s* in Volker Berghahn, 123, in Volker R. Berghahn, *Quest for Economic Empire,* (1996)
[707] Charles Williams, *Adenauer,* 441

708 Charles Williams, *Adenauer*, 412-418
709 Townsend Hoopes *The Devil and J F Dulles*, (1973), 301-2
710 G B Foreign Office, selected docs. 188-9
711 Charles Williams, *Adenauer*, 442-3
712 J L Gaddis, *The Cold War* (paper ed), 69
713 Charles Williams, *Adenauer*, 465-467
714 *Der Spiegel* 10 04 2011
715 *New York Times* 18 May 1963
716 UN Doc ENDC/84 8 April 1963
717 For treaties made under Johnson and Nixon see Dennis L Bark & David R Gress *A History of West Germany 2*, 162
718 Mark Walker in *Nova* 11 08 2005
719 Freidrich Georg, *Hitlera Siegeswaffen Band 1; Luftaffe und Marine Geheim Nuclearwffen des Dritten Reich und ihre Traegersysteme* (2000) Henry Stevens, *Hitler's Suppressed and Still-Secret Weapons, Science and Technology* 76
720 Henry Stevens, *Hitler's Suppressed and Still-Secret Weapons, Science and Technology* 232
721 Dennis Piskiewicz *The Nazi Rocketeers, Dreams of Space and Crimes of War* 184, 195
722 Beate Klarsfeld, *Wherever they may Be*, (1975) 55-56
723 Stephen A Schuker *American 'Reparations' to Germany, Implications for the Latin American debt crisis* (1988) 131
724 *Economist* 10 July 1972
725 Peter Uwe Schliemann, *The Strategy of British and German investors in Brazil* (1981) 106
726 On 27 June 1975 the Kraftwerk Union company (KWU) of Germany, owned by Siemens and AEG, concluded a giant order with Brazil for the *purchase* of up to eight nuclear reactors A fuel fabrication plant was to be built by the KWU Nukem General Electric subsidiary Reaktor Brennelment Union, a nozzle separation enrichment plant was to be built by the Steag utility and a reprocessing plant was to be built by Kewa-Kernbrennstoff-Wiederaufarbeitungs-Gesellschaft mbH – which is a joint subsidiary of Bayer, Hoeschst, Gelsenberg and Nukem. The equipment and technology package was said to be worth $4.5 billion. *Nucleonics Week*, 20.12.1975. *Nucleonics Week*, 16.11.1976 reported that AEG was leaving the consortium, leaving Siemens as the sole owner of Kraftwerk Union, AG, effective from 1 January 1977.
727 *Nucleonics Week*, 1.1.1976 'since nations like Brazil would clandestinely protect themselves from the possibility of attack by their neighbours.'
728 *Nucleonics Week*, 10.2.1977.
729 Charles Williams, *Adenauer* 507
730 Cited in Wilharm (ed.), *Deutsche Geschichte 1962-1983*, 2: 200 also in Bark & Gress, 313.

731 *The Times* Obituary of Helmut Schmidt, material taken from Jonathan Carr's biography of Schmidt
732 Dennis L. Bark & David R. Gress, *A History of West Germany*, 2, 'Democracy and its Discontents', 309.
733 Andrew Alexander *America and the Imperialism of Ignorance* 196
734 Bark & Gress, *A History of West Germany*, 2, 313-14.
735 Bark & Gress, *A History of West Germany*, 2, 315.
736 *Nucleonics Week*, 31.5.1979. Brazil declared that it wished to export her nuclear technology (just before the signing of the SALT II Treaty). *Nucleonics Week* reassured its readers, however, that the Germans still held effective control of Nuclen through key technological and commercial directors, although KWU held only 25% of the stock to Nuclebras's 75%.
737 On 15 November 1979
738 *Neucleonics Week*, 29 11 1979
739 *Annual Register*, 85.
740 John Lewis Geddes, *The Cold War* (paper ed) 84
741 Bark & Gress, *A History of West Germany*, 2, 316-317.
742 At the end of December an estimated 50,000 Russian troops invaded Afghanistan (24-26 December) and installed a puppet dictator (27 December).
743 Niall Ferguson, *The Ascent of Money, A Financial History of the World* (2008), 165
744 *The Times* Overseas News
745 *Daily Express* 13 10 2014
746 Christopher Lee, *Carrington, An Honourable Man* (2018), 503 Carrington, A
747 T W Carr, lecture 'German and US involvement in the Balkans
748 Christopher Lee, *Carrington An Honourable Man*, 506
749 T W Carr, 'German and US involvement in the Balkans.
750 *Der Spiegel* 09 30 2010 'Was the deutsche Mark Sacrificed for Reunification?'
751 David Marsh, *The Bundesbank, The Bank that rules Europe* (1992) 18
752 T W Carr, 'German and US involvement in the Balkans
753 *The Guardian*
754 *Guardian 3 February 2005*
755 Adam Tooze, *Prospect Magazine*, 'The Secret History of the Banking Crisis'
756 *The New York Times* 21 08 2011 Gordon Brown *The Euro Zone's Cure starts with Germany*
757 *Daily Telegraph* Ambrose Evens-Pritchard, May 2007 *France and Germany clash over inflation as north-south divide widens*
758 Micky Levy 19 01 2012
759 *Daily Telegraph* 18 05 2007 Ambrose Evans-Pritchard 'France and Germany clash over inflation as north-south divide widens'

[760] Major Coleman 1V, Michael LaCour-Little, Kerry D Vandell, *Subprime lending and the Housing Bubble, Tail Wags Dog?* 4-5
[761] *Daily Telegraph,* 12 07 2007, Ambrose Evans-Pritchard, 'Sarkozy drafts fresh plans to hobble the ECB as euro nears $1.40
[762] Financial Post *Bank Fiasco began with Northern Rock* 18 12 12
[763] RTE news, 05 12 2017, *ECB 'will not hesitate'* on interest hike
[764] *Reuters* 23 09 2007, Francois Murphy and Jon Boyle, *Trichet brushes off French Criticism of ECB*
[765] *Daily Telegraph* Ambrose Evens-Pritchard 19 10 2007 *Dollar dives as US slump spreads*
[766] *Daily Telegraph* Ambrose Evans-Pritchard 09 11 2007 *Eurozone at Loggerheads over interest rates*
[767] *Wikepedia World Oil Price chronology*
[768] *Economist Intelligence Unit* June 2008
[769] Adam Tooze, *Crashed*, 241
[770] Vanity Fair/business/features/2011/09/Europe-201109
[771] *Telegraph* 02 10 2008, Ambrose Evans-Pritchard, 'So much for tirades against American greed'
[772] *Die Welt* 7 02 09 'Under the pressure of the economic crisis the government and Länder have given themselves until 2020 to reduce their borrowings to nothing. ... For the government the new regulations will reduce in stages to the whole country borrowing only 0.35% of gross national product in the budgetary year of 2011 till 2016. That is about 8.5 billion euros a year. The Länder must reduce their net borrowings between 2011 and 2020 to zero.'
[773] *The New York Times,* 21 08 2011, Gordon Brown, *The Euro Zone Cure Starts with Germany*
[774] Paul Krugman *End this Depression Now!* (paper-back ed) 19
[775] Nicolai Hubble, (Southbank Research) *How the Euro Dies*, 48,53
[776] Fritz Fischer, *Germany's Aims in the First World War*, (p.ed), 538
[777] Samuel Charap, Timothy J Coltman, *Everyone Loses,* 2017, 122
[778] Samuel Charap, Timothy J Coltman, *Everyone Loses,* 2017,
[779] Wikepedia War in Ukraine, Timeline
[780] Lev Golinkin, Forward, 20 May 2018
[781] Apnews 04 01 2025
[782] NATO Press Conference, 03 10 2024
[783] 'What does victory look like for Ukraine?' Owen Matthews, Spectator
[784] *War of Illusions,* 504, Geiss, No 1001, Hammann to Ballin, 1.8.14
[785] Martin Kitchen, *Political Economy of Germany 1815-1914* (1978) 278

[786] Frye Alton, *Nazi Germany and the American Hemisphere 1933-1941*, 132-133
[787] Kenneth S Davies, *FDR: Into the Storm 1937-1940 (1993)*, 621
[788] William L Shirer, *The Rise and Fall of the Third Reich*, 894
[789] W Manchester *The Arms of Krupp 1587-1968*, 513
[790] Directive issued by the Chief of the Intelligence Division of the German High Command, Admiral Walter Wilhelm Canaris, on 15 03 1944.
[791] Victor Sebastyen, *1946 The Making of the Modern World*, (paperback ed), 91
[792] David Marsh, *The Bank that rules Europe*, 139
[793] T H Tetens, *Germany plots with the Kremlin*, (1953), 5
[794] Eric Toussaint, *Solidarity*, 15th March 2019, 'Why the 1953 cancellation of German debt won't be reproduced for Greece and Developing Countries.'
[795] Andrew Roberts, *The Holy Fox, A Biography of Lord Halfax*, 48
[796] G B Foreign Office, selected docs. 188-9
[797] Bark & Gress, *A History of West Germany*, 2, 313-14.
[798] Micky Levy 19 01 2012
[799] RTE news, 05 12 2017, *ECB 'will not hesitate'* on interest hike
[800] Paul Krugman *End this Depression Now!* (paper-back ed) 19

About the Author

Sara Moore is in independent political and economic historian whose research is gaining increasing recognition. Her new book takes a broad sweep through history from Bismarck till the present day to reveal the continuity of 'Prussian ambitions.'

Sara's other books include *Peace without Victory for the Allies 1918-1932, How Hitler Came to Power, The Fourth Reich?* And *The EU – An Emerging German Empire.* She is the author of a recent article published by *The Cobden Centre* (economics magazine) October 2024, asking *Did Germany cause the Great Depression?*

Sara lives in London and Shropshire with her husband and has two daughters and a son.

THE BRUGES GROUP

The Bruges Group is an independent all-party think tank. Set up in 1989, its founding purpose was to resist the encroachments of the European Union on our democratic self-government. The Bruges Group spearheaded the intellectual battle to win a vote to leave the European Union and against the emergence of a centralised EU state. With personal freedom at its core, its formation was inspired by the speech of Margaret Thatcher in Bruges in September 1988 where the Prime Minister stated, "We have not successfully rolled back the frontiers of the State in Britain only to see them re-imposed at a European level."

We now face a more insidious and profound challenge to our liberties – the rising tide of intolerance. The Bruges Group challenges false and damaging orthodoxies that suppress debate and incite enmity. It will continue to direct Britain's role in the world, act as a voice for the Union, and promote our historic liberty, democracy, transparency, and rights. It spearheads the resistance to attacks on free speech and provides a voice for those who value our freedoms and way of life.

WHO WE ARE

Founder President:
The Rt Hon. The Baroness Thatcher of Kesteven LG, OM, FRS

Former President:
The Rt Hon. The Lord Tebbit CH PC

Vice-President:
The Rt Hon. The Lord Lamont of Lerwick, PC (1993 – 2024)

Chairman:
Barry Legg

Director:
Robert Oulds MA, FRSA

Washington D.C. Representative:
John O'Sullivan CBE

Founder Chairman:
Lord Harris of High Cross

Former Chairmen:
Dr Brian Hindley, Dr Martin Holmes & Professor Kenneth Minogue

Academic Advisory Council:
Professor Tim Congdon
Dr Richard Howarth
Professor Patrick Minford
Andrew Roberts
Martin Howe, KC
John O'Sullivan, CBE

Sponsors and Patrons:
E P Gardner Dryden
Gilling-Smith
Lord Kalms
David Caldow
Andrew Cook
Lord Howard
Brian Kingham
Lord Pearson of Rannoch
Eddie Addison
Ian Butler
Thomas Griffin
Lord Young of Graffham
Michael Fisher
Oliver Marriott
Hon. Sir Rocco Forte
Michael Freeman
Richard E.L. Smith

MEETINGS

The Bruges Group holds regular high–profile public meetings, seminars, debates, and conferences. These enable influential speakers to contribute to the European debate. Speakers are selected purely by the contribution they can make to enhance the debate.

For further information about the Bruges Group, to attend our meetings, or join and receive our publications, please see the membership form at the end of this paper. Alternatively, you can visit our website www.brugesgroup.com or contact us at info@brugesgroup.com.

Contact us
For more information about the Bruges Group please contact:
Robert Oulds, Director
The Bruges Group, 246 Linen Hall, 162-168 Regent Street, London W1B 5TB
Tel: +44 (0)20 7287 4414 Email: info@brugesgroup.com

www.brugesgroup.com

www.ingramcontent.com/pod-product-compliance
Lightning Source LLC
Chambersburg PA
CBHW030300080526
44584CB00012B/382